T0291405

RESPONSIBLE FIRMS

INTERNATIONAL FINANCE REVIEW

Series Editor: J. Jay Choi

INTERNATIONAL FINANCE REVIEW   VOLUME 23

RESPONSIBLE FIRMS: CSR, ESG, AND GLOBAL SUSTAINABILITY

EDITED BY

J. JAY CHOI

Temple University, USA

AND

JIMI KIM

University of New South Wales, Australia

United Kingdom – North America – Japan
India – Malaysia – China

Emerald Publishing Limited
Emerald Publishing, Floor 5, Northspring, 21-23 Wellington Street, Leeds LS1 4DL.

First edition 2024

Reprints and permissions service
Contact: www.copyright.com

British Library Cataloguing in Publication Data
A catalogue record for this book is available from the British Library

ISBN: 978-1-83753-963-5 (Print)
ISBN: 978-1-83753-962-8 (Online)
ISBN: 978-1-83753-964-2 (Epub)

ISSN: 1569-3767 (Series)

INVESTOR IN PEOPLE

CONTENTS

LIST OF CONTRIBUTORS

Nakano Chiaki	*Japan International University, Japan*
Jongmoo Jay Choi	*Temple University, PA, USA*
Taehee Choi	*KDI School of Public Policy and Management, Korea*
Marco Simões-Coelho	*Federal University of Rio de Janeiro, Brazil*
Bengi Ertuna	*Bogazici University, Istanbul, Türkiye*
Ariane Roder Figueira	*Federal University of Rio de Janeiro, Brazil*
Xian Gong	*University of Technology Sydney, Australia*
Ilham Haouas	*Abu Dhabi University, United Arab Emirates*
Burcin Hatipoglu	*University of New South Wales, Canberra, Australia*
J.H. John Kim	*College of Charleston, SC, USA*
Jimi Kim	*University of New South Wales, Sydney, Australia*
Paul X. McCarthy	*University of New South Wales, Sydney, Australia*
Alain Naef	*ESSEC Business School and THEMA, France*
Ankit Nyati	*NMIMS University, Mumbai, India*
Sebeom Oh	*Temple University, PA, USA*
Bora Ozkan	*Temple University, PA, USA*
Michael Parker	*PRAXIS Communication University of Technology Sydney, Australia*
Palak Rathi	*NMIMS University, Mumbai, India*
Robert A. Rodrigues	*Saint Mary's College of California, USA*
Eduardo Russo	*Tecnológico de Monterrey, Mexico*
Henrik Skaug Sætra	*University of Oslo, Norway*
Julianne Sellin	*Temple University, PA, USA*
Rushina Singhi	*NMIMS University, Mumbai, India*
Anubha Srivastava	*Christ University, Bangalore, India*
Tien Thi Thuy Tran	*Massey University, New Zealand*
Hai Hong Trinh	*Massey University, New Zealand*
Zhou Zucheng	*Shanghai Jiao Tong University, China*

PART I

AN OVERVIEW: CONCEPTS AND MEASUREMENTS

CHAPTER 1

RESPONSIBLE FIRMS AND GLOBAL SUSTAINABILITY: TOWARD AN INTEGRATED FRAMEWORK

Jongmoo Jay Choi[a] and Jimi Kim[b]

[a]Temple University, PA, USA
[b]University of New South Wales, Sydney, Australia

ABSTRACT

The apparent contemporary corporate model is that of a "responsible firm" – a firm that pursues not only profit and shareholder return but also considers the concerns and interests of its social and environmental stakeholders. Research on corporate social responsibility (CSR), investor recognition via environmental, social, and governance (ESG) issues, and long-term sustainability has developed into an established field of study. We attempt to clarify the terminologies and models of this field by conducting a brief review of the existing work and suggesting an integrated conceptual framework for CSR, ESG, and sustainability in a domestic and global context. We suggest that externality and temporality are the drivers of this integrated framework.

Keywords: Sustainability; CSR; ESG; externality; temporality

JEL codes: M14, M16, G34

Responsible Firms: CSR, ESG, and Global Sustainability
International Finance Review, Volume 23, 3–15
Copyright © 2025 by Jongmoo Jay Choi and Jimi Kim
Published under exclusive licence by Emerald Publishing Limited
ISSN: 1569-3767/doi:10.1108/S1569-376720240000023001

1. INTRODUCTION

The purpose of a corporation has been the subject of debate for decades. Traditionally, the dominant view argues that a firm's sole responsibility is to maximize profits for its shareholders (Friedman, 1970). This perspective emphasizes that corporations exist within a free market system, and their primary function is to generate financial returns for shareholders who invest capital. This focus on profits and shareholder returns incentivizes efficiency and innovation, driving economic growth and prosperity.

However, many now challenge this view and argue that corporations have a broader purpose that extends beyond profit maximization (Business Roundtable, 2019; Jensen, 2001). This perspective highlights the interconnectedness of businesses with society and the environment. Corporations can be seen as having a responsibility to these stakeholders (Donaldson & Preston, 1995). Corporations rely on a healthy and educated workforce, as well as stable communities where they operate; investing in employee well-being, fair wages, and supporting local communities fosters loyalty and creates a positive social impact. Business activities can have a significant impact on the environment. Thus, sustainable practices, such as reducing waste and pollution, are not simply good for the planet, but can also lead to long-term cost savings and improved brand reputation of the firm (Joly, 2021).

The contemporary global model is that of a "responsible firm" – a firm that not only pursues profit and shareholder return but also considers the concerns and interests of its social and environmental stakeholders. Thus, research on CSR and/or, its investor-specific dimension, ESG, has developed into an established field of study.[1] A related development from a policy perspective is the notion of sustainability, which evolves into the same field because sustainability overlaps with CSR and ESG. However, despite significant research on these areas in business and economics, the basic results remain mixed and fragmented. Starks (2013) argues that the differences between investors' and managers' motivations, along with confused terminologies and complex models in sustainable finance, contribute to misunderstandings. In this work, we attempt to clarify the terminologies and models in responsible firms and sustainability by conducting a brief review of existing work and by suggesting a conceptual framework for CSR, ESG, and sustainability. We also consider the case of multinational enterprises (MNE) that contextualize the discussion from domestic to global economy. We do not attempt to be exhaustive in this review, only to sketch an overview. However, we do make an initial attempt to combine the fragmented pieces of corporate, investor, and societal perspectives on CSR, ESG, and sustainability into an integrated framework of responsible firms and global sustainability.

2. SUSTAINABILITY, CSR, AND STAKEHOLDER MODELS

Various researchers have explored how and when firms address the concerns of stakeholders (e.g., Carroll, 1991; Freeman, 1984) and how firms differ in balancing interests between shareholder and social stakeholders, such as communities and employees – the "S" (social) in ESG (e.g., Clarkson, 1995). By building trust with stakeholders and fostering a positive brand image, firms can attract and retain talent, improve customer loyalty, and maintain a competitive advantage. Simultaneously, environmental concerns impact firms, and combined with studies in economics and environmental science, this led to research on the "E" (environmental) in ESG. In this section, we discuss these streams of research on social and environmental sustainability with CSR activities as primary tools. Later, we will discuss ESG as an instrument to address market recognition and investor perspectives.

The definition of sustainability most frequently cited originates from the UN World Commission on Environment and Development (1987), which defines sustainable development as "development that meets the needs of the present without compromising the ability of future generations to meet their own needs."

Regarding specific outcomes, there are three types of sustainability: corporate sustainability, social sustainability, and environmental sustainability. *Corporate sustainability* is the effect of a firm's CSR activities, or ESG ratings, on its own sustainability. This includes enhanced reputation and brand value, reduced risks and costs, improved access to capital, innovation, and long-term growth as well as the likelihood of the firm's legitimacy and survival. This can be estimated by predicted proxies of firm bankruptcy and financial stress and the firm's reputation, legitimacy, and social acceptability.

The other two concepts of sustainability address the effects on CSR contributions to society and the earth. *Environmental sustainability* (E) denotes concerns regarding reduced greenhouse gas emissions; resource conservation, efficiency, and innovation; and climate change mitigation. *Social sustainability* (S) pertains to improved employee relations and stronger community relationships including philanthropy. It should be stressed that some business functions such as supply chain management (SCM) may involve both social and environmental sustainability, as these influence the implementation of responsible sourcing practices and supplier codes of conduct, as well as the promotion of ethical labor practices (S) and environmental sustainability (E) through the SCM process.

The academic field has developed related constructs that describe firms' social engagement to achieve sustainability, with similar but slightly different emphasis, such as corporate social performance (Clarkson, 1995), the triple bottom line (Elkington, 1997), corporate citizenship (Matten & Crane, 2005), as well as corporate social responsibility (Carroll, 1999), and others. CSR, in particular, refers to voluntary organizational practices that seek to improve social and environmental sustainability (Carroll, 1999; McWilliams & Siegel, 2001). While each construct was developed from varied backgrounds, the overarching notion that moves the model of firms from a shareholder-centric view to that of the stakeholders pertains to how various stakeholder perspectives can be harmoniously incorporated into corporate operations and strategies.

Carroll (1999) defines CSR as a firm's voluntary actions and initiatives to address social and environmental issues beyond their legal requirements. CSR can include philanthropic activities, community engagement, ethical sourcing, sustainability programs, and employee volunteer programs, among others. CSR is often viewed as a way for companies to build and maintain their reputation, mitigate risks (Godfrey, 2005; Godfrey et al., 2009; Kim et al., 2021), improve stakeholder relationships, and contribute to the well-being of society and the environment. Underlying motivations for CSR initiatives are numerous, including instrumental, relational, and moral motivations from individuals, organizations, and institutions (e.g., Aguilera et al., 2007; Aguinis & Glavas, 2012).

3. ESG AND INVESTOR PERSPECTIVES

Environmental, social, and governance factors are used by investors to evaluate companies' long-term sustainability and potential risks and opportunities. The term "ESG" was coined to define a series of issues to be integrated into investment analysis and was first devised in the 2004 report by financial institutions from multiple countries in response to a call from Kofi Anon, Secretary-General of the United Nations (for a historical summary, see Pollman, 2022; and IFC website). The report notes that the goal is for a "better inclusion of ESG factors in investment decisions" and that "companies with better ESG performance can increase shareholder value by better-managing risks related to emerging ESG issues, by anticipating regulatory changes or consumer trends, and by accessing new markets or reducing costs." A recent development of ESG posits that it is a mainstream practice rather than a niche subfield (Edmans, 2023) and clarifies the term by differentiating investment approaches, investor preferences, and expected returns with a *value* versus *values* framework, e.g., financial value vs. multiple manager preferences (Starks, 2023). In her presidential address, Starks (2023), president of the American Finance Association, posits that ESG investments are a way to pursue nonpecuniary motivations with a willingness to accept lower returns from a *values* perspective, whereas ESG investments can also be employed by sole financially oriented investors from a *value* perspective.

Reflecting the investor focus, many authors have examined the impact of ESG investments on firm alpha, the abnormal rate of return in relation to a benchmark after adjustment for risk. A study by Khan et al. (2016) shows that firms improving on material ESG issues significantly outperform firms with poor ratings. In contrast, addressing the issue of correlated omitted factors, Ahn et al. (2024) report that the materiality portfolio does not outperform, once accounting for its exposure to profitability and growth factors. Attig et al. (2024) indicate that firms oversell CSR by hyping up their CSR narratives at year-end earnings conference calls.

Among the most examined questions in the literature is the relationship between CSR/ESG and financial performance (e.g., Margolis & Walsh, 2003; Orlitzky et al., 2003). For example, several studies support the agency-based perspective that CSR/ESG enhance managers' utility (e.g., Benabou & Tirole, 2010) even when it does not produce market valuation (Di Giuli & Kostovetsky, 2014; Masulis & Reza, 2015). However, most studies document a positive association between CSR/ESG and the financial performance of the firm (e.g., Borghesi et al., 2014; Flammer, 2015; Gao & Zhang, 2015; Liang & Renneboog, 2017), suggesting mechanisms such as an increase in tangible or intangible assets or a decrease in the cost of capital.

Broadly, ESG (or CSR) is fundamentally related to the notion of stakeholder theory (Donaldson & Preston, 1995), consistent with not only shareholder profits but also the interests of social and environmental stakeholders. Given the identity and context of stakeholders and firms, applications vary. CSR pertains to a firm's voluntary social and environmental practices, while ESG focuses on the evaluation of these voluntary practices by market or investors aiming to manage risks pertaining to ESG. Recently, there has been some skepticism about the overselling of CSR (Attig et al., 2024). Nevertheless, both CSR and ESG are instruments that highlight the importance of firms taking responsibility for their impact on society and the environment and for being transparent about their actions and performance (Campbell, 2007; McWilliams & Siegel, 2001).

4. TEMPORAL ORIENTATION OF S VS. E

In management and finance research within the CSR and ESG domain, little attention has been directed to how the social (S) and environmental (E) components of ESG distinctly contribute to intergenerational and intragenerational equity, respectively. Although the temporal dimension has been explored in CSR/ESG research (e.g., Flammer & Bansal, 2017; Slawinski & Bansal, 2015), it is seldom linked to distinct social and environmental dimensions and their potential conflicts. A recent review of CSR and ESG research (Gillan et al., 2021) shows that the majority of sustainability studies utilize CSR or ESG as a singular construct and measure, masking the important differences between the two.

Within the ESG/CSR framework, social (S) and environmental (E) corporate activities differ in two respects. One is the difference in intertemporal context. S prioritizes intragenerational equity, emphasizing fair distribution of resources and equal opportunities for people within the present generation. This includes addressing issues such as fair labor practices, diversity and inclusion initiatives, or addressing social issues impacting specific communities within a given time period. The social dimension generally addresses primary stakeholders such as employees, customers, suppliers, and communities, which helps develop intangible and tangible assets, increasing shareholder value (Hillman & Keim, 2001).

On the other hand, E primarily focuses on intergenerational (i.e., intertemporal) equity, concerned about the responsible stewardship of natural resources and the mitigation of climate change impact to ensure a sustainable outcome for future generations. Intergenerational equity involves organizational actions, such as reducing carbon emissions, preserving biodiversity, and developing renewable energy sources to safeguard the environment for the future. The different time frame between S and E is supported by findings that more long-term oriented firms demonstrate greater E performance than S engagement (Choi et al., 2023).

Despite some attempts about the potential tradeoffs between S and E strategies (Beckmann et al., 2014; Hahn et al., 2015), only the surface has been sketched. Fundamentally, this line of inquiry over time and space is a matter of intertemporal economic choice (Loewenstein & Thaler, 1989) and its application in sustainability theory and management remains an open issue.

5. ENVIRONMENT AS A STAKEHOLDER WITH EXTERNALITY

Traditionally, businesses have not viewed the environment as a stakeholder. However, a growing understanding of our interconnectedness with the natural world necessitates a broader perspective. The environment is a crucial "stakeholder," whose concerns must be incorporated into corporate decisions now given the intertemporal gaps between emissions and outcomes. This is also because of the notion of externality, which does not enter typical corporate cost and benefit analysis.

The theory of *externality* explains how a company's activities can create costs or benefits for society, which are not reflected in market prices. Jiang et al. (2023) examine the negative externalities of mandatory ESG disclosure through the lens of regulatory salience and report that mandatory disclosure may induce trade-offs of different ESG goals by prioritizing more conspicuous ESG practices at the cost of trivializing other longer-term issues. Moreover, aside from the disclosure effect, businesses often generate negative environmental externalities such as pollution, resource depletion, and climate change. The negative externalities must be included in cost-benefit analysis of all corporate investments and operations, as well as their impacts on social and environmental sustainability in both national and supranational policy debates.

Many challenges are related to environments, some expected and some unexpected. Conflict resolutions are key to the successful navigation through the vagaries and uncertainties of the future – both horizontally across divergent interests and stakeholders and vertically across agents and institutions over time. To explain the dynamic business decisions pertaining to environments, theories of institutional change (North, 1990) and intertemporal choice (Loewenstein & Thaler, 1989) seem relevant as foundational pieces before application.

6. GOVERNANCE (G) AND INSTITUTIONS

Parenthetically, another ESG factor pertaining to social environmental practices is "G" (governance). The United National Environment Programme Finance Initiative, in its original report, provides the rationale for including G as part of ESG by noting: "Sound corporate governance and risk management systems are crucial prerequisites to successfully implementing policies and measures to address environmental and social challenges." The governance (G) factor functions as a foundation for firms, which underlies all corporate decisions including the environmental (E) and social (S) initiatives.

Various scholars have documented the effects of G on the firm, in both CSR and ESG domains. To wit, board directors' gender (Brammer et al., 2009;

Cronqvist & Yu, 2017; McGuinness et al., 2017), CEO altruism (Borghesi et al., 2014), CEO pay (Ferrell et al., 2016; Ikram et al., 2019), and liberal organizational culture (Gupta et al., 2017) are shown to increase CSR performance. As the role of board of directors evolves beyond mere oversight of management to providing access to information and resources (Boivie et al., 2021; Hillman & Dalziel, 2003), they actively advise managers on whether and to what extent the firm engage in CSR (e.g., Aguilera et al., 2021; De Villiers et al., 2011; Walls et al., 2012). Additionally, Choi et al. (2018) find that group affiliation is positively related to CSR, which may buffer the bad events for group firms arising from group-wide negative reputational externalities.

Ownership, a G factor, influences CSR, including institutional investors' engagement (e.g., Dyck et al., 2019; Johnson & Greening, 1999; Neubaum & Zahra, 2006), and long-term orientation of the firm and culture on CSR (Choi et al., 2023; Gloßner, 2019). The effects of government ownership, however, are mixed. Hsu et al. (2018) suggest that state-owned firms exhibit greater engagement in CSR. McGuinness et al. (2017) find a nonlinear relationship between state ownership and CSR, while a study by Kim and Jo (2022) suggests a negative association between state ownership and CSR, but a positive association between a sovereign wealth fund and CSR. These findings indicate that state capital is subject to government policies and ideologies embedded in institutions and culture. Further research is necessary to uncover the deep factors underlying corporate ownership and CSR.

7. GLOBAL SUSTAINABILITY: MULTINATIONAL ENTERPRISES (MNE) AND INSTITUTIONS

Organizational decisions, including whether and how firms engage in socially or environmentally responsible activities or the way in which firms interact with their stakeholders, are subject to the cultural, socioeconomic, and political institutions in which the firms operate (Aguilera et al., 2007; Hall & Soskice, 2001; Matten & Moon, 2008). Institutional norms, rules, and conventions are essential for a holistic understanding of organizational decisions and behaviors (e.g., Avetisyan & Ferrary, 2013; Meyer & Rowan, 1977). As organizations adopt and align with institutional norms and conventions, they can benefit from becoming accepted as legitimate. The degree of organizational legitimacy, in turn, depends on cultural and societal traits underlying institutional norms (Meyer & Rowan, 1977).

Building on this theoretical construct, several researchers have identified various institutional factors that shape CSR/ESG, including political and education systems, government labor policies (Ioannou & Serafeim, 2012; Young & Makhija, 2014), cultural factors, such as collectivism and power distance (Waldman et al., 2006), and language (Liang et al., 2018), among others. At the intersection of formal and informal institutions and CSR, scholars have emphasized the role of institutions that serve as a filter through which CSR is shaped and implemented. This literature suggests that cultural and socioeconomic contexts can either constrain or enable socially responsible practices (Aguilera et al., 2007; Höllerer, 2013; Jackson & Apostolakou, 2010; Matten & Moon, 2008).

International agreements, such as the Kyoto Protocol, the Paris Agreement on climate change, global partnerships for sustainable development, and the United Nations Sustainable Development Goals (SDG), which provide a framework for achieving global sustainability, are typical examples that directly and indirectly affect a firm's CSR. The UN has described these goals as "development that meets the needs of the present without compromising the ability of future generations to meet their own needs" (UN SDG). The goals emphasize the interconnectivity of economic, social, and environmental systems and the need for businesses to consider the long-term impacts of their operations. Since 2015 when the Sustainable Development Goals (SDGs) were adopted by the United Nations, each member country has been called upon to pledge and achieve these SDGs, with environmental sustainability being the primary component. Accordingly, extensive national and international policies have emerged to shape sustainable outcomes, including the European Green Deal, a set of policy initiatives by the European Commission with the overarching aim of making the European Union climate-neutral by 2050, along with India's 2% CSR rules, and Australia's Net Zero Plan, which strives for zero net emissions by 2050.

From a national government perspective, a country's sustainability – addressing social and environmental issues – is a critical agenda pursued along with economic growth, which needs to be fostered by government policies such as renewable energy incentives, social welfare programs, and environmental regulations. Firms operating within this boundary increasingly interact with their governments through various means, including state capital (Musacchio et al., 2015; Wood & Wright, 2015), political activism (Chatterji & Toffel, 2019), and addressing social value and grand societal challenges (George et al., 2016).

From a corporate standpoint, the choice of location is a critical decision firms make in internationalizing their business. Dam and Scholtens (2008) hypothesize that some firms might choose pollution havens, seeking countries with lax environmental or labor regulations. Berry et al.(2021), indeed, document the pollution-haven effect by showing that the stringency of environmental regulations in a country leads firms to reduce their share in sourcing, especially in industries with higher toxic emissions. More broadly, MNEs integrate, coordinate, and share knowledge among their geographically and culturally dispersed institutions (Bartlett & Ghoshal, 1988; Rugman & Verbeke, 1992), engaging in institutional arbitrage (Jackson & Deeg, 2008; Surroca et al., 2013). Depending on their industry-level inducements and constraints (Berry et al., 2021), the institutional arbitrage can create an opportunity for multinational firms to combine seemingly unrelated social contexts (labor) with environmental or governance issues across national boundaries.

Similarly, governance practices might be embedded within the institutional context of the home country, i.e., headquarters' location. For instance, an MNE from the United States might adopt different governance practices compared to one headquartered in the UK, even though they have operations in the same country (Aguilera & Jackson, 2003; Aguilera et al., 2006). The composition of

MNE's board of directors and the level of oversight they exert can be influenced by the norms and expectations of the headquarters' location (Choi et al., 2007; Peng, 2004). The way in which decisions are made might also be shaped by the headquarters' culture. For instance, a more centralized decision-making model might be prevalent in a hierarchical corporate culture, while a more decentralized approach might be favored in a more collaborative organization. The complexity of MNE governance, with or without sustainability, is another area ripe for opportunities for future studies.

8. CONCLUSIONS

The role of firms in society is likely to continue evolving. However, it seems clear that firms that embrace a broader purpose, those that integrate stakeholder considerations into their strategies, and those that prioritize sustainability are well-positioned for success in the future. Existing academic studies on CSR, ESG, and sustainability are fragmented and scattered. We have reviewed the gist of these streams of research with an eye toward developing an integrated conceptual framework, which permits dynamic interactions over time and space. As a point of departure, we suggested the perspectives of externality and temporality, and the resulting framework is one that can differentiate social and environmental sustainability horizontally across different fields as well as address the dynamic interactions vertically over time. In addition, we discussed a similar nexus focusing on global sustainability with multinational enterprises and global climate institutions as dynamic drivers. This is but a crude initial attempt, which can be refined and fine-tuned in future research.

We also stress that having a multidisciplinary perspective is crucial for research on CSR, ESG, and sustainability due to the complexity and interconnectedness of these issues. By integrating perspectives from various disciplines, such as economics, finance, sociology, environmental science, and management, researchers can gain a holistic understanding of the challenges and opportunities surrounding CSR engagements and their market recognition via ESG, as well as long-term sustainability at the level of firms, countries, and the world. One future avenue could explore the intersection of sustainability and green technology based on science or engineering; for example, water management and its effect on the firm and society. By crossing these multidisciplinary topics, researchers can contribute valuable insights to the ongoing discourse on CSR, ESG, and sustainability, fostering sustainable business practices and desirable societal and global outcomes.

NOTE

1. An aspect of ESG that arises from investments is called "socially responsible investments" (SRI). In this work, we assume SRI is a subset of ESG, and it will not be discussed separately.

REFERENCES

Aguilera, R. V., Aragón-Correa, J. A., Marano, V., & Tashman, P. A. (2021). The corporate governance of environmental sustainability: A review and proposal for more integrated research. *Journal of Management*, *47*(6), 1468–1497.

Aguilera, R. V., & Jackson, G. (2003). The cross-national diversity of corporate governance: Dimensions and determinants. *Academy of Management Review*, *28*(3), 447–465.

Aguilera, R. V., Rupp, D. E., Williams, C., & Ganapathi, J. (2007). Putting the S back in corporate social responsibility: A multilevel theory of social change in organizations. *Academy of Management Review*, *32*(3), 836–863.

Aguilera, R. V., Williams, C. A., Conley, J. M., & Rupp, D. E. (2006). Corporate governance and social responsibility: A comparative analysis of the UK and the US. *Corporate Governance: An International Review*, *14*(3), 147–158.

Aguinis, H., & Glavas, A. (2012). What we know and don't know about corporate social responsibility: A review and research agenda. *Journal of Management*, *38*(4), 932–968.

Ahn, B. H., Patatoukas, P. N., & Skiadopoulos, G. S. (2024, February 8). Material ESG alpha: A fundamentals-based perspective. *The Accounting Review*, 1–27.

Attig, N., Hu, W., Rahaman, M. M., & Zaman (2024). Overselling corporate social responsibility. *Financial Management*, Forthcoming.

Avetisyan, E., & Ferrary, M. (2013). Dynamics of stakeholders' implications in the institutionalization of the CSR Field in France and in the United States. *Journal of Business Ethics*, *115*(1), 115–133.

Bartlett, C. A., & Ghoshal, S. (1988). Organizing for worldwide effectiveness: The transnational solution. *California Management Review*, *31*(1), 54–74.

Beckmann, M., Hielscher, S., & Pies, I. (2014). Commitment strategies for sustainability: How business firms can transform trade-offs into win-win outcomes. *Business Strategy and the Environment*, *23*(1), 18–37.

Bénabou, R., & Tirole, J. (2010). Individual and corporate social responsibility. *Economica*, *77*(305), 1–19.

Berry, H., Kaul, A., & Lee, N. (2021). Follow the smoke: The pollution haven effect on global sourcing. *Strategic Management Journal*, *42*(13), 2420–2450.

Boivie, S., Withers, M. C., Graffin, S. D., & Corley, KG. 2021. Corporate directors' implicit theories of the roles and duties of boards. *Strategic Management Journal*, *42*, 1662–1695.

Borghesi, R., Houston, J. F., Naranjo, A. (2014). Corporate socially responsible investments: CEO altruism, reputation, and shareholder interests. *Journal of Corporate Finance*, *26*(C), 164–181.

Brammer, S., Millington, A., & Pavelin, S. (2009). Corporate reputation and women on the board. *British Journal of Management*, *20*(1), 17–29.

Business Roundtable. (2019). Statement on the Purpose of a Corporation. https://www.businessroundtable.org/business-roundtable-redefines-the-purpose-of-a-corporation-to-promote-an-economy-that-serves-all-americans.

Cambpbell, J. I. (2007). Why would corporations behave in socially responsible ways? An institutional theory of corporate social responsibility, *Academy of Management Review*, *32*(3), 946–967.

Carroll, A. B. (1991). The pyramid of corporate social responsibility: toward the moral management of organizational stakeholders. *Business Horizons*, *34*(4), 39–48.

Carroll, A. (1999). Corporate social responsibility evolution of a definitional construct. *Business & Society*, *38*(3), 268–295.

Chatterji, A. K., & Toffel, M. W. (2019). Assessing the Impact of CEO Activism. *Organization & Environment*, *32*(2), 159–185.

Choi, J. J., Jo, H., Kim, J., & Kim, M.S. (2018). Business groups and corporate social responsibility. *Journal of Business Ethics*, *153*, 931–954.

Choi, J. J., Kim, J., & Shenkar, O. (2023). Temporal Orientation and Corporate Social Responsibility: Global Evidence. *Journal of Management Studies*, *60*(1), 82–119.

Choi, J. J., Park, S. W., & Yoo, S. S. (2007). The value of outside directors: evidence from corporate governance reform in Korea. *Journal of Financial and Quantitative Analysis*, *42*, 941–962.

Clarkson, M. E. (1995). A stakeholder framework for analyzing and evaluating corporate social performance. *Academy of Management Review*, *20*(1), 92–117.

Cronqvist, H., Yu, F. (2017). Shaped by their daughters: Executives, female socialization, and corporate social responsibility. *Journal of Financial Economics, 126*(3), 543–562.

Dam, L., Scholtens, B. (2008). Environmental regulation and MNEs location: Does CSR matter? *Ecological Economics, 67*(1), 55–65.

Di Giuli, A., Kostovetsky, L. (2014). Are red or blue companies more likely to go green? Politics and corporate social responsibility. *Journal of Financial Economics, 111*, (1), 158–180.

De Villiers, C., Naiker, V., & Van Staden, C. J. (2011). The effect of board characteristics on firm environmental performance. *Journal of Management, 37*(6), 1636–1663.

Donaldson, T. & Preston, L. (1995). The stakeholder theory of the corporation. *Academy of Management Review, 20*(1), 65–91.

Dyck, A., Lins, K., Roth, L., Wagner, H. (2019). Do institutional investors drive corporate social responsibility? International evidence. *Journal of Financial Economics, 131*(3), 693–714.

Edmans, A. (2023). The end of ESG. *Financial Management, 52*(1), 3–17. https://doi.org/10.1111/fima.12413

Elkington, J. (1997). *Cannibals with forks: The triple bottom line of 21st century business.* Capstone.

Ferrell, A., Liang, H., & Renneboog, L. (2016). Socially responsible firms. *Journal of Financial Economics, 122*(3), 585–606. https://doi.org/10.1016/j.jfineco.2015.12.003

Flammer, C. (2015). Does corporate social responsibility lead to superior financial performance? a regression discontinuity approach. *Management Science, 61*(11), 2549–2568. https://doi.org/10.1287/mnsc.2014.2038

Flammer, C., & Bansal, P. (2017). Does a long-term orientation create value? Evidence from a regression discontinuity. *Strategic Management Journal, 38*(9), 1827–1847. https://doi.org/10.1002/smj.2629

Freeman, R. E. (1984). *Strategic Management: A Stakeholder Approach.* Pitman, Boston.

Friedman, M. (1970). The social responsibility of business is to increase its profits. *New York Times Magazine, 32–33*, 122–124.

Gao, L., Zhang, J. (2015). Firms' Earnings Smoothing, Corporate Social Responsibility, and Valuation. *Journal of Corporate Finance, 32*(C), 108–127. https://doi.org/10.1016/j.jcorpfin.2015.03.004

George, G., Howard-Grenville, J., Joshi, A., & Tihanyi, L. (2016). Understanding and tackling societal grand challenges through management research. *Academy of Management Journal, 59*(6), 1880–1895.

Gillan, S. L., Koch, A., & Starks, L. T. (2021). Firms and social responsibility: A review of ESG and CSR research in corporate finance. *Journal of Corporate Finance, 66*(September 2019), 101889.

Glößner, S. (2019). Investor horizons, long-term blockholders, and corporate social responsibility. *Journal of Banking & Finance, 103*, 78–97.

Godfrey, P. C., Merrill, C. B., & Hansen, J. M. (2009). The relationship between corporate social responsibility and shareholder value: An empirical test of the risk management hypothesis. *Strategic Management Journal, 445*(December 2008), 425–445.

Godfrey, P. C. (2005). Philanthropy and shareholder wealth: The relationship between corporate a risk management perspective. *Academy of Management Review, 30*(4), 777–798.

Gupta, A., Briscoe, F., & Hambrick, D. C. (2017). Red, blue, and purple firms: Organizational political ideology and corporate social responsibility. *Strategic Management Journal, 38*(5), 1018–1040.

Hahn, T., Pinkse, J., Preuss, L., & Figge, F. (2015). Tensions in Corporate Sustainability: Towards an Integrative Framework. *Journal of Business Ethics, 127*, 297–316.

Hall, P. A., & Soskice, D. (Ed.). (2001). *Varieties of capitalism: The institutional foundations of comparative advantage.* Oxford University Press

Hillman, A. J., & Dalziel, T. (2003). Boards of directors and firm performance: Integrating agency and resource dependence perspectives. *Academy of Management Review, 28*, 383–396.

Hillman, A. J., & Keim, G. D. (2001). Shareholder value, stakeholder management, and social issues: What's the bottom line? *Strategic Management Journal, 22*(2), 125–139.

Höllerer, M. (2013). From taken-for-granted to explicit commitment: The rise of CSR in a corporatist country. *Journal of Management Studies, 50*(4), 573–606.

Hsu, P., Liang, H., Matos, P. (2021). Leviathan Inc. and corporate environmental engagement. *Management Science, 69*(12), 7719–7758.

Ikram, A., Li, Z., & Minor, D. (2019). CSR-contingent executive compensation contracts. *Journal of Banking & Finance, 151*, 105655.

Ioannou, I., & Serafeim, G. (2012). What drives corporate social performance? The role of nation-level institutions. *Journal of International Business Studies*, *43*(9), 834–864.

Jackson, G., & Apostolakou, A. (2010). Corporate social responsibility in Western Europe: An institutional mirror or substitute? *Journal of Business Ethics*, *94*(3), 371–394.

Jackson, G., & Deeg, R. (2008). Comparing capitalisms: Understanding institutional diversity and its implications for international business. *Journal of International Business Studies*, *39*(4), 540–561.

Jensen, M. C. (2001). Value maximization, stakeholder theory, and the corporate objectives function. *European Financial Management*, *7*, 297–317.

Jiang, Y., Kang, Y., & Liang, H. (2023). The externalities of ESG disclosure. European Corporate Governance Institute, Finance working paper No. 880.

Johnson, R. A., & Greening, D. W. (1999). The effects of corporate governance and institutional ownership types on corporate social performance. *Academy of Management Journal*, *42*(5), 564–576.

Joly, H. (2021). Creating a Meaningful Corporate Purpose. *Harvard Business Review*. (Oct. 28, 2021). https://hbr.org/2021/10/creating-a-meaningful-corporate-purpose

Khan, M., Serafeim, G., & Yoon, A. (2016). Corporate sustainability: First evidence on materiality. *Accounting Review*, *91*(6), 1697–1724.

Kim, J., & Jo, H. (2022). Controlling owner type, state capitalism, and corporate social responsibility in Africa. *Corporate Governance: An International Review*, *30*(6), 765–782.

Kim, S., Lee, G., & Kang, H. G. 2021. Risk management and corporate social responsibility. *Strategic Management Journal*, *42*, 202–230.

Liang, H., Marquis, C., Renneboog, L., & Sun, S. L. (2018). Future-time framing: The effect of language on corporate future orientation. *Organization Science*, *29*(6), 1093–1111.

Liang, H., & Renneboog, L. (2017). The foundations of corporate social responsibility the foundations of corporate social responsibility. *Journal of Finance*, *72*(2), 853–910.

Loewenstein, G. & Thaler, R.H. (1989). Intertemporal choice. *Journal of Economic Perspectives*, *3*(4), 181–199.

Margolis, J. D., & Walsh, J. P. (2003). Misery loves companies: Rethinking social initiatives by business. *Administrative Science Quarterly*, *48*(2), 268–305.

Masulis, R., & Reza, S. W. (2015). Agency Problems of Corporate Philanthropy. *The Review of Financial Studies*, *28*(2), 592–636.

Matten, D., & Crane, A. (2005). Corporate citizenship: Toward an extended theoretical conceptualization. *Academy of Management Review*, *30*(1), 166–179.

Matten, D., & Moon, J. (2008). "Implicit" and "explicit" CSR: A conceptual framework for a comparative understanding of corporate social responsibility. *Academy of Management Review*, *33*(2), 404–424.

McGuinness, P. B., Vieito, J. P., & Wang, M. (2017). The role of board gender and foreign ownership in the CSR performance of Chinese listed firms. *Journal of Corporate Finance*, *42*(C), 75–99.

McWilliams, A., & Siegel, D. (2001). Profit-maximizing corporate social responsibility. *Academy of Management Review*, *26*(4), 504–505.

Meyer, J. W., & Rowan, B. (1977). Institutionalized organizations: Formal structure as myth and ceremony. *American Journal of Sociology*, *83*(2), 340–363.

Musacchio, A., Lazzarini, S. G., & Aguilera, R. V. (2015). New varieties of state capitalism: strategic and governance implications. *Academy of Management Perspectives*, *29*, 115–131.

Neubaum, D. O., & Zahra, S. A. (2006). Institutional Ownership and Corporate Social Performance: The Moderating Effects of Investment Horizon, Activism, and Coordination. *Journal of Management*, *32*(1), 108–131.

North, D. C. (1990). *Institutions, Institutional Change and Economic Performance*. Cambridge University Press, MA.

Orlitzky, M., Schmidt, F. L., & Rynes, S. L. (2003). Corporate Social and Financial Performance: A Meta-Analysis. *Organization Studies*, *24*.

Peng, M. W. 2004. Outside directors and firm performance during institutional transitions. *Strategic Management Journal*, *25*, 453–471.

Pollman, E. (2022). The making and meaning of ESG. U of Penn, Inst for Law & Econ Research Paper, 22–23.

Rugman, A. M., & Verbeke, A. (1992). A Note on the Transnational Solution and the Transaction Cost Theory of Multinational Strategic Management. *Journal of International Business Studies*, *23*(4), 761–771.

Slawinski, N., & Bansal, P. (2015). Short on time: Intertemporal tensions in business sustainability. *Organization Science*, *26*(2), 531–549.

Starks, L. T. (2023). Presidential Address: Sustainable Finance and ESG Issues—Value versus Values. *Journal of Finance*, *78*(4), 1837–1872.

Surroca, J., Tribó, J. A., & Zahra, S. A. (2013). Stakeholder pressure on MNEs and the transfer of socially irresponsible practices to subsidiaries. *Academy of Management Journal*, *56*(2), 549–572.

Waldman, D. A., Sully de Luque, M., Washburn, N., House, R. J., Adetoun, B., Barrasa, A., … Wilderom, C. P. M. (2006). Cultural and leadership predictors of corporate social responsibility values of top management: a GLOBE study of 15 countries. *Journal of International Business Studies*, *37*(6), 823–837.

Walls, J., Berrone, P., & Phan, P. 2012. Corporate governance and environmental performance: is there really a link? *Strategic Management Journal*, *33*, 885–913.

Wood, G., & Wright, M. (2015). Corporations and new statism: Trends and research priorities. *Academy of Management Perspectives*, *29*(2), 271–286.

World Commission on Environment and Development (WCED) (1987). *Our common future*. Oxford and New York: Oxford University Press.*

Young, S. L., & Makhija, M. V. (2014). Firms' corporate social responsibility behavior: An integration of institutional and profit maximization approaches. *Journal of International Business Studies*, *45*(6), 670–698.

CHAPTER 2

MEASURING CSR, ESG, AND SUSTAINABILITY

J.H. John Kim[a] and Sebeom Oh[b]

[a]College of Charleston, SC, USA
[b]Temple University, PA, USA

ABSTRACT

We examine the spectrum of sustainability, corporate social responsibility (CSR), and environmental, social, and governance (ESG) databases, highlighting the variety of methodologies for generating ESG scores and their consequences for empirical finance research and investment strategy development. We begin by exploring the conceptual distinctions and overlaps among CSR, ESG, and sustainability initiatives, moving to address the challenges associated with measuring and applying these databases. We present a comparative analysis of these databases, which directly contribute to the discourse on sustainable finance. Furthermore, we acknowledge the prevalent challenges in ESG metric development, such as data availability, comparability issues, and the dynamic nature of ESG factors. Through our review, we find that, although there are efforts toward accurate representation, significant discrepancies exist in the extent to which these databases capture the complexities of CSR, ESG, and sustainability. We uncover a lack of comparability among these databases and the empirical studies leveraging them, which complicates the synthesis of research findings and the development of a coherent investment strategy based on these principles. The study advocates for future research to refine ESG scoring methodologies, improve metrics' comparability across databases, and foster a more sustainable and responsible investment ecosystem.

Keywords: Corporate sustainability; corporate social responsibility; ESG; sustainable finance; metrics

JEL Classification: M14; Q56

Responsible Firms: CSR, ESG, and Global Sustainability
International Finance Review, Volume 23, 17–34
Copyright © 2025 by J.H. John Kim and Sebeom Oh
Published under exclusive licence by Emerald Publishing Limited
ISSN: 1569-3767/doi:10.1108/S1569-376720240000023002

1. INTRODUCTION

The landscape of sustainable investing has undergone a profound transformation, transitioning from a niche interest to a mainstream priority of modern finance. This evolution signifies a pivotal moment in finance research, integrating sustainable investment principles at the core of financial analysis and signaling the emergence of a new paradigm in responsible investing. However, the widespread embrace of CSR, ESG standards, and sustainability indices has unveiled a critical challenge: a gap in understanding their methodological foundations and the impact of their diversity across different databases due to these constructs' inherent complexity and multidimensionality, leading to scholarly debate and practical confusion. These challenges underscore the need for a refined comprehension of these metrics, advocating for enhanced transparency, standardization, and methodological precision in creating and utilizing ESG scores.

Our study delves into various databases dedicated to sustainability, CSR, and ESG. We highlight the myriad methodologies utilized in generating ESG scores and discuss the significant repercussions these methodologies have on empirical finance research and the crafting of investment strategies, thereby enriching the discourse on sustainable investing. Empirical studies have consistently highlighted that discrepancies in ESG scoring often originate from differences in measurement approaches, further compounded by conceptual variations. Notably, Chatterji et al. (2015) observed that measurement discrepancies are more pronounced than the conceptual ones. Similarly, Kotsantonis and Serafeim (2019) identified several sources of these variances, including inconsistent data provision, subjective determination of peer groups, mishandling of missing data, and disagreements on conceptual understandings of ESG. Berg et al. (2022) further reinforced this perspective, pointing out that the challenges posed by measurement intricacies extend beyond the conceptual scope of ESG, leading to inconsistencies. Amidst this backdrop, Starks (2023) revisits the fundamental reasons for the differences in CSR, ESG, and CS scores, offering a timely conceptual clarification and shedding light on the extensive terminologies prevalent in this sphere. This contribution underscores the nuanced motivations and perspectives that underlie the complexity of CSR and ESG issues.

Our investigation reveals a significant inconsistency among various databases, despite considerable efforts to align their metrics with ESG, CSR, and sustainability principles. This inconsistency may stem from attempts to maintain marketability or uniqueness, leading to the adoption of diverse sources and methodologies in developing these databases. The competitive landscape might make the methodologies opaque, often using broad descriptions like "a variety of sources were used." Given the expansive nature of ESG, CSR, and sustainability, it is understandable that the databases embody these concepts. However, from both an empirical and practical standpoint, the application of these databases may yield conflicting results because of low correlations on each aggregated score highlighted by previous scholarly work (e.g., Chatterji et al., 2015; Berg et al., 2022). This discord complicates synthesizing research findings and formulating a cohesive investment strategy based on these principles.

The ramifications extend beyond academic inquiry and investment strategies. Without uniform evidence or consistent results, challenges may arise for governments, lawmakers, and companies aiming to enhance their engagement with and implement ESG, CSR, and sustainability strategies. Variances in reports and databases can signal either the success or failure of these initiatives. Such discrepancies underscore the need for a collaborative endeavor to harmonize or underscore the commonalities among these databases rather than merely identifying which databases are in alignment with CSR, ESG, and sustainability criteria.

Building on understanding these complexities, it becomes crucial to explore the distinction between corporate and community/global sustainability, another critical area of conceptual confusion within the sustainability domain. Community sustainability, which spans social groups to the global community, focuses on three principles as identified by Berkowitz (1996): the comprehensive use of community resources (especially human resources), building strong social networks with shared interests, and fulfilling the community's non-material needs, emphasizing values beyond profitability. Corporations within these communities possess unique insights into community sustainability and may lean toward sustainable practices influenced by cultures with a long-term orientation. Marrewijk and Werre (2003) suggest embedding sustainability in all corporate operations despite the company's inherent focus on profit and financial viability. This focus often leads to divergent strategies and objectives between corporate and community sustainability efforts. However, this distinction allows corporations to significantly contribute to the community or global sustainability, engaging in efforts that align their long-term success with the welfare of their communities and environment. This alignment is framed within the "triple bottom line" approach, balancing social, environmental, and financial responsibilities. It reflects the evolving phases of sustainability development from profit-driven to caring and synergistic approaches, as in Marrewijk and Werre (2003), echoing the values-based emphasis discussed by Starks (2023).

The debate between shareholder and stakeholder theories enriches our understanding of corporate governance by challenging traditional models and highlighting how sustainable practices can create long-term value for all stakeholders. Under Milton Friedman's theory, Shareholder theory prioritizes maximizing shareholder wealth, presenting a clear but narrow pathway to corporate success. Contrastingly, stakeholder theory, formulated by R. Edward Freeman (Freeman, 1984), argues for a more inclusive approach to corporate responsibility that encompasses a broader array of interests beyond the financial bottom line. This theory advocates for the corporation's accountability to shareholders, employees, customers, suppliers, the community, and the environment, presenting a multifaceted perspective on success. Here, ESG criteria emerge as the practical embodiment of stakeholder theory, emphasizing the corporation's role in fostering sustainable and ethical business practices. ESG criteria challenge and expand the traditional shareholder-focused model, illustrating how sustainable practices enhance long-term value for all stakeholders, including shareholders.

This nuanced interplay between shareholder and stakeholder suggests a comprehensive approach integrating ethical, sustainable practices to pursue financial profitability.

Our study makes three key contributions to the existing literature. First, we dissect the conceptual distinctions and synergies between CSR, ESG, and sustainability frameworks by recalling previous discussions on corporate sustainability (CS) and showing why disparities arise. Second, our comprehensive comparative analysis of ESG databases illuminates the methodological divergences, acknowledging the existing hurdles in ESG metric formulation, such as the issues of data accessibility, metric comparability, and the fluidity of ESG. Lastly, we extend the discourse by introducing several of the most popular and newer databases that have yet to be used and can be helpful. Our analysis aims to elevate the discourse in sustainable finance, offering a refined lens through which academics and industry stakeholders can assess and navigate the evolving paradigms of corporate responsibility and sustainable investing.

The remainder of the work is structured as follows: Section 2 presents the difference in concept and measurement, Section 3 examines the various databases, and Section 4 concludes the paper.

2. DIFFERENCE IN CONCEPT AND MEASUREMENT

Few studies have explored the distinctions between CS, CSR, and ESG concepts, despite their frequent interchangeable use in both academic and industry contexts. Kaptein and Wempe (2002) argue that CS represents "the ultimate goal" of a firm, with CSR as "an immediate stage where companies try to balance" competing interests. Similarly, authors depict CS as a broad concept, considering corporate responsibility as an intermediate concept encompassing economic, social, and environmental responsibilities (Panapanaan et al., 2003). Marrewijk (2003) further differentiates these concepts by associating CSR with the communion of people and organizations and emphasizing phenomena such as transparency, stakeholder dialogue, and sustainability reporting. In contrast, CS focuses on value creation, environmental management, eco-friendly production systems, and human capital management.

Building on these foundational ideas, Marrewijk and Werre (2003) propose a nuanced classification of firms' sustainability motivations, identifying six hierarchical levels that range from pre-CS, characterized by minimal external pressures, to holistic CS, seamlessly integrating sustainability into the fabric of the organization. This framework provides a detailed examination of how firms evolve in their sustainability journey, moving beyond regulatory compliance and profit motivations to embrace a comprehensive, values-driven approach to business and societal well-being.

Starks (2023) employs a similar approach to Marrewijk and Werre (2003), defining value as financial value and values as diverse non-financial preferences. This framework categorizes various finance literature terminologies based on their orientation toward value or values. As illustrated in Fig. 2.1, it is evident

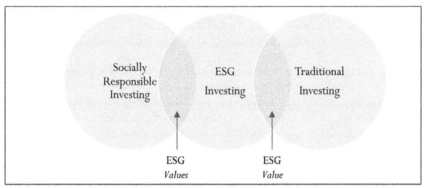

Panel A. *Values* versus *Value* in Investment Approaches

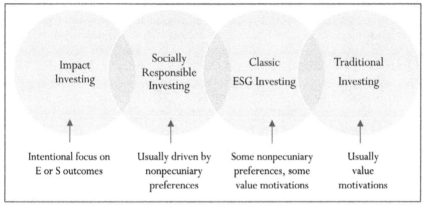

Panel B. *Values* versus *Value* in Investment Approaches: Investor Preferences

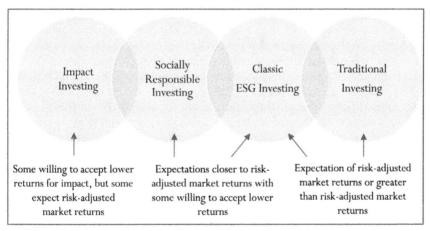

Panel C *Values* versus *Value* in Investment Approaches: Expected Returns

Fig. 2.1.   Values vs. Value Concept (Adapted from Starks, 2023).

that non-financial preferences weigh more heavily in impact investing than in traditional investing. Within this framework, socially responsible investing (or CSR-based investing) aligns more closely with diverse values than ESG investing, suggesting that these concepts share a common dimension.

The measurement and evaluation of CSR, ESG, and CS concepts have prompted further empirical investigation, as demonstrated by Chatterji et al. (2015) and Berg et al. (2022). Chatterji et al. (2015) explore the variability and low correlation among CSR scores across different rating agencies, finding that these discrepancies are primarily due to divergent measurement methodologies rather than conceptual differences. Kotsantonis and Serafeim (2019) further elucidate the challenges in this domain, identifying four primary difficulties: the inconsistency of data and formats provided by companies, the subjective setting of peer groups for comparison by rating agencies, the handling of missing data, and the varied perspectives of rating firms on what constitutes CSR and ESG. Berg et al. (2022) show inconsistent correlations among academic databases academics frequently use (see Section 3 and Table 2 for a detailed low correlation table). They extend the previous analysis, attributing 56% of the variation in ESG ratings to differences in measurement approaches, 38% to variations in the scope of ESG components, and 6% to differences in scoring weights.

Our analysis of databases centered on ESG, CSR, and sustainability has identified marked inconsistencies despite concerted attempts to align their metrics with the core ideals of these domains. These discrepancies likely stem from efforts to distinguish databases through unique features or market positioning, leading to adopting varied methodologies and sources. Given the comprehensive nature of ESG, CSR, and sustainability, databases are expected to encapsulate these concepts. Yet, their divergent applications pose challenges in collective research outcomes and developing integrated investment strategies.

Beyond academic exploration and strategy development, these inconsistencies bear significant implications for government agencies, legislative bodies, and corporations aiming to enhance their ESG, CSR, and sustainability initiatives. The lack of uniform data can skew perceptions regarding the efficacy of such initiatives, with disparate reports potentially signaling both triumphs and setbacks. This highlights an imperative for concerted action to bridge these disparities, emphasizing the need to draw out and reinforce the shared elements among these databases. Moving forward, aligning these resources with the essence of CSR, ESG, and sustainability becomes critical in furnishing stakeholders with dependable data that underpins sound decision-making and the successful execution of sustainability agendas across diverse sectors. These findings highlight the importance of a deeper understanding and standardization of measurement methodologies to ensure the reliability and comparability of CSR and ESG evaluations.

2.1. Corporate Sustainability vs. Community Sustainability

It is vital to clarify a common area of conceptual confusion within the domain of sustainability: the distinction between CS and community and global sustainability. The term "community" encompasses a broad spectrum of entities from social groups and neighborhoods to entire countries or the global community. Community sustainability, a significant focus within community psychology as highlighted by Berkowitz (1996), operates on three foundational principles aimed at achieving sustainability at the community levels: (1) the ongoing utilization of all community resources, with a particular emphasis on human resources; (2) the creation of strong social networks characterized by shared interests and a collective sense of destiny; (3) addressing the more profound, non-material needs of the community. Importantly, these principles underscore values that extend beyond financial gains or profitability.

As integral parts of the broader community, corporations have unique insights into what constitutes community sustainability. Firms deeply embedded in cultures emphasizing long-term orientation are more inclined toward engaging in sustainable practices (Choi et al., 2022). Marrewijk and Werre (2003) explore the possibilities of embedding sustainability into every aspect of corporate operations and decision-making processes. Nonetheless, the inherent nature of a company's existence is closely tied to profitability and financial viability (Elkington, 1998), which means that, although corporate and community sustainability efforts may align in their overarching goals, their strategies and immediate objectives often differ, mainly due to the profit imperative driving CS.

Nevertheless, this dichotomy allows corporations to contribute substantially to community or global sustainability initiatives. Corporations, as participants in a larger ecosystem, actively engage in efforts to support community sustainability, recognizing the inextricable link between their long-term success and the welfare of their communities and environments. This concept is often framed within the "triple bottom line" approach, advocating a balance among social, environmental, and financial responsibilities aptly encapsulated as "profit, people, and the planet" (Elkington, 1998; Hussain et al., 2016). Such perspectives are in harmony with the phases of sustainability development identified by Marrewijk and Werre (2003) ranging from profit-driven to caring and synergistic sustainability and complement the emphasis on "values" discussed by Starks (2023).

2.2. Shareholder Value vs. Stakeholder Value

Stakeholder and shareholder theories provide distinct frameworks for understanding corporate governance, each with its unique emphasis on the objectives and beneficiaries of corporate actions. The finance and business ethics literature has explored these theories.

Shareholder theory, closely linked to Milton Friedman, asserts that the primary objective of a corporation is to maximize shareholder wealth, positing that prioritizing shareholder interests leads to optimal economic efficiency and societal wealth (Milton, 1970). On the other hand, stakeholder theory, formulated by R. Edward Freeman and others, advocates for a more inclusive approach to corporate responsibility (Freeman, 1984). This theory extends the corporation's accountability beyond shareholders to include employees, customers, suppliers, the community, and the environment, arguing that attending to the diverse interests of these groups fosters sustainable success and ethical business operations.

The juxtaposition of these theories highlights a pivotal shift in corporate governance from a singular focus on financial returns to a broader engagement with ethical considerations and the creation of long-term value.

ESG criteria inherently align with stakeholder theory by addressing the wide-ranging interests of stakeholders. Environmental criteria underscore a company's duty toward ecological sustainability and the impacts of its operations. Social criteria emphasize the importance of nurturing relationships with employees, customers, suppliers, and communities, advocating for their well-being and interests. Governance criteria are focused on promoting ethical conduct, accountability, and transparency, ensuring that decisions benefit all stakeholders, including minority shareholders. In this context, ESG emerges as a tangible manifestation of stakeholder theory principles, signaling a move toward more inclusive and sustainable business practices that contemplate the extended effects of corporate actions on various stakeholder groups.

Merging ESG with shareholder theory reveals a complex interplay with the traditional emphasis on shareholder value maximization. ESG initiatives can reconcile with shareholder theory by demonstrating how sustainable practices mitigate risks, enhance brand reputation, and unlock new opportunities, thus contributing to long-term shareholder value (Jensen, 2010; Syed, 2017). This synthesis challenges the conventional dichotomy between profit maximization and investment in sustainable, ethical practices.

The evolving dialogue in corporate governance suggests a reevaluation toward balancing shareholder value maximization with stakeholder wealth maximization. This recalibration acknowledges that ethical and sustainable business practices are compatible with and contribute to enhancing profitability and shareholder returns over time. This development signifies a refined understanding of corporate responsibility, blending traditional models with contemporary societal and environmental well-being concerns.

3. EXAMINING DATABASES

This section outlines an overview of various databases dedicated to CS, ESG, and CSR metrics. It underscores the prevalent engagement of scholars with ESG scores while highlighting a general oversight regarding the underlying methodologies that differentiate these scores across numerous dimensions. The compilation of databases under review offers insights into diverse facets of ESG/CSR, tailored to distinct objectives such as ESG investment analysis or the identification of ESG compliance lapses. These databases exhibit various strengths and limitations, collectively encompassing a broad spectrum of coverage and progressively expanding to encapsulate a more comprehensive dataset. The emergent interest in ESG/CSR themes has precipitated the development of these databases; however, a notable limitation is their relatively short span of historical data. The dynamic nature of the corporate landscape, coupled with increasing corporate initiatives toward addressing ESG/CSR concerns, necessitates regular updates to these databases. Table 2.1 presents a comparative analysis of some of the predominant databases utilized in academic research. It details their access points, temporal

Table 2.1. Overview of ESG Data Sources.

DB Name	Focus	Institution	Available at	Data Coverage	Companies Covered
SASB Materiality	Industry-level (firm-level available)	SASB, IFRS	Bloomberg	2007~	–
Major Characteristics			**Methodology**		**Sample paper**
Environment, Social Capital, Human Capital, Business Model and Innovation, Leadership and Governance' – Industry-specific recommendations – Integrated with the IFRS Foundation			– Moderated by technical staffs – Propose standard update – Incorporate public comments		Grewal et al. (2020)
DB Name	**Focus**	**Institution**	**Available at**	**Data Coverage**	**Companies Covered**
MSCI KLD	Firm-level	MSCI	WRDS	1991~2019	Top 3,000 US companies by market capitalization
Major Characteristics			**Methodology**		**Sample Paper**
– Comprehensive coverage – Data depth – Historical data			– Draws data from various sources – Subdivides ESG into numerous categories		Lins et al. (2017)
DB Name	**Focus**	**Institution**	**Available at**	**Data Coverage**	**Companies Covered**
Sustainalytics	Firm-level	Morningstar	Morningstar, WRDS	2018~2023	17,000 private and public companies from 110 countries
Major Characteristics			**Methodology**		**Sample Paper**
– Global coverage – Detailed ESG ratings – Materiality focused analysis			– Pinpoints material ESG issues – Rates companies based on exposure and management of ESG risk		Lins et al. (2017)

(Continued)

Table 2.1. (*Continued*)

DB Name	Focus	Institution	Available at	Data Coverage	Companies Covered
Robeco SDG	Firm-level	Robeco	Robeco	2017	11,000 key players in global equity and fixed income benchmarks
Major Characteristics			**Methodology**		**Sample Paper**
– Alignment with UN SDGs – Quantitative and qualitative analysis – Materiality focused analysis			– Three-step analysis – Determines company's influence on ESG		Hartzmark and Sussman (2019)

DB Name	Focus	Institution	Available at	Data Coverage	Companies Covered
Refinitiv ESG	Firm-level	Thompson Refinitiv	WRDS	2002~	15,000 global companies across 76 countries
Major Characteristics			**Methodology**		**Sample Paper**
– Global scope – Quantitative and qualitative analysis – Standardized scoring system			– Focus on key themes deemed most critical for specific industries		Albuquerque et al. (2020)

coverage, the scope of companies surveyed, and examples of academic works employing these databases for empirical investigation. While not exhaustive, this compilation showcases recent scholarly contributions to the field.

Table 2.2, adapted from Berg et al. (2022), illuminates the strikingly low correlations among various ESG scores discussed in this work. This comparison of pairwise correlation coefficients highlights the lack of consistency in ESG assessments, revealing that even within the common sample, the overall ESG scores exhibit surprisingly weak correlations. A more troubling observation arises when considering the individual pillars or components of ESG scores – governance scores, in particular, sometimes demonstrate negative correlations. This indicates significant discrepancies in the methodologies and measurements employed by different rating agencies, contributing to a fragmented ESG landscape. As previously discussed, these variations in measurement contribute to the difficulty of achieving a standardized approach to evaluating and interpreting ESG performance.

3.1. Databases on Sustainability

3.1.1 SASB Materiality

The Sustainability Accounting Standards Board (SASB) is a non-profit organization that aims to establish industry standards for sustainability scores. Beginning in 2022, integrating SASB standards into the IFRS Foundation marked their broad acceptance within the accounting community. The SASB Standards discern distinct sustainability issues pertinent to investor decision-making across 77 industries. As a result, a firm is evaluated based on industry-specific standards, encompassing 2–11 issues (see Table 2.3). We classify these issues into five dimensions: Environment, Social Capital, Human Capital, Business Model, Innovation, and Leadership and governance.

These standards are unique in that they provide guidelines suggesting that not all firms must address every aspect of sustainability. For instance, the casino gaming industry has four relevant issues: Energy Management in the Environment, Customer Welfare in Social Capital, Employee Health and safety in Human Capital, and Business Ethics in Leadership and Governance. The Software and IT Services industry should consider six issues: Energy Management, Customer Privacy, Data Security, Employee Engagement, Diversity and inclusion, Competitive Behavior, and Systemic Risk Management. This approach offers valuable industry standards or firm-level recommendations for consideration. However, a challenge for academics is that these standards act as guidelines for firms rather than as evaluated scores.

Table 2.2. Correlations Between ESG Ratings Adapted from Berg et al. (2022).

	KLD and Sustainalytics	KLD and Refinitiv	Sustainalytics and Refinitiv
Overall ESG	0.53	0.42	0.67
Environment	0.59	0.54	0.64
Social	0.31	0.22	0.55
Governance	0.02	−0.05	0.49

Table 2.3. SASB Materiality.

Dimension	Issues
Environment	GHG emissions
	Air quality
	Energy management
	Water & wastewater management
	Waste & hazardous materials management
	Ecological impacts
Social Capital	Human rights & community relations
	Customer privacy
	Data security
	Access & affordability
	Product quality & safety
	Customer welfare
	Selling practices & product labeling
Human Capital	Labor practices
	Employee health & safety
	Employee engagement, diversity, & inclusion
Business Model and Innovation	Product design & lifecycle management
	Business model resilience
	Supply chain management
	Materials sourcing & efficiency
	Physical impacts of climate change
Leadership and Governance	Business ethics
	Competitive behavior
	Management of the legal & regulatory environment
	Critical incident risk management
	Systemic risk management

Grewal et al. (2020) demonstrated the application of these materiality standards to firm-level corporate finance research. They constructed a material sustainability disclosure variable using data from the Bloomberg terminal. Grewal et al. (2020) provide a detailed procedure for utilizing Excel. Bloomberg aligns ESG data items with SASB's topics and issues, enabling the calculation of a disclosure score based on the proportion of non-missing fields to the total number of fields.

3.1.2 Sustainalytics

Sustainalytics, a subsidiary of Morningstar, offers a detailed database dedicated to ESG research, ratings, and data. This resource explores various ESG issues and controversies, covering corporate governance, business ethics, carbon emissions, human rights, product governance, and efficient resource utilization. Central to its services, Sustainalytics's ESG Risk Ratings evaluate a company's vulnerability to ESG risks beyond mitigation and assess the effectiveness of its management of controllable ESG risks.

The primary goal of the ESG Risk Ratings is to quantify a company's exposure to specific material ESG risks and assess how well it manages these risks. This effort seeks to equip investors with comprehensive insights into the ESG factors that could impact a company's financial stability and long-term sustainability.

The information provided is essential for making informed investment decisions, evaluating risks, and engaging with stakeholders.

Sustainalytics analyses over 17,000 entities, including public and private companies and fixed-income issuers from developed, emerging, and frontier markets. The firm focuses particularly on Chinese enterprises listed with A and B shares. The firm's industry coverage spans an extensive range, from energy and mining to technology and consumer goods, highlighting the wide range of ESG challenges encountered across various sectors.

Sustainalytics' approach to ESG Risk Ratings begins by pinpointing Material ESG Issues (MEIs) vital to each industry. Following the identification of these MEIs, the process involves assessing a company's vulnerability to these issues and the efficacy of its strategies for managing such risks. The process concludes with the scoring and rating of companies based on their exposure to and management of ESG risks, placing them within a defined spectrum from negligible to severe risks.

Sustainalytics employs a detailed method that blends numerical data and narrative insights, sourcing information from corporate reports, non-governmental organization (NGO) publications, and media stories. This transparent and open method guarantees that investors grasp the reasoning behind the ESG Risk Rating assigned to each company. By aggregating diverse issues into one comprehensive rating, the database facilitates easy comparison among companies, enabling users to efficiently evaluate the ESG concerns most pertinent to specific businesses and their operational environments. Sustainalytics caters to industry experts, focusing on identifying the ESG factors most likely to influence financial outcomes.

3.1.3 Robeco SDG

The Robeco SDG Database, created by Robeco, is a comprehensive tool designed to assess corporate contributions toward the United Nations' Sustainable Development Goals (SDGs). These goals aim to tackle global challenges, including poverty, inequality, and environmental degradation, by 2030. The database evaluates over 11,000 companies, key players in global equity and fixed income benchmarks, to provide insights into their sustainability impacts. This effort is part of Robeco's initiative to enhance sustainability data quality and establish common standards in the investment industry.

Robeco's scoring framework employs a detailed three-step analysis to determine a company's influence on the SDGs, resulting in scores ranging from -3 (highly negative impact) to $+3$ (highly positive impact). This scoring reflects a rigorous evaluation of a company's sustainability performance, offering investors a clear and consistent basis for decision-making. However, the database does not include a long historical time series of data, focusing instead on recent years. Data sources include corporate reports and information from external providers, ensuring the accuracy and reliability of the SDG scores. This approach enables comprehensive assessments of companies' sustainability efforts. Robeco targets industry professionals and emphasizes a materiality-centric approach, prioritizing events and developments with significant financial implications. Furthermore, Robeco features a dynamic update mechanism, meaning that a company's score is fluid and adjusted to mirror the latest news. This continuous updating process can present challenges for researchers seeking to utilize the database, as the evolving nature of the data may complicate longitudinal studies or comparisons over time.

3.2. Databases on ESG and CSR

3.2.1 MSCI (KLD) ESG Scores

The MSCI KLD ESG Database, developed through a collaboration between Morgan Stanley Capital International (MSCI) and KLD Research & Analytics, Inc., is a comprehensive ESG data series that has provided insights since 1991. It is a critical tool for integrating ESG considerations into investment strategies and research. The MSCI ESG KLD STATS, a vital database component, offers an extensive historical record and analysis of public companies through a wide range of ESG performance indicators.

Drawing from various sources, including academic research, data from governmental and NGOs, and company-specific disclosures like annual reports and sustainability disclosures, MSCI's ESG research adopts a thorough approach to evaluating a company's ESG risk management and opportunities. MSCI promotes transparency and accuracy in its research process by allowing companies to review the data collected on them.

The database is structured around the core pillars of ESG, subdivided into numerous categories that include positive and negative performance indicators. This structure provides a detailed view of a company's ESG performance, allowing for nuanced analysis. What distinguishes this dataset is its extensive scope and the level of detail it provides. It covers a broad spectrum of ESG factors across various components, offering a comprehensive view of a company's ESG performance. Unlike other databases that offer a generalized ESG score, the MSCI KLD ESG Database provides detailed indicators for specific aspects of ESG. This detail enables investors to compare companies based on distinct ESG factors directly.

Researchers and analysts have utilized this dataset to develop custom ESG scores for companies, focusing on relevant aspects of their interests. This methodological approach allows for the creation of tailored assessments of a company's ESG performance, facilitating precise and direct comparisons. MSCI is designed for industry professionals, but it stands out from many other contemporary databases by offering access to historical data. This feature makes it particularly valuable for academic researchers, enabling them to conduct longitudinal studies and analyze trends.

3.2.2 Thompson/Refinitiv ESG Company Scores

The Refinitiv ESG Database scrutinizes the ESG performance of over 15,000 global entities across 76 countries, representing a significant share of the world's market capitalization with a dataset that extends back to 2002. This comprehensive resource, incorporating upward of 700 metrics, underpins the integration of ESG considerations into investment strategies, aiding in identifying potential risks and opportunities. It spans a broad spectrum of the financial market, detailing the ESG practices of many officers, directors, equity issuers, and fixed-income securities.

Refinitiv's scoring methodology, aligned with LSEG standards, systematically evaluates ESG performance through a detailed analysis of publicly sourced and directly reported data. By focusing on 10 key themes and employing over 630 specific measures, of which 186 are deemed most critical for industry-specific assessments, the database offers a nuanced ESG score for each company. These scores result from a percentile ranking across categories, consolidated into ESG pillars, culminating in a composite score that reflects relative ESG performance. This approach benchmarks sustainability efforts and adjusts for industry relevance and company scale, facilitating a standardized comparison of CS practices. The Refinitiv ESG database primarily targets investors and corporations seeking to assess and enhance their sustainability practices. It is a critical tool for investors looking to integrate ESG considerations into their investment strategies and for companies aiming to understand and improve their ESG performance.

3.3 Other Supplemental Data

3.3.1 Climate TRACE

Climate TRACE reports annual human-caused greenhouse gas emissions at the country-sector-source level starting from 2015. It details emissions across 10 sectors: agriculture, buildings, fluorinated gases, forestry and land use, fossil fuel operations, manufacturing, mineral extraction, power, transportation, and waste. Specifically, within the transportation sector, the database distinguishes between types of gases (e.g., CO_2 and CH_4) and various emission sources such as domestic and international aviation, domestic and international shipping, and road transportation. Climate TRACE also provides insights into the geographic locations of emission sources, offering a unique opportunity to analyze the international aspects of greenhouse gas emissions.

As a relatively new resource, Climate TRACE has yet to be widely adopted in economic research, presenting a unique opportunity for pioneering work in this area. Researchers seeking to delve into the intricacies of global emissions data are encouraged to explore Gore (2022) and Haines et al. (2023) for an in-depth understanding of this tool's potential applications.

3.3.1 Violation Tracker

Violation Tracker compiles an extensive database containing records of corporate violation fines that exceed $5,000 in the United States, dating from 2000 onward. The database categorizes these records into nine offenses: competition, consumer protection, employment, environment, financial, government contracts, healthcare, safety, and other offenses. Each record specifies the federal regulatory agency responsible, such as the Department of Justice, and incorporates information about certain class action lawsuits. A notable feature of Violation Tracker is its detailed presentation of the financial penalties involved, offering researchers and policymakers a quantitative basis to gauge the severity of corporate transgressions. Such quantification is crucial for those analyzing the effectiveness of regulatory measures and the extent of corporate malfeasance.

For instance, Heese and Pérez-Cavazos (2019) utilized this dataset to examine the influence of managerial site visits on facility misconduct. More recently, Raghunandan (2021) leveraged data related explicitly to wage violations from this resource to explore the connection between corporate incentives and wage theft.

4. CONCLUSION

The profound transformation of sustainable investing from a niche to a mainstream priority in modern finance signifies a critical evolution toward embedding CSR, ESG, and sustainability principles at the heart of financial analysis and investment strategy. This indicates the emergence of a new paradigm in responsible investing that challenges traditional models by integrating sustainable investment principles. Our comprehensive exploration of various databases dedicated to sustainability, CSR, and ESG unveils the indispensable role these resources play in deepening our understanding of such principles despite the inherent challenges presented by their complexity and the diversity of methodologies employed in ESG scoring. Through examination of critical databases, including SASB Materiality, Sustainalytics, MSCI KLD ESG, and Refinitiv ESG, complemented by insights from supplementary databases like Climate TRACE and Violation Tracker, this study maps out the extensive data landscape pivotal for conducting nuanced analysis and making informed decisions in the realm of sustainable finance.

Our findings highlight the essential need for enhanced transparency, standardization, and methodological precision in creating and applying ESG scores to address the methodological foundations and the impact of their diversity across different platforms. Significant inconsistencies persist across various databases. These discrepancies arise from divergent methodologies and sources, often a byproduct of attempts to differentiate through unique features or strategic market positioning. Such variance complicates the aggregation of research findings and the formulation of cohesive investment strategies. The absence of standardized data can distort perceptions of the effectiveness of initiatives tied to ESG, CSR, and sustainability, underscoring the imperative to mitigate these differences and highlight commonalities within these databases. Establishing standardized measurement methodologies emerges as a critical endeavor to provide reliable data that facilitates informed decision-making and the effective implementation of sustainability strategies. By navigating through the complexities of these databases, we aim to bridge the gaps in understanding and methodological approaches, contributing significantly to the discourse on sustainable investing.

Furthermore, our study enriches the academic discourse on sustainable finance by introducing several of the most popular and newer databases that have yet to be widely used. This contribution offers a refined lens through which academics and industry stakeholders can navigate the evolving paradigms of corporate responsibility and sustainable investing, thus facilitating a more informed and sustainable financial future. We uncover discrepancies within these databases and the empirical investigations leveraging them, rendering the amalgamation of research outcomes and formulating a unified investment strategy grounded in these tenets challenging.

This work's contributions to the existing literature are threefold: providing a clear understanding of the conceptual distinctions within CSR, ESG, and sustainability; offering a comprehensive comparative analysis of ESG databases to highlight methodological divergences; and introducing underutilized databases that hold potential for future research. In doing so, we enrich the academic discourse on sustainable finance and provide practical insights for industry professionals seeking to align their operations with sustainability goals.

4.1. Limitations and Future Work

Our study explores the intricate inconsistencies among databases concerning ESG, CSR, and sustainability. We thoroughly examine the methodologies employed by these databases and assessed the implications of their differences on strategic decision-making. Despite these efforts, there is room for broader exploration. Future research could build on this foundation by delving deeper into the methodologies of these databases, evaluating their direct impact on corporate and governmental sustainability initiatives, and identifying how these influences materialize in practice.

Additionally, our analysis highlights the need for greater harmonization among these databases to address their discrepancies. However, it stops short of investigating the specific models or frameworks that could facilitate such alignment. Delving into sector-specific dynamics furthers our understanding, revealing how methodological variations influence sustainability strategies within distinct industries.

Given the dynamic nature of ESG, CSR, and sustainability, our findings are limited by the current conceptualizations of these terms. As the field evolves, future research should pivot to accommodate new trends and insights, exploring innovative methodologies for database alignment that resonate with these developments. Such inquiries are vital for enhancing the effectiveness and relevance of ESG, CSR, and sustainability databases in both scholarly and practical realms. Progress in this area is essential for harmonizing the myriad sustainability efforts with the broader objectives of environmental stewardship, social responsibility, and governance excellence.

REFERENCES

Albuquerque, R., Koskinen, Y., Yang, S., & Zhang, C. (2020). Resiliency of environmental and social stocks: An analysis of the exogenous COVID-19 market crash. *Review of Corporate Finance Studies 9*, 593–621.

Berg, F., Kölbel, J. F., & Rigobon, R. (2022). Aggregate confusion: The divergence of ESG ratings. *Review of Finance, 26*, 1315–1344.

Berkowitz, B. (1996). Personal and community sustainability. *American Journal of Community Psychology, 24*, 441–459.

Chatterji, A. K., Durand, R., Levine, D. I., & Touboul, S. (2015). Do ratings of firms converge? Implications for managers, investors and strategy researchers. *Strategic Management Journal, 37*, 1597–614.

Choi, J. J., Kim, J., & Shenkar, O. (2022). Temporal orientation and corporate social responsibility: Global evidence. *Journal of Management Studies*, *60*, 82–119.

Elkington, J. (1998). *Cannibals with Forks: The triple bottom line of 21st century business*. ISBN 0865713928.

Freeman, R. E. (1984). *Strategic management: A stakeholder approach*. ISBN 9780273019138.

Gore, A. (2022). Measure emissions to manage emissions. *Science*, *378*, 455.

Grewal, J., Hauptmann, C., & Serafeim, G. (2020). Material sustainability information and stock price informativeness. *Journal of Business Ethics*, *171*, 513–544.

Haines, A., Whitmee, S., & Anton, B. (2023). Accountability for carbon emissions and health equity. *Bulletin of the World Health Organization*, *101*, 83–83A.

Hartzmark, S. M., & Sussman, A. B. (2019). Do investors value sustainability? A natural experiment examining ranking and fund flows. *Journal of Finance*, *74*, 2789–2837.

Heese, J., & Pérez-Cavazos, G. (2019). When the boss comes to town: The effects of headquarters' visits on facility-level misconduct. *The Accounting Review*, *95*, 235–261.

Hussain, N., Rigoni, U., & Orij, R. P. (2016). Corporate governance and sustainability performance: Analysis of triple bottom line performance. *Journal of Business Ethics*, *149*, 411–432.

Jensen, M. C. (2010). Value maximization, stakeholder theory, and the corporate objective function. *Journal of Applied Corporate Finance*, *22*, 32–42.

Kaptein, M., & Wempe, J. F. D. B. (2002). *The balanced company: A theory of corporate integrity*. ISBN 9780199255504.

Kotsantonis, S., & Serafeim, G. (2019). Four things no one will tell you about ESG data. *Journal of Applied Corporate Finance*, *31*, 50–58.

Lins, K. V., Servaes, H., & Tamayo, A. (2017). Social capital, trust, and firm performance: The value of corporate social responsibility during the financial crisis. *Journal of Finance*, *72*, 1785–1824.

Marrewijk, M. V. (2003). Concepts and definitions of CSR and corporate sustainability: Between agency and communion. *Journal of Business Ethics*, *44*, 95–105.

Marrewijk, M. v., and M. Werre. 2003. Multiple levels of corporate sustainability. *Journal of Business Ethics*, *44*, 107–119.

Milton, F. (1970, Sept 13). The social responsibility of business is to increase its profits. *New York Times Magazine*.

Panapanaan, V. M., Linnanen, L., Karvonen, M.-M., & Phan, V. T. (2003). Roadmapping corporate social responsibility in Finnish companies. *Journal of Business Ethics*, *44*, 133–148.

Raghunandan, A. (2021). Financial misconduct and employee mistreatment: Evidence from wage theft. *Review of Accounting Studies*, *26*, 867–905.

Starks, L. T. (2023). Presidential address: Sustainable finance and ESG issues value versus values. *Journal of Finance*, *78*, 1837–1872.

Syed, A. M. (2017). Environment, social, and governance (ESG) criteria and preference of managers. *Cogent Business & Management*, *4*, 1340820.

PART II

CSR, ETHICS, AND SUPPLY CHAINS

CHAPTER 3

CORPORATE SOCIAL RESPONSIBILITY STRATEGY: THE EFFECTS OF LEGITIMACY AND AUTHENTICITY ON CORPORATE REPUTATION*

Robert A. Rodrigues

Saint Mary's College of California, USA

ABSTRACT

Aggressive corporate practices have damaged the reputation of many firms and industries. While the media and the Internet improve stakeholder transparency and influence social expectations for responsible business, firms have found an increasing need to manage their corporate reputation. One-way firms have responded is by adopting voluntary corporate social responsibility (CSR) programs to live up to expectations set by the firm's history, identity (core business), and image. However, conformance to evolving external isomorphic forces has encouraged many firms to adopt similar CSR programs without understanding their motives, resource constraints, and capabilities resulting in fragmented strategies and ineffective implementation approaches. The result has been inconclusive results in practice and inconsistent findings in extant literature on the link between CSR, corporate reputation, and financial performance. This chapter examines how the synthesis of stakeholder theory and

---

*A Book Chapter Presented to International Finance Review, March 24, 2024

Responsible Firms: CSR, ESG, and Global Sustainability
International Finance Review, Volume 23, 37–72
Copyright © 2025 by Robert A. Rodrigues
Published under exclusive licence by Emerald Publishing Limited
ISSN: 1569-3767/doi:10.1108/S1569-376720240000023003

resource-based view theory can provide tighter boundaries with corporate identity and shared value as the heart of a CSR strategy to direct top management's resource allocation. The chapter introduces four CSR micro-strategies as a response to external forces based on a blend of two essential dimensions including internal authenticity and external legitimacy. The study examines the impact of authenticity, legitimacy, and the intensity of their interactions on corporate reputation of 107 publicly traded US firms. Through three models, the study found internal authenticity as the dominant dimension while external legitimacy contributed inconsistently to corporate reputation. Implications for CSR strategy suggest that CSR programs with higher authenticity levels improve corporate reputation consistently more than those focused on external legitimacy.

Keywords: Corporate social responsibility; strategy; strategic choice; shared value; authenticity; legitimacy; reputation; resource-based view; stakeholder theory

JEL Codes: D21; D91; D81; D84; L21; M14; O21

INTRODUCTION

Environmental accidents, corporate scandals, and aggressive business practices have damaged the reputation and trust of many firms and industries (Lins et al., 2017). Government regulations and professional standards exert coercive and normative forces that guide corporate conduct away from socially irresponsible behavior by encouraging similar business forms and practices (DiMaggio & Powell, 1983). With improved visibility through the media and the Internet, powerful stakeholders have acquired greater insight into a firm's activities that influence their expectations for acceptable, proper, and appropriate business conduct (Bitektine, 2011). These rapidly changing social expectations influenced by the media, professional organizations, and special interest groups encourage firms to respond strategically based on their position of power, resource dependency, regulatory environment, and visibility (Oliver, 1991). One strategic response is a voluntary CSR program that can be used to balance financial performance, environmental concerns, and social expectations to avoid reputational damage (Bertels & Peloza, 2008). However, as firms conform to evolving social expectations, many have adopted fragmented CSR programs without coherent strategies and ineffective implementation approaches due to a lack of understanding of differing motives, resource constraints, and competencies that results in the decoupling of a firm's motives from action level activities (Hawn & Ioannou, 2016; Porter & Kramer, 2006). Stakeholders perceive this decoupling as greenwashing which has exposed companies to litigation, reputational damage, and social sanctions. Greenwashing occurs when a firm spends more time, resources, and marketing efforts to disclose their products to be environmentally safe and their practices are socially conscious than completing the CSR activities with meaningful results (Bams et al., 2022).

The intersection of strategic management and CSR literature presents an opportunity to advance CSR strategy by exploring how a program's external legitimacy, internal authenticity, and their interaction levels impact corporate reputation through an alignment of program motives and action-level activities (Hengst et al., 2020; Morgeson et al., 2013). CSR programs support a company's efforts to conform to laws, regulations, professional standards, and social expectations through external legitimacy-seeking activities while remaining true to its history, identity (core business), and values. This chapter finds four CSR micro-strategies (compliance, strategic, authentic, integrated) based on the interaction levels of two essential CSR dimensions including external legitimacy and internal authenticity by examining their impact on corporate reputation. With a better understanding of how these essential dimensions impact nuanced CSR strategies, firms can modify their CSR programs based on their position of power (size, resource control, visibility) and internal strengths (competencies and capabilities) around relevant stakeholder needs. In particular, this chapter aims to answer the following research questions:

- Does a CSR strategy focused on internal authenticity have a larger positive impact on corporate reputation than one focused on external legitimacy (and vice versa)? If so, which components of each dimension should a firm focus on for effective implementation?
- What blend (intensity level) of internal authenticity and external legitimacy has the largest positive impact on corporate reputation as it manifests in the four CSR micro-strategies (compliance, strategic, authentic, integrated)?

This chapter suggests the synthesis of stakeholder theory and resource-based view theory (RBV) can serve as an effective framework to capture the value of a CSR program through corporate reputation. The synthesis of these theories allows firms to observe external trends, opportunities, and social expectations to inform top management team's (TMTs) financial strategies and social opportunities they are best able to execute (Freeman et al., 2021). The chapter's findings could inform TMTs on how to focus their CSR strategies to maximize its impact on corporate reputation, strengthen stakeholder relationships, and create a sustainable competitive advantage that is unique, valuable, imitable, and non-substitutable (Barney, 1991; McWilliams & Siegel, 2011).

Section 1 of this chapter provides an overview of CSR literature including definitions, boundaries, and key constructs of a conceptual model including internal authenticity, external legitimacy, and corporate reputation through the lens of stakeholder theory and the RBV framework. Section 2 introduces hypotheses to explore the impact of authenticity, legitimacy, components of each, and their interaction effect on corporate reputation. Section 3 describes the methodology and hypotheses testing. Lastly, Section 4 discusses the theoretical and managerial insights alongside limitations and future research opportunities.

LITERATURE REVIEW

CSR Definitions and Empirical Clarity

CSR is a partnership between business and society that employs a broad focus on stakeholders rather than a narrow emphasis on shareholders (Jones et al., 2018). CSR can be broadly defined as a program that includes voluntary company policies and practices that go beyond maximizing economic outcome for shareholders and include actions that meet the social needs and expectations of other stakeholders (Shin et al., 2016). Carroll's (1991) corporate social responsibility pyramid provides a hierarchy of business responsibilities with economic and legal requirements at the base of the pyramid increasing to a normative expectation for ethical business, and finally a desire for philanthropic activities at the top. The base of the pyramid aligns with a firm's traditional objectives of profitability and compliance with laws and regulations. Ethical expectations are associated with normative expectations for a firm to willingly conduct business fairly, responsibly, and to avoid harm. The top of the pyramid reflects society's desire for profitable firms to demonstrate corporate citizenship through philanthropic activities.

Firms need a strong stakeholder orientation to balance conflicting needs, expectations, and desires that occur at different times and intensities (Freeman, 1984). The multi-level, multi-discipline, and diverse CSR perspectives have resulted in ambiguous measurement instruments that have constrained clarity in empirical findings on the link between CSR, corporate reputation, and financial performance. The primary issue with measuring CSR outcomes such as reputation is the subjective nature of the constructs and ambiguity in providing a direct link to intangible benefits that offset upfront costs in the future without clearly establishing boundaries and controls over confounding factors (Nizamuddin, 2018). This lack of clarity has contributed to the prolonged philosophical debate in CSR literature on whether it is appropriate for corporate leaders to allocate time, attention, and resources to social activities that may not accrue to measurable shareholder value (Friedman, 1970). Empirical findings with a financial link to CSR would improve the business case to pursue CSR programs (Herold et al., 2019). However, to accomplish this task we need a granular understanding of how CSR strategies align with opportunities for effective implementation. This chapter's essential CSR dimensions of internal authenticity and external legitimacy can serve as boundaries to test their impact on corporate reputation as support for long-term profitability.

Stakeholder Theory and Shared Value

According to stakeholder theory, a firm's ability to focus on primary stakeholder needs while balancing conflicting demands of secondary stakeholders is essential to the health of the firm (Freeman, 1984). A strong stakeholder orientation provides firms with the ability to recognize opportunities and manage stakeholder needs (Peloza & Papania, 2008). In other words, clear boundaries on which stakeholders are relevant to the firm can be identified as those who are involved with the co-creation of value between society, the firm, and employees. Porter and Kramer (2006) suggest that shared value with relevant stakeholders can serve as an overarching theme for a firm's CSR strategy to direct the allocation of resources and activities.

INTEGRATION OF STAKEHOLDER THEORY AND RESOURCE-BASE VIEW FRAMEWORK

While prior literature focused on resource dependency as a basis for strategic responses to institutional forces (Oliver, 1991), this chapter synthesizes stakeholder theory and RBV framework to provide a dynamic exploration of CSR as an integrative mechanism that meets external stakeholder expectations through complex social relationships with relevant stakeholders as a competitive advantage. The synthesis provides a broader understanding than resource dependency theory alone. Barney (1991) suggests that RBV can establish a sustainable competitive advantage that is unique, valuable, imitable, and nonsubstitutable by aligning external opportunities with a firm's internal strengths while neutralizing its weaknesses relative to competitors. RBV's focus on both the external and internal business environment aligns with a CSR program's wide stakeholder orientation. The alignment allows a firm to evaluate stakeholder needs, trends, inform strategies, build complex relationships, and reduce uncertainty associated with evolving social expectations. Over time, a CSR program creates a competitive advantage through unique path-dependent relationships that reduces information asymmetry with stakeholders through an improved reputation (Fombrun & Shanley, 1990; McWilliams & Siegel, 2011).

The synthesis of stakeholder theory and the RBV framework supports the integration of CSR strategies with a firm's identity (core business), strategy, competencies, and business practices to reduce the decoupling of CSR motives from action-level activities. Fig. 3.1 presents the synthesis of both theories.

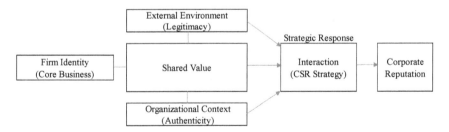

Fig. 3.1. Integration of Stakeholder Theory, RBV, and CSR Strategy.

CSR Strategy as a Response to Isomorphic Forces

A firm's reputation can be impacted by how it responds to external pressures such as coercive forces (regulations) and normative expectations (social norms). Oliver (1991) focused on resource dependency theory to explain how firms respond to

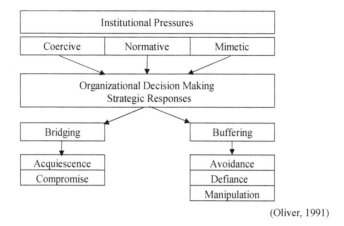

(Oliver, 1991)

Fig. 3.2.   Oliver's Strategic Responses to Isomorphic Forces.

external stakeholders to obtain productive resources based on their position of power, influence, and visibility. Meznar and Nigh (1995) suggest that firms respond by bridging or buffering their business structures and practices based on their resource dependency. Bridging occurs when firms conform to external pressures by adapting internal business practices that align with external stakeholder expectations. Conversely, buffering involves protecting the firm's operating efficiency from the external environment by insulating its operating structure or actively influencing external forces in its favor. Oliver (1991) suggests the firm's ultimate response ranges from unconscious conformance to active resistance that includes actions ranging from acquiescence, compromise, avoidance, defiance, or manipulation. Oliver's strategic decision-making process model shown in Fig. 3.2 reflects the dynamic interplay between external institutional forces, a firm's decision-making process, and potential strategic responses based on its capabilities.

This chapter examines CSR programs as a strategic response to meet stakeholder expectations while staying true to its identity (core business). The interaction of internal authenticity and external legitimacy is expected to manifest in CSR micro-strategies that support a firm's choice to meet the needs of external stakeholders, the firm, and employees.

CORPORATE REPUTATION

Many firms develop CSR strategies to create a positive reputation, build relationships, and establish trust by linking internal and external stakeholders through ongoing interactions (Jones et al., 2018). CSR programs allow firms to establish a positive reputation by setting expectations, creating an image, and then demonstrating its character by living up to them by conducting business responsibly overtime (Sen & Bhattacharya, 2001). Barnett et al. (2006) suggest that corporate identity can be defined as a representation of who the firm is based on its

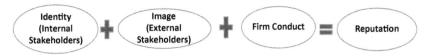

Fig. 3.3. Stakeholder Reputation Evaluation Process.

history and core business. In contrast, corporate image is the representation of what the firm wants its evaluators to have of the firm. Lastly, a firm's reputation is influenced by an observer's judgment of the alignment between a firm's identity, image, and conduct (Barnett et al., 2006). The stakeholder evaluation process is illustrated in Fig. 3.3.

In contrast with corporate identity, the definition of reputation in extant literature has been imprecise due to its close association with corporate identity and image. Barnett et al. (2006) define corporate reputation as the collective judgement of stakeholders based on their assessment of the firm's financial, social, and environmental impact over time. Fombrun and Shanley (1990) suggest that corporate reputation is a multiperspective construct viewed by stakeholders through multiple disciplines and perspectives contributing to various dimensions in measuring corporate reputation.

A positive corporate reputation can serve as an intangible asset capable of reducing informational asymmetry during a stakeholder's evaluation of the firm. As a firm meets expectations set by its identity and image, stakeholder relationships are strengthened and information acquisition costs are reduced during contract development (Fombrun & Shanley, 1990). Moreover, a positive corporate reputation attracts employees and creates loyal customers (Mitchell et al., 2007). When a CSR program meets the expectations of relevant stakeholders, a positive reputation can support a sustainable competitive advantage (Barney, 1991; Fombrun & Shanley, 1990; McWilliams & Siegal, 2011). This chapter aims to examine the impact of external legitimacy, internal authenticity, and their interaction effects on corporate reputation.

ESSENTIAL DIMENSIONS OF CSR STRATEGY

Internal Authenticity

Authenticity can be defined as being true to oneself, acting in accordance with the true self, and expressing oneself in ways that are consistent with inner thoughts and feelings (Liedtka, 2008). From an organizational perspective, authenticity of a CSR program is related to employee perceptions of whether CSR motives and activities are aligned with the firm's identity (core business), values, and business practices. When CSR activities are genuine to the firm and aligned with its espoused values, employees perceive the CSR program as being authentic (Cording et al., 2014). According to McShane and Cunningham (2012), employee perceptions of CSR authenticity are based on several cues used to compare how the motives of a CSR program align with a firm's socially constructed organizational identity. The cues include the integration of CSR strategy with a firm's core business, a sustained commitment of resources, the engagement of management, and a sense of justice in terms of fair administrative processes and equitable distribution of program resources. The perception of a CSR program's authenticity by employees contributes to their intrinsic motivation to participate in CSR program activities through social identification with the firm resulting in engagement, organizational commitment, and lower turnover (Graafland & Van de Ven, 2006; Story & Neves, 2015). Moreover, a firm's CSR commitment can be demonstrated through its organizational structure and policies such as a CSR board committee and CSR-linked compensation that provides management with authority, motivation, and funding (Flammer et al., 2019).

A high degree of internal authenticity assumes that the CSR strategy is linked to its identity (core business), values, and business practices (Aquinis & Glavas 2013; McShane & Cunningham, 2012). Furthermore, management's commitment and involvement can reduce decoupling of CSR motives through consistent and fair allocation of resources (Siltaloppi et al., 2021).

External Legitimacy

According to Bitektine (2011), organizational legitimacy is a multi-perspective construct related to the perception, judgment, and endorsement of a firm's compliance with laws, regulations, professional standards, and social expectations of stakeholders. Legitimacy can be viewed as property awarded to a firm for its adoption of policies and practices that align with stakeholder interests or those of society. If a firm's conduct is desirable, proper, and appropriate social actors award legitimacy that can provide differentiated access to markets and productive resources (Suchman, 1995). This chapter focuses on two components of legitimacy including regulatory legitimacy and sociopolitical legitimacy. Regulatory legitimacy emphasizes a firm's compliance with laws, regulations, and professional standards. Sociopolitical legitimacy entails a social actor's evaluation of a firm's business practices against prevailing social norms (Bitektine, 2011). In accordance with sociopolitical legitimacy, external actors render judgment as to whether the firm's business practices and outcomes are desirable, proper, and appropriate. Lee and Yoon (2018) suggest that external stakeholders compare formal CSR disclosures with observable results, actions, and behaviors of the firm. If the activities are reported accurately and the firm performs to stated goals, external stakeholders award legitimacy to the organization.

Disclosure Adequacy

Communication of CSR goals, progress, and impact is essential to establishing external legitimacy with relevant stakeholders (Lee & Yoon, 2018). The perceived quality of CSR communication is improved when reports are prepared by third-party firms with established reporting standards such as the Global Reporting Initiative (GRI) and Sustainability Accounting Standards Board (SASB) which can increase a CSR program's legitimacy (García-Sánchez et al., 2022). Formal external CSR communication is conducted through ESG audits and financial reports.

A high degree of external legitimacy is defined here as sociopolitical legitimacy that assumes that the firm exceeds regulations and meets external social expectations, norms, and values through desirable, proper, and appropriate conduct. With a high degree of external legitimacy, firms are awarded differentiated access to markets, productive resources, and a positive reputation (Bietkine, 2011; Fombrun & Shanley, 1990). Conversely, a violation of social expectations could damage stakeholder trust in a firm and adversely impact its corporate reputation.

CONCEPTUAL MODEL AND HYPOTHESES DEVELOPMENT

A firm's ability to find the optimal blend of external legitimacy and internal authenticity in CSR strategy enhances its durability and resilience. While external institutional forces encourage firms to conform with similar business practices such as CSR programs (DiMaggio & Powell, 1983), a CSR program's authenticity enables it to differentiate from competitors when integrated with its history, identity (core business), and business strategy. This chapter introduces a conceptual model to explore three hypotheses associated with the impact of internal authenticity, external legitimacy, and their interaction on corporate reputation. Fig. 3.4 provides a diagram of the conceptual model.

Hypothesis 1 (External Legitimacy)

External legitimacy is explored through two degrees of compliance. A low degree of external legitimacy is examined through regulatory legitimacy. A high degree of external legitimacy is examined through sociopolitical legitimacy.

Regulatory Legitimacy
A firm that conforms to coercive forces including laws, regulations, and professional standards while minimizing harm to society is awarded regulatory legitimacy by stakeholders (Bitektine, 2011; Carroll, 1991). The exchange of regulatory legitimacy for compliance with laws and regulations ensures stakeholders have recourse in the event of business failure, contract violations, and

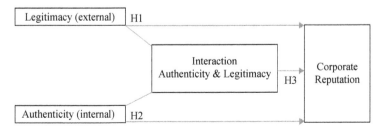

Fig. 3.4. Conceptual Model.

service disruptions. With standardized expectations, stakeholders are provided a benchmark to judge a firm's behavior. A firm's consistent compliance and minimal violations provide stakeholders with an indicator of a firm's regulatory legitimacy.

Sociopolitical Legitimacy

Stakeholders reward firms with a high degree of legitimacy for compliance with social expectations, societal norms, and the adoption of business practices that are desirable and appropriate (Bitektine, 2011). When awarding sociopolitical legitimacy, a social actor's perception, judgment, and endorsement of a firm's behavior consists of an on-going evaluation of whether the firm's conduct is appropriate (Suchman, 1995). If a firm's actions meet social expectations, sociopolitical legitimacy is granted providing differentiated access to markets and productive resources. As social expectations of stakeholders evolve, a firm's CSR program can act as a way to acquire external information to inform strategic initiatives that meet evolving social demands to improve stakeholder relationships and corporate reputation.

> *H1: A firm's corporate reputation is positively impacted by the degree of external legitimacy.*

Hypothesis 2 (Internal Authenticity)

This chapter explores internal authenticity through degrees of commitment. A low degree of internal authenticity is measured by whether CSR motives are decoupled from action-level activities. A high degree of internal authenticity is measured by the congruence of CSR motives with a firm's identity (core business), sustained commitment of resources, and managerial involvement in the program.

CSR Decoupling

Decoupling is defined as the adoption of policies and practices symbolically to achieve legitimacy regardless of their contributions to efficiency (DiMaggio & Powell, 1983; Hengst et al., 2020; Meyer & Rowen, 1977). Hengst et al. (2020) suggest that conflicting financial and social goals can result in decoupling when social policies are not integrated with a firm's business practices. When organizational leaders are not actively involved with a CSR program and do not consistently allocate resources for its integration with business routines, decoupling is more likely (Hengst et al., 2020; McShane & Cunningham, 2012). When decoupled, firms could fail to meet social commitments resulting in sanctions by salient stakeholders. For example, employees may adopt cynical or apathetic behaviors and lower their support for the firm (Story & Neves, 2015). External stakeholders may become skeptical increasing the likelihood of greenwashing claims, litigation, and potentially damaging a firm's reputation for violation of its implicit social contract. Conversely, when a CSR program is integrated with a firm's identity (core business) and competitive strategy, the firm is more likely to achieve both financial and social goals while meeting stakeholder expectations (Aquinis & Glavas, 2013). The integration of a CSR program with its identity, strategy, and business practices supports a positive reputation.

CSR Commitment

When CSR programs are integrated with a firm's business practices, management can establish a shared value between society, the firm, and workplace. McShane and Cunningham (2012) suggest that employee perception of CSR authenticity is enhanced through cues including a sustained resource commitment, management commitment, and a sense of justice.

H2: A firm's corporate reputation is positively impacted by the degree of internal authenticity.

Hypothesis 3 (Interaction Effects)

The interaction effects of internal authenticity and external legitimacy on corporate reputation depend on their intensity level. Evolving regulations and social expectations increase uncertainty and a need for a firm to modify its strategy continuously. A CSR program that balances both external and internal stakeholder needs, wants, and desires is better positioned to create shared value (Porter & Kramer, 2006). Shared value allows a firm to focus its CSR strategy on activities the firm is most capable of achieving while staying true to its unique history, identity (core business), and character, thereby enhancing employee perception of authenticity. The optimal blend of internal authenticity and external legitimacy allows a firm to conform with changing regulations and expectations in ways that can differentiate the firm through unique social relationships that place the firm in a position to acquire financial and physical resources to execute strategic initiatives and improve corporate reputation.

H3: A firm's reputation is positively impacted by the interaction between internal authenticity and external legitimacy at low and high intensity levels.

METHODOLOGY

Data Sample

A positivist research design with linear regression models and longitudinal databases was applied in this study to examine the impact of internal authenticity, external legitimacy, and their interaction on corporate reputation. The study's data sample consists of 107 publicly traded US firms with $10 billion or more in revenues listed on the S&P 500 and NASDAQ index across eight sectors and 78 industries. Data sources include the highly cited Refinitiv Assets 4 ESG database, version 1 ("Refinitiv"), Fortune Most Admired Companies Survey ("FMAC"), and Compustat. All three databases were matched to arrive at the final sample with FMAC scores over a five-year period from 2017

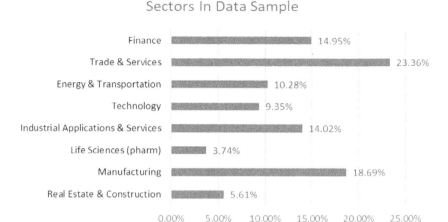

Fig. 3.5.   Data Sample Sectors.

to 2022. The US context ensures that firms have similar economic, legal, polit-ical, and cultural norms. Fig. 3.5 provides a summary of the sectors included in the data sample.

Data Sources

The Refinitiv database (version 1) is a comprehensive and broadly used database in academia that includes scored social performance dimensions to monitor a firm's CSR activities including environmental, community, human rights, govern-ance, workforce, and product innovation. This study reorganizes 14 of the data-base's main categories, underlying indicators, and data points to measure internal authenticity and external legitimacy as defined in this chapter and extant literature (Bitektine, 2011; McShane & Cunningham, 2012; Suchman, 1995). The Refinitiv categories were combined to form higher-order indexes to measure the compo-nents of authenticity and legitimacy by bifurcating the categories into internal (substantive and authentic) and external (symbolic and legitimacy-seeking) dimensions (Villiers et al., 2022). Furthermore, litigation costs and media contro-versies associated with each category were provided. Table 3.1 demonstrates how the Refinitiv categories were reorganized for this study.

FMAC Survey is an established and highly cited corporate reputation survey used in industry and academia to rank firms based on corporate reputation since 1997 by Fortune magazine in partnership with Korn Ferry. The survey includes firms with $10 billion or more in revenue and ranked among the larg-est in their industry by revenue (Fortune, 2022). The ranking is based on ques-tionnaires distributed to experts in the field including senior executives, outside board directors, and industry analysts (Flanagan et al., 2011). The annual sur-vey is rated on nine attributes that contribute to an overall corporate reputa-tion score used in this study. Brown and Perry (1994) identified concerns with

Table 3.1. Bifurcation of Refinitiv Categories.

Legitimacy (External Dimension)			Authenticity (Internal Dimensions)		
Community	Environment	Human Rights	Corporate Governance	Workforce	Product
Product Responsibility	Emission Reduction		Integration Vision/Strategy	Employment Quality	Product Innovation
	Resource Reduction		Board Functions	Diversity	
			Compensation Policy	Health & Safety	
			Board Structure	Training & Develop	

FMAC data associated with the high degree of influence of financial performance on the overall score. Later, Flanagan et al. (2011) conducted a follow-up study with more recent FMAC data to examine whether the influence of financial performance persists. They conclude that the FMAC survey continues to be a valid data source for studies in organizational reputation when controlling for financial performance. Based on the findings, this study controlled for industry and financial performance.

Compustat is a comprehensive corporate financial database published by S&P Global Market Intelligence covering companies worldwide since 1950 across 12 industries. The database is broadly used by financial professionals and academia for annual financial data and industry classifications. This study used Compustat for financial information related to the control variables.

VARIABLE DEFINITIONS AND MEASUREMENT METHODS

Legitimacy

Suchman (1995) defined legitimacy as a "generalized perception of organizational actions that are desirable, proper, or appropriate within a socially constructed system of values, norms, and beliefs." In this chapter, legitimacy is operationalized by the perception, judgment, and endorsement of a firm's compliance with regulations and social expectations of stakeholders (Bitektine, 2011). For example, when firms incur penalties and fines related to lost court cases and settlements, they fail to meet stakeholder expectations for compliance with regulatory requirements. Moreover, when firms are targeted in the media for controversies it reflects a stakeholder group's dissatisfaction with a firm for its failure to live up to expectations through desirable and appropriate conduct. Although various stakeholder groups have different perspectives that change over time, a strong stakeholder orientation can assist a firm with evaluating expectations to reduce regulatory infractions and meet social expectations (Mitchell et al., 1997).

Regulatory legitimacy was measured by Refinitiv data (version 1) associated with all real litigation costs, provisions, fines, and penalties associated with lost court cases (Refinitiv, 2023). The total amount of litigation, fines, and penalties costs indicate the degree of regulatory legitimacy.

Sociopolitical legitimacy was measured through equally weighted components including (1) the number of controversial media events, (2) the degree of a firm's external CSR focus measured by an external CSR index comprised of categories such as environmental, community, and human rights, (3) the number of nationally recognized awards which indicates desirable conduct, and (4) CSR disclosure adequacy measured by voluntary standards used in ESG audits such as the GRI, SASB, and United Nations (UN) Global Compact that provide transparency (Garcia-Sanchez et al., 2021). Quality CSR disclosures form a link of awareness between internal and external stakeholders for social actors to compare a firm's actions against its claims and prevailing social norms. If the firm performs and reports accurately, it reflects positively on the firm's commitment to its CSR program (Lee & Yoon, 2018). Table 3.2 provides a summary of legitimacy and its component measurements.

Table 3.2.   Legitimacy and Component Measurements.

External Legitimacy	Dimension	Measure	Scale	Method of Calculation
Regulatory				
Litigation costs	Settlement, fine, penalty (−) (reverse code)	$ amt	1–3	Compare to sample percentile.
Sociopolitical				
Media controversies	Perception (-), rev code	Count	1–3	Compare to sample percentile.
CSR external focus	External Index (+)	Score	0–4	Average 3-year external index ≥ current year internal index. Y(1)/N(0). Compare to sample percentile.
Disclosure adequacy	Perception (+)	Count	1–3	Compare to sample percentile.
Awards	Perception (+)	Count	1–3	Compare to sample percentile.
Total legitimacy			4–16	

Authenticity

Driver (2006) describes authenticity as being true to the organizational self as determined by the firm and employees through ongoing interactions codified in its core values, mission statement, and code of ethics. Authenticity is observed by the alignment of a firm's identity (core business), CSR activities (image), and conduct. This study examined authenticity through two components including (1) CSR decoupling measured by the degree of integration between a CSR program and the firm's core strategy and (2) CSR commitment measured by a sustained commitment of resources, management commitment, and sense of justice. The components were measured through indexes created from Refinitiv database (version 1) categories consistent with extant literature (Villiers et al., 2022; Tang et al., 2012).

Decoupling of CSR Strategy

Decoupling of CSR motives from action level activities was observed in two ways: (1) Refinitiv's integrated vision/strategy category score that measures a firm's capacity to integrate its CSR program into its day-to-day decision-making. The category captures data associated with a firm's overarching strategy that integrates financial and nonfinancial goals through policies, processes, and monitoring mechanisms (Refinitiv, 2023), (2) CSR internal focus was measured through an embedded index determined by whether a firm's three-year average internal CSR activities ("internal index") exceeds its current year external CSR activities ("external index") (Villiers et al., 2022; Tang et al., 2012). Internal index scores were based on Refinitiv categories including (1) governance sub-categories comprised board strategy, structure, functions, and compensation, (2) workforce subcategory comprised employee quality, diversity/opportunity, health/safety, and training/development, and (3) product innovation score that addresses environmental concerns and consumer protection (Lougee & Wallace, 2008; Refinitiv, 2023).

CSR Commitment

McShane and Cunningham (2012) suggest that employees observe a firm's CSR commitment through cues including a sustained commitment of resources, management commitment, and a sense of justice.

Sustained Resource Commitment. Sustained commitment of resources was measured as total CSR score ("CSR intensity") including external and internal indexes. If the current year total CSR score exceeds the prior three-year average CSR score, it indicates a sustained resource commitment signaling a firm's commitment to the program and contributing to the perception of internal authenticity (Lins et al., 2017; McShane & Cunningham, 2012).

Management Commitment. A firm's support for management involvement in the CSR program includes authority, motivation, and transparency. Firm level support was measured through a management index including (1) authority granted through a CSR committee, (2) motivation encouraged through a compensation policy that links incentives to CSR targets (Hong et al., 2016), (3) involvement supported by participation in a CSR sustainability index, ESG supplier training, environmental teams, and (4) transparency through voluntary adoption of CSR certifications, standards, and initiatives.

Fair Administration of CSR Resources. Fair stakeholder treatment contributes to the perception of CSR authenticity (McShane & Cunnigham, 2012). Procedural

justice is associated with transparency, communication, and process administration that provides equal access to organizational members. CSR procedural
justice was examined by Refinitiv's board structure category that measures how
well the board supports the exchange of ideas and independent decision-making
by an experienced and diverse board (Refinitiv, 2023). The second measure is a
culture of trust index formed through Refinitiv indicators that observe policies
for employee communication such as whistleblower protection and trade union
relations.

Distributive justice in CSR programs was observed through the balanced
distribution of program resources between external and internal stakeholders. Balance was measured by dividing a three-year average external index by
a three-year internal index and comparing the result to other sample firms. It
was then assigned a score based on whether the balance fell within one standard deviation of the mean. The score indicates whether a firm follows an integrative strategy (balanced) or one that is more externally focused (legitimacy
seeking) or internally focused (authentic) (Tang et al., 2012). Mallory and
Rupp (2015) suggest that employee perception of fairness is not based solely
on how they are treated but how the firm treats others. When a firm's stakeholder treatment is balanced, employee's perception of a firm's authenticity is
improved. Table 3.3 provides a summary of authenticity and its component
measurements.

Table 3.3. Authenticity and Component Measurements.

Internal Authenticity	Dimension	Measure	Scale	Method of Calculation
CSR-decoupling (embedded strategy)				
CSR strategy integration	Strategy/vision	Score	1–3	Compare to sample percentile.
CSR embeddedness	Internal index	Score	0–4	Average 3-year internal index $>$ = current year external index. Y(1)/N(0). Compare to sample.
CSR-commitment				
Sustained resource commit	Total CSR score	Score	0–4	Three-year average total CSR score $<$ = CY total CSR score Y(1)/N(0). Compare to sample percentile.
Management commit/fair	Motiv, authority, Involvement	Score	1–2	Compare to sample percentile.
Procedural justice	Board struct + trust	Score	1–3	Compare to sample percentile.
Distributive justice	Balance (int/ext)	Binary	0–1	Three-year external index vs. 3yr internal index within ½ SD of mean. (1) N(0).
Total authenticity			3–17	

Corporate Reputation

Corporate reputation is defined as an observer's judgment of a firm's conduct, achievements, or failures to perform in accordance to its identity and image (Barnett et al., 2006). Corporate reputation is established by ongoing interactions between the firm and stakeholders that, over time, reduce information asymmetry, improve creditability, and acquires legitimacy. The FMAC overall reputation score was used in this study.

DATA ANALYSIS

Three linear regression models were conducted to test the hypotheses. Model 1 included the main effects of internal authenticity and external legitimacy on corporate reputation with all control variables. Model 2 included a regression analysis for insight into which components of authenticity and legitimacy impact corporate reputation the most. Lastly, Model 3 (post hoc) utilized ANOVA analysis based on categorical interactions to test how the intensity levels bifurcated at low and high levels of authenticity and legitimacy impact corporate reputation. The separate models provide insight into CSR strategy development and implementation approaches while reducing the potential for confounding between the aggregated main variables and their component measurements. Fig. 3.6 summarizes the progression of the linear regression models used in the study.

Control variables included industry, firm size, profitability, and discretionary expenses such as marketing and R&D expenses (Lins et al., 2017). Flanagan et al. (2011) recommend controlling for financial performance and industry when using FMAC data due to their potential influence on the overall reputation score. Moreover, Bitekine (2011) suggest that a stakeholder's taken-for-granted bias toward an industry's reputation, norms, and regulations could impact a firm's current reputation. In agreement with extant literature, industry was controlled for due to its explanatory power. Firm size measured by total assets (log) was controlled due to their higher visibility and power to influence stakeholder

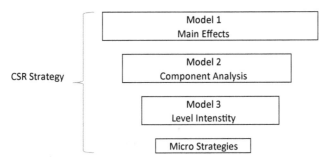

Fig. 3.6. Linear Regression Models.

perceptions. Profitability measured by net income (log) was controlled based on its influence on CSR program funding. Profitable firms with financial slack are more likely to spend on discretionary items such as a CSR program. Lastly, discretionary expenses such as advertising, marketing, and R&D were controlled as they often compete for CSR funding.

Scoring System and Measured Dimensions

Multi-dimensional measurements were used to capture the dynamic interplay between external legitimacy and internal authenticity. This study used a parsimonious scoring system with percentiles to categorize variables as low, medium, or high. Component scores were then added to determine the aggregate authenticity and legitimacy score. Negative polarity of data points was accounted through reverse coding where a low count is better for negative events. Conversely, negative events with a higher count were assigned a low score. Neutral measurements were considered binary with a score of 1 for meeting the requirement or 0 if not. Table 3.4 provides a summary of the scoring system.

Table 3.4. Scoring System.

Positive Polarity	Percentile	Score
Low	0–0.33	1
Mid	0.34–0.66	2
High	0.67–100	3

Negative polarity	Percentile	Score
Low	0.67–100	1
Mid	0.34–0.66	2
High	0–0.33	3

Descriptive Statistics

Based on the data sample's descriptive statistics, firms are more internally focused with authentic CSR activities ($M = 10.09$) than outward looking with legitimacy seeking activities ($M = 9.96$). Volatility associated with internal authenticity was primarily related to a firm's embedded strategy ($SD = 1.39$) which highlights an opportunity for firms to differentiate by integrating their CSR strategy with their core business. Management commitment and management fairness ($SD = 0.86$) present a smaller opportunity to differentiate while resource commitment alone ($SD = 0.797$) had the smallest opportunity as it is a complementary component that enhances the perception of authenticity when it exists concurrently with other components.

Volatility associated with external legitimacy was primarily related to a CSR program's external focus ($SD = 1.116$), media controversy ($SD = 0.849$), disclosure adequacy ($SD = 0.641$), litigation costs ($SD = 0.496$), and awards ($SD = 0.479$). Based on this variability, opportunities to differentiate through legitimacy

Table 3.5. Descriptive Statistics: Main Variables and Components.

	N	Mean	SD	Min	Max	Skewness	Kurtosis
Fortune most admired	529	6.835	0.677	5.3	8.63	0.412	2.825
Authenticity	529	10.089	2.600	4	16	−0.158	2.192
Legitimacy	529	9.958	1.624	6	15	−0.031	3.242
Embedded strategy	529	4.327	1.386	2	7	0.012	2.058
Resource commitment	529	2.425	0.797	1	4	−0.036	2.513
Management fairness	529	2.117	0.862	1	4	0.305	2.33
Management commitment	529	1.219	0.856	0	2	−0.435	1.506
Litigation cost	529	1.936	0.496	1	3	−0.137	3.971
Media controversy score	529	2.164	0.849	1	3	−0.319	1.463
Disclosure adequacy	529	1.934	0.641	1	3	0.059	2.428
External focus	529	2.758	1.116	1	4	−0.341	1.747
Awards	529	1.166	0.479	1	3	2.907	10.451

are associated with a program's external CSR focus and a reduction of media controversies. Conversely, there are lower opportunities to differentiate through disclosure adequacy and reduction of litigation costs. Table 3.5 provides a summary of the descriptive statistics for each major construct and its component.

Correlation Analysis & Measurement Validity

A correlation analysis was conducted for two purposes: (1) to demonstrate measurement validity of higher order constructs and (2) to demonstrate the independence of predictor variables. Based on the nonfinancial and subjective nature of CSR in business, this study considers lower correlation coefficients as relevant (Schober et al., 2018). For example, correlation coefficients less than 0.10 are considered nonmaterial, 0.11–0.25 weak, 0.26–0.50 moderate, and greater than 0.51 as strong. Table 3.6 provides a summary of correlations between main variables (Model 1) and components (Model 2).

The correlation between the main variables and their respective components were moderate to strong ($r > 0.30$) and statistically significant ($p < 0.05$). The higher correlations confirm validity of the main variables (authenticity and legitimacy). Table 3.7 below summarizes the strength and direction (+ or −) between the main variables and their components.

For Model 2 (components), stronger relationships between components (independent variables, $r > 0.25$) were evaluated for combination (or elimination) to reduce the potential for confounding. For example, embedded strategy combines the Refinitiv integrated strategy/vision category and this study's embedded index variable. Moreover, management fairness combines the components of management commitment and fairness to reflect a firm's support for management involvement in the CSR program. For legitimacy, external CSR focus, is reflected by this study's external CSR index and eliminates disclosure adequacy and awards due to similar undying data.

Table 3.6. Correlations of Main Variables (Model 1) and Components (Model 2).

Variables	(1)	(2)	(3)	(4)	(5)	(6)	(7)	(8)	(9)	(10)	(11)
(1) Authenticity	1.000										
(2) Legitimacy	0.099*	1.000									
	(0.023)										
(3) Embedd Strat	0.864*	0.078	1.000								
	(0.000)	(0.072)									
(4) Resource Com	0.681*	0.080	0.493*	1.000							
	(0.000)	(0.068)	(0.000)								
(5) Fairness Mgmt	0.319*	0.116*	0.076	-0.086*	1.000						
	(0.000)	(0.008)	(0.082)	(0.047)							
(6) Litigation Cost	-0.185*	0.458*	-0.148*	-0.156*	0.035	1.000					
	(0.000)	(0.000)	(0.001)	(0.000)	(0.417)						
(7) Media Controv	-0.344*	0.473*	-0.282*	-0.176*	-0.021	0.336*	1.000				
	(0.000)	(0.000)	(0.000)	(0.000)	(0.627)	(0.000)					
(8) Ext Focus	0.092*	0.701*	0.021	0.063	0.157*	0.054	0.022	1.000			
	(0.034)	(0.000)	(0.636)	(0.150)	(0.000)	(0.215)	(0.612)				
(9) Lg Assets	0.330*	-0.180*	0.327*	0.261*	-0.130*	-0.335*	-0.472*	0.006	1.000		
	(0.000)	(0.000)	(0.000)	(0.000)	(0.003)	(0.000)	(0.000)	(0.884)			
(10) Lg NI	0.346*	-0.171*	0.316*	0.291*	-0.093*	-0.267*	-0.441*	-0.009	0.761*	1.000	
	(0.000)	(0.000)	(0.000)	(0.000)	(0.038)	(0.000)	(0.000)	(0.843)	(0.000)		
(11) Lg Discr. Exp.	0.351*	-0.071	0.301*	0.336*	-0.092*	-0.142*	-0.373*	0.051	0.240*	0.456*	1.0
	(0.000)	(0.105)	(0.000)	(0.000)	(0.033)	(0.001)	(0.000)	(0.245)	(0.000)	(0.000)	

***$p < 0.01$, **$p < 0.05$, *$p < 0.1$.

Table 3.7. Correlation Between Main Variables and Components.

Component	Authenticity	Legitimacy
Embedded strategy	$r = 0.86^*$	–
Resource commitment	$r = 0.68^*$	–
Management fairness	$r = 0.32^*$	–
Litigation costs	–	$r = 0.45^*$
Media controversy	–	$r = 0.47^*$
External focus	–	$r = 0.70^*$

Statistically significant at $^*p < 0.05$.

Authenticity Correlations
Measurement of overall internal authenticity variable was supported by a strong correlation with its sub-components including embedded strategy ($r = 0.86$, $p < 0.01$), resources commitment ($r = 0.68$, $p < 0.01$), and management fairness ($r = 0.32$, $p < 0.01$). Low-to-moderate correlation of the components with each other enables their use as independent variables in Model 2. Lastly, overall authenticity is moderately correlated with all control variables ($r < 0.35$, $p < 0.01$). These correlations indicate a firm's ability to implement an embedded strategy that is moderately dependent on firm's size, profitability, and available CSR funding.

Legitimacy Correlations
Measurement of the overall legitimacy variable is supported by the moderate to strong correlation with its components including external CSR focus ($r = 0.70$, $p < 0.01$), media controversy ($r = 0.47$, $p < 0.01$), and litigation costs ($r = 0.45$, $p < 0.01$). For legitimacy components, the litigation costs component was moderately correlated with media controversy component ($r = 0.34$, $p < 0.01$) indicating that lower violation costs could reduce media's controversies and, conversely, that violation costs could enhance the newsworthiness of controversies.

Lastly, the separation of Model 1 (main variables) from Model 2 (components) reduced the potential for multicollinearity between the main variables (authenticity/legitimacy) with its components. Internal authenticity and external legitimacy are not materially correlated with each other ($r = 0.09$, $p < 0.01$) reducing confounding of the main variable's regression on reputation (Model 1). Moreover, variance inflation factors reflected collinearity tolerance levels at acceptable levels below 10 for the main components of authenticity and legitimacy. As such, splitting the main variable regression analysis from its components provides a more nuanced insight into the impact of each component on corporate reputation. This insight identifies which components contribute to micro-CSR strategies and nuanced implementation approaches.

I next examine the main variables and their components with regression modeling. I then discuss how authenticity and legitimacy can serve as guardrails to develop four micro-CSR strategies that managers could adopt based on their position of power, resource dependency, and competencies.

HYPOTHESES TESTING

The impact of internal authenticity and external legitimacy (main variables) on corporate reputation was explored through three models including the main variables, a component analysis, and a categorical grouping at different intensity levels. First, Model 1 (main variables) includes internal authenticity and external legitimacy as independent variables with size, industry, and financial performance as control variables. Model 2 (components) identifies which components of the main variables impact corporate reputation the most. Lastly, Model 3 explores how the intensity level combinations of the main variables impact corporate reputation. Table 3.8 provides a summary of the variables used in linear regression Model 1, Model 2, and Model 3.

Table 3.8.   Comparison of Linear Regression Model Variables.

Purpose	Model 1 (Main Variables)	Model 2 (Components)	Model 3 (Intensity Categories)	
Primary variables	Internal authenticity External legitimacy	Embedded strategy Resource commitment Management fairness	Compliance Strategic Authentic	Low A # Low L Low A # High L High A # Low L
		Litigation costs Media controversies External focus	Integrated	High A # High L *A = Authenticity *L = Legitimacy
Control variables	Log Assets, Log Net Income, Log Discr. Exp, Fiscal Year, Industry	Same as Model 1	Fiscal year, industry	

FINDINGS

Model 1 (Main Variables)

Hypothesis 1, that a firm's reputation is always positively impacted by the degree of a firm's legitimacy was not supported ($\beta = 0.011$, $p = 0.411$). Legitimacy holds a weak and inconsistent relationship with corporate reputation where the results do not reliably fall in the same causal direction. Hypothesis 2, that a firm's reputation is always positively impacted by the degree of authenticity was confirmed ($\beta = 0.031$, $p < 0.05$). Company size (log assets) was found to be statistically significant with a moderately positive relationship strength ($\beta = 0.21$, $p < 0.05$), profitability (log net income) was not statistically significant ($\beta = 0.14$, $p = 0.08$), and discretionary expenses was not statistically significant and held a weak relationship ($\beta = 0.03$, $p = 0.62$). In summary, corporate reputation consistently increased with internal authenticity while external legitimacy contributes inconsistently to corporate reputation. These relationships hold when a company's size, profitability, and discretionary expenses are controlled.

Table 3.9. Linear Regression Results.

Variables	Model (1) (Main)	SE	Model (2) (Components)	SE	Model (3) (Intensity)	SE
Authenticity	0.0312**	(0.01)	–	–	–	–
Legitimacy	0.0115	(0.01)	–	–	–	–
Embedded strategy	–	–	0.143***	(0.03)	–	–
Sustain resource commitment	–	–	0.103**	(0.04)	–	–
Fairness management	–	–	0.069**	(0.03)	–	–
Litigation cost	–	–	0.171***	(0.05)	–	–
Media controversy score	–	–	0.012	(0.04)	–	–
External focus score	–	–	0.078***	(0.03)	–	–
Compliance (Low A# Low L)	–	–	–	–	base	–
Strategic (Low A# High L)	–	–	–	–	−0.041	(0.06)
Authentic (High A# Low L)	–	–	–	–	0.163**	(0.07)
Integrated (High A # High L)	–	–	–	–	0.136**	(0.07)
Log Assets	0.213**	(0.09)	0.219**	(0.10)	–	–
Log NI	0.136	(0.08)	0.158**	(0.08)	–	–
Log Discretionary Expense	0.0312	(0.06)	0.0093	(0.06)	–	–
Constant	4.664***	(0.51)	4.061***	(0.56)	6.386***	(0.22)
Industry	78-various		78-various		78-various	
Fiscal Year	5-various		5-various		5-various	
Observations	502		502		502	
R-squared	0.698		0.715		0.669	
ANOVA – F-test	10.827***		10.983***		10.249***	

**indicates p-value < 0.05 and ***indicates p-value < 0.01.

Model 2 (Components)

Model 2 examined the components of internal authenticity and external legitimacy to ascertain their effect on corporate reputation while controlling for size, financial condition, and industry. For authenticity, all components in the model were statistically significant ($p < 0.05$) of which the strongest predictor of corporate reputation was an embedded strategy ($\beta = 0.143$, $p < 0.001$) and a sustained commitment of resources ($\beta = 0.103$, $p < 0.05$). Management commitment/fairness was statistically significant with a weaker relationship ($\beta = .069, p < 0.05$). In terms of legitimacy, litigation costs (reduction in) held the strongest statistically significant relationship ($\beta = 0.171$, $p < 0.05$), media controversies (reduction in) was surprisingly not significant ($\beta = 0.012$, $p = 0.76$), and external CSR focus held a weak impact on corporate reputation ($\beta = 0.078, p < 0.05$).

Model 3 (Intensity Levels)

Model 3 examines how the intensity levels of internal authenticity and external legitimacy (main variables) impact corporate reputation. The model identifies the combination of intensity levels with the highest impact on corporate reputation through an ANOVA and margins analysis at high and low limits split at their means. Interestingly, the findings demonstrate how authenticity always improves corporate reputation but can be influenced by the intensity and inconsistency of legitimacy that could either enhance or detract from authenticity's impact on corporate reputation. The results, as shown in Table 3.9, suggest that a combination of high authenticity and low legitimacy (authentic micro-strategy) has the strongest positive relationship with corporate reputation ($\beta = 0.163$, $p < 0.05$). The combination of high authenticity and high legitimacy (integrated micro-strategy) has the second largest positive relationship with corporate reputation ($\beta = 0.136$, $p < 0.05$). Lastly, the combination of low authenticity and high legitimacy (strategic CSR) has a negative and weak relationship with corporate reputation that is not statistically significant ($\beta = -0.041$, $p = 0.48$). This analysis provides a framework for TMTs to develop CSR micro-strategies and programs.

DISCUSSION

While institutional forces encourage firms to conform with similar CSR programs, managers can respond strategically by bridging or buffering based on their position of power, resource dependence, and visibility (Meznar & Nigh, 1995). A CSR program can be used by firms to strategically respond to evolving stakeholder expectations. A firm's shared value with relevant stakeholders can set expectations and serve as an overarching theme for its CSR strategy, to coordinate activities, and guide resource allocation (Porter & Kramer, 2006). When a CSR program is integrated with its competitive strategy, the perception of the program's authenticity is improved enhancing stakeholder legitimacy. Moreover, the CSR program becomes durable as it consistently lives up to stakeholder expectations by achieving financial and social objectives consistently, concurrently, and cost-effectively. Overtime, a firm's reputation is established.

I next explore the original research questions including, What blend of internal authenticity and external legitimacy has the largest impact on corporate reputation? What type of CSR program is the best fit for firms to improve their corporate reputation? These questions were explored as potential strategic choices for firms to respond to external isomorphic forces. First, I summarize each model's findings. Second, I discuss the implications of the components and intensity levels analysis of the two essential dimensions. Third, I explain its significance in relation to CSR micro-strategy development and implementation.

OVERVIEW OF FINDINGS

Main Variables (Model 1 Discussion)

A CSR program focused on authenticity is more effective in improving corporate reputation than one focused on external legitimacy. When a CSR program is authentic, it has an embedded strategy with program activities aligned with its identity (core business), culture, and business practices that improve stakeholder trust and resilience during economic downturns (Cording et al., 2014; Lins et al., 2017). A firm has more control over internal operations than external social expectations associated with legitimacy. The impact of these constructs could be affected by varying stakeholder perspectives of how a CSR program is implemented and more clearly understood by examining the underlying components of authenticity and legitimacy.

Components (Model 2 Discussion)

Authenticity

CSR strategies that move beyond aspirations by integrating its CSR program through substantive business practices improve its reputation. Internal authenticity components that enhance corporate reputation include (1) an embedded CSR strategy, (2) a sustained commitment of resources, and (3) management commitment/fairness. Stakeholders with expert knowledge of the firm such as employees, customers, and vendors perceive authenticity based on cues including (1) sustained commitment of resources, (2) management involvement, and (3) fair administrative processes with balanced distribution of program resources through procedural and distributive justice. Procedural justice ensures that administrative procedures are transparent, accessible, and applied consistently to all involved (Sun et al., 2012). Distributive justice ensures the fair distribution of resources. An incongruence between how a firm treats internal and external stakeholders affects their evaluation of the firm (Chun, 2005). The dynamic interplay between the perception of internal (authentic) and external (legitimacy) highlights how these boundaries impact reputation at differing intensity levels.

Legitimacy

Expectations of external stakeholders set by a firm's history, identity (core business), and CSR claims (image) were evaluated through regulatory legitimacy and sociopolitical legitimacy. Regulatory legitimacy positively impacts corporate reputation through legal compliance while remaining profitable. According to Carroll's pyramid of corporate social responsibility, compliance with economic and legal responsibilities by firms are basic requirements of society (Carroll, 1991). Legal compliance reduces the risk for primary stakeholders by providing legal recourse should the firm fail. In exchange, protected stakeholders purchase the firm's products and provide access to productive resources.

Media accessibility through improved technology has amplified stakeholder expectations for responsible business. Rapid changes in social expectations increase uncertainty and the risk of social sanctions such as negative press, boycotts, and strikes when expectations are unmet (McDonell & King, 2013). According to the pyramid of corporate responsibility, society expects a firm to conduct business ethically and to avoid harm by meeting normative expectations (Carroll, 1991). This study observed sociopolitical legitimacy as a firm's conformance to social expectations through appropriate business practices based on a socially constructed system of common values, norms, and beliefs (Suchman, 1995). Media controversies complicate a firm's ability to manage external social expectations as the impact could benefit or impair a firm's reputation based on the perspective of the stakeholder group evaluating the firm. Moreover, the degree of impact depends on a firm's ability to control the incident and whether a firm manages the event through appropriate actions based on accepted values, norms, and beliefs (Nickerson et al., 2022; Suchman, 1995). This was demonstrated by the weak and inconsistent impact from a reduction in media controversies. Although external pressure for firms to conduct business responsibly continues to intensify, a clear method for compliance remains underexplored. This study suggests that a firm's history, identity (core business), and shared value with relevant stakeholders can serve as boundaries for a firm to focus its external CSR activities on those in which it is most capable of solving. For legitimacy, the degree of a firm's external CSR focus was shown to have a positive impact on reputation which overtime can reduce the weaker and inconsistent effects of media controversies.

In summary, this study finds that the authenticity's impact on corporate reputation is more consistent than legitimate. With this information, I now answer the research question, What blend of internal authenticity and external legitimacy impacts corporate reputation the most? Model 3 (post hoc) explores this interaction at low and high levels of the main variables with four groupings identified here as CSR micro-strategies.

Interaction Intensity Levels and CSR Micro-Strategies (Model 3 Discussion)

Categorical interactions of authenticity and legitimacy at low and high levels were examined through an ANOVA analysis with a two-way tabulation. The interaction creates four micro-strategies (combinations) that impact corporate reputation. Fig. 3.7 illustrates the interactional relationship through a margins plot at high and low levels of authenticity and legitimacy split at their means.

The graph depicts that CSR strategies with high legitimacy have a lower reputation score at any level of authenticity. CSR programs with high authenticity

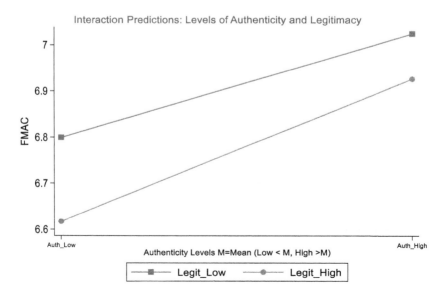

Fig. 3.7. Effect of Intensity Levels on Corporate Reputation.

also have a higher reputation score consistently. The interaction of legitimacy and authenticity as continuous variables is reflected by the unparallel lines suggesting that CSR programs with low authenticity have a greater gap in reputational score than those with high authenticity (smaller gap). In another words, a CSR program focused on authenticity has a stronger relationship with corporate reputation than one focused on legitimacy. A two-way tabulation of internal authenticity and external legitimacy at low and high intensity levels further demonstrates this relationship through four CSR micro-strategies. The micro-CSR strategies include a compliance strategy (low authenticity, low legitimacy), authentic strategy (high authenticity, low legitimacy), strategic micro-strategy (low authenticity, high legitimacy), and integrated strategy (high authenticity, high legitimacy). These micro-strategies are referenced throughout the remainder of the chapter for simplicity. Fig. 3.8 shows the two-way tabulation on the relationship between the micro-CSR strategies with corporate reputation.

As shown in Fig. 3.8, corporate reputation is highest with a mean score of 7.02 with an authentic strategy (high authenticity/low legitimacy) demonstrated in the lower right box. The second highest reputation score at 6.93 occurs with an integrated strategy (high authenticity/high legitimacy) demonstrated in the upper right box. The third highest reputation score at 6.80 occurred with a compliance strategy (low authenticity/low legitimacy) as reflected in the lower left box. Lastly, the lowest reputation score of 6.62 occurs with a strategic micro-strategy (low authenticity/high legitimacy) reflected in the upper left box.

		Buffering	Bridging
External legitimacy	High	4th Strategic Strategy Reputation: Mean = 6.62	2nd Integrated Strategy Reputation: Mean = 6.93
	Low	3rd Compliance Strategy Reputation: Mean = 6.80	1st Authentic Strategy Reputation: Mean = 7.02
		Low	High
		Internal authenticity	

Note: $p < 0.05$. Mean: low = below mean and high = above mean.

Fig. 3.8. CSR Micro-Strategy: Impact on Reputation Scores.

CONTRIBUTION

This chapter establishes internal authenticity as an essential dimension of CSR strategy. The consistent impact of internal authenticity on corporate reputation can guide TMTs to align their CSR strategy with a firm's identity (core business), culture, and business practices to coordinate activities around an overarching purpose. The boundaries allow firms to focus their resources on CSR issues they are most capable of addressing by using complementary resources (Aguinis & Glavas, 2013; Tang et al., 2012). A CSR strategy with a coordinated implementation approach can maximize financial and social performance (Siltaloppi et al., 2021). Moreover, a firm's sustained commitment and management involvement improves the perception of authenticity and demonstrates a firm's character as honest, sincere, genuine, and consistent. This study found internal authenticity as a critical component of CSR strategy that allows it to differentiate from competitors within the constraints of legitimacy.

Significance of Contribution

CSR programs contribute to a firm's corporate reputation that serves as a mechanism for stakeholders to predict a firm's behavior. An authentic CSR strategy that demonstrates consistency and integrity lowers informational asymmetry, increases creditability, and forms long-term relationships that place the firm in a position to acquire financial and physical assets to execute strategic initiatives. Path-dependent relationships formed through authentic CSR activities become a valuable intangible asset that contributes to a sustainable competitive advantage (Barney, 1991; Defillippi & Reed, 1990). Authentic CSR strategies can serve as a strategic response to stakeholder expectations by adapting business practices. Adapting ensures its durability and resilience while reducing employee cynicism and stakeholder skepticism.

Moreover, authentic CSR strategies improve corporate reputation by lowering perceived risk through strong governance, value alignment, and a perception of integrity. For example, customers that value a firm's environmentally friendly products and socially conscious business practices are willing to absorb price premiums and demonstrate loyalty through repeat business (Fombrun & Shanley, 1990). Vendor relationships based on a firm's favorable reputation reduces information asymmetry, a costly information search, or protective contract provisions that can lower a firm's cost of goods sold (Jones et al., 2018). Authentic CSR strategies contribute to employee social identification with the firm improving engagement, productivity, and turnover (Lee & Yoon, 2018). A CSR strategy designed around a shared value with relevant stakeholders provides a perception of fairness by balancing the needs of internal and external stakeholders. Lastly, an authentic CSR program can serve as a sustainable competitive advantage when linked to its unique identity, aligns with internal competencies, and utilizes complementary resources to achieve financial and social goals.

Internal authenticity and external legitimacy as essential dimensions provide insight into which CSR components are important for effective implementation. These insights address the research question: What type of CSR program is the best fit for firms to improve their reputation? With an understanding of how the interaction of authenticity and legitimacy at different intensity levels impacts corporate reputation, a firm can strategically respond to changing regulations, social expectations, and workforce needs with a consistent and coordinated approach. Fig. 3.9 describes the four basic CSR programs under buffering or bridging approaches that align with the micro-CSR strategies described in this study.

		Buffering Programs	Bridging Programs
External legitimacy	High Sociopolitical legitimacy	4th **Strategic** Mean reputation = **6.62**	2nd **Integrated** Mean Reputation = **6.93***
	Low regulatory legitimacy	3rd **Compliance** Mean reputation = **6.80***	1st **Authentic** Mean Reputation = **7.02***
		Low (espoused values)	High (embedded practices)
		Internal authenticity	

*P < 0.01.

Fig. 3.9. CSR Programs as a Strategic Response.

CSR PROGRAMS AS A STRATEGIC RESPONSE
Bridging CSR Programs
Authentic CSR Program
Authentic CSR programs are embedded in the network of internal stakeholders, culture, and norms of the firm as determined by organizational members over time. In the context of business, authenticity is being true to the organizational self whereby a firm's identity, image, and conduct align consistently by including employee perspectives in the strategy making process (Driver, 2006). An authentic program has the highest positive impact on corporate reputation with a mean reputation score of 7.02. The authentic program is integrated with its identity (core business) through a sustained commitment of complementary resources. Furthermore, these programs have a supportive governance structure with policies that encourage management's involvement through CSR committees, monitoring tools, and compensation linked to CSR objectives. The congruence between a firm's core business and values of authentic CSR program contributes to the perception of its authenticity and enhances employee social identification, engagement, and organizational learning (Aguinis & Glavas, 2013; McShane & Cunningham, 2012). In the long term, a firm can better respond to external opportunities through socially complex relationships as a sustainable competitive advantage (Freeman et al., 2021; Reed & Defillippi, 1990; Story & Neves, 2015).

Integrated CSR Program
Integrated CSR programs are well-balanced and integrated into a firm's core business that goes beyond regulations to meet social expectations and maximize economic outcome (Shin et al., 2016). The program's high authenticity reflects a commitment to activities that support the firm's alignment of espoused values and its external image (Cording et al., 2014). In terms of legitimacy, the program focuses on external social activities that it is most capable of performing (Hawn & Ioannou, 2016). High intensity levels on both dimensions balance the tension between financial and social goals while enhancing employee engagement through a shared value with salient stakeholders (Aguinis & Glavas, 2013;

Siltaloppi et al., 2021). Essentially, the program's authenticity differentiates the firm through unique financial, social, and cognitive capabilities acquired through program activities (McWilliams & Siegel, 2011). The result is a durable CSR program with enhanced reputation.

Interestingly, the integrated CSR program was found to have the second highest impact on corporate reputation with a mean reputation score of 6.93. Based on this finding, it is plausible that the lower and inconsistent impact of external legitimacy compared to authenticity's consistency and strength tilts the balance toward a stronger reputation for authenticity when both dimensions are at high levels. For example, the inconsistency of legitimacy's impact could detract from authenticity's impact on corporate reputation. The impact is demonstrated by the difference in reputation scores between the authentic CSR program ($M = 7.02$) and integrated CSR program ($M = 6.93$).

Buffering CSR Programs

Strategic CSR Program
Strategic CSR programs focus on buffering internal operating efficiencies through external CSR activities that align with powerful stakeholders (Graafland & Van de Ven, 2006; McWilliams & Siegel, 2001). In other words, a strategic CSR program focuses on creating strategic partnerships enhanced by social exchange and reciprocity. Activities are allocated to stakeholders that support a firm's desired economic outcome which could be decoupled from action-level activities (Siegel, 2009). This chapter adopts this definition and found that the strategic program has the lowest reputation score of 6.62 as it could be perceived as insincere without leadership's communication of the program's motives.

Compliance CSR Program
A compliance CSR program meets basic requirements by espousing core values but not embedding them into its culture. Externally, the firm complies with regulations but does not go beyond the requirements to meet social expectations. A compliance program has the second lowest mean FMAC score of 6.80. Low authenticity reflects a low integration of program activities with a firm's culture. Likewise low legitimacy indicates the program's focus on compliance but not meet external social expectations. The program avoids disruption of operational efficiencies and may reduce the risk of litigation, employee cynicism, and stakeholder skepticism associated with the perception of insincere CSR activities.

THEORETICAL CONTRIBUTION

Integration of stakeholder theory, RBV, and CSR strategy is an opportunity to narrow broad theories by establishing boundaries around shared value as an overarching theme. This chapter contributes to CSR literature by establishing internal authenticity and external legitimacy as two essential dimensions that capture the value of CSR programs through an improved corporate reputation. Furthermore, by identifying internal authenticity as the dominant dimension, the four CSR micro-strategies introduced demonstrate how a firm can respond to external isomorphic forces and reduce the risk of sanctions by social actors. This study contributes to CSR strategic management literature by identifying a CSR micro-strategy that is aligned with a firm's identity (core business), integrated in their routines, and uses complementary resources consistently to satisfy differing stakeholder expectations while improving corporate reputation as a sustainable competitive advantage. By staying true to its organizational self, a CSR program can become durable and resilient to resource allocation questions during an economic downturn. While external legitimacy encourages firms to adopt similar CSR programs to conform (DiMaggio & Powell, 1983), an authentic CSR program allows firms to differentiate through its unique history and relationship with relevant stakeholders and employees through shared value. This chapter contributes to the ongoing philosophical debate on whether it is appropriate to allocate resources to social needs by supporting the business case for CSR programs. An authentic CSR program could offset upfront costs by integrating CSR activities with existing business practices that contribute to organizational learning, innovation, and operating efficiencies. Moreover, a firm's understanding of how employees judge authenticity of a CSR program is essential to its acceptance by employees (McShane & Cunningham, 2012; Rodrigo & Arenas, 2008).

MANAGERIAL IMPLICATIONS

This study established internal authenticity and external legitimacy as essential dimensions in a parsimonious framework that could guide TMTs with adjusting their CSR strategy and implementation approach. Authenticity uncovered as the dominant CSR dimension can assist managers by identifying a blend of authenticity and legitimacy that fits their financial and social position to positively impact corporate reputation. The four micro-CSR strategies focus on activities that improve corporate reputation based on a firm's power, resource constraints, and competencies. Powerful firms can respond by buffering efficient operations from external pressures through a compliance program or strategic program. Conversely, weaker firms that lack power can respond by compromising with powerful stakeholders by adapting internal operations through an authentic or integrated CSR program that aligns CSR motives with core business practices. A positive reputation can improve market value by reducing information asymmetry, improving credibility, and providing differentiated access to markets and productive resources (Fombrun & Shanley, 1990; Suchman, 1995).

Management Discretion, Industry, and Reputation

A firm's industry has a strong impact on corporate reputation. Industry membership influences how stakeholders perceive, evaluate, and judge a firm's legitimacy by providing recognizable standards to evaluate the firm including compliance with similar regulations, standards, and norms. Suchman (1995) suggests that cognitive legitimacy influences social actors with a taken-for-granted bias when judging a firm based on its industry's reputation. Based on this suggestion, a firm's industry should be a salient factor in management's CSR strategy when seeking to differentiate from competition. In particular, authenticity can serve as the differentiating factor within the homogeneous constraints of acquiring legitimacy in an industry.

As firms create CSR strategies within their industry group, industry reputation should be considered when seeking a sustainable competitive advantage. Consistent with McShane and Cunningham (2012), this study found that managers can differentiate their firms by integrating their CSR strategy, committing resources consistently, and managing the program through transparent administrative processes with fair (balanced) distribution of program resources.

LIMITATIONS

CSR is a multilevel construct with extant literature using a mixture of unidimensional and multidimensional measures (Nizamuddin, 2018). The result has been inconsistent in the CSR field on the relationship between CSR, reputation, and financial performance (Chun, 2005). This study establishes boundaries for CSR strategy within the RBV framework using stakeholder theory to examine how the dynamic interplay between external and internal CSR activities improves corporate reputation by comparing CSR conduct (database) to corporate reputation (perceptual measure). While Model 1 (main variables), Model 2 (component analysis), and Model 3 (intensity level) arrived with statistically significant results, industry was found to absorb much of the model's explanatory power. FMAC's reputation survey is influenced by using survey respondents composed of industry executives, external board members, and analysts that have more industry and financial expertise than the general public that could skew the results toward industry characteristics and weaken the evaluation of social responsibility (Liston-Heyes & Ceton, 2008). Despite this limitation, this study found that statistically significant results in the expected causal direction provide insight into nuanced CSR strategy when controlling for industry. Moreover, an analysis based on the mean scores of each dimension allowed for groupings into micro-CSR strategies that provide insight on which intensity levels are most impactful on corporate reputation. Future studies should consider focusing on FMAC's social responsibility components to reduce the effect of industry in the FMAC survey. Future research could also consider using a reputational survey that includes a broader base of stakeholder perspectives.

FUTURE RESEARCH

The multilevel focus of CSR strategy contributed to the use of longitudinal databases and the FMAC survey. Although FMAC is a well-established survey for corporate reputation in academia, this study's limitations highlight the need for future reputation research to establish boundaries around key stakeholder perspectives to inform which FMAC components are essential. Moreover, future CSR studies should consider reputation databases that use a variety of survey respondents, questionnaires, or other methods to acquire data specific to corporate social responsibility.

Comparing social conduct (CSR activities) against perception (FMAC reputation score) highlights a need for future research to incorporate this distinct difference to capture a true comparison. This study's use of a social performance database and a perceptual-based reputation survey highlights a method that could be used more in organizational studies with financial and nonfinancial disclosures. Although this study focused on alignment (decoupling) between identity (core business), image (CSR claims), and conduct (databases), a qualitative study as an alternative research design could provide insight into how TMTs view their initial CSR motives compared to what their disclosures communicate. The insight could inform marketing strategies, social performance reporting standards, and accounting procedures for CSR activities. Better understanding of CSR motives could shape more nuanced CSR strategies that involve the use of external and internal CSR activities.

With CSR research trends shifting from firm-level to micro-CSR strategies that account for differing stakeholder perspectives, future studies should test hypotheses that differentiate stakeholder perspectives to understand how their perceptions impact the formation, management, and improvement of corporate reputation over time. Lastly, future studies should continue exploring multilevel boundaries around shared value to improve measurability by narrowing the level of analysis, disciplinary approach, and stakeholder perspectives for improved clarity.

CONCLUSION

The dynamic interaction between internal authenticity and external legitimacy was explored to identify a CSR strategy that can improve corporate reputation as a sustainable competitive advantage. This study uncovered internal authenticity as the dominant dimension to consistently impact corporate reputation positively. This insight informs TMTs that a CSR program bounded by its unique history, identity (core business), and complementary capabilities will maximize its financial and social performance through a balance of stakeholder needs, wants, and desires. Moreover, the chapter can assist TMTs by identifying the components and intensity levels of authenticity and legitimacy that are the most valuable and effective in improving corporate reputation while considering their resource constraints to focus on activities they are best capable of performing. CSR micro-strategies with distinct components were examined for their impact on a corporate reputation and uncovered a framework to guide CSR strategy ranging from compromising with powerful stakeholders to buffering their operating efficiencies. Based on the consistency of authenticity over legitimacy, authentic and integrated CSR strategies that adapt to external forces provide the highest impact on corporate reputation by improving stakeholder perception of authenticity. Furthermore, these CSR programs that bridge business practices allow firms to differentiate from competitors within the constraints of external isomorphic forces. Although an authentic CSR strategy requires a sustained commitment of resources to integrate structural changes, the outcome is a durable CSR program with consistent delivery of financial and social performance while creating an enlightened workplace.

REFERENCES

Aguinis, H., & Glavas, A. (2013). Embedded versus peripheral corporate social responsibility: Psychological foundations. *Industrial and Organizational Psychology, 6*(4), 314–332. https://doi.org/10.1111/iops.12059

Bams, D., van der Kroft, B., & Maas, K. (2022). Connecting the dots: An integrative framework of CSR antecedents, heterogeneous CSR approaches, and sustainable and financial performance. Available at SSRN 3906715.

Barnett, M. L., Jermier, J. M., & Lafferty, B. A. (2006). Corporate reputation: The definitional landscape. *Corporate Reputation Review, 9*(1), 26–38. https://doi.org/10.1057/palgrave.crr.1550012

Barney, J. (1991). Firm resources and sustained competitive advantage. *Journal of Management, 17*(1), 99–120. https://doi.org/10.1177/014920639101700108

Bertels, S., & Peloza, J. (2008). Running just to stand still? Managing CSR reputation in an era of ratcheting expectations. *Corporate Reputation Review, 11*(1), 56–72. https://doi.org/10.1057/crr.2008.1

Bitektine, A. (2011). Toward a theory of social judgments of organizations: The case of legitimacy, reputation, and status. *The Academy of Management Review, 36*(1), 151–179. https://doi.org/10.5465/amr.2009.0382

Brown, B., & Perry, S. (1994). Removing the financial performance halo from Fortune's "Most Admired" companies. *Academy of Management Journal, 37*(5), 1347–1359. https://doi.org/10.5465/256676

Carroll, A. B. (1991). The pyramid of corporate social responsibility: Toward the moral management of organizational stakeholders. *Business Horizons, 34*(4), 39–48. https://doi.org/10.1016/0007-6813(91)90005-G

Cording, M., Harrison, J. S., Hoskisson, R. E., & Jonsen, K. (2014). Walking the talk: A multistakeholder exploration of organizational authenticity, employee productivity, and post-merger performance. *Academy of Management Perspectives, 28*(1), 38–56. https://doi.org/10.5465/amp.2013.0002

Chun, R. (2005). Corporate reputation: Meaning and measurement. *International Journal of Management Reviews, 7*(2), 91–109. https://doi.org/10.1111/j.1468-2370.2005.00109.x

DiMaggio, & Powell, W. W. (1983). The iron cage revisited: Institutional isomorphism and collective rationality in organizational fields. *American Sociological Review, 48*(2), 147–160. https://doi.org/10.2307/2095101

Driver, M. (2006). Beyond the stalemate of economics versus ethics: Corporate social responsibility and the discourse of the organizational self. *Journal of Business Ethics, 66*(4), 337–356. https://doi.org/10.1007/s10551-006-0012-7

Flammer, C., Hong, B., & Minor, D. (2019). Corporate governance and the rise of integrating corporate social responsibility criteria in executive compensation: Effectiveness and implications for firm outcomes. *Strategic Management Journal, 40*(7), 1097–1122. https://doi.org/10.1002/smj.3018

Flanagan, D. J., O'Shaughnessy, K. C., & Palmer, T. B. (2011). Re-assessing the relationship between the fortune reputation data and financial performance: Overwhelming influence or just a part of the puzzle? *Corporate Reputation Review, 14*(1), 3–14. https://doi.org/10.1057/crr.2011.4

Freeman, R. E. (1984). *Strategic management: A stakeholder approach.* Pitman.

Freeman, R. E., Dmytriyev, S. D., & Phillips, R. A. (2021). Stakeholder theory and the resource-based view of the firm. *Journal of Management, 47*(7), 1757–1770. https://doi.org/10.1177/0149206321993576

Friedman, M. (1970, September 13). A Friedman doctrine: The social responsibility of business is to increase its profits. *New York Times*, 17.

Fombrun, C., & Shanley, M. (1990). What's in a name? Reputation building and corporate strategy. *Academy of Management Journal, 33*(2), 233–258. https://doi.org/10.5465/256324

Fortune.com (2022). https://fortune.com/franchise-list-page/methodology-worlds-most-admired-companies-2022

García-Sánchez, I., Hussain, N., Aibar-Guzmán, C., & Aibar-Guzmán, B. (2022). Assurance of corporate social responsibility reports: Does it reduce decoupling practices? *Business Ethics, the Environment & Responsibility, 31*(1), 118–138. https://doi.org/10.1111/beer.12394

Graafland, J., & van de Ven, B. (2006). Strategic and moral motivation for corporate social responsibility. *The Journal of Corporate Citizenship, 22*, 111–123. https://doi.org/10.9774/gleaf.4700.2006.su.00012

Hengst, I.-A., Jarzabkowski, P., Hoegl, M., & Muethel, M. (2020). Toward a process theory of making sustainability strategies legitimate in action. *Academy of Management Journal, 63*(1), 246–271. https://doi.org/10.5465/amj.2016.0960

Herold, D. M., Farr-Wharton, B., Lee, K., & Groschopf, W. (2019). The interaction between institutional and stakeholder pressures: Advancing a framework for categorising carbon disclosure strategies. *Business Strategy & Development, 2*(2), 77–90. https://doi.org/10.1002/bsd2.44

Hong, B., Li, Z., & Minor, D. (2016). Corporate governance and executive compensation for corporate social responsibility. *Journal of Business Ethics, 136*(1), 199–213. https://doi.org/10.1007/s10551-015-2962-0

Jones, T. M., Harrison, J. S., & Felps, W. (2018). How applying instrumental stakeholder theory can provide sustainable competitive advantage. *The Academy of Management Review, 43*(3), 371–391. https://doi.org/10.5465/amr.2016.0111

Lee, S., & Yoon, J. (2018). Does the authenticity of corporate social responsibility affect employee commitment? *Social Behavior and Personality, 46*(4), 617–632. https://doi.org/10.2224/sbp.6475

Liedtka, J. (2008). Strategy making and the search for authenticity. *Journal of Business Ethics, 80*(2), 237–248. https://doi.org/10.1007/s10551-007-9415-3

Lins, K. V., Servaes, H., & Tamayo, A. (2017). Social capital, trust, and firm performance: The value of corporate social responsibility during the financial crisis. *The Journal of Finance (New York), 72*(4), 1785–1823. https://doi.org/10.1111/jofi.12505

Liston-Heyes, C., & Ceton, G. (2009). An investigation of real versus perceived CSP in S&P-500 firms. *Journal of Business Ethics, 89*(2), 283–296. https://doi.org/10.1007/s10551-008-9999-2

Lougee, B., & Wallace, J. (2008). The Corporate Social Responsibility (CSR) trend. *Journal of Applied Corporate Finance, 20*(1), 96–108. https://doi.org/10.1111/j.1745-6622.2008.00172.x

Mallory, D. B., & Rupp, D. E. (2015). "Good" leadership: Using corporate social responsibility to enhance leader–member exchange. In B. Erdogan & T. N. Bauer (Eds.), *The Oxford handbook of leader-member exchange.* Oxford University Press. https://doi.org/10.1093/oxfordhb/9780199326174.013.0013

McDonnell, M.-H., & King, B. (2013). Keeping up appearances: Reputational threat and impression management after social movement boycotts. *Administrative Science Quarterly, 58*(3), 387–419. https://doi.org/10.1177/0001839213500032

McShane, L., & Cunningham, P. (2012). To thine own self be true? Employees' judgments of the authenticity of their organization's corporate social responsibility program. *Journal of Business Ethics, 108*(1), 81–100. https://doi.org/10.1007/s10551-011-1064-x

McWilliams, A., & Siegel, D. (2001). Corporate social responsibility: A theory of the firm perspective. *The Academy of Management Review, 26*(1), 117–127.

McWilliams, A., & Siegel, D. S. (2011). Creating and capturing value: Strategic corporate social responsibility, resource-based theory, and sustainable competitive advantage. *Journal of Management, 37*(5), 1480–1495. https://doi.org/10.1177/0149206310385696

Meznar, M. B., & Nigh, D. (1995). Buffer or bridge? Environmental and organizational determinants of public affairs activities in American firms. *Academy of Management Journal, 38*(4), 975–996. https://doi.org/10.5465/256617

Meyer, J. W., & Rowan, B. (1977). Institutionalized organizations: Formal structure as myth and ceremony. *The American Journal of Sociology, 83*(2), 340–363. https://doi.org/10.1086/226550

Mitchell, R. K., Agle, B. R., & Wood, D. J. (1997). Toward a theory of stakeholder identification and salience: Defining the principle of who and what really counts. *The Academy of Management Review, 22*(4), 853–886. https://doi.org/10.2307/259247

Morgeson, F. P., Aguinis, H., Waldman, D. A., & Siegel, D. S. (2013). Extending corporate social responsibility research to the human resource management and organizational behavior domains: A Look to the future. *Personnel Psychology, 66*(4), 805–824. https://doi.org/10.1111/peps.12055

Nickerson, D., Lowe, M., Pattabhiramaiah, A., & Sorescu, A. (2022). The impact of corporate social responsibility on brand sales: An accountability perspective. *Journal of Marketing, 86*(2), 5–28. https://doi.org/10.1177/00222429211044155

Nizamuddin, M. (2018). Corporate social responsibility and corporate financial performance: An exploratory study of measurement-approach selection issues. *IUP Journal of Corporate Governance, 17*(2), 36–54.

Hawn, O., & Ioannou, I. (2016). Mind the gap: The interplay between external and internal actions in the case of corporate social responsibility. *Strategic Management Journal*, *37*, 2569–2588. https://doi.org/10.1002/smj.2464

Oliver, C. (1991). Strategic responses to institutional processes. *The Academy of Management Review*, *16*(1), 145–79. https://doi.org/10.2307/258610

Peloza, J., & Papania, L. (2008). The missing link between corporate social responsibility and financial performance: Stakeholder salience and identification. *Corporate Reputation Review*, *11*(2), 169–181. https://doi.org/10.1057/crr.2008.13

Porter, M. E., & Kramer, M. R. (2006). Strategy and society: The link between competitive advantage and corporate social responsibility. *Harvard Business Review*, *84*(12), 78–163.

Refintiv.com (2023). https://www.refinitiv.com/en/financial-data/company-data/esg-data

Reed, R., & DeFillippi, R. J. (1990). Casual ambiguity, barriers to imitation, and sustainable competitive advantage. *The Academy of Management Review*, *15*(1), 88.

Rodrigo, P., & Arenas, D. (2008). Do employees care about CSR programs? A typology of employees according to their attitudes. *Journal of Business Ethics*, *83*(2), 265–283. https://doi.org/10.1007/s10551-007-9618-7

Schober, P., Boer, C., & Schwarte, L. A. (2018). Correlation coefficients: Appropriate use and interpretation. *Anesthesia & Analgesia*, *126*(5), 1763–1768.

Sen, S., Bhattacharya, C. B. (2001). Does doing good always lead to doing Better? Consumer reactions to corporate social responsibility. *Journal of Marketing Research*, *38*(2), 225–243. https://doi.org/10.1509/jmkr.38.2.225.18838

Shin, I., Hur, W.-M., & Kang, S. (2016). Employees' perceptions of corporate social responsibility and job performance: A sequential mediation model. *Sustainability (Basel, Switzerland)*, *8*(5), 493. https://doi.org/10.3390/su8050493

Siegel, D. S. (2009). Green management matters only if it yields more green: An economic/strategic perspective. *Academy of Management Perspectives*, *23*(3), 5–16. https://doi.org/10.5465/amp.2009.43479260

Siltaloppi, J., Rajala, R., & Hietala, H. (2021). Integrating CSR with business strategy: A tension management perspective. *Journal of Business Ethics*, *174*(3), 507–527. https://doi.org/10.1007/s10551-020-04569-3

Story, J., & Neves, P. (2015). When corporate social responsibility (CSR) increases performance: exploring the role of intrinsic and extrinsic CSR attribution. *Business Ethics (Oxford, England)*, *24*(2), 111–124. https://doi.org/10.1111/beer.12084

Suchman, M. C. (1995). Managing legitimacy: Strategic and institutional approaches. *The Academy of Management Review*, *20*(3), 571–610. https://doi.org/10.2307/258788

Sun, L.-Y., Chow, I. H. S., Chiu, R. K., & Pan, W. (2013). Outcome favorability in the link between leader–member exchange and organizational citizenship behavior: Procedural fairness climate matters. *The Leadership Quarterly*, *24*(1), 215–226. https://doi.org/10.1016/j.leaqua.2012.10.008

Tang, Z., Hull, C. E., & Rothenberg, S. (2012). How corporate social responsibility engagement strategy moderates the CSR–financial performance relationship. *Journal of Management Studies*, *49*(7), 1274–1303. https://doi.org/10.1111/j.1467-6486.2012.01068.x

Villiers, C., Jia, J., & Li, Z. (2022). Corporate social responsibility: A review of empirical research using Thomson Reuters Asset4 data. *Accounting and Finance (Parkville)*, *62*(4), 4523–4568. https://doi.org/10.1111/acfi.13004

CHAPTER 4

A COMPARISON OF BUSINESS ETHICS IN CHINA, JAPAN, AND KOREA

Taehee Choi[a], Nakano Chiaki[b] and Zhou Zucheng[c]

[a]KDI School of Public Policy and Management, Korea
[b]Japan International University, Japan
[c]Shanghai Jiao Tong University, China

ABSTRACT

This study investigates business ethics (BE) practices in three East-Asian countries (China, Japan, and South Korea) through a questionnaire survey conducted in the years of 2014 and 2015. Specifically, ethical attitudes of employees working in major native companies in each mentioned country are studied. In detail, the study examines (1) respondents' responsibility felt toward various stakeholder groups, (2) the existence of unethical practices in respondents' industries, (3) respondents' experience of ethical conflicts, (4) factors influencing ethical and unethical decisions, (5) respondents reactions to hypothetical situations involving ethical dilemmas, (6) institutionalization of BE in respondents' companies, and (7) the change of ethical standards compared with ten years ago. We find that a number of similarities as well as differences exist regarding BE practices in the three countries, which can be partially attributed to different political, economic, and socio-cultural backgrounds. It can also be observed that in a number of cases, Chinese practices differ from those that are similar for Japan and Korea. This can be explained by the ongoing transition of Chinese economic system toward market economy and the fact that, compared with Japan and Korea, China is less economically

Responsible Firms: CSR, ESG, and Global Sustainability
International Finance Review, Volume 23, 73–92
Copyright © 2025 by Taehee Choi, Nakano Chiaki and Zhou Zucheng
Published under exclusive licence by Emerald Publishing Limited
ISSN: 1569-3767/doi:10.1108/S1569-376720240000023004

developed, and the local business environment, including BE management, is less mature. This study significantly contributes to the existing literature on BE and has practical implications for any agents interested in ethical aspects on business environment in the investigated countries.

Keywords: Business ethics; survey; China; Japan; Korea

JEL classification: M14; O57

1. INTRODUCTION

In the current world of business, ethical aspects of enterprises are becoming increasingly more important. The importance of business ethics (henceforth BE) has recently been highlighted by Global Economic Crisis of 2009 and its negative effect on the world economy and company profits, which has also resulted in changed perceptions of the role of BE in domestic as well as international business. Recently, BE is beginning to be understood as one of the important factors influencing companies' competitiveness; nevertheless, at the same time, companies' ability and effort toward higher ethical standards tend to suffer when companies experience economic difficulties. Until now, BE has been studied by a number of authors among whom a significant portion have focused on BE and ethical attitudes of respondents working at various managerial levels of organizations in different countries (Al-Khatib et al.,2004; Baumhart, 1961; Beekun et al., 2003; Brenner & Molander, 1977; Cacioppe et al., 2008; Choi & Nakano, 2008; Choi et al., 2014, 2015, 2018, 2023; Christie et al., 2003; Handerson et al., 2001; Jackson & Artola, 1997; Jackson et al., 2000; Lee & Yoshihara, 1997; Milton-Smith, 1997; Nakano, 1997, 1999; Okleshen & Hoyt, 1996; Palazzo, 2002; Schwarts, 2012; Sims & Gegez, 2004).

However, only few studies have provided direct comparison of Chinese, Japanese, and Korean BE attitudes. This is especially surprising considering the fact that these three countries are economic powers from a regional and global perspective (for example, in 2015, China, Japan, and Korea were the second, third, and eleventh largest economies in the world in terms of GDP) and have strong mutual business ties. The bilateral trade among the three neighboring countries is among the most important for them. In 2015, China was Japan's second biggest importer and the biggest exporter, China was Korea's biggest importer and exporter, Japan was Korea's second biggest exporter, and Korea was Japan's third biggest importer. Thorough knowledge of BE practices in the three mentioned countries is also important for foreign enterprises doing business in the territory, emphasized by the increasing significance of the three countries in international trade and international business relations.

Culturally speaking, the mentioned three countries are commonly perceived to have similarities and differences in the business environment, including their ethical and socio-cultural aspects, which are even more significant from the perspective of foreign business partners. To our knowledge, only one study

(Zhou et al., 2011) that is based on questionnaire survey and also involves BE practices in China exists. In the study, the authors investigated the teaching, research, and training in the three countries as seen by experts in the field of BE. As far as we know, this is also the only study that includes comparison of China, Japan, and Korea through such a survey.

Our research contributes to the existing literature on BE in two significant ways. First, we present the results of the first survey of BE practices of this type conducted in China, along with the most recent results of the same survey conducted in Japan and Korea. Second, we compare the findings for the three countries and make an explanation regarding the similarities and differences found in the survey.

The paper unfolds as follows. After the introduction, in Section 2, economic, political, and cultural backgrounds to our study are discussed, followed by methodology in Section 3 and results in Section 4. Section 5 lists our major findings organized as the most important commonalities and differences among BE practices in the three countries. Section 6 concludes the study.

2. ECONOMIC, POLITICAL, AND CULTURAL BACKGROUNDS

In this section, the economic, political, and cultural backgrounds of BE in China, Japan, and Korea are discussed. We consider such discussion relevant, as we believe these factors may serve as explanatory factors to some of our findings and provide better idea of similarities and differences in the business environment in the three investigated countries.

Institutional theory suggests that the unique political, economic, and cultural landscapes of China, Japan, and Korea significantly shape their BE countries (Campbell, 2007; Donaldson & Preston, 1995; North, 1990). For instance, China's centralized governance and rapid market shifts may foster practices that prioritize social harmony but struggle with transparency. Japan's mature economy and value for hierarchy support ethical behaviors aligned with long-term sustainability yet may inhibit whistleblowing. In Korea, the influence of business conglomerates could promote rapid development but potentially at the expense of transparency. Understanding these institutional contexts provides a framework for anticipating the differences in BE observed across these three countries.

Regarding the economic perspective, it is generally known that the system of economy has influence on companies' ethical decision-making (Campbell, 2007). From this viewpoint, all the three countries employ a market economy system, with some deviation in China. However, one of the important differences is that Japan and Korea have a longer history of market economy than China, which formally introduced socialist market economy in 1993 when the Communist Party of China released the Decision on Issues Concerning to Perfect the Socialist Market Economy System. China is in the transition from the planned economy to socialist market economy, resulting in an immature market economy. Considering these facts, it might be tentatively expected that companies in all the three countries will have strong incentive to satisfy their stakeholders, among whom customers will hold an important place as the only direct source of profit, and that existence of unethical industry practices and experience of ethical conflicts might be higher in China than in Japan and Korea.

As for political perspective, corruption is one of the important aspects that deserve attention (Schleifer & Vishny, 1993). With the development of market economy in China, corruption has become a major issue. This trend remained unchanged until the end of 2012, when a country-wide fight against corruption was launched. The fight against corruption is so strong and enduring that the deteriorating trend has been gradually contained since then, but corruption and its effect on business practices still existed by the time the survey was conducted in 2014. Similarly, in Japan and Korea, corruption is considered a serious problem; however, as in China systematic fight against corruption started later, in the two other countries the problem can be expected to be less eminent.

Finally, to take into consideration the cultural perspective and cultural similarity, we can borrow the six-dimensional tool developed by Hofstede et al. (2010). The model suggests that, contrary to the belief that China, Japan, and Korea share similar culture, the three countries show significant differences in four out of the six dimensions (Power Distance, Individualism, Uncertainty Avoidance, Masculinity, Long-Term Orientation, and Indulgence). All the three countries share a high score on the Long-Term Orientation dimension and low score on Indulgence, but they display different scores on the remaining four dimensions. While the sample composition (e.g., low Uncertainty Avoidance in China commonly attributed to a higher proportion of SME in the Chinese sample than in the Korean and Japanese ones) can help explain some of these differences, it is still true that cultural differences among the three countries are significant. According to Hofstede, cultures that score high on Long-Term Orientation take a more pragmatic approach, and in societies with such an orientation, people believe that truth depends on the situation, context, and time. Thus, it can be expected that "Depends on the situations" will be high regarding what contributes to employees' ethical decision-making in all three countries. Regarding Power Distance, China (80) is the most power-distant country among the three, followed by Korea (60) and Japan (54), which may influence the understanding of authorities and hierarchy in BE enforcement. The scores of Individualism for China, Japan, and Korea are 20, 46, and 18, respectively; China and Korea are thus highly collectivist cultures, while Japan is collectivist by Western standards and individualist by Asian standards. In line with that, it can be expected that the pressure to follow the collective and act in favor of an in-group will be more strongly felt in China and Korea, whereas the Japanese might tend toward more individualistic behavior by comparison. People in a society with low UAI are comfortable with ambiguity, while those in high UAI are not. China has a low score of 30 on UAI, while Japan has a high score of 92 and Korea a score of 85, which make Japan and Korea among the most uncertainty avoiding countries on earth. With the significant differences in UAI among the three countries in mind, one would expect an acceptance of a western ethics program in Japan and Korea, but not in China. Finally, we do not see much of significance on Indulgence and Masculinity dimensions in relation to our survey and its results, so we do not discuss them here in detail.

3. METHODOLOGY

This study uses a questionnaire instrument that is taken from previous studies (Choi & Nakano, 2008; Nakano, 1997, 2005), with its basic framework created by Baumhart (1961), Brenner and Molander (1977), Vitell and Festervand (1987), and the Center for Business Ethics at Bentley College (1986, 1992). We translated the questionnaire into the official language of each investigated country, and performed any other necessary revisions, such as expressing the financial amount in the local monetary unit. Since this is the first time to conduct such a survey in China, we performed a pilot test based on the sample of five enterprises, and we made further minor language-type adjustments according to the respondent responses. In order to obtain a clear picture of BE practices as typical for each of the investigated countries, we only surveyed native companies in each country.

In China, the sample was composed of native companies from east, middle, and west of Mainland China, containing state-owned and private enterprises. We called all potential respondents from the selected companies before sending out the questionnaires. The respondents were informed of the aims of the survey, and we assured them that the results of this survey would only be used for academic purposes. To deliver the questionnaire and collect the data, we used an online survey website called SoJump. The participants filled out the questionnaire online themselves. For each company, there was only one participant. The questionnaire was anonymous and strictly confidential. The survey was conducted from November 28 to December 27, 2014; in total, 212 copies of questionnaire were collected and considered effective.

In Japan, we mailed the questionnaire on August 1, 2014 to 3,600 companies listed in the summer 2014 issue of "Toyo Keizai Quarterly Corporate Report CD-ROM version." The deadline for responses was September 1, 2014. The response rate was extremely low, and valid responses were received only from 141 companies, which was an effective response rate of 3.9%.

In Korea, the survey was conducted in 2015. Questionnaires were partially distributed through mail/e-mail and partially by personal visits of survey administrators; in total, 321 of usable questionnaires were returned.

Descriptive statistics of the samples can be found in Table 4.1. As indicated in the table, usable questionnaires were submitted by 212, 141, and 321 respondents from China, Japan, and Korea, respectively. The respondents are business managers at various organizational levels. The majority of the Chinese respondents (62.3%) work in the non-manufacturing sector. In contrast, the majority of Korean respondents (77.2%) are employed in the manufacturing sector, while more than half of the Japanese respondents (59.6%) work for non-manufacturing companies

Table 4.1. Descriptive Statistics: Respondents.

Descriptive Statistics	China 2014	Japan 2014	Korea 2015
Industry	$N = 212$	$N = 141$	$N = 321$
Manufacturing	37.7%	40.4%	77.2%
Non-manufacturing	62.3%	59.6%	22.8%
Management position	$N = 212$	$N = 137$	$N = 321$
Top management	20.8%	6.6%	1.9%
Middle management	34.4%	73.7%	20.6%
First-line management	25.9%	14.6%	27.4%
Non-management	18.9%	5.1%	50.2%

4. EMPIRICAL RESULTS

In the following part, we discuss the survey results as focused on in different parts of the questionnaire.

4.1. Company Responsibility to Different Stakeholder Groups

In the first part of the questionnaire, we focused on respondents' responsibility to different stakeholders. Table 4.2 presents the results we obtained when we asked the respondents to rank different stakeholder groups in the order of importance (1 – the most important; 7 – the least important).

Customers, employees, and stockholders ranked on top of the list in all the three investigated countries. A slight difference can be observed between China and the other two countries' results in that Chinese respondents ranked stockholders higher than employees. Interestingly, customers were ranked first among all the three countries, which revealed that companies in all the three countries recognized the important role customers played in successfully running a business. One significant difference in the results is that in China, much more emphasis is put on society in general rather than local community (ranked No. 4 and No. 7 in the list), while in Japan society in general is deemed less important than local community (No. 6 and No. 4). Society in general also ranked above local community in Korea, but both groups are considered the least important in the list (Nos. 6 and 7).

One more finding is also worth noting. In China, responsibility toward government is ranked No. 6, suggesting that the government is not valued as highly as one may think. In Korea, respondents feel slightly stronger responsibility toward government than society in general and local community. Unlike that, in Japan, government is not only ranked No. 7, but also the mean rank (6.68) is much higher than No. 6 (4.72), indicating that the responsibility felt toward the government is much weaker than the responsibility felt toward other stakeholders.

It should also be noted that the results of the studies carried out in the three East Asian countries in 2014 and 2015 are quite similar to those of the 1985 U.S. study; the Japanese result being especially close to that (not tabulated).

Table 4.2. To Whom Should a Company Most Responsible?

	Mean Ranks		
	China (2014) (N = 212)	Japan (2014) (N = 138)	Korea (2015) (N = 321)
Customers	1.33 (1)	1.70 (1)	2.55 (1)
Stockholders	1.77 (2)	3.12 (3)	3.56 (3)
Employees	1.82 (3)	2.52 (2)	3.28 (2)
Society in general	3.45 (4)	4.72 (6)	4.79 (6)
Suppliers	3.80 (5)	4.63 (5)	4.10 (4)
Government	4.15 (6)	6.68 (7)	4.67 (5)
Local community	4.69 (7)	4.48 (4)	5.05 (7)

4.2. Unethical Business Practices

Table 4.3 shows the results when we asked respondents whether unethical practices exist in their industry. As the table reveals, in China, 61.7% of the participants responded "A few" and 10.9% responded "Many." These numbers were much greater than in Japan (20.6% and 1.5%, respectively) and Korea (39.3% and 2.2%, respectively). In China, only 10.9% of the participants responded "None," which was much lower than in 56.6% in Japan and 42.7% in Korea. It is interesting to note that as many as 16.5% (China), 21.3% (Japan), and 15.9% (Korea) respondents choose "Do not know."

We further asked those who responded "Yes" to the existence of unethical business practices which practices they thought needed to be eliminated. Table 4.4 presents their preferences.

The top three unethical business practices from the list that participants would like to see eliminated are the same across all the three countries: "Giving of gifts, gratuities, and bribes," "Unfairness to employees," "Price discrimination and unfairness," although the number of rank varies. "Giving of gifts, gratuities, and bribes" is ranked No. 1 in China and Korea, but No. 3 in Japan. In China, a large a share of respondents (58.44%) would like to see "Giving of gifts, gratuities, and bribes" eliminated. This number, which showed that the majority of Chinese respondents found this behavior annoying, is much higher than the number for "Unfairness to employees," which ranked second. Unlike that, in Japan and Korea, more than half of the respondents in each country chose no such behavior. In all three countries, "Unfairness to employees" is ranked No. 2, which coincides with the results of the question "To whom should the company be responsible" (Table 4.2). One possible reason is that, as all the respondents are

Table 4.3. Existence of Unethical Industry Practices.

	China (2014) (N = 212)	Japan (2014) (N = 136)	Korea (2015) (N = 321)
None	10.9%	56.6%	42.7%
A few	61.7%	20.6%	39.3%
Many	10.9%	1.5%	2.2%
Do not know	16.5%	21.3%	15.9%

Table 4.4.   Unethical Business Practices Participants Would
Like to See Eliminated.

	China (2014) ($N = 154$?	Japan (2014) ($N = 30$)	Korea (2015) ($N = 321$)
Giving of gifts, gratuities, and bribes	58.44% (1)	16.7% (4)	26.7% (1)
Price discrimination and unfairness	31.82% (3)	20.0% (3)	17.6% (4)
Cheating customers	29.87% (4)	16.7% (4)	5.3% (8)
Collusion by competitors (price, etc.)	17.53% (8)	3.3% (9)	13.7% (6)
Unfairness to employees	44.81% (2)	26.7% (2)	26.0% (2)
Dishonesty in making or keeping a contract	27.27% (5)	6.7% (8)	16.0% (5)
Dishonest advertising	11.69% (9)	10.0% (6)	0.0% (10)
Unfair credit practices	20.13% (7)	0.0% (11)	0.0% (10)
Miscellaneous unfair competitive practices	27.27% (5)	3.3% (9)	5.3% (8)
Overselling	11.04% (10)	10.0% (6)	7.6% (7)
Other	7.14% (11)	33.3% (1)	19.1% (3)

employees, they know and understand companies' treatment of employees better than the way companies treat other stakeholders. Another possible reason is that employees' awareness of fairness is increasing.

Among Chinese respondents, unfair credit practices (20.13%, ranked No. 7) and miscellaneous unfair competitive practices (27.27%, ranked No. 5) were also chosen by a large share of respondents, while both mentioned practices were not so important in Japan (0.0% ranked No. 11, and 3.3% ranked No. 9, respectively) and Korea (0.0% ranked 10 and 5.3% ranked 8, respectively).

One interesting finding is that less than 10% of Chinese respondents chose "Other" (7.14, ranked No. 11), compared to 33.3% in Japan (ranked No. 1) and 19.1% in Korea (ranked No. 3). It may indicate that other unethical business practices are receiving more respondents' attention in Japan and Korea when the unethical business practices listed in Table 4.4 become less prevalent. One explanation may also be that the survey uses the list of unethical practices as first developed by Baumhart (1961). While the unethical business practices identified by Baumhart (1961) are still relevant, new unethical business practices have emerged during the past 50 years. Future studies may provide an updated list that better reflects the current business environment.

4.3. Managers' Experience of Ethical Conflicts

Table 4.5 suggests that in China (49.06%), respondents experience ethical conflicts significantly more often than in Japan (28.1%) and Korea (25.9%).

Table 4.6 provides a detailed view of the type of ethical conflicts respondents have experienced. The results show that Chinese respondents have experienced more different types of ethical conflicts than Japanese and Korean respondents. In China, over 40% of respondents reported four different types of conflicts, while over 40% respondents in Japan and Korea reported only one type of conflict. The fact that China is still in the stage of economic and social transition may

Table 4.5. Experience of Ethical Conflicts.

	China (2014) (N = 212)	Japan (2014) (N = 135)	Korea (2015) (N = 321)
Yes	49.06%	28.1%	25.9%
No	50.04%	71.9%	74.1%

Table 4.6. Ethical Conflicts Participants Ever Experienced.

	China (2014) (N = 104)	Japan (2014) (N = 38)	Korea (2015) (N = 321)
Gifts, entertainment, and kickbacks	40.38% (4)	13.2% (5)	19.8% (3)
Price collusion and pricing practices	22.12% (5)	23.7% (3)	9.9% (7)
Unfairness and discrimination to customers and employees	44.23% (2)	36.8% (1)	50.6% (1)
Honesty in internal communication	43.27% (3)	15.8% (4)	34.6% (2)
Honesty in external communication	18.27% (6)	7.9% (6)	11.1% (6)
Honesty in executing contracts and agreement	16.35% (7)	5.3% (8)	13.6% (5)
Firings and layoffs	48.08% (1)	26.3% (2)	18.5% (4)
Other	0.96% (8)	7.9% (6)	2.5% (8)

help explain this outcome. During transition, old and new ethical beliefs coexist, which may result in a higher occurrence and larger variety of ethical conflicts.

"Unfairness and discrimination to customers and employees" is ranked No. 2 in China, and No. 1 in both, Japan and Korea, indicating that being fair is a common need for employees in all the three countries. This may also indicate that employees' ethical conflicts might be reduced if more attention is paid to fairness.

Table 4.7. In relation to which group ethical conflicts happened.

	China (2014) (N = 104)	Japan (2014) (N = 42)	Korea (2015) (N = 321)
Customers	40.38% (2)	35.7% (2)	27.7% (4)
Suppliers	20.19% (7)	21.4% (3)	47.0% (2)
Competitors	22.12% (5)	7.1% (7)	43.4% (3)
Superiors	38.46% (3)	59.5% (1)	55.4% (1)
Employees	28.85% (4)	19.0% (4)	26.5% (5)
Colleagues	41.35% (1)	4.8% (8)	18.1% (7)
Stockholders	10.58% (8)	4.8% (8)	9.6% (9)
The law and government	21.15% (6)	11.9% (5)	19.3% (6)
Local community/Society in general	1.92% (10)	9.5% (6)	14.5% (8)
Other	2.88% (9)	4.8% (8)	1.2% (10)

Regarding the groups that were involved in the ethical conflicts respondents experienced (Table 4.7), similar responses occur in relation to "Stockholders," "Employees," and "The law and government." As for the differences, "Suppliers" ranked No. 7 in China, while it was No. 3 in Japan and No. 2 in Korea. A remarkable difference is also found regarding "Colleagues," which ranked No. 1 in

China, but No. 8 in Japan, and No. 7 in Korea. Another interesting difference can be observed regarding "Superiors," both in terms of percentage (38.46% in China, 59.5% in Japan, and 55.4% in Korea) and rank (No. 3 in China and No. 1 in Japan and Korea).

4.4. Factors Influencing Ethical Decisions of Managers

In terms of the factors that influence the decisions of respondents to act ethically (Table 4.8), the results are quite similar for all the three investigated countries. "One's personal code of behavior," "Company policy," and "The behavior of one's superiors" are the top three factors, and "Ethical climate of the industry" and "The behavior of one's equals in the company" are the least important factors. It is understandable that "One's personal code of behavior" is ranked No. 1; however, it may not be that obvious why "Company policy" comes second, before "The behavior of one's superiors," which is No. 3. Previous research shows that ethical leadership has a positive effect on employees' attitudes and behavior. It has also been found that company policy (e.g., code of conduct) has a positive effect on employees' attitudes and behavior. However, it has not been clear which factor between "The behavior of one's superiors" and "Company policy" has more important effect on employees' attitudes and behaviors. The results of our study shed light on the issue.

Unlike factors influencing ethical decisions, there is less consensus among the three countries as for the factors influencing unethical decisions (Table 4.9). The pattern of importance given to the factors by Chinese respondents is different from that by Japanese and Korean respondents.

Table 4.8. Factors Influencing Ethical Decisions.

	Mean Ranks		
	China (2014) (N = 212)	Japan (2014) (N = 137)	Korea (2015) (N = 321)
One's personal code of behavior	1.19 (1)	1.97 (1)	2.54 (1)
Company policy	1.42 (2)	2.07 (2)	2.85 (2)
The behavior of one's superiors	1.84 (3)	2.63 (3)	3.01 (3)
Ethical climate of the industry	2.47 (4)	4.14 (5)	3.48 (5)
The behavior of one's equals in the company	3.08 (5)	4.12 (4)	3.11 (4)

Table 4.9. Factors Influencing Unethical Decisions.

	Mean Ranks		
	China (2014) (N = 212)	Japan (2014) (N = 137)	Korea (2015) (N = 321)
Ethical climate of the industry	1.57 (1)	3.07 (3)	2.80 (3)
The behavior of one's superiors	1.57 (1)	2.19 (1)	2.71 (2)
One's personal financial needs	1.82 (3)	3.30 (4)	3.61 (5)
Company policy or lack thereof	2.07 (4)	2.20 (2)	2.63 (1)
The behavior of one's equals in the company	2.98 (5)	4.21 (5)	3.27 (4)

Similarities exist in terms of "The behavior of one's superiors," which was deemed important in all the three countries, while "The behavior of one's equals in the company" is among the least important. Overall, "One's personal financial needs" is not very important, though it is more important in China than in Japan and Korea. This may be explained by the fact that China is less economically developed than Japan and Korea. Differences can be observed in relation to "Company policy", which is not as important in China (No. 4) as in Japan (No. 2) and Korea (No. 1). This result is consistent with the findings in "Methods of instilling ethical values in the organization" (Table 4.16) that company policy regarding ethics is not less established in China than in Japan and Korea. An interesting finding is that "Ethical climate of the industry" is not as important for ethical decisions as for unethical decisions. "The behavior of one's equals in the company" is the least important factor for both, ethical and unethical decisions.

It is interesting to note that factors influencing ethical decisions and factors influencing unethical decisions are not exactly the same. According to fundamental attribution error, people tend to attribute ethical decisions to internal factors and unethical decisions to external factors. Of the factors listed, "One's personal code of behavior" is the only internal factor among the factors influencing ethical decisions, and "One's personal financial needs" is the only internal factor among factors influencing unethical decisions; therefore, it is not surprising that "One's personal code of behavior" is considered the most important factor and "One's personal financial needs" is not ranked as high as "The behavior of one's superiors" and "Ethical climate of the industry."

We further tried to find out whether employees' ethical decision-making is influenced by company interests or personal ethics. Table 4.10 documents that respondents from different countries value different aspects. While "Depends on the situation" is the most common answer among Chinese (43.27%) and Japanese respondents (50.0%), "Company interests" is No. 1 answer for Korean respondents (50.9%). Among Chinese and Korean respondents, "Personal ethics" is the least common answer (23.08% for Chinese and 12.3% for Korean), while Japanese respondents chose "Company interests" (21.3%) as the least common answer. The answers to this question reveal the diversity of ethical decision-making principles people follow when making ethics-related decisions.

Table 4.10. Ethical Preference – Company Interests or Personal Ethics.

	China (2014) ($N = 104$)	Japan (2014) ($N = 42$)	Korea (2015) ($N = 57$)
Company interests	33.65% (2)	21.4% (3)	50.9% (1)
Personal ethics	23.08% (3)	28.6% (2)	12.3% (3)
Depends on the situations	43.27% (1)	50.0% (1)	36.8% (2)

4.5. Hypothetical Situations

In another section of the questionnaire, we examined respondents' reaction to four hypothetical situations involving unethical practices. Respondents were

asked to report their own choice and the choice they believe an average manager would make. In all four cases, the results show that respondents believe
themselves much more ethical than others, which is consistent with the results
of former researchers (e.g., Brenner & Molander, 1977; Choi & Nakano, 2008).

- **Case 1**: An executive earning $100,000 a year has been padding his expense
  account by about $5,000 a year. What do you think?

Table 4.11 shows the result for the situation of embezzling funds of a company (Case 1). While more than 60% of the respondents in the three countries
think it is "Unacceptable regardless of the circumstances," in Japan, the result
was 89.9%, which is much higher than the result for China (68.87%) and Korea
(63.2%.) Interestingly, in Japan and China more than 50% of respondents
believe an average manager will find it unacceptable, while in Korea only 37.4%
respondents believe so. More Chinese respondents (11.79%) found embezzling
funds "Acceptable if other executives in the company do the same thing" than in
Japan (1.4%) and Korea (5.3%). In Korea, much more respondents (31.5%) chose
"Acceptable if the executive's superior knows about it and says nothing" than
those in China (19.34%) and Japan (8.7%).

Table 4.11. Embezzling Funds of a Company.

	China (2014)		Japan (2014)		Korea (2015)	
	Oneself ($N = 212$)	Average Manager ($N = 212$)	Oneself ($N = 138$)	Average Manager ($N = 139$)	Oneself ($N = 321$)	Average Manager ($N = 321$)
Acceptable if other executives in the company do the same thing	11.79%	23.11%	1.4%	10.8%	5.3%	17.8%
Acceptable if the executive's superior knows about it and says nothing	19.34%	24.53%	8.7%	21.6%	31.5%	44.9%
Unacceptable regardless of the circumstances	68.87%	52.36%	89.9%	67.6%	63.2%	37.4%

- **Case 2**: Imagine that you are the president of a company in a highly competitive
  industry. You learn that a competitor has made an important scientific discovery
  that will give him an advantage that will substantially reduce the profits of your
  company for about a year. If there were some hope of hiring one of the competitor's employees who knew the details of the discovery, what would you do?

As for the situation of hiring employees to acquire competitor's discovery (Case 2), as shown in Table 4.12, more than half of the respondents in
China (77.36%) and Korea (59.4%) think they "probably would" do that, while only

Table 4.12. Hiring Employees to Acquire Competitor's Discovery.

	China (2014) (N = 212)		Japan (2014) (N = 137)		Korea (2015) (N = 321)	
	Oneself	Average Manager	Oneself	Average Manager	Oneself	Average Manager
Probably would	77.36%	91.04%	42.3%	66.4%	59.4%	81.9%
Probably would not	22.64%	8.96%	57.7%	33.6%	40.7%	18.1%

42.3% of Japanese respondents chose the same answer. The results show that hiring employees to acquire competitor's discovery is quite acceptable in the three countries.

- **Case 3**: The minister of a foreign nation, where extraordinary payments to lubricate the decision-making machinery are common, asks you, as a company executive, for a $300,000 consulting fee. In return, he promises special assistance in obtaining a $100 million contract which should produce, at least, a $5 million profit for your company.

Case 3 (Table 4.13) involved extraordinary payments to lubricate the decision-making for a sale. In this case, more than 50% of the respondents from all the three countries chose "Pay the fee, feeling it was ethical in the moral climate of the foreign nation," which seemed to be the most preferred choice among all the three options. Among Japanese respondents, "Refuse to pay" is the second most common option as 41.3% of them think they will do so, while the numbers in China and Korea are only 14.6% and 29.6%, respectively. Among Chinese respondents, the next best option after "Pay the fee, feeling it was ethical in the moral climate of the foreign nation" is "Pay the fee, feeling it was unethical but necessary to help insure the sale" (17.5%). Unlike that, this option is only the third preference among Japanese (5.8%) and Korean (18.4%) respondents. It should also be noted that a smaller share of Chinese and Korean respondents think that an average manager will choose "Pay

Table 4.13. Extraordinary Payments to Lubricate the Decision-Making for a Sale.

	China (2014)		Japan (2014)		Korea (2015)	
	Oneself (N = 212)	Average Manager (N = 212)	Oneself (N = 138)	Average Manager (N = 137)	Oneself (N = 321)	Average Manager (N = 321)
Refuse to pay, even if sale is lost	14.62%	7.08%	41.3%	21.9%	29.6%	12.5%
Pay the fee, feeling it was ethical in the moral climate of the foreign nation	67.92%	43.4%	52.9%	59.9%	52.0%	47.0%
Pay the fee, feeling it was unethical but necessary to help insure the sale	17.46%	49.52%	5.8%	18.2%	18.4%	40.5%

the fee, feeling it was ethical in the moral climate of the foreign nation" or "Refuse to pay" than they thought about themselves. However, the results for "Pay the fee, feeling it was ethical in the moral climate of the foreign nation" in Japan showed the opposite pattern (52.9% for oneself, 59.9% for an average manager). "Pay the fee, feeling it was unethical but necessary to help insure the sale" is little preferred option when respondents talk about their own behavior in all the three countries, but the scores for average managers in China and Korea are quite high.

- **Case 4**: Imagine that you are a regional sales manager for a large industrial supply company and your salespeople are giving money to purchasing agents to obtain sales. This is beyond the generally acceptable meal or promotional item. Assuming that no laws are being violated, what would you do?

Case 4 (Table 4.14) reveals respondents' reaction to salespeople's bribing behavior. Most respondents from all the three countries chose "Issue an order stopping future payments" as their own behavior. As shown in Table 4.14, however, "Issue an order stopping future payments, but do not reduce sales people's pay" is more preferred among Chinese (52.36%) and Japanese (66.9%) than Korean respondents (38.9%). It seems that Korean respondents react to this behavior more strongly, as 55.1% of Korean respondents chose to "Issue an order stopping future payments and reduce salespeople's pay in the amount equal to their commissions on the sales gained as a result of future payments." In China, 51.42% think an average manager would "Say and do nothing," while in Japan and Korea only 16.7% and 34.3% of respondents think so, respectively.

Table 4.14.   Reaction to a Salesman's Bribing Behavior.

	China (2014)		Japan (2014)		Korea (2015)	
	Oneself ($N = 212$)	Average Manager ($N = 212$)	Oneself ($N = 138$)	Average Manager ($N = 137$)	Oneself ($N = 321$)	Average Manager ($N = 321$)
Issue an order stopping future payments and reduce salespeople's pay in the amount equal to their commissions on the sales gained as a result of future payments	27.83%	17.45%	30.9%	16.7%	55.1%	34.0%
Issue an order stopping future payments, but do not reduce sales people's pay	52.36%	31.13%	66.9%	66.7%	38.9%	31.8%
Say and do nothing	19.81%	51.42%	2.2%	16.7%	5.9%	34.3%

4.6. Institutionalization of Business Ethics

The effort companies make to institutionalize BE is documented by Table 4.15. The results show that most respondents in all the three countries chose "Very

Table 4.15. Company Eagerness to Instill Ethical Values in the Organization.

	China (2014) (N = 212)	Japan (2014) (N = 137)	Korea (2015) (N = 321)
Very eagerly	20.75%	51.1%	35.5%
To some extent	64.15%	42.3%	54.8%
Very little	11.79%	4.4%	8.1%
Not at all	3.31%	2.2%	1.6%

Table 4.16. Methods of Instilling Ethical Values in the Organization.

	China (2014) (N = 205)	Japan (2014) (N = 138)	Korea (2015) (N = 321)
Corporate philosophy including ethics	50.24% (2)	34.1% (8)	40.3% (6)
Following parent company's philosophy	48.78% (3)	24.6% (9)	27.5% (8)
Ethics committee	8.78% (8)	55.8% (5)	24.0% (9)
Code of ethics	37.07% (5)	79.0% (2)	73.8% (1)
Employee training in ethics	41.95% (4)	68.8% (3)	41.2% (5)
CEO's frequent statements on ethics	17.07% (7)	43.5% (6)	55.6% (3)
Anonymous reporting hotline for unethical or illegal conduct	8.78% (8)	79.7% (1)	47.3% (4)
Punishment for unethical conduct	29.27% (6)	67.4% (4)	57.5% (2)
Contribution to social/cultural activities	52.2% (1)	37.0% (7)	39.6% (7)
Other	6.34% (10)	0.0% (10)	1.9% (10)

eagerly" and "To some extent" (84.9% in China, 93.4% in Japan, 90.3% in Korea, the two answers combined). As for the major differences, only 20.75% of respondents chose "Very eagerly" in China compared to as many as 51.1% in Japan and 35.5% in Korea. Furthermore, in China, about 15% of respondents chose "Very little" and "Not at all" if the two answers are combined, while the numbers in Japan and Korea are only 6.6% and 9.7%.

We further asked the respondents what methods of instilling ethical values their companies use. As shown in Table 4.16, practices usually included in an ethics program (or compliance program) such as ethics committee, code of ethics, employee training in ethics, CEO's frequent statements on ethics, anonymous reporting hotline for unethical conduct, and punishment for unethical conduct, were not yet common in China, but they are more widely employed in Japan and Korea. In China, "Contribution to social/cultural activities" (52.2%, No. 1) is the most popular method, which is significantly different from Japan (37.0%, No. 7) and Korea (39.6%, No. 7). "Corporate philosophy including ethics" is also more prevalent in China (50.24%, No. 2) than in Japan (34.1%, No. 8) and Korea (40.3%, No. 6). Similar patterns also apply to "Following parent company's philosophy."

4.7. Ethical Standards of the Business Community

When asked to compare ethical standards today and 10 years ago (Table 4.17), only 36.8% of Chinese respondents chose "Higher standards today," while 68.6% respondents in Japan and 72.3% of respondents in Korea did so.

Table 4.18 summarizes the factors that respondents consider responsible for higher ethical standards today. Among them, "New social expectations for

Table 4.17.   Recent Ethical Standards in the World of Business: Comparison with 10 Years Ago.

	China (2014) (N = 212)	Japan (2014) (N = 137)	Korea (2015) (N = 321)
Higher standards today	36.8%	68.6%	72.3%
About the same	16.5%	19.0%	3.7%
Lower standards today	46.7%	12.4%	24.0%

Table 4.18.   Factors Resulting in Higher Ethical Standards.

	China (2014) (N = 78)	Japan (2014) (N = 130)	Korea (2015) (N = 321)
New social expectations for business's role in society	67.95% (2)	96.2% (1)	60.4% (1)
Public disclosure, publicity and media coverage	65.38% (3)	71.5% (2)	53.3% (4)
Increased public awareness and scrutiny	84.62% (1)	63.8% (3)	59.8% (2)
Top management's emphasis on ethical action	65.38% (3)	48.5% (4)	58.3% (3)
Increased commitment of corporations to cultural and environmental protection activities	43.59% (7)	32.3% (5)	25.2% (6)
Government regulation, legislation and intervention	55.13% (5)	15.4% (6)	31.2% (5)
Increase in manager professionalism and education	50.00% (6)	9.2% (7)	19.6% (7)
Other	1.28% (8)	2.3% (8)	0.9% (8)

business's role in society" is ranked No. 2 in China and No. 1 in Japan and Korea. Close to that is "Increased public awareness and scrutiny," which is ranked No. 1 in China, No. 3 in Japan, and No. 2 in Korea. "Public disclosure, publicity and media coverage" is also commonly cited as a factor, along with "Top management's emphasis on ethical action," which is also quite important in all the three countries. Looking at the mentioned factors, we may notice that all these are related to corporate social responsibility (henceforth CSR). It is encouraging to know that CSR does play a role in enhancing ethical behavior. "Increased commitment of corporations to cultural and environmental protection activities," "Government regulation, legislation and intervention," and "Increase in manager professionalism and education," do not seem to be very significant, especially in Japan and Korea.

The factors resulting in the worsening of ethical standards are listed in Table 4.19. Among the most influential factors, "Increase in pressure from excessive competition" is ranked No. 1 in Japan, No. 2 in Korea, and No. 3 in China. Following that, "Greed and the desire for gain" is also deemed an important factor. The answers differ significantly for "Political corruption and loss of confidence in government," which is the most important factor in China and Korea, but not very important in Japan. Similarly, "Society's standards are lower" is an important factor in China (No. 2), but not very important in Japan and Korea (No. 5 in both countries). "Pressure for survival in slow economy" is a more important factor in Japan (No. 2) than in China (No. 4) and Korea (No. 6), reflecting the general economic situations in the three countries.

Table 4.19. Factors Resulting in Lower Ethical Standards.

	China (2014) ($N = 99$)	Japan (2014) ($N = 100$)	Korea (2015) ($N = 321$)
Increase in pressure from excessive competition	71.72% (3)	61.0% (1)	63.9% (2)
Pressure for survival in slow economy	57.58% (4)	52.0% (2)	31.2% (6)
Greed and the desire for gain	54.55% (5)	40.0% (3)	61.7% (3)
Lack of personal integrity	36.36% (6)	38.0% (4)	33.3% (4)
Society's standards are lower	77.78% (2)	32.0% (5)	31.8% (5)
Political corruption and loss of confidence in government	83.84% (1)	27.0% (6)	70.7% (1)
Other	1.01% (7)	3.0% (7)	0.3% (7)

5. MAJOR FINDINGS (COMMONALITIES AND DIFFERENCES)

The survey in our study is the first survey on BE in China, Japan, and Korea using the same questionnaire instrument. In this section, we would like to use the opportunity this fact provides to make comparison among China, Japan, and Korea and list the most important similarities and differences among the three neighboring countries regarding BE as suggested by our findings.

5.1. Commonalities

1. The top three stakeholders to whom a company should be responsible are customers, employees, and stockholders. Customers are unanimously deemed the first stakeholder to whom a company should be responsible.
2. Fairness belongs among the top priorities. Among the eight types of ethical conflicts as presented in Table 4.6 of this study, "Unfairness and discrimination to customers and employees" comes out as No. 1 in both Japan and Korea and No. 2 in China. In line with that, "Unfairness to employees" is a No. 2 unethical business practice respondents would like to see eliminated in all the three countries (No. 1 being different for each country).
3. "One's personal code of behavior," "Company policy," and "The behavior of one's superiors" are the top three factors influencing ethical decisions, and "The behavior of one's superiors" is the most important factor influencing unethical decisions.
4. As indicated by Case 1 (embezzling funds of a company), respondents from none of the three surveyed countries are willing to accept behavior that would harm their company. In contrast, unethical practices that benefit their own company are tolerated, as suggested by Case 2 (hiring employees to acquire competitor's discovery) and Case 3 (extraordinary payments to lubricate the decision-making for a sale).
5. Respondents' ethical decision-making is quite strongly situational, as shown in Table 4.10, where a large portion of respondents from each country (43.27% in China, 50.0% in Japan, and 36.8% in Korea) chose "Depends on the

situations" regarding what contributes to employees' ethical decision-making. This is supported by Case 3 (Table 4.13, extraordinary payments to lubricate the decision-making for a sale), where more than half of respondents (67.92% in Chinese, 52.9% in Japan, and 52.0% in Korean) report they would "Pay the fee, feeling it was ethical in the moral climate of the foreign nation."

6. "New social expectations for business's role in society," "Public disclosure, publicity and media coverage," "Increased public awareness and scrutiny," and "Top management's emphasis on ethical action" are the four most influential factors resulting in higher ethical standards. This may also indicate positive effect of CSR movement on higher ethical standards in business.

7. The three investigated countries share three interesting patterns. First, respondents from all the three countries believe that they themselves are more ethical than others working in the same industry. Second, factors influencing ethical decisions are almost the same, but factors influencing unethical decisions are more diversified; the same pattern is also found for factors resulting in higher ethical standards and factors resulting in lower ethical standards. Third, while respondents attribute their ethical decisions to "One's personal code of behavior" as the strongest factor, as for unethical decisions, they blame external factors such as "The behavior of one's superiors," "Ethical climate of the industry," and "Company policy or lack thereof."

5.2. Differences

1. Respondents' responses to hypothetical situations suggest that ethical standards in Japan are higher than in China and Korea. Chinese respondents experience more ethical conflicts and unethical industry practices than Japanese and Korean respondents.

2. "Giving of gifts, gratuities, and bribes" is the No. 1 unethical business practice Chinese and Korean participants would like to see eliminated, while it is No. 4 for Japanese respondents.

3. Chinese respondents consider "Ethical climate of the industry" as one of the two most important factors influencing unethical decisions, while it is No. 3 and No. 5 factors for Japanese and Korean respondents.

4. It seems that the superior has a greater influence on subordinates in Korea than in China and Japan. In Korea, much a larger portion of respondents (31.5%) chose "Acceptable if the executive's superior knows about it and says nothing" than those in China (19.34%) and Japan (8.7%).

5. Once an employee's unethical behavior is disclosed, the punishment is more severe in Korea than in China and Japan, as indicated in Case 4 (Table 14, Reaction to a salesman's bribing behavior).

6. The methods commonly included in a typical western BE program such as ethics committee, code of ethics, employee training in ethics, CEO's frequent statements on ethics, anonymous reporting hotline for unethical conduct, and punishment for unethical conduct, are widely employed in Japan and Korea, but not in China.

6. CONCLUSION

In our study, we examined BE practices in three important East Asian countries – China, Japan, and South Korea. Our findings suggest that the three neighboring countries share a number of similarities in BE attitudes and practices, but also that a number of differences exist. The differences in results can be tentatively explained to some extent by various economic, political, and cultural backgrounds. Differences may be also partially because of the different sample compositions (e.g. a higher proportion of SME in the Chinese sample than in the Korean and Japanese ones). Our research is the first case of a BE questionnaire survey conducted in the three countries with the use of the same questionnaire instrument. We hope that as such, our research helps shed light on BE practices in the three countries, especially because it allows for direct comparison of practices in the investigated countries. We suggest that future research might focus on how BE practices in the three countries evolve in time. It would also be worthwhile to look at more detail into the question of what new BE tools have been recently developed and whether and how BE and its enhancement are influenced by rapidly developing internet and computer technologies.

ACKNOWLEDGMENTS

This research was funded by a research grant from the KDI School of Public Policy and Management awarded to the first author (grant number 20140044) and the Grant-In-Aid for Scientific Research, Japan Society for the Promotion of Science, to the second author (grant number 26380474).

REFERENCES

Al-Khatib, J. A., Rawwas, M. Y. A., & Vitell, S. J. (2004). Organizational ethics in developing countries: A comparative analysis. *Journal of Business Ethics, 55*(4), 307–320.

Baumhart, R. C. (1961). How ethical are businessmen? *Harvard Business Review, 39*, 6–17.

Beekun, R. I., Sedham, Y., Yamamura, J. H., & Barghouti, J. A. (2003). Comparing business ethics in Russia and the US. *International Journal of Human Resource Management, 14*(8), 1333–1349.

Brenner, S. N., & Molander, E. A. (1977). Is the ethics of business changing? *Harvard Business Review, 55*, 57–71.

Cacioppe, R., Forster, N., & Fox, M. (2008). A survey of managers' perceptions of corporate ethics and social responsibility and actions that may affect companies' success. *Journal of Business Ethics, 82*(3), 681–700.

Campbell, J. L. (2007). Why would corporations behave in socially responsible ways: An institutional theory of corporate social responsibility. *Academy of Management Review, 32*(3), 946–967.

Center for Business Ethics at Bentley College (1986). Are corporations institutionalizing ethics? *Journal of Business Ethics, 5*, 85–91.

Center for Business Ethics at Bentley College (1992). Instilling ethical values in large corporations. *Journal of Business Ethics, 11*, 867–883.

Choi, J., Kim, H., Kim, J., & Kim, M. S. (2018). Business group and social responsibility. *Journal of Business Ethics, 153*(4), 931–954.

Choi, J., Kim, J., & Shenkar, O. (2023). Temporal orientation and corporate social responsibility: Global evidence. *Journal of Management Studies, 60*(1), 82–119.

Choi, J., Jiang, C., & Shenkar, O. (2015). The quality of local government and firm performance: The case of China's provinces. *Management and Organization Review, 11*(4), 679–710.

Choi, T. H., & Nakano, C. (2008). The evolution of business ethics in Japan and Korea over the last decade. *Human Systems Management, 27,* 183–199.

Christie, P. M. J., Kwon, I.-W. G., Stoeberl, P. A., & Baumhart, R. (2003). A cross-cultural comparison of ethical attitudes of business managers: India, Korea and the United States. *Journal of Business Ethics, 46,* 263–287.

Donaldson, T., & Preston, L. E. (1995). The stakeholder theory of the corporation: Concepts, evidence, and implications. *Academy of Management Review, 20*(1), 65–91.

Handerson, J. N. C., Fraedrich, J. P., & Yeh, Q. J. (2001). An investigation of moral value and the ethical content of the corporate culture: Taiwanese versus U.S. sales people. *Journal of Business Ethics, 30*(1), 73–85.

Hofstede, G., Hofstede, G. J., & Minkov, M. (2010). *Cultures and organizations: Software of the mind* (3rd ed.). McGraw-Hill.

Jackson, T., Artola, M. C. (1997). Ethical beliefs and management behaviour: A cross-cultural comparison. *Journal of Business Ethics, 16,* 1163–1173.

Jackson, T., David, C., Jones, J., Joseph, J., Lau, K., Matsuno, K., Nakano, C., Park, H., Piounowska-Kokoszko, J., Taka, I., & Yoshihara, H. (2000). Making ethical judgments: A cross-cultural management study. *Asia Pacific Journal of Management, 17*(3), 443–472.

Lee, C. Y., & Yoshihara, H. (1997). Business ethics of Korean and Japanese managers. *Journal of Business Ethics, 16*(1), 7–21.

Milton-Smith, J. (1997). Business ethics in Australia and New Zealand. *Journal of Business Ethics, 16,* 1485–1479.

Nakano, C. (1997). A survey study on Japanese managers' views of business ethics. *Journal of Business Ethics, 16,* 1737–1751.

Nakano, C. (1999). Attempting to institutionalize ethics: Case studies from Japan. *Journal of Business Ethics, 18,* 335–343.

Nakano, C. (2005). *Survey data on business ethics.* Reitaku Business Ethics Center (R-bec).

North, D. C. (1990). *Institutions, institutional change and economic performance.* Cambridge University Press.

Okleshen, M., & Hoyt, R. (1996). A cross-cultural comparison of ethical perspectives and decision approaches of business students: United States of America versus New Zealand. *Journal of Business Ethics, 15,* 537–549.

Palazzo, B. (2002). U.S.-American and German business ethics: An intercultural comparison. *Journal of Business Ethics, 41,* 195–216.

Schleifer, A., & Vishny, R. W. (1993). Corruption. *Quarterly Journal of Economics, 108,* 599–617.

Schwartz, M. S. (2012). The state of business ethics in Israel: A light unto the nations? *Journal of Business Ethics, 105*(4), 429–446.

Sims, R., & Gegez, A. (2004). Attitudes towards business ethics: A five nation comparative study. *Journal of Business Ethics, 50,* 253–265.

Vitell, S. T., & Festervand, T. A. (1987). Business ethics: Conflicts, practices, and beliefs of industrial executives. *Journal of Business Ethics, 6,* 111–122.

Zhou, Z., Nakano, C., & Luo, B. N. (2011). Business ethics as a field of training, teaching & research in East Asia. *Journal of Business Ethics, 104*(Suppl 1), 19–27.

CHAPTER 5

CHALLENGES OF CSR IMPLEMENTATION IN SUPPLY CHAINS: A THEMATIC REVIEW IN THE EMERGING MARKET CONTEXT

Julianne Sellin

Loyola University Maryland, MD, USA

ABSTRACT

Encouraged by a variety of stakeholders and the benefits that could derive from corporate social responsibility (CSR), multinational corporations (MNCs) are increasingly concerned with limiting the social and environmental costs of their operations. Yet, they are often accused of not walking the talk on sustainability. Since offshoring and outsourcing became mainstream in international business, concerns have particularly emerged around MNCs' ability to implement credible and efficient sustainability strategies along increasingly complex and dispersed global supply chains. Evidence on the effectiveness of private initiatives to socially and environmentally upgrade supplier practices remains mixed, and the different insights from the literature, siloed. This work aims to provide a survey of the literature documenting the challenges MNCs face trying to implement more sustainable policies in supplier networks located in developing countries, where sustainability standards and certifications are likely to be poorly enforced. We integrate insights from multiple disciplines, provide an overview of the existing body of research on the topic, and propose

Responsible Firms: CSR, ESG, and Global Sustainability
International Finance Review, Volume 23, 93–115
ISSN: 1569-3767/doi:10.1108/S1569-376720240000023005

an analysis structured around three recurring themes: the policy tools available to MNCs and their limitations, the obstacles to suppliers' compliance, and the different governance mechanisms available to MNCs to shape their suppliers' practices. By providing a comprehensive picture of CSR policy implementation challenges, we contribute to practice and highlight potential avenues for future research.

Keywords: Global supply chains; corporate social responsibility; multinational corporations; emerging market; policy implementation

JEL Codes: F23; L23; M14; M16

1. INTRODUCTION

Both research and practice have extensively discussed the idea of strategic CSR for large, vertically integrated firms. However, over the past decade, the conversation has grown to encompass the critical role played by MNCs in addressing social and environmental challenges beyond their organizational boundaries (Schrempf-Stirling & Palazzo, 2016). Contemporary events such as the catastrophic Rana Plaza collapse (Sinkovics et al., 2016), or the disruptive onset of the COVID-19 pandemic (Crane & Matten, 2021), along with the growing threat of climate change (Ghadge et al., 2020), have collectively underscored the fragility inherent within global supply chains and the imperative for proactive mitigation measures. Accordingly, MNCs have increasingly recognized the strategic advantages inherent in enhancing the social and environmental practices of their suppliers (e.g., improved brand image, Mayer & Gereffi, 2010; Ponte, 2020 for a review). This realization has manifested in the adoption of various CSR policies, ranging from the promulgation of comprehensive codes of conduct to the formulation of internal standards governing global supply chains. Simultaneously, MNCs have faced heightened scrutiny from stakeholders demanding tangible improvements in supply chains (e.g., Delmas & Burbano, 2011).

Although the importance and specificity of CSR implementation in global supply chains are increasingly recognized, the topic has been mostly overlooked in mainstream CSR research. As an illustration, Aguinis and Glavas (2012)'s extensive review of the literature highlights a focus on the firm-level motivations, gains, and losses associated with CSR. Instead, attention to the implications of MNCs' CSR strategies for supply chain partners, along with an assessment of the societal outcomes of such strategies at the supplier-level has been limited. Yet, these questions require closer examination, as they bring about new and unique challenges (e.g., Koberg & Longoni, 2019). Indeed, the topic calls for an extension of the traditional analysis beyond MNCs' organizational boundaries as it involves a multitude of actors across different industries and tiers of the chain. It also calls for an analysis of complex relationships between geographically and culturally distant, but irremediably interdependent partners. Finally, the topic requires taking a multidisciplinary approach, as it engages with many different academic fields, including International Business, (Sustainable) Supply Chain Management, Strategic Management, Business Ethics, or again, Risk Management.

The existing literature on the specificity of CSR in the context of supply chains puts notable emphasis on the challenge of assessing the tangible impact of MNCs' CSR initiatives on supplier sustainability risks, beyond the environmental, social, and governance (ESG) metrics usually scrutinized by investors, but which can sometimes be seen as a smokescreen. In effect, while some scholars have suggested that MNCs may voluntarily "hide" their pollution in their supply chain (e.g., Shi et al., 2023), others have assumed that engagement with suppliers would automatically lead to an environmental, social, and economic upgrade of their practices (Gereffi et al., 2005). Empirically, the evidence is mixed. Some scholars have found a positive spillover effect of corporate customers' CSR efforts on that of their suppliers (e.g., Dai et al., 2021; Schiller, 2018; She, 2022; Tang et al., 2023). Yet, many others have pointed out the lack of, or limited effectiveness of MNCs' efforts and have been skeptical about the fact that they lead to significant and sustained improvements in CSR standards (Locke et al., 2007, 2009; Lund-Thomsen & Lindgreen, 2014).

At the same time, scholars have discussed the growing complexity of building more sustainable supply chains. They argue that the advent of global value chains (Gereffi et al., 2005) has dramatically increased the difficulty of setting up global and efficient CSR policies, as CSR issues expand beyond the traditional limits of ownership and control (Kim & Davis, 2016). This reflects what Davis et al. (2010) refer to as a the "responsibility paradox": while demand for CSR spikes, companies' ability to deliver shrinks. In view of this phenomenon, Villena and Gioia (2018) note:

> Although multinational companies (MNCs) have increasingly embraced a sustainability strategy for their own operations, fewer have tried to engage their (tier-one) suppliers in their sustainability initiatives. It is even rarer that MNCs engage their suppliers' suppliers (lower-tier suppliers), despite the latter having a higher incidence of violations with more acute environmental and social impacts that can jeopardize the MNCs' operations and reputation. (p. 65)

In this context, scholars have called for a deepening of our understanding of CSR diffusion in global supply chains, especially when MNCs and suppliers are operating in very different business environments. The literature, mostly focused on (1) the MNCs perspective and (2) the opportunities and ways to improve CSR adoption in global supply chains offers valuable insights. However, we argue that by focusing our attention on the pitfalls, roadblocks, and other challenges faced by both MNCs and suppliers in the context of supply networks' upgrading, we can gain another set of powerful insights on how firms can more efficiently work together to achieve mutually beneficial outcomes. Indeed, some authors have highlighted the lack of studies on the existence and nature of, and mechanisms behind suppliers' responses to MNCs' pressures in developing countries (Zhu & Lai, 2019), or the interplay in developed/emerging country dyads and networks (Khan & Nicholson, 2014). Surprisingly, the lack of studies on the specificities of sustainable value chains in developing countries is observed across fields (Silvestre & Neto, 2014). Existing studies sometimes ignore the international dimension of the issue, and usually don't answer our full problematic. This gap is evidenced by Asif's (2020) review of the literature on the antecedents of standards decoupling in global supply chains, which fails to account for the antecedents directly related to suppliers' environment/location.

In sum, besides calls for a greater theoretical integration to better assess the potential of CSR initiatives as a regulatory tool (Wahl & Bull, 2013), research on the effective implementation of sustainable global supply chains is dispersed and does not form a cohesive body of knowledge. Hence, in an effort to integrate relevant studies, analyze, and synthesize existing research and encourage future research on the challenges of CSR implementation in supply networks located in emerging countries, we develop a survey of the literature on the topic. We ask: To which extent can multinational companies successfully implement CSR policies in their network of suppliers, especially those located in developing countries? We provide a description of the surveyed literature in terms of disciplines. We then provide a summary of the literature along the following themes: first, we provide an overview of MNCs' available resources to implement CSR policies in their global supply chains and their respective limitations. Second, we consider the barriers to compliance from the suppliers' perspective. Third, we examine possible ways for MNCs' to overcome the challenge of CSR policies implementation in their value chains.

Our work contributes to advancing the research on sustainable supply chain development in many ways. First, by integrating existing research from very different fields, we build a framework on which future research can build upon and on which practitioners and/or policymakers can rely to think about how to overcome the potential pitfalls and roadblocks in supply chain upgrading. Second, we emphasize the shortcomings of existing firms' initiatives, as we believe that identifying them forms the basis of our understanding of supplier engagement and compliance with such initiatives. As such, we answer the calls to shift the main research focus from understanding "what" to "how" companies can implement sustainable practices along their value chains, a question that has greater practical relevance (Basu & Palazzo 2008; Porter & Kramer, 2006). Finally, we emphasize the importance of accounting for supplier characteristics, and their location in particular, as it (1) adds another layer of complexity to the phenomenon (2) that is considerable in practice. Indeed, the complexity and the length of MNCs' supply chains increase their difficulty to fully implement responsible practices, but this is especially true when operating in distant, developing countries where a large part of MNCs' sub-suppliers – those who are frequently involved in unsustainable actions – are located (Wilhelm et al., 2016).

2. REVIEW METHOD

We limited our search to academic research works including working papers, books, and book chapters in order to guarantee reliability. To retrieve relevant works, we first searched the Science Direct database using keywords. Since the topic of our literature is relatively narrow, we came up with a list of words for each specific dimensions of the problem at stake and combined them in different ways to gather an initial corpus (see Table 5.1). We supplemented our search with the snowball technique (i.e., finding relevant papers from the bibliography of other relevant works). We then read through the articles and discarded those which did not directly relate to (1) specific challenges in implementing/adopting CSR voluntary private initiatives (2) in supply chains. Given the multidisciplinary nature of supply chain research, this review process led to the inclusion of academic works from a multitude of disciplines: supply chain and operations management, but also international business, strategic management, business ethics, finance, accounting, marketing, human resources, legal studies, and economics. This resulted in a corpus of 209 documents. Finally, both (1) the identification of challenges to CSR implementation and adoption in global supply chains and (2) their organization in a framework were performed following an inductive approach (i.e., they were not defined a priori, but resulted from the search).

3. OVERVIEW OF THE BODY OF RESEARCH

To get a better understanding of the literature, we proceed to an analysis of the corpus. We categorize research articles following the Academic Journal Guide (AJG) list of journals, and field categories. The results of the analysis are summarized in Fig. 5.1. Not surprisingly given the topic, half of the articles included in the review came from two main fields: 30% of works were published in Operations and Technology Management outlets, and 21% in General Management, Ethics, Gender, and Social Responsibility outlets. Interestingly, fewer works (11%) were derived from International Business and Area Studies, which suggests that there could be some opportunities for future research focused on the contextual nature of CSR adoption and implementation. Because we focus on firm-led initiatives and firm interactions, the body of research is logically derived mostly from macro fields. However, focusing on micro-level interactions between managers, employees, or again psychological processes could also lead to valuable insights. Similarly, future research could pay more attention to the interactions between MNCs, and other stakeholders' initiatives aimed at improving suppliers' CSR.

Table 5.1. Keywords in the Literature Review.

	Keywords
Buyer	"buyer," "corporate customer," "MNC/Multinational Company," "MNE/ Multinational Enterprise"
Supplier	"supplier," "supply chain," "supply network"
CSR	"CSR/corporate social responsibility," "ESG," "sustainability"
Issue	"Issue," "problem," "challenge," "limitations"
Implementation	"Implementation," "decoupling," "compliance"
Context	"Emerging country/economy," "Developing country/economy"

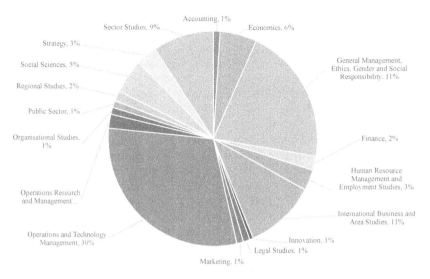

Fig. 5.1.   Distribution of Articles, by Field.

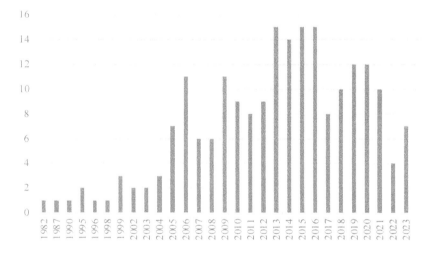

Fig. 5.2.   Yearly Number of Studies Published.

Finally, publications in the *Journal of Cleaner Production* (i.e., Sector Studies) make up 9% of the corpus.

Figs. 5.2 and 5.3 provide additional insights on the surveyed literature. Fig. 5.2 shows a peak of studies published in the mid-2010s, driven by supply chain management scholarship. Although it does not fully trace the evolution of the literature Fig. 5.3 seems to confirm a steady interest in supply chain and general management, a growing interest in international business and more unexpected,

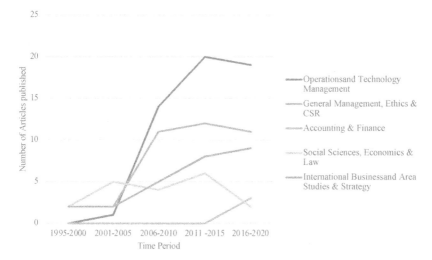

Fig. 5.3. Number of Articles Published, by Year and Field.

in accounting and finance. In fact, it should be noted that when finance and accounting studies represent only 3% of the body of research, the field produces most of the empirical, large-scale quantitative studies on the diffusion, or spillover effect of CSR in global supply chains.

4. CHALLENGES OF CSR IMPLEMENTATION IN SUPPLIER NETWORKS: A THEMATIC REVIEW IN THE EMERGING MARKET CONTEXT

4.1 MNC-Side Pitfalls: Available Policies and Their Limitations

Scholars have noted a proliferation of private voluntary regulatory systems by MNCs since the 1990s (e.g., Christmann & Taylor, 2002). Supply chain scholars, in particular, have documented how companies increasingly engage their suppliers in their environmental (Jira & Toffel 2013; Wu & Pagell, 2011), labor, and ethical initiatives (Huq et al., 2016; Jacobs & Singhal, 2017). Many MNCs, indeed, have developed tools to embark suppliers in their CSR journey, increase their competitive advantage, and protect their brands. This phenomenon is largely explained by (1) the failure of international treaties and intergovernmental organizations to regulate international business (Abbott & Snidal, 2009; Parmigiani & Rivera-Santos, 2015) and (2) the inadequacy of national legislations on labor rights or pollution in developing countries due to lack of regulation or enforcement (Acutt et al., 2004; Perry, 2012). In such context, MNCs have started to address concerns along their supply chains through the development of directive orchestration instruments (Ponte, 2019). We discuss the most popular initiatives and their limitations in this section.

4.1.1 Codes of Conduct

In the wake of well-publicized scandals, companies massively introduced their own "codes of conduct" or "codes of ethics." These codes constitute a concrete effort to fill institutional voids, especially from MNCs who have to operate across moral and regulatory borders, where cultural and institutional distance is relatively high (Kostova & Zaheer, 1999). They are meant to establish new rules, guide, and/or restrict suppliers' behavior to improve CSR. They set recommendations on a range of issues including child and forced labor, wages, and benefits, working hours, health and (product) safety, or again, environmental impact (Mamic, 2005; Strange & Humpfrey, 2019). But besides these efforts, many scholars have pointed out the general lack of codes' effectiveness as mechanism to address CSR-related issues (Barrientos & Smith, 2007; Locke et al., 2007). Empirical evidence has shown that many MNCs have struggled with how to implement their codes of conduct in their value chains (Leigh & Waddock, 2006). In practice, studies tend to show that they are vague and lack clear monitoring mechanisms, sometimes leading to inconsistent interpretations (see Kolk & van Tuldner, 2005 for an extensive discussion on this matter). For instance, scholars have shown that standardized codes of conduct can be translated in different ways depending on the contexts, as if negotiable (Babri et al., 2021; Helin & Babri, 2015). Finally, scholars underline the fact that codes are non-legally binding (Sanders, 1982) and stress that they would be easier to enforce if they did not consist in incomplete contracts (Pedersen & Andersen, 2006).

4.1.2. Internal Monitoring

Internal monitoring is defined as "the practice of conducting audits of suppliers to determine the level of compliance by supplier factories with codes of conduct" (Mamic, 2005, p. 95). The issue is that codes have historically lacked efficient monitoring systems (Pedersen & Andersen, 2006), with a minority of firms stipulating compliance mechanisms or monitoring systems and processes (Kolk et al., 1999). Such a lack of enforcement generally rises suspicion toward codes of conduct which may become public relations and "alibis" rather than a genuine attempt at improving CSR (Kolk & van Tulder, 2005). A second debate over monitoring revolves around its nature as a supposed objective governance mechanism (Hatanaka & Busch, 2008). In practice, critics observe that auditors are subject to serious conflicts of interest (Esbenshade, 2004), or lack transparency (Short et al., 2016). These concerns apply to both internal and external monitoring (i.e., conducted by third-party organizations; O'Rourke, 2003). Indeed, firms' self-assessment can be positively biased and superficial but private firms acting as third-party auditors could also be tempted to please their clients (both big brands and their suppliers) who pay for these services. Finally, when audits are conducted by NGOs, the concern becomes how the latter can assess technical issues, such as air quality (Andersen & Skjoett-Larsen, 2009; Locke et al., 2007).

4.1.3. Certifications and Third-Party Monitoring

Besides introducing codes of conduct and monitoring systems, MNCs also rely on other tools. The most common one is certification or standards on production and process methods (e.g., ISO 9000 and 14000). CSR standards can be defined as "the substantive rules that determine what is considered responsible behavior by business with regard to one or more social, environmental and ethical concerns, including human rights" (Fransen & Kolk, 2007, p. 668). Like codes of conduct, most of these standards develop implementation programs and compliance instruments, and often provide firm certifications as a sign of assurance (Fransen et al., 2019). Ponte and Gibbon (2005) note that with a growing demand for product information (i.e., origin, transformation, and composition) and increasing control and quality requirements, "hands-off quality management" is paradoxically preferred to direct control of suppliers. Indeed, resorting to third-party assessments allows MNCs to be less involved, reduce their monitoring costs, maintain their control over the procurement and production of products, but also ensure independence, objectivity, transparency, and thus, credibility of the audits (Humphrey, 2014). Yet again, when firms outsource monitoring functions, it creates potential agency problems because third-party monitors often have different incentive structures from the principals that hire them (Khalil & Lawarrée, 2006). As a result, they may behave opportunistically (Schuessler et al., 2019). What is more, Anner (2012) argues that programs to monitor workers' rights and standards in global value chains are more likely to emphasize detection of violations of minimal standards. Yeung and Mok (2005) finally point out the shortage of qualified auditors, which weakens the efficiency of standards monitoring and ultimately, questions the efficacy of certification tools to upgrade the chains.

4.1.4. Information and Communication Technologies
To address these challenges, MNCs have started to re-internalize sustainability management to better manage supplier risks (Wagner & Bode, 2006). They have started to massively invest in information and communication technologies and develop internal supply chain analytics programs to gain detailed insights on the composition of sourced products (Hofmann et al., 2018) and obtain more information from suppliers that can be used to better manage value chains without necessarily resorting to vertical integration. Some firms identify critical products and suppliers based on life-cycle analysis, risk/supplier assessment, and risk management (Matook et al., 2009; Strange & Humpfrey, 2019). Resource planning system or sustainability performance databases can also help firms collect and share sustainability performance data (Chen et al., 2012). These technologies ultimately serve as critical drivers of relationship management, collaboration, and integration, which is in turn a key driver of supply chain sustainability performance (Silvestre, 2015; Vachon & Klassen, 2006). Additionally, scholars have started to investigate the role that big data, predictive analytics (Hazen et al., 2016), or even blockchain technology (Saberi et al., 2019) could play in sustainable supply chain management. However, while these technologies can greatly help MNCs monitor their supply chains, they are extremely costly. Full-chain responsibility is made even more cost-prohibitive when formal suppliers are intricately linked to a multitude of informal sector suppliers and depend on informally employed unskilled labor (Narula, 2019).

4.2. Supplier-Side Pitfalls: Firm and Institutional Level Barriers to Compliance

Besides MNCs' substantial efforts to mitigate supplier sustainability risk, there is limited empirical evidence to ascertain whether value chains are truly sustainable (Montabon et al., 2016). To understand why MNCs fail in enforcing CSR guidelines over their suppliers, scholars have taken another perspective and dug deeper into the reasons why suppliers would be tempted not to comply, or unable to do so (Zorzini et al., 2015). In this section, we review studies that investigate the firm-level but also institutional-level barriers to CSR adoption/compliance (e.g., Marquis & Raynard, 2015). Some scholars specifically highlight the lack of research on the role of institutions in influencing how CSR is manifested in emerging markets, in contrast with developed markets, where CSR standards are usually designed (Boubakri et al., 2021; Jamali et al., 2017; Pisani et al., 2017).

4.2.1. Monitoring Fatigue

Faced with a growing number and diversity of codes of conduct and auditing protocols, many suppliers complain about "monitoring fatigue" (or "audit fatigue"): they must endure audits multiple times a year on behalf of each – or many – of the global brands they work with. Locke et al. (2007), for instance, interviewed Nike employees who revealed that numerous codes of conduct are accompanied by increasingly detailed guides which specify, for instance, the exact position of fire extinguishers. As a result, suppliers are placed in "compliance limbo" between different, sometimes conflicting requirements, continuously moving fire extinguishers back and forth as different brands' auditors perform plant inspections. Critics have thus questioned the usefulness of factory and plant monitoring (Pruett, 2005) especially since a multiplicity of standards, when incongruent with one another, contributes to confusion (Fransen et al., 2019) and sometimes, symbolic compliance through falsification of records (Huq et al., 2016).

4.2.2. Economic Barriers

Beyond confusion, having to comply with a multiplicity of rules increases transaction costs for the actors involved. Yet, Kolk and van Tuldner (2005) argue that the biggest challenge for suppliers arises from the costs associated with (extra) requirements that suppliers, themselves, often have to bear (i.e., charges for certification by an independent agency). This issue is particularly stringent for actors in the informal sector, who are often constrained in terms of economic resources. Said differently, the upfront costs (the diversion of scarce resources, time, money) may just be too high for small and medium firms and/or suppliers in developing countries, and the return on investment may not be obvious or quick enough to achieve (Chiu & Sharfman, 2011; Li et al., 2015), especially when they lack preparation before implementation (Yeung & Mok, 2005). As a result, suppliers tend to think that upgrading will not be economically beneficial in the long run (Kasim & Ismail, 2012). Indeed, scholars have pointed out that while buyers create significant pressure to reduce suppliers' prices (Huq et al., 2016), most of the costs are often pushed towards upstream suppliers, with benefits mostly staying at buying firms' level (Fransen et al., 2019). The prohibitive costs of CSR can in turn trigger opportunism or even give economic incentives to cut down standards or symbolically adopt codes of conduct to achieve financial gains without bearing the associated costs (Mena & Palazzo, 2012; Wijen, 2014). Additionally, access to additional resources from financial institutions is often limited for these firms (Claessens & Yurtoglu, 2013). Under such circumstances, some MNCs resort to financial and/or technical support to help suppliers overweight the cost of CSR (Ben Brik et al., 2013). They cover, for instance, training/consultancy costs and certification labels (Li et al., 2015). MNCs also engage in cost-sharing contracts and other financial incentives to alleviate the economic burden of their suppliers and incentivize them to invest (Hsueh, 2014; Slotnick & Sobel, 2022). The adoption, and the benefits of such collaborative financing initiatives, however, greatly depend on factors such as market demand uncertainty, the bank premia, and the supplier's bankruptcy risk (Moraux et al., 2023).

4.2.3. Political and Regulatory Environments

Along with economic barriers, suppliers in developing countries deal with a generalized lack of political support, the existence of institutional voids (Doh et al., 2015), weak institutions (Clarke & Boersma, 2017), unconducive business environments (Wrana & Revilla Diez, 2018), and relatively undemanding environmental and social regulations (Tachizawa & Wong, 2014). Such environments make it difficult for MNCs to convince suppliers to change their practices. In particular, policy enforcing is made more difficult due to insufficient resources available for inspection and monitoring (Azmat & Ha, 2013), or greater informality (Marquis & Raynard, 2015). MNCs also have to adapt regulations to local contexts (Bartley, 2010). Cheung et al. (2015) for instance, observe that while China is currently the world's manufacturing center, most Chinese factories are struggling with the implementation of standards imposed by Western companies. Related to the climate in which suppliers evolve, there is also the issue of corruption, or "mock compliance" (Jia et al., 2018) that questions the existence of sustainable supply chains, with firms bribing private auditors instead of implementing the standard in environments with high levels of general corruption (Montiel et al., 2012). Empirical research also finds evidence for suppliers resisting changes, resorting to irregular payments to government agencies (Azmat & Ha, 2013) or again, transfers of fake documentation during audits to acquire certifications (Huq et al., 2016). Yeung and Mok (2005) reveal that, in China, where the regulation of certification agencies is an issue, number of the managers they interviewed were used to "buying" certification in countries such as Bangladesh or Indonesia. In light of this phenomenon, MNCs have started not only to request their suppliers to get certified but also demand that they get certified and audited by reputable auditors from foreign countries with low general corruption (Montiel et al., 2012) rather than by some of the established auditors based in developing countries.

4.2.4. Social and Cultural Barriers

A recurring argument in the literature is the necessity for MNCs to translate, or at least, contextualize, the standardized, Western concept of CSR to emerging markets (Khan et al., 2021). Codes of conduct may fail in practice because of suppliers' traditions, or beliefs (Soundararajan & Brown, 2016). Many scholars observe that such barriers translate into employees' resistance to change in supplier's facilities. Again, this can be explained by a misalignment between global standards and local needs (Huq et al., 2016). Indeed, not all managers may be convinced of the real benefits that can be derived from certification, but all are (indirectly or directly) "forced" to implement them (Yeung & Mok, 2005). Similarly, scholars have found evidence for a lack of awareness and support from the workers which often result in the discontinuation of training programs and welfare schemes (Uttam et al., 2022). What is more, there is a growing understanding that the benefits of CSR are not equally distributed along the value chain. This, in turn, creates tensions, lack of trust, and thus, further resistance (Chiles & McMackin 1996). Ponte (2019, p. 78) speaks about "sustainability-driven supplier squeeze": "under the mantle of achieving environmental sustainability, lead firms in global value chains capture value for themselves, while extracting more demands from their suppliers and promoting a further consolidation of their supply base." Thus, enforcement of CSR policies does not only consist in a simple transmission of guidelines from MNCs to suppliers, but is also entangled in the continuous negotiation over rights, responsibilities, and struggles over the nature of the problem and its appropriate solutions (Andonova et al., 2009). Ultimately, factors such as language, culture, and education can affect not only the process of negotiation and decision-making (Nyuur et al., 2014), but also the access to information, the process of reporting and verification (Acutt et al., 2004), etc.

4.2.5. Lack of Awareness and Other Resources

Finally, suppliers in developing countries may lack awareness regarding CSR standards, but also, guidance and expertise to adopt complex sustainable practices (Busse et al., 2016). Similarly, local consumers may have a low demand for sustainable products (Ehrgott et al., 2013) as a result of both a lack of awareness about environmental issues and a low buying power which makes them more concerned with meeting their basic needs than with the quality of their purchases (Morris & Dunne, 2004). Pressures from external stakeholders (e.g., media and NGOs) are also much lower compared to the ones experienced in developed countries (e.g., Hamann et al., 2017). This is reinforced when suppliers play a more peripheral role in the supply network. Small or medium firms that produce intermediate products, in particular, are less likely to feel strong pressures to change since they are far from and invisible to stakeholders and final consumers. This contributes to their passivity in addressing their environmental and labor issues: they might consider environmental concerns as irrelevant, even perceive minimal consequences from non-compliance (Villena & Gioia, 2018). In fact, some scholars suggest that board connectedness could help firms acquire relevant information in this context (Amin et al., 2020). Finally, the small-scale, capital-poor, and labor-intensive nature of many actors in a developing country does not allow for monitoring through IT systems integration (Locke et al., 2013). Indeed, lower-tier suppliers often do not have the information available or are reluctant to share it as they fear competitive drawbacks. In developing countries, the lack of adequate infrastructures can also become a major barrier for the adoption of CSR practices (see Jia et al., 2018 for a review).

4.3 Buyer-Supplier Relationship-Level Antecedents: Governance Mechanisms

Although MNCs implement strategies to prevent sustainability breaches along their supply chains, the unique environment in which their suppliers located in developing countries evolve renders their task difficult, sometimes vain. Confronted with the issues of withdrawal and non-compliance, MNCs can ultimately resort to different styles of governance based on the power distribution along the supply chain, and their willingness to engage with their upstream partners. The literature mostly refers to "collaboration or assessment," also referred to as the "transactional vs. relational approaches," or "buyer-to-supplier vs. peer-to-peer" governance (Jiang, 2009). How MNCs engage with their lower-tier suppliers is also discussed.

4.3.1. Power Imbalance and The Transactional Approach

Governance is a centerpiece of value chains analysis (Gereffi, 2014). Power, in particular, is a key element to consider when studying CSR in value chains. Indeed, who has the largest influence dramatically impacts the extent to which CSR practices are implemented. In the first "scenario," the power can be exerted by (some, one) supplier(s) who can leverage their bargaining power. For example, it has been argued that lower-tier suppliers are less governable not only because they are geographically or culturally distant but also because a deal with one MNC might only represent a small fraction of their total business (Plambeck, 2012; Tachizawa & Wong, 2014). In some markets (rare and valuable resources, e.g., minerals), MNCs might simply be tied to problematic suppliers. According to Hofmann et al. (2018), such setting may leave firms unable to implement sophisticated compliance processes. Ultimately, MNCs are also constrained in their choice of suppliers as economic factors force them to operate in specific countries. Indeed, when sourcing from developing and poor countries, they often seek low costs that are only achieved by lower wages and poorer safety conditions. In a "buyer-dependence" setting (Pedersen & Andersen, 2006), persuading a partner to act responsibly might thus prove difficult (Hoejmose et al., 2013). In the second scenario, the power is exerted by MNCs, often referred to as "lead firms." Gereffi et al. (2005) refer to hierarchical (vertically integrated) and captive value chains. In the latter, networks are frequently characterized by a high degree of monitoring and control by lead firms, topics that have been the focus of the Supplier Sustainability Management literature. Here, scholars highlight that, by providing firm-specific (technological, reputational) advantages (Kano, 2018), MNCs increase suppliers' switching (or termination) costs. In such circumstances, suppliers that do not adhere to compliance regimes take the risk to be severely pressured, sanctioned, even immediately replaced (Andersen & Skjoett-Larsen, 2009; Locke et al., 2009) or disqualified (Bondareva & Pinker, 2019). This phenomenon is particularly salient for lower-tier suppliers, who tend to have a less stable relationship with the rest of the value chain, exactly because they can be replaced more easily. What is more, MNCs often have parallel value chains in several countries which enable to shift production wherever best suit them (Narula, 2019). But this "arm-strong"-type of approach has its limits, in particular if the MNC still wants to do business with a particular supplier. While Chen et al. (2016) find that supplier dependence to its corporate customer can positively influence suppliers' motivation, excessive pressure can backfire (Baden et al., 2009), decrease trust (Homburg et al., 2013) and ultimately undermine the relationship (Dwyer et al., 1987; Zhang et al., 2021). Finally, cutting ties with suppliers may require looking for alternative partners. Not only is it costly, but there is no guarantee that the new supplier will perform better (Bondareva & Pinker, 2019).

4.3.2. The Relational Approach

Although lead firms in position of power might coerce their suppliers to achieve CSR goals, it rarely happens this way. If, for new suppliers, non-compliance might result in their immediate elimination from the qualification process (Foerstl et al., 2010), management of already established suppliers is quite different. In practice, lead firms engage in more collaborative, supportive and adaptative strategies with their suppliers (Foerstl et al., 2015), and studies suggest that it leads to better outcomes than pure assessment strategies (Sancha et al., 2019). Indeed, highly turbulent business environments in those countries seriously hamper suppliers' capabilities and performance (Silvestre, 2015). Research now suggests that sustainable supply chains are the result of a complex and dynamic process that actively engages and supports suppliers toward fulfilling requirements for due diligence, and which can only occur through learning and innovative solutions (Hofmann et al., 2018, Pagell & Wu, 2009). This is well exemplified by Andersen and Skjoett-Larsen (2009) who observe that, as long as suppliers show a willingness to improve their practices, IKEA tends to grant additional time for suppliers to come up with corrective action plans. In fact, research shows that MNCs tend to move away from CSR standards as devices to implement their CSR programs, to, instead, invest more time and money in supplier development (Gualandris et al., 2014) through capability-building corporate programs, internal employee trainings including online learning library, courses, workshops, job shadowing, mentoring, self-development books and videos (Leigh & Waddock, 2006), or again, knowledge transfer (Vachon & Klassen, 2008).

Beyond training and education, MNCs have recognized the importance of doing business with "partners" with whom they "collaborate." Hence, they invest in their relationship with suppliers, focusing on positive values such as mutual respect (Locke et al., 2009) or trust (van Hoof & Thiell, 2015) to make the network become the source of power (Nye, 2011). In such context, MNCs have tried to make it more fluid, setting up cooperative information systems throughout the supply network (van Bommel, 2011), organizing supplier conventions, using intranet and e-communication systems to maintain up to date information between all parties, etc. (van Hoof & Thiell, 2015). In effect, studies have found that collaboration practices are more likely to improve suppliers' social and environmental performance (Alghababsheh & Gallear, 2021; Allenbacher & Berg, 2023; Venkatesh et al., 2020). Ultimately, scholars have suggested that MNCs' formal control for CSR practices adoption should be supported by cultivating relational ties with their suppliers from emerging country (Zhu & Lai, 2019). In other words, scholars have suggested that a middle-ground governance mechanism between assessment and collaboration should be achieved (see Asif, 2020). Sancha et al. (2016, 2019), for instance, find that auditing and monitoring suppliers on social issues (e.g., working conditions or child employment) does not directly lead to improvements in their facilities, but does so through the implementation of collaborative activities.

4.3.3. (In)Direct-Contracting Reasoning

Monitoring and/or engaging with direct suppliers can be costly and time-consuming for MNCs. Thus, it is even more complex when MNCs are pushed to assume the same responsibilities in wider, more dispersed supplier networks; especially when concentrated in emerging economies characterized by the presence of large informal sectors. Scholars highlight that although lower-tier suppliers are more likely to behave unsustainably, they are seldom integrated to MNCs' CSR development/monitoring programs (Villena & Gioia, 2018). Meinlschmidt et al., (2018) use the iceberg analogy, whose greatest threat remains invisible. Instead, MNCs rely on "direct contract reasoning" or "cascading" (Narula, 2019) – when the buyer delegates the authority for managing T2 suppliers to the T1 supplier (Choi & Hong, 2002; Wilhelm et al., 2016) – since they often don't have contractual relationships with lower-tier suppliers (Choi & Linton, 2011) who are increasingly located in geographically and institutionally distant countries (Awaysheh & Klassen, 2010). Yet, solely upgrading close and visible first-tier suppliers does little to prevent unsustainable behavior of lower tier, or nexus suppliers (Rauer & Kaufmann, 2015) who play an important role within supply networks (Yan et al., 2015). As a result, many firms have decided to dig deeper into their upstream supply networks and to conduct lower-tier sustainability management (see Tachizawa & Wong, 2014 for a review). Yet, moving from a "don't bother" multi-tier supply chain management strategy (only focusing on first-tier suppliers) to a "closed" one (establishing formal or informal relationships with tier-2 suppliers, Mena et al., 2013) does not solve the issue of unsustainable supply chains. Many problems subsist. A stringent issue is information. With all this complexity, lower-tier suppliers are the suppliers about whom buyers have the least information (Choi & Hong, 2002). In a 2015 study of 525 companies across 71 countries, 73.5% of the respondents reported they ignored who were their tier-two and tier-three suppliers (Business Continuity Institute. 2015). These numbers, although improving, raise concerns for MNCs claiming to build sustainable supply chains as "a supply chain is only as strong as its weakest link" (Villena & Gioia, 2020, p. 93).

What is more, supplier networks are often dominated by informal relationships, making MNCs even more boundedly rational (Narula, 2019). Finally, such governance approach has the potential to reinforce the economic burden imposed on first-tier suppliers, as MNCs not only transfer them the responsibility but also the costs of greater levels of monitoring of other upstream actors. In fact, in a recent study, van Assche and Narula (2023) argue that such approach would create significant economic benefits to MNCs, at the expense of creating disincentives for suppliers.

5. DISCUSSION AND FUTURE RESEARCH

This study summarizes the literature documenting the challenges MNCs face while trying to implement CSR policies in their network of suppliers located in developing countries. We articulate the review around three recurring themes. First, we discuss the strategies that MNCs can adopt to prevent CSR breaches along their value chains. From codes of conducts to audits, the review highlights the potential behind the many tools MNCs have started to use but also points out their limitations. Second, we consider the suppliers' perspective and list the different barriers that prevent them from (fully) implementing MNCs' CSR policies. From a lack of economic resources to a lack of awareness around CSR standards and environmental and social issues more generally, suppliers located in developing countries are likely to suffer from numerous handicaps which ultimately impede them from strictly following Western MNCs' (often) strict guidelines. Finally, we review the different governance mechanisms that can be adopted in the context of buyer-supplier relationships, their benefits, and limitations.

The resulting framework could serve as a basis for future research and provide useful insights for practice and policymaking. Managers, in particular, could see it as a basic guide to either (1) reassess their criteria for selecting suppliers or (2) rethink the way in which they currently engage with their suppliers in accordance with their specific sustainability goals and timelines. This may imply pre-screening suppliers, prioritizing those that demonstrate a commitment to CSR principles. It could also involve investing in training and capacity-building programs for suppliers to help them address CSR implementation challenges. Our framework is also an invitation for policymakers to grasp the extent of the difficulty some suppliers and MNCs might face while trying to do better. In effect, it calls for greater collaboration amongst all stakeholders – including NGOs, industry associations, and regulators – to help identify common challenges, share best, and promote new practices, and foster collective action to drive positive change in global supply chains.

We also contribute to scholarship by providing an overview of the building blocks of the existing literature, but also, by identifying where it falls short. Overall, we observe that, although at the crossroads of many different fields, the topic has rarely been tackled from a multidisciplinary perspective (e.g., Abbasi & Nilsson, 2012). As evidenced by Fig. 1, the Supply Chain Management and Business Ethics fields appear to monopolize the discussion. Studies in international business are less common, however, and those in HRM, or again, finance are almost anecdotical in terms of volume. This can be explained by the default unit(s) of analysis and phenomena specific to each field. As a result, isolated theoretical contributions fail to provide a homogenous and coherent framework that could substantially advance research and practice. At the empirical level, case studies provide the most holistic view of the phenomenon. Yet, they usually focus on one aspect of CSR (e.g., labor rights), a single MNC tool or initiative (e.g., codes of conduct), often in single country and/or firm contexts. A large chunk of the literature also relies on a limited set of theoretical lenses, such as agency theory, or institutional theory.

Finally, we identify some avenues for future research. Future research could further focus on the specificities of the relationship between Western MNCs and their suppliers in developing countries, taking on a more salient international business perspective. It should also consider the suppliers' perspective to a greater extent (e.g., Glover & Touboulic, 2020), question the relevance, and applicability of the Western definition of CSR in global value chains. Similarly, future research could investigate further the plurality of perspectives on CSR, paying more attention to the micro (i.e., individual) level.

The review also highlights the potential for further research on international business policy. In fact, scholars have recently called for greater research on the issue of sustainability in supply chains (e.g., Goerzen et al., 2023). Indeed, the various strategies available to MNCs to implement CSR policies in their supply chains are everything but perfect. In reaction to the failure of self-regulation, future research might want to explore the interactions between private and public initiatives, or how policy efforts could be redirected to think of ways to overcome the limitations of MNCs' current strategies. One example could be the instauration of a formal liability system which would force MNCs to gather information on their most remote suppliers and hold them legally accountable for activities taking place within their supply chains, something that was included in the 2017 French Duty of Vigilance law, the first comprehensive law on human rights and environmental due diligence requiring firms to disclose detailed information about their supply chain risks and to come up with an elaborate, long-term plan to eradicate ethical breaches throughout their supply chains.

Another avenue for future research could be the study of CSR diffusion patterns in supplier networks. Few but promising studies have already started to examine, through quantitative studies using supply chain data, CSR policies could trickle down value chains from MNCs to suppliers (Dai et al., 2021; de Góes et al., 2021; Schiller, 2018). By using a large amount of data, these authors are able to identify more systematic impediments to or enablers of CSR policies adoption, and the evolution of their impact over time. One could also look into patterns of diffusion across countries, or regions, to identify more localized impediments to CSR policies adoption.

REFERENCES

Abbasi, M., & Nilsson, F. (2012). Themes and challenges in making supply chains environmentally sustainable. *Supply Chain Management: An International Journal, 17*(5), 517–530.

Abbott, K. W., & Snidal, D. (2009). Strengthening international regulation through transnational new governance: Overcoming the orchestration deficit. *Vanderbilt Journal of Transnational Law, 42*, 501–578.

Acutt, N. J., Medina-Ross, V., & O'Riordan, T. (2004). Perspectives on corporate social responsibility in the chemical sector: A comparative analysis of the Mexican and South African cases. *Natural Resources Forum, 28*(4), 302–316.

Aguinis, H., & Glavas, A. (2012). What we know and don't know about corporate social responsibility: A review and research agenda. *Journal of Management, 38*(4), 932–968.

Alghababsheh, M., & Gallear, D. (2021). Socially sustainable supply chain management and suppliers' social performance: The role of social capital. *Journal of Business Ethics, 173*(4), 855–875.

Allenbacher, J., & Berg, N. (2023). How assessment and cooperation practices influence suppliers' adoption of sustainable supply chain practices: An inter-organizational learning perspective. *Journal of Cleaner Production*, *403*, 136852.

Amin, A., Chourou, L., Kamal, S., Malik, M., & Zhao, Y. (2020). It's who you know that counts: Board connectedness and CSR performance. *Journal of Corporate Finance*, *64*, 101662.

Andersen, M., & Skjoett-Larsen, T. (2009). Corporate social responsibility in global supply chains. *Supply Chain Management: An International Journal*, *14*(2), 75–86.

Andonova, L. B., Betsill, M. M., & Bulkeley, H. (2009). Transnational climate governance. *Global Environmental Politics*, *9*(2), 52–73.

Anner, M. (2012). Corporate social responsibility and freedom of association rights: The precarious quest for legitimacy and control in global supply chains. *Politics & Society*, *40*(4), 609–644.

Asif, M. (2020). Supplier socioenvironmental compliance: A survey of the antecedents of standards decoupling. *Journal of Cleaner Production*, *246*, 118956.

Awaysheh, A., & Klassen, R. D. (2010). The impact of supply chain structure on the use of supplier socially responsible practices. *International Journal of Operations & Production Management*, *30*(12), 1246–1268.

Azmat, F., & Ha, H. (2013). Corporate social responsibility, customer trust, and loyalty-perspectives from a developing country. *Thunderbird International Business Review*, *55*(3), 253–270.

Babri, M., Davidson, B., & Helin, S. (2021). An updated inquiry into the study of corporate codes of ethics: 2005–2016. *Journal of Business Ethics*, *168*(1), 71–108.

Baden, D. A., Harwood, I. A., & Woodward, D. G. (2009). The effect of buyer pressure on suppliers in SMEs to demonstrate CSR practices: An added incentive or counterproductive? *European Management Journal*, *27*(6), 429–441.

Barrientos, S., & Smith, S. (2007). Do workers benefit from ethical trade? Assessing codes of labour practice in global production systems. *Third World Quarterly*, *28*(4), 713–729.

Bartley, T. (2010). Transnational private regulation in practice: The limits of forest and labor standards certification in Indonesia. *Business and Politics*, *12*(3), 1–34.

Basu, K., & Palazzo, G. (2008). Corporate social responsibility: A process model of sensemaking. *Academy of Management Review*, *33*(1), 122–136.

Ben Brik, A., Mellahi, K., & Rettab, B. (2013). Drivers of green supply chain in emerging economies. *Thunderbird International Business Review*, *55*(2), 123–136.

Bondareva, M., & Pinker, E. (2019). Dynamic relational contracts for quality enforcement in supply chains. *Management Science*, *65*(3), 1305–1321.

Boubakri, N., El Ghoul, S., Guedhami, O., & Wang, H. (Helen). 2021. Corporate social responsibility in emerging market economies: Determinants, consequences, and future research directions. *Emerging Markets Review*, *46*, 100758.

Business Continuity Institute. (2015). *Supply chain resilience survey*. https://www.riskmethods.net/resourc es/research/bci-supply-chain-resilience-2015.pdf.

Busse, C., Schleper, M. C., Niu, M., & Wagner, S. M. (2016). Supplier development for sustainability: contextual barriers in global supply chains. *International Journal of Physical Distribution and Logistics Management*, *46*, 442–468.

Chen, C., Zhu, J., Yu, J.-Y., & Noori, H. (2012). A new methodology for evaluating sustainable product design performance with two-stage network data envelopment analysis. *European Journal of Operational Research*, *221*(2), 348–359.

Chen, J., Zhao, X., Lewis, M., & Squire, B. (2016). A multi-method investigation of buyer power and supplier motivation to share knowledge. *Production and Operations Management*, *25*(3), 417–431.

Cheung, Y.-L., Kong, D., Tan, W., & Wang, W. (2015). Being good when being international in an emerging economy: The case of China. *Journal of Business Ethics*, *130*(4), 805–817.

Chiles, T. H., & Mcmackin, J. F. 1996. Integrating Variable Risk Preferences, Trust, and Transaction Cost Economics, 28.

Chiu, S.-C., & Sharfman, M. (2011). Legitimacy, visibility, and the antecedents of corporate social performance: An investigation of the Instrumental Perspective. *Journal of Management*, *37*(6), 1558–1585.

Choi, T. Y., & Hong, Y. (2002). Unveiling the structure of supply networks: case studies in Honda, Acura, and DaimlerChrysler. *Journal of Operations Management*, *20*(5), 469–493.

Choi, T. Y., & Linton, T. (2011). Don't let your supply chain control your business. *Harvard Business Review, 89*(12), 112–117.

Christmann, P., & Taylor, G. (2002). Globalization and the environment: Strategies for international voluntary environmental initiatives. *Academy of Management Perspectives, 16*(3), 121–135.

Claessens, S., & Yurtoglu, B. B. (2013). Corporate governance in emerging markets: A survey. *Emerging Markets Review, 15*, 1–33.

Clarke, T., & Boersma, M. (2017). The governance of global value chains: Unresolved human rights, environmental and ethical dilemmas in the apple supply chain. *Journal of Business Ethics, 143*(1), 111–131.

Crane, A., & Matten, D. (2021). COVID-19 and the future of CSR research. *Journal of Management Studies, 58*(1), 280–284.

Dai, R., Liang, H., & Ng, L. (2021). Socially responsible corporate customers. *Journal of Financial Economics, 142*(2), 598–626.

Davis, G. F., von Neumann Whitman, M., & Zald, M. N. (2010). Political agency and the responsibility paradox: Multinationals and corporate social responsibility. IPC Working Paper Series 107.

de Góes, B. B., Kotabe, M., & Geleilate, J. M. G. (2021). The diffusion of corporate sustainability in global supply networks: An empirical examination of the global automotive industry. In A. Verbeke, R. van Tulder, E. L. Rose, & Y. Wei (Eds.), *The multiple dimensions of institutional complexity in international business research* (vol. 15, pp. 435–458). Emerald Publishing Limited.

Delmas, M. A., & Burbano, V. C. 2011. The drivers of greenwashing. *California Management Review, 54*(1), 64–87.

Doh, J. P., Littell, B., & Quigley, N. R. (2015). CSR and sustainability in emerging markets: Societal, institutional, and organizational influences. *Organizational Dynamics, 44*(2), 112–120.

Dwyer, F. R., Schurr, P. H., & Oh, S. (1987). Developing buyer-seller relationships. *Journal of Marketing, 51*(2), 11–27.

Ehrgott, M., Reimann, F., Kaufmann, L., & Carter, C. R. (2013). Environmental development of emerging economy suppliers: Antecedents and outcomes. *Journal of Business Logistics, 34*(2), 131–147.

Esbenshade, JL. (2004). *Monitoring sweatshops: Workers, consumers, and the global apparel industry.* Temple University Press.

Foerstl, K., Azadegan, A., Leppelt, T., & Hartmann, E. (2015). Drivers of supplier sustainability: Moving beyond compliance to commitment. *Journal of Supply Chain Management, 51*(1), 67–92.

Foerstl, K., Reuter, C., Hartmann, E., & Blome, C. (2010). Managing supplier sustainability risks in a dynamically changing environment—Sustainable supplier management in the chemical industry. *Journal of Purchasing and Supply Management, 16*(2), 118–130.

Fransen, L. W., & Kolk, A. (2007). Global rule-setting for business: A critical analysis of multi-stakeholder standards. *Organization, 14*(5), 667–684.

Fransen, L., Kolk, A., & Rivera-Santos, M. (2019). The multiplicity of international corporate social responsibility standards: Implications for global value chain governance. *Multinational Business Review, 27*(4), 397–426.

Gereffi, G. (2014). Global value chains in a post-Washington Consensus world. *Review of International Political Economy, 21*(1), 9–37.

Gereffi, G., Humphrey, J., & Sturgeon, T. (2005). The governance of global value chains. *Review of International Political Economy, 12*(1), 78–104.

Ghadge, A., Wurtmann, H., & Seuring, S. (2020). Managing climate change risks in global supply chains: A review and research agenda. *International Journal of Production Research, 58*(1), 44–64.

Glover, J., & Touboulic, A. (2020). Tales from the countryside: Unpacking "passing the environmental buck" as hypocritical practice in the food supply chain. *Journal of Business Research, 121*, 33–46.

Goerzen, A., Sartor, M., Brandl, K., & Fitzsimmons, S. 2023. Widening the lens: Multilevel drivers of firm corporate social performance. *Journal of International Business Studies, 54*(1), 42–60.

Gualandris, J., Golini, R., & Kalchschmidt, M. (2014). Do supply management and global sourcing matter for firm sustainability performance? An international study. *Supply Chain Management: An International Journal, 19*(3), 258–274.

Hamann, R., Smith, J., Tashman, P., & Marshall, R. S. (2017). Why do SMEs Go green? An analysis of wine firms in South Africa. *Business & Society, 56*(1), 23–56.

Hatanaka, M., & Busch, L. (2008). Third-party certification in the global agrifood system: An objective or socially mediated governance mechanism? *Sociologia Ruralis, 48*(1), 73–91.

Hazen, B. T., Skipper, J. B., Ezell, J. D., & Boone, C. A. (2016). Big data and predictive analytics for supply chain sustainability: A theory-driven research agenda. *Computers & Industrial Engineering, 101*, 592–598.

Helin, S., & Babri, M. 2015. Travelling with a code of ethics: A contextual study of a Swedish MNC auditing a Chinese supplier. *Journal of Cleaner Production, 107*, 41–53.

Hoejmose, S., Grosvold, J., & Millington, A. (2013). Socially responsible supply chains: Power asymmetries and joint dependence. *Supply Chain Management: An International Journal, 18*(3), 277–291.

Hofmann, H., Schleper, M. C., & Blome, C. (2018). Conflict Minerals and Supply Chain Due Diligence: An Exploratory Study of Multi-tier Supply Chains. *Journal of Business Ethics, 147*(1), 115–141.

Homburg, C., Stierl, M., & Bornemann, T. (2013). Corporate social responsibility in business-to-business markets: How organizational customers account for supplier corporate social responsibility engagement. *Journal of Marketing, 77*(6), 54–72.

Hsueh, C.-F. (2014). Improving corporate social responsibility in a supply chain through a new revenue sharing contract. *International Journal of Production Economics, 151*, 214–222.

Humphrey, J. (2014). Internalisation theory, global value chain theory and sustainability standards. *Progress in International Business Research, 8*, 91–114.

Huq, F. A., Chowdhury, I. N., & Klassen, R. D. (2016). Social management capabilities of multinational buying firms and their emerging market suppliers: An exploratory study of the clothing industry. *Journal of Operations Management, 46*(1), 19–37.

Jacobs, B. W., & Singhal, V. R. (2017). The effect of the Rana Plaza disaster on shareholder wealth of retailers: Implications for sourcing strategies and supply chain governance*. *Journal of Operations Management, 49–51*(1), 52–66.

Jamali, D., Karam, C., Yin, J., & Soundararajan, V. (2017). CSR logics in developing countries: Translation, adaptation and stalled development. *Journal of World Business, 52*(3), 343–359.

Jia, F., Zuluaga-Cardona, L., Bailey, A., & Rueda, X. (2018). Sustainable supply chain management in developing countries: An analysis of the literature. *Journal of Cleaner Production, 189*, 263–278.

Jiang, B. (2009). The effects of interorganizational governance on supplier's compliance with SCC: An empirical examination of compliant and non-compliant suppliers. *Journal of Operations Management, 27*(4), 267–280.

Jira, C. (Fern), & Toffel, M. W. (2013). Engaging supply chains in climate change. *Manufacturing & Service Operations Management, 15*(4), 559–577.

Kano, L. (2018). Global value chain governance: A relational perspective. *Journal of International Business Studies, 49*(6), 684–705.

Kasim, A., & Ismail, A. (2012). Environmentally friendly practices among restaurants: drivers and barriers to change. *Journal of Sustainable Tourism, 20*(4), 551–570.

Khalil, F., & Lawarree, J. (2006). Incentives for corruptible auditors in the absence of commitment. *Journal of Industrial Economics, 54*(2), 269–291.

Khan, M., Lockhart, J., & Bathurst, R. (2021). The institutional analysis of CSR: Learnings from an emerging country. *Emerging Markets Review, 46*, 100752.

Khan, Z., & Nicholson, J. D. (2014). An investigation of the cross-border supplier development process: Problems and implications in an emerging economy. *International Business Review, 23*(6), 1212–1222.

Kim, Y. H., & Davis, G. F. (2016). Challenges for global supply chain sustainability: Evidence from conflict minerals reports. *Academy of Management Journal, 59*(6), 1896–1916.

Koberg, E., & Longoni, A. (2019). A systematic review of sustainable supply chain management in global supply chains. *Journal of Cleaner Production, 207*, 1084–1098.

Kolk, A., & van Tulder, R. (2005). Setting new global rules? TNCs and codes of conduct. *Transnational Corporations, 14*(3), 28.

Kolk, A., van Tulder, R., & Welters, C. (1999). International codes of conduct and corporate social responsibility: Can transnational corporations regulate themselves? *Transnational Corporations, 8*(1), 36.

Kostova, T., & Zaheer, S. (1999). Organizational legitimacy under conditions of complexity: The case of the multinational enterprise. *The Academy of Management Review, 24*(1), 64–91.

Leigh, J., & Waddock, S. (2006). The emergence of total responsibility management systems: J. Sainsbury's (plc) voluntary responsibility management systems for global food retail supply chains. *Business and Society Review, 111*(4), 409–426.

Li, J., Pan, S.-Y., Kim, H., Linn, J. H., & Chiang, P.-C. (2015). Building green supply chains in eco-industrial parks towards a green economy: Barriers and strategies. *Journal of Environmental Management, 162*, 158–170.

Locke, R., Amengual, M., & Mangla, A. (2009). Virtue out of necessity? Compliance, commitment, and the improvement of labor conditions in global supply chains. *Politics & Society, 37*(3), 319–351.

Locke, R. M., Qin, F., & Brause, A. (2007). Does monitoring improve labor standards? Lessons from Nike. *Industrial and Labor Relations Review, 61*(1), 3–31.

Locke, R. M., Rissing, B. A., & Pal, T. (2013). Complements or substitutes? Private codes, state regulation and the enforcement of labour standards in global supply chains: Complements or substitutes? *British Journal of Industrial Relations, 51*(3), 519–552.

Lund-Thomsen, P., & Lindgreen, A. (2014). Corporate social responsibility in global value chains: Where are we now and where are we going? *Journal of Business Ethics, 123*(1), 11–22.

Mamic, I. (2005). Managing global supply chain: The sports footwear, apparel and retail sectors. *Journal of Business Ethics, 59*(1–2), 81–100.

Marquis, C., & Raynard, M. (2015). Institutional strategies in emerging markets. *The Academy of Management Annals, 9*(1), 291–335.

Matook, S., Lasch, R., & Tamaschke, R. (2009). Supplier development with benchmarking as part of a comprehensive supplier risk management framework. *International Journal of Operations & Production Management, 29*(3), 241–267.

Mayer, F., & Gereffi, G. (2010). Regulation and economic globalization: Prospects and limits of private governance. *Business and Politics, 12*(3), 1–25.

Meinlschmidt, J., Schleper, M. C., & Foerstl, K. (2018). Tackling the sustainability iceberg: A transaction cost economics approach to lower tier sustainability management. *International Journal of Operations & Production Management, 38*(10), 1888–1914.

Mena, C., Humphries, A., & Choi, T. Y. (2013). Toward a theory of multi-tier supply chain management. *Journal of Supply Chain Management, 49*(2), 58–77.

Mena, S., & Palazzo, G. (2012). Input and output legitimacy of multi-stakeholder initiatives. *Business Ethics Quarterly, 22*(3), 527–556.

Montabon, F., Pagell, M., & Wu, Z. (2016). Making sustainability sustainable. *Journal of Supply Chain Management, 52*(2), 11–27.

Montiel, I., Husted, B. W., & Christmann, P. (2012). Using private management standard certification to reduce information asymmetries in corrupt environments. *Strategic Management Journal, 33*(9), 1103–1113.

Moraux, F., Phan, D. A., & Vo, T. L. H. (2023). Collaborative financing and supply chain coordination for corporate social responsibility. *Economic Modelling, 121*, 106198.

Morris, M., & Dunne, N. (2004). Driving environmental certification: Its impact on the furniture and timber products value chain in South Africa. *Geoforum, 35*(2), 251–266.

Narula, R. (2019). Enforcing higher labor standards within developing country value chains: Consequences for MNEs and informal actors in a dual economy. *Journal of International Business Studies, 50*(9), 1622–1635.

Nye, J. (2011). *The Future of Power*. Public Affairs.

Nyuur, R., F. Ofori, D., & Debrah, Y. (2014). Corporate social responsibility in Sub-Saharan Africa: Hindering and supporting factors. *African Journal of Economic and Management Studies, 5*(1), 93–113.

O'Rourke, D. (2003). Outsourcing regulation: Analyzing nongovernmental systems of labor standards and monitoring. *Policy Studies Journal, 31*(1), 1–29.

Pagell, M., & Wu, Z. (2009). Building a more complete theory of sustainable supply chain management using case studies of 10 exemplars. *Journal of Supply Chain Management, 45*(2), 37–56.

Parmigiani, A., & Rivera-Santos, M. (2015). Sourcing for the base of the pyramid: Constructing supply chains to address voids in subsistence markets. *Journal of Operations Management, 33–34*(1), 60–70.

Pedersen, E. R., & Andersen, M. (2006). Safeguarding corporate social responsibility (CSR) in global supply chains: how codes of conduct are managed in buyer-supplier relationships. *Journal of Public Affairs*, *6*(3–4). 228–240.

Perry, P. (2012). Exploring the influence of national cultural context on CSR implementation. In T. Choi (Ed.) *Journal of Fashion Marketing and Management: An International Journal*, *16*(2), 141–160.

Pisani, N., Kourula, A., Kolk, A., & Meijer, R. 2017. How global is international CSR research? Insights and recommendations from a systematic review. *Journal of World Business*, *52*(5), 591–614.

Plambeck, E. L. (2012). Reducing greenhouse gas emissions through operations and supply chain management. *Energy Economics*, *34*, S64–S74.

Ponte, S. (2019). *Business, power and sustainability in a world of global value chains*. Zed Books.

Ponte, S. (2020). Green capital accumulation: Business and sustainability management in a world of global value chains. *New Political Economy*, *25*(1), 72–84.

Ponte, S., & Gibbon, P. (2005). Quality standards, conventions and the governance of global value chains. *Economy and Society*, *34*(1), 1–31.

Porter, M. E., & Kramer, M. R. (2006). Strategy and society: The link between competitive advantage and corporate social responsibility. *Harvard Business Review*, *23*(5), 76–93.

Pruett, D. (2005). *Looking for a quick fix: How weak social auditing is keeping workers in sweatshops*. Clean Clothes Campaign.

Rauer, J., & Kaufmann, L. (2015). Mitigating external barriers to implementing green supply chain management: A grounded theory investigation of green-tech companies' rare earth metals supply chains. *Journal of Supply Chain Management*, *51*(2), 65–88.

Saberi, S., Kouhizadeh, M., Sarkis, J., & Shen, L. (2019). Blockchain technology and its relationships to sustainable supply chain management. *International Journal of Production Research*, *57*(7), 2117–2135.

Sancha, C., Gimenez, C., & Sierra, V. (2016). Achieving a socially responsible supply chain through assessment and collaboration. *Journal of Cleaner Production*, *112*, 1934–1947.

Sancha, C., Wong, C. W. Y., & Gimenez, C. (2019). Do dependent suppliers benefit from buying firms' sustainability practices? *Journal of Purchasing and Supply Management*, *25*(4), 100542.

Sanders, P. (1982). Implementing international codes of conduct for multinational enterprises. *The American Journal of Comparative Law*, *30*(2), 241.

Schiller, C. (2018). Global supply-chain networks and corporate social responsibility. In: *13th Annual mid-Atlantic research conference in finance (MARC) paper*, March 23, 2018, Villanova, PA. doi: 10.2139/ssrn.3089311.

Schrempf-Stirling, J., & Palazzo, G. (2016). Upstream corporate social responsibility: The evolution from contract responsibility to full producer responsibility. *Business & Society*, *55*(4), 491–527.

Schuessler, E., Frenkel, S. J., & Wright, C. F. (2019). Governance of labor standards in Australian and German garment supply chains: The impact of Rana Plaza. *ILR Review*, *72*(3), 552–579.

She, G. (2022). The real effects of mandatory nonfinancial disclosure: Evidence from supply chain transparency. *The Accounting Review*, *97*(5), 399–425.

Shi, Y., Tang, C. S., & Wu, J. (2023, December 8). Are firms voluntarily disclosing emissions greener? Rochester, NY. https://doi.org/10.2139/ssrn.4426612.

Short, J. L., Toffel, M. W., & Hugill, A. R. (2016). Monitoring global supply chains: Monitoring global supply chains. *Strategic Management Journal*, *37*(9), 1878–1897.

Slotnick, S. A., & Sobel, M. J. (2022). Collaboration with a supplier to induce fair labor practices. *European Journal of Operational Research*, *302*(1), 244–258.

Silvestre, B. S. (2015). Sustainable supply chain management in emerging economies: Environmental turbulence, institutional voids and sustainability trajectories. *International Journal of Production Economics*, *167*, 156–169.

Silvestre, B. S., & Neto, R. (2014). Capability accumulation, innovation, and technology diffusion: Lessons from a base of the pyramid cluster. *Technovation*, *34*(5), 270–283.

Sinkovics, N., Hoque, S. F., & Sinkovics, R. R. (2016). Rana Plaza collapse aftermath: Are CSR compliance and auditing pressures effective? *Accounting, Auditing & Accountability Journal*, *29*(4), 617–649.

Soundararajan, V., & Brown, J. A. (2016). Voluntary governance mechanisms in global supply chains: Beyond CSR to a stakeholder utility perspective. *Journal of Business Ethics*, *134*(1), 83–102.

Strange, R., & Humphrey, J. (2019). What lies between market and hierarchy? Insights from internalization theory and global value chain theory. *Journal of International Business Studies, 50*(8), 1401–1413.

Tachizawa, E., & Wong, C. (2014). Towards a theory of multi-tier sustainable supply chains: A systematic literature review. *Supply Chain Management: An International Journal, 19*(5/6), 643–663.

Tang, J., Wang, X., & Liu, Q. (2023). The spillover effect of customers' ESG to suppliers. *Pacific-Basin Finance Journal, 78*, 101947.

Uttam, N., Dutta, P., & Singh, A. (2022). Micro, small, and medium suppliers' perspectives on supply chain social sustainability: New evidence from India. *Journal of Cleaner Production, 379*, 134473.

Vachon, S., & Klassen, R. D. (2006). Extending green practices across the supply chain: The impact of upstream and downstream integration (P. D. Cousins. Co-Editors: Benn Lawson, Ed.) *International Journal of Operations & Production Management, 26*(7), 795–821.

Vachon, S., & Klassen, R. D. (2008). Environmental management and manufacturing performance: The role of collaboration in the supply chain. *International Journal of Production Economics, 111*(2), 299–315.

Van Assche, A., & Narula, R. (2023). Internalization strikes back? Global value chains, and the rising costs of effective cascading compliance. *Journal of Industrial and Business Economics, 50*(1), 161–173.

van Bommel, H. (2011). A conceptual framework for analyzing sustainability strategies in industrial supply networks from an innovation perspective. *Journal of Cleaner Production, 19*(8), 895–904.

van Hoof, B., & Thiell, M. (2015). Anchor company contribution to cleaner production dissemination: Experience from a Mexican sustainable supply programme. *Journal of Cleaner Production, 86*, 245–255.

Venkatesh, V. G., Zhang, A., Deakins, E., & Mani, V. (2020). Drivers of sub-supplier social sustainability compliance: An emerging economy perspective. *Supply Chain Management: An International Journal, 25*(6), 655–677.

Villena, V. H., & Gioia, D. A. (2018). On the riskiness of lower-tier suppliers: Managing sustainability in supply networks. *Journal of Operations Management, 64*(1), 65–87.

Wagner, S. M., & Bode, C. (2006). An empirical investigation into supply chain vulnerability. *Journal of Purchasing and Supply Management, 12*(6), 301–312.

Wahl, A., & Bull, G. Q. (2013). Mapping research topics and theories in private regulation for sustainability in global value chains. *Journal of Business Ethics, 124*(4), 585–608.

Wijen, F. (2014). Means versus ends in opaque institutional fields: Trading off compliance and achievement in sustainability standard adoption. *Academy of Management Review, 39*(3), 302–323.

Wilhelm, M., Blome, C., Wieck, E., & Xiao, C. Y. (2016). Implementing sustainability in multi-tier supply chains: Strategies and contingencies in managing sub-suppliers. *International Journal of Production Economics, 182*, 196–212.

Wrana, J., & Revilla Diez, J. (2018). Multinational enterprises or the quality of regional institutions – What drives the diffusion of global CSR certificates in a transition economy? Evidence from Vietnam. *Journal of Cleaner Production, 186*, 168–179.

Wu, Z., & Pagell, M. (2011). Balancing priorities: Decision-making in sustainable supply chain management. *Journal of Operations Management, 29*(6), 577–590.

Yan, T., Choi, T. Y., Kim, Y., & Yang, Y. (2015). A theory of the nexus supplier: A critical supplier from a network perspective. *Journal of Supply Chain Management, 51*(1), 52–66.

Yeung, G., & Mok, V. (2005). What are the impacts of implementing ISOs on the competitiveness of manufacturing industry in China? *Journal of World Business, 40*(2), 139–157.

Zhang, Z., Hu, D., & Liang, L. (2021). The impact of supplier dependence on suppliers' CSR: The moderating role of industrial dynamism and corporate transparency. *Journal of Purchasing and Supply Management, 27*(5), 100702.

Zhu, Q., & Lai, K. (2019). Enhancing supply chain operations with extended corporate social responsibility practices by multinational enterprises: Social capital perspective from Chinese suppliers. *International Journal of Production Economics, 213*, 1–12.

Zorzini, M., Hendry, L. C., Huq, F. A., & Stevenson, M. (2015). Socially responsible sourcing: reviewing the literature and its use of theory. *International Journal of Operations & Production Management, 35*(1): 60–109.

PART III

ESG, CLIMATE RISK, AND POLITICS

CHAPTER 6

ASSESSING FIRM'S ESG PERFORMANCE USING THE TOPSIS

Palak Rathi[a], Ankit Nyati[a], Rushina Singhi*[a] and Anubha Srivastava[b]

[a]NMIMS University, Mumbai, India
[b]Christ University, Bangalore, India

ABSTRACT

Environment, social and governance (ESG) criteria are a quantum of a company's performance in the environmental, social and governance aspects. A company's worth may be determined not only by its earnings but also by its knowledge and sensitivity towards its stakeholders and society. The study aims to rank the companies and determine which company is superior based on ESG criteria. The authors employed the Technique for Order of Preference by Similarity to Ideal Solution (TOPSIS) in this study. The companies are ranked with this standardized method comprehending which company is the best taking into consideration the various environmental, social and governance factors. The authors have evaluated four companies in the electric utilities and IPPs industry. The results of the study rank these four companies on the basis of ESG criteria. Interestingly, the rankings calculated for ESG criteria are identical to the rankings calculated by a well-known ESG rating agency. To the best of author's knowledge, this work is among the first to use the TOPSIS method to find rankings of the companies on the basis on ESG criteria. The work provides practical implications regarding convenient to use when finding

Responsible Firms: CSR, ESG, and Global Sustainability
International Finance Review, Volume 23, 119–136
Copyright © 2025 by Palak Rathi, Ankit Nyati, Rushina Singhi and Anubha Srivastava
Published under exclusive licence by Emerald Publishing Limited
ISSN: 1569-3767/doi:10.1108/S1569-376720240000023006

ESG rankings for companies. This might be the most effective way for investors or other parties to learn which firm is the greatest for sustainable investing.

Keywords: Decision-making; ESG; environment; social; governance; TOPSIS; ranking

JEL codes: D81; G11; G24; M14; Q01

1. INTRODUCTION

ESG criteria have been the talk of the town for quite a good time now. Post-pandemic, it has become increasingly more important in the industry as it is the reflection of company's performance on the environmental, social and governance factors and the related exposure to their risks. Farnham (2023) states that ESG scores explain the company's situation to anticipate the future risks and make more informed decisions that are beneficial for the firm in the short as well as long term.

Depletion of resources, climate change and public health have made sustainability a global concern (Menon & Ravi, 2022). A company's worth is influenced by its commitment to strong corporate governance, social responsibility and sensitivity for its stakeholders going way beyond its financial metrics (Pfajfar et al., 2022). Prioritizing transparency, fairness and accountability can help companies foster trust and integrity among the stakeholders and consumers. The stakeholders build long-term relationships only with companies that work towards their beneficence keeping in mind their needs and concerns. Embracing social responsibility through ethical practices and community engagement build stronger reputations and long-term sustainability for the company (Nimani et al., 2022).

Investors and shareholders have become more responsible and sensitive as they tend to inspect each and every aspect before investing in a company. They are taking into account the non-financial factors to analyse the risks and achieve favourable returns (Parrado et al., 2020; Sood et al., 2023). ESG scores help the investors and shareholders to make a sustainable investment. By integrating ESG criteria, momentum investors can lower their overall portfolio risk even when there is bearish trend in the market (Kaiser & Welters, 2019; Lamanda & Tamásné Vőneki, 2024; Sciarelli et al., 2021). For the populace, ESG scores are easy to understand and are readily available and have become a very crucial factor to obtain a peek into company's work in the short period of time (Popescu et al., 2021). Companies can also use these ratings to scrutinize areas that require further attention with the intent of getting an improved ESG rating. It arouses a competitive spirit among the companies and in the aftermath, companies take suitable measures to refine their work to entice the people connected with the company and reduce exposure to risk (Makridou et al., 2023). A company with a lower environmental score focuses on designing better waste management policies and strategize on creating environmental impact to establish brand handle

(Emerick, 2021). On the basis of a survey conducted by MIT Sloan Management Review, Kiron (2012) stated that two third of companies view sustainability as a necessary component to being competitive in today's marketplace.

The environmental (E) factor in ESG incorporates details relating to the company's awareness towards the environmental issues it may cause and their reciprocating actions towards the same. The social (S) factor includes company's behaviour towards its workforce and consumers, their rights and the efforts towards giving them a better experience. Various stakeholders in the company have different goals and managing all of them together is a challenging task for the company (Menon & Ravi, 2022). The governance (G) factor revolves around the management and shareholders of the company. Other than the financial information, ESG scores explain pertinent information about the challenges and the performances of the company. Studies show that environmental, social and governance factors are interrelated. Participation of executives is advantageous for good environment performance and investments in CSR might affect internal governance of the company (Abukari et al., 2023; Li et al., 2021). A similar study by Chininga et al. (2023) observed that the environmental pillars and corporate financial performance were positively related. A good ESG score reflects better innovation, profitability and productivity of the company. Emerick (2021) discusses that a good ESG score helps the company get better investments as they can win the trust of the investors and the new employees become optimistic to join the company as the score also reflects the company's behaviour and care towards its employees.

Calculating ESG ratings is a time-consuming procedure that necessitates extensive data processing. There are third-party firms that create ESG scores for corporations based on data provided to rating companies or publicly available data. According to Escrig-Olmedo et al. (2019), the rising significance of sustainable and responsible investment has given a boom to the ESG rating agencies. Refinitiv, the financial and risk business of Thomson Reuters, is a rating agency that calculates the ESG scores using their self-developed model (Refinitv, 2022). These rating companies use different qualitative and quantitative methods and various formulas to calculate ESG scores for each company and compare it with other companies in the industry (Farnham, 2023). Thus, for a particular sector the companies are ranked on the basis of their ESG score. The objective of this study is to rank companies using the TOPSIS process simplifying it to understand which company is better on the basis of ESG criteria. TOPSIS stands for Technique for Order of Preference by Similarity to Ideal Solution. It is a process used for Multi-Criteria Decision-Making (MCDM) problems. It was proposed by Hwang and Yoon in 1981. It is used to rank the alternatives (choices) on the basis of various criteria that affect the decision-making process (Zulqarnain et al., 2020). In this work, the method of TOPSIS is used to investigate which company is the best in the industry on the basis of various environmental, social and governance criteria. We can categorize this as a MCDM problem and employ the TOPSIS process to find the required results.

TOPSIS method has several advantages over the composite score methods which are generally used by the rating agencies. Statistically, the method is quite simple to comprehend and implement and so it requires minimal technical expertise for interpretation. TOPSIS accommodates both qualitative and quantitative criteria and thus facilitates its applicability across diverse decision-making problems (Alsalem et al., 2018). It incorporates the subjective preferences of the decision maker through the weights that are assigned to each of the criteria on the basis of its importance. In our case, this is of importance as the significance of few criteria may change from industry to industry or from investor to investor. TOPSIS demonstrates robustness against outliers and variations in data, as it focuses on the relative distances between alternatives rather than absolute values. It allows to evaluate a greater number of alternatives and so there is no restriction on the number of companies that can be ranked. Practically, there is no universally accepted methodology that is used for ESG calculations. Different rating providers consider different sets of attributes and use different methods to calculate the ESG scores. Thus, the divergence of ratings occurs and it makes it difficult for investors to take decisions (Berg et al., 2019). TOPSIS helps to standardize the process as it provides ESG rankings that the investor uses in its decision-making process. In this case, it may also happen that companies try to improve their score based on the specific methodology of a particular rating agency rather than making genuine improvements in their ESG performance.

The work is further divided into following sections, Section 2 explains the existing literature, Section 3 provides the research methodology, Section 4 expresses analysis and Section 5 exhibits the final conclusion.

2. LITERATURE REVIEW

Empirical studies have been published on the relation between ESG criteria and corporate financial performance which traces back to the beginning of 1970s. The study by Friede et al. (2015) has collected all the important data from these studies allowing for generalized statements. There has been an increasing significance of non-financial factors like ESG for financial valuation of a company in the long term (Barman, 2018). Many of these factors are qualitative in nature and their disclosure becomes difficult. These factors may be the key performance indicators along with the company's financial information and so quantification of these factors helps companies in providing more reliable information to the investors in the capital markets. Though there is no conclusive evidence of direct link between ESG performance and company's performance, ESG performance provides information about management quality, company's response to long-term trends, etc. This additional information allows for more differentiated investment judgements by enabling investors to assess risks and opportunities in a better way (Bassen & Kovács, 2008; Lamanda & Tamásné Vőneki, 2024).

ESG rating providers have become influential institutions for investors. Investors representing $100 trillion in combined assets have come together to integrate ESG information for investment decision making. Whelan et al. (2021) in their research found that ESG investing helps in providing downside protection, especially during a social or economic crisis. To assess environmental risks and sustainable finance strategy, disclosure of ESG factors becomes very important (European Banking Authority, 2021). There are no standard frameworks to disclose the ESG data hampering the comparability among the companies. This becomes one of the biggest problems to use the disclosed data for investment decisions. There exist providers who have advanced at designing frameworks but there are no internationally approved set of standards for ESG calculations at present (Boffo & Patalano, 2020). Recent studies about ESG information conclude that ESG is associated with numerous meaningful effects like stock price movements, lower capital constraints, and cost of capital. Though these have significant economic effects, we still lack the knowledge about how investors use and understand ESG information (Khemir, 2019). Many of the ESG factors are qualitative in nature and thus quantification of this information is a challenge to the rating agencies. Reliability of data is a very important factor to keep in mind during the entire process. The analysis by Amel-Zadeh and Serafeim (2017) states that the future practices in ESG are to be driven by the materiality of the actions undertaken.

Socially responsible investors have moved towards sustainable investing over the period of time. However, there is a lack of sufficient development to incorporate investors' preferences, particularly those investors who are sensitive to social issues. Therefore, the challenge lies in effectively combining these preferences into investment decisions. Escrig-Olmedo et al. (2017) use the MCDM technique to integrate ESG investors' preferences. Paradowski et al. (2021) have analysed and compared MCDM techniques like COMET, TOPSIS, VIKOR and PROMETHEE II. The research concluded that real-life problems could be successfully solved using appropriate MCDM methods. For example, MCDM techniques were used for the assessment of service quality in teaching hospitals of medical sciences by Shafii et al. (2016). Ogonowski (2022) has used the TOPSIS method to study internet activities while Jayant et al. (2014) used the same approach for the selection of reverse logistics service providers. A case study to compare the similarities in the rankings obtained by VIKOR and TOPSIS processes was done by Shekhovtsov and Sałabun (2020). Chou and Chang (2008) have discussed a methodology to tackle the qualitative and quantitative decision factors effectively using the Fuzzy approach. To rank the countries in context of participation finance, Yüksel et al. (2023) have used a CRITIC (criteria importance through intercriteria correlation)-based TOPSIS model. They developed this tool to ensure transparency and objectivity in participation finance.

3. DATA

3.1 Factors Used for Calculation of ESG

The European Banking Authority states that 'Environmental, social or governance matters that may have a positive or negative impact on the financial performance or solvency of an entity, sovereign or individual' (EBA, 2021).

For our research, we have identified 21 critical ESG factors (refer Table A1).

3.2 Data Collection

This work examined four companies in the electric utilities and independent power producers (IPPs) industry. These are companies that are not public utilities but own and operate their own power plants. The companies were chosen as the data was readily available for them in accordance with the preferred layout. The data was gathered from the company's factsheets available on the website of ESG Churchgate Partners (Churchgate. 2023), the annual reports and the public disclosures made by the company. The data was collected for ESG disclosures for the financial year 2021–2022. Churchgate Partners is an investor relations firm offering financial services to its corporate clients. It publishes ESG data and provides ESG profiles for various companies. Company names have not been disclosed as we respect the privacy and reputation of all organizations and do not intend to engage in any negative or defamatory commentary. To maintain homogeneity, the available data in different units was converted to the same units (refer Table A2). The data constitutes the finalized dataset of ESG variables utilized for subsequent analysis (refer Table A3).

3.3. Method

TOPSIS uses the concept of Euclidean distance to rank the alternatives. The best alternative is the one which is closest to the positive ideal solution (PIS) and farthest from the negative ideal solution (NIS). It maximizes the benefit criteria and minimizes the cost criteria (Sevkli et al., 2010).

The flowchart presented in Figure 3.1 below explains at a glance the steps used for calculations in the TOPSIS process.

To evaluate a MCDM problem with m alternatives $(A_1, A_2,..., A_m)$ and n decision criteria $(C_1, C_2,..., C_n)$, the following steps are used (Sevkli et al., 2010):

Step 1: Construct the decision matrix (X)

The data is entered with for each company with companies being the rows and the criteria being the columns thus forming a data matrix for calculations ahead. The data for each criterion should be in the same unit to get correct results:

$$X = \left(x_{ij}\right)_{m*n} \tag{i}$$

Step 2: Calculate the normalized decision matrix (NDM)

The normalized matrix R is calculated to get the relative performance of the alternatives using vector normalization using the given formula:

$$r_{ij} = \frac{x_{ij}}{\sqrt{\sum_{k=1}^{m} x_{kj}^2}} \tag{ii}$$

Step 3: Calculate the weighted NDM

The weighted NDM V is calculated by multiplying the columns of the NDM by the associated weights satisfying $\sum_{j=1}^{n} w_j = 1$:

$$V = \left(v_{ij}\right),$$
$$\text{where } v_{ij} = r_{ij} * w_j$$

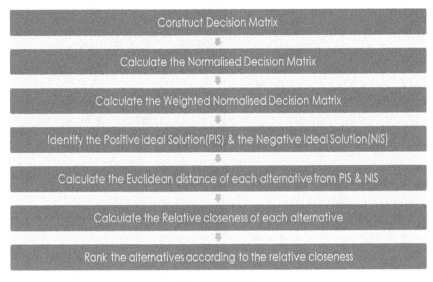

Fig. 6.1. TOPSIS Process

where

$$v_{ij} = r_{ij} * w_j \qquad \text{(iii)}$$

Step 4: Identify the PIS and the NIS

Each criterion is either a benefit criterion or a cost/non-benefit criterion. Benefit criteria is a criterion for which more the value better is the result for the company. Cost criterion is a criterion for which lesser the value better it is. All the factors have thus been classified in these two categories.

3.3.1 Positive Ideal Solution (PIS)

$$A^+ = \left(v_1^+, v_2^+, \ldots, v_n^+ \right)$$

where

$$v_j^+ = \left\{ \left(\max_i v_{ij} \, if \, j \in B \right), \left(\min_i v_{ij} \, if \, j \in C \right) \right\} \qquad \text{(iv)}$$

that is, the maximum value of benefit criteria and the minimum value of the cost criteria are taken for **PIS** (Menon & Ravi, 2022).

3.3.2 Negative Ideal Solution (NIS)

$$A^- = \left(v_1^-, v_2^-, \ldots, v_n^- \right)$$

where

$$v_j^- = \left\{\left(\min_i v_{ij} \, if \, j \in B\right), \left(\max_i v_{ij} \, if \, j \in C\right)\right\} \qquad \text{(v)}$$

that is, the minimum value of benefit criteria and the maximum value of the cost criteria are taken for NIS (Menon & Ravi, 2022).

Step 5: Calculate the Euclidean distance of each alternative from PIS and NIS.

$$\text{Euclidean distance from PIS} : S_i^+ = \sqrt{\sum_{j=1}^{n}\left(v_{ij} - v_j^+\right)^2} \qquad \text{(vi)}$$

$$\text{Euclidean distance from NIS} : S_i^- = \sqrt{\sum_{j=1}^{n}\left(v_{ij} - v_j^-\right)^2} \qquad \text{(vii)}$$

Step 6: Calculate the relative closeness of each alternative.
The relative closeness of each alternative from the PIS:

$$RC_i = \frac{S_i^-}{S_i^+ + S_i^-} \qquad \text{(viii)}$$

Step 7: Rank the alternatives according to the relative closeness.
Larger the value of RC_i, better is the alternative A_i. Thus, the best alternative is the one which has the biggest RC_i and one with the smallest RC_i is the worst.

4. RESULTS AND DATA INTERPRETATION

The TOPSIS process as explained in the previous section is used to study the performance of the company.

The decision matrix is the data collected and summarized in Table A3. Using eq. (ii) on the decision matrix, the NDM is found (refer Table 6.1).

Equation (iii) is used to calculate the weighted NDM. Twenty-one criteria/factors have been considered for the TOPSIS process. Each of these criteria has been given equal weightage. Thus, $w_{ij} = \frac{1}{21} \, \forall j$ (refer Table 6.2).

The PIS and the NIS are calculated using the eqs. (iv) and (v). After calculating PIS and NIS, eqs. (vi) and (vii) are used to calculate the distance between the best and worst solutions (refer Tables 6.3 and 6.4).

Equation (viii) gives the value for coefficient for relative closeness for the four companies (refer Table 6.5).

After this, the companies are ranked on the basis of the coefficients calculated. The final ranks for the four companies are given in Table 6.6. It can be seen that the calculated RC for Company 1 is the highest. Thus, out of the four alternatives, it has been ranked on the top. Similarly, Company 2 is ranked second and Company 4 third. Company 3 has the smallest RC and so it holds the last place.

Table 6.1. Normalized Decision Matrix

Variables	Company 1	Company 2	Company 3	Company 4
E1	0.08086	0.98452	0.15322	0.02676
E2	0.46263	0.01925	0.84938	0.25330
E3	0.09787	0.98329	0.15142	0.02532
E4	0.26278	0.89676	0.34671	0.08106
E5	0.52305	0.00581	0.84245	0.12909
S1	0.75188	0.40100	0.15038	0.50125
S2	0.64232	0.29440	0.58879	0.39253
S3	0.00000	1.00000	0.00000	0.00000
S4	0.66735	0.65106	0.03542	0.35988
S5	0.05835	0.98857	0.00000	0.13898
S6	0.17669	0.60798	0.67304	0.38230
S7	0.55873	0.03585	0.00973	0.82852
S8	0.83875	0.32096	0.01848	0.43947
G1	0.18599	0.52518	0.68822	-0.46470
G2	0.92604	-0.11037	0.07907	0.35217
G3	0.58381	0.38532	0.59462	0.39638
G4	0.55898	0.31769	0.51240	0.56927
G5	0.53882	0.53882	0.35921	0.53882
G6	0.50000	0.50000	0.50000	0.50000
G7	0.50000	0.50000	0.50000	0.50000
G8	0.49999	0.50002	0.49999	0.49999

Table 6.2. Weighted NDM

Variables	Company 1	Company 2	Company 3	Company 4	Weights
E1	0.00385	0.04688	0.00730	0.00127	0.04762
E2	0.02203	0.00092	0.04045	0.01206	0.04762
E3	0.00466	0.04682	0.00721	0.00121	0.04762
E4	0.01251	0.04270	0.01651	0.00386	0.04762
E5	0.02491	0.00028	0.04012	0.00615	0.04762
S1	0.03580	0.01910	0.00716	0.02387	0.04762
S2	0.03059	0.01402	0.02804	0.01869	0.04762
S3	0.00000	0.04762	0.00000	0.00000	0.04762
S4	0.03178	0.03100	0.00169	0.01714	0.04762
S5	0.00278	0.04707	0.00000	0.00662	0.04762
S6	0.00841	0.02895	0.03205	0.01820	0.04762
S7	0.02661	0.00171	0.00046	0.03945	0.04762
S8	0.03994	0.01528	0.00088	0.02093	0.04762
G1	0.00886	0.02501	0.03277	-0.02213	0.04762
G2	0.04410	-0.00526	0.00377	0.01677	0.04762
G3	0.02780	0.01835	0.02832	0.01888	0.04762
G4	0.02662	0.01513	0.02440	0.02711	0.04762
G5	0.02566	0.02566	0.01711	0.02566	0.04762
G6	0.02381	0.02381	0.02381	0.02381	0.04762
G7	0.02381	0.02381	0.02381	0.02381	0.04762
G8	0.02381	0.02381	0.02381	0.02381	0.04762

Table 6.3. Calculation of S_i^+

Variables	Company 1	Company 2	Company 3	Company 4
E1	0.00001	0.00208	0.00004	0.00000
E2	0.00045	0.00000	0.00156	0.00012
E3	0.00001	0.00208	0.00004	0.00000
E4	0.00007	0.00151	0.00016	0.00000
E5	0.00061	0.00000	0.00159	0.00003
S1	0.00082	0.00014	0.00000	0.00028
S2	0.00000	0.00027	0.00001	0.00014
S3	0.00227	0.00000	0.00227	0.00227
S4	0.00000	0.00000	0.00091	0.00021
S5	0.00196	0.00000	0.00222	0.00164
S6	0.00000	0.00042	0.00056	0.00010
S7	0.00068	0.00000	0.00000	0.00152
S8	0.00000	0.00061	0.00153	0.00036
G1	0.00057	0.00006	0.00000	0.00301
G2	0.00000	0.00244	0.00163	0.00075
G3	0.00000	0.00010	0.00000	0.00009
G4	0.00000	0.00014	0.00001	0.00000
G5	0.00000	0.00000	0.00007	0.00000
G6	0.00000	0.00000	0.00000	0.00000
G7	0.00000	0.00000	0.00000	0.00000
G8	0.00000	0.00000	0.00000	0.00000
S^+	0.08632	0.09928	0.11211	0.10259

Table 6.4. Calculation of S_i^-

Variables	Company 1	Company 2	Company 3	Company 4
E1	0.00185	0.00000	0.00157	0.00208
E2	0.00034	0.00156	0.00000	0.00081
E3	0.00178	0.00000	0.00157	0.00208
E4	0.00091	0.00000	0.00069	0.00151
E5	0.00023	0.00159	0.00000	0.00115
S1	0.00000	0.00028	0.00082	0.00014
S2	0.00027	0.00000	0.00020	0.00002
S3	0.00000	0.00227	0.00000	0.00000
S4	0.00091	0.00086	0.00000	0.00024
S5	0.00001	0.00222	0.00000	0.00004
S6	0.00056	0.00001	0.00000	0.00019
S7	0.00017	0.00142	0.00152	0.00000
S8	0.00153	0.00021	0.00000	0.00040
G1	0.00096	0.00222	0.00301	0.00000
G2	0.00244	0.00000	0.00008	0.00049
G3	0.00009	0.00000	0.00010	0.00000
G4	0.00013	0.00000	0.00009	0.00014
G5	0.00007	0.00007	0.00000	0.00007
G6	0.00000	0.00000	0.00000	0.00000
G7	0.00000	0.00000	0.00000	0.00000
G8	0.00000	0.00000	0.00000	0.00000
S^-	0.11063	0.11273	0.09818	0.09681

Table 6.5. Relative Closeness

Company	RC_i
Company 1	0.561700116
Company 2	0.531717686
Company 3	0.466884768
Company 4	0.485491109

Table 6.6. TOPSIS Rankings V/S Refinitiv Rankings

Company	RC_i	Rank (by TOPSIS)	Rank (by Refinitiv)
Company 1	0.561700116	1	38/295
Company 2	0.531717686	2	145/295
Company 3	0.466884768	4	190/295
Company 4	0.485491109	3	153/295

5. CONCLUSION

This study introduces the TOPSIS approach for calculating ESG rankings for a comparative comparison of different organizations. Four businesses in the electric utilities and IPPs industry were analysed for research purposes. This method can be extended to companies in any other industry and to any number of companies in each of these industries. The performance of the firms on the basis of ESG variables was determined using a TOPSIS model. The firms were rated using the RC_i score, as previously indicated. The firm at the top might be deemed ideal for long-term investment. Surprisingly, the scores for ESG criteria are similar to those determined by a well-known ESG rating firm.

Because various rating agencies employ different ways to determine ESG scores, the rankings for each organization may differ from one another. TOPSIS assists in overcoming this issue by providing a comparable ranking for all firms. When computing ESG scores for comparing firms, the recommended approach is simple to apply.

ESG scores and rankings are of great importance not only for the investors but also for the company itself. It helps investors make sustainable investments and companies build sustainable brands. Responsible investors or third parties can efficiently find out which company can be given priority for investment. And so instead of the complicated models used by rating agencies, TOPSIS process could serve as an alternative method to calculate the ESG rankings. This model also allows the investor to assign more weight to the criteria that are more important for them and less weight to the criteria that are less important. Thus, this model helps to make personalized decisions for every investor.

Even though this approach overcomes a few limits encountered by ESG computations, it is not without limitations. The restriction of corporations' inadequate data disclosure prevails in the TOPSIS model employed in this work. Improved data accessibility and dependability can lead to more robust and precise outcomes. Because many businesses reveal their data in multiple units, bringing the data to homogeneity for computation is critical. This approach may be expanded to determine separate rankings for corporations based on environmental, social and governance factors by running the TOPSIS procedure for each parameter. This aids in determining which organization excels in each of these areas. This methodology may also be used to rank ESG aspects in other sectors with minor variations in the influencing factors.

DECLARATION

The authors declare that they have no known competing financial interests or personal relationships that could have appeared to influence the work reported in this paper.

REFERENCES

Abukari, K., Musah, A., & Assaidi, A. (2023). The role of corporate sustainability and its consistency on firm financial performance: Canadian evidence*. *Accounting Perspectives*, *22*(1), 55–86. https://doi.org/10.1111/1911-3838.12309

Aich, S., Thakur, A., Nanda, D., Tripathy, S., & Kim, H.-C. (2021). Factors affecting ESG towards impact on investment: A structural approach. *Sustainability*, *13*(19), 10868. https://doi.org/10.3390/su131910868

Alsalem, M. A., Zaidan, A. A., Zaidan, B. B., Hashim, M., Albahri, O. S., Albahri, A. S., Hadi, A., & Mohammed, K. I. (2018). Systematic review of an automated multiclass detection and classification system for acute leukaemia in terms of evaluation and benchmarking, open challenges, issues and methodological aspects. *Journal of Medical Systems*, *42*(11), 204. https://doi.org/10.1007/s10916-018-1064-9

Amel-Zadeh, A., & Serafeim, G. (2017). Why and how investors use ESG information: Evidence from a global survey. *SSRN Electronic Journal*, *74*(3), 87–103. https://doi.org/10.2139/ssrn.2925310

Barman, E. (2018). Doing well by doing good: A comparative analysis of ESG standards for responsible investment. In S. Dorobantu, R. V. Aguilera, J. Luo, & F. J. Milliken (Eds.), *Advances in strategic management* (Vol. 38, pp. 289–311). Emerald Publishing Limited. https://doi.org/10.1108/S0742-33222018000038016

Bassen, A., & Kovács, A. M. (2008). Environmental, social and governance key performance indicators from a capital market perspective. *Zeitschrift Für Wirtschafts- Und Unternehmensethik*, *9*(2), 182–192. https://doi.org/10.5771/1439-880X-2008-2-182

Berg, F., Kölbel, J., & Rigobon, R. (2019). Aggregate confusion: The DIVERGENCE of ESG ratings. *SSRN Electronic Journal*. https://doi.org/10.2139/ssrn.3438533

Bernoville, T. (2022, July). What are Scopes 1, 2 and 3 of carbon emissions? *Plana Academy*. https://plana.earth/academy/what-are-scope-1-2-3-emissions

Boffo, R., & Patalano, R. (2020). *ESG investing: Practices, progress and challenges*. https://www.oecd.org/finance/ESG-Investing-Practices-Progress-Challenges.pdf

Brunner, P. H., & Rechberger, H. (2015). Waste to energy – Key element for sustainable waste management. *Waste Management*, *37*, 3–12. https://doi.org/10.1016/j.wasman.2014.02.003

Chininga, E., Alhassan, A. L., & Zeka, B. (2023). ESG ratings and corporate financial performance in South Africa. *Journal of Accounting in Emerging Economies*, *14*(3), 692–713. https://doi.org/10.1108/JAEE-03-2023-0072

Chou, S., & Chang, Y. (2008). A decision support system for supplier selection based on a strategy-aligned fuzzy SMART approach. *Expert Systems with Applications*, *34*(4), 2241–2253. https://doi.org/10.1016/j.eswa.2007.03.001

Churchgate. (2023). *ESG world*. Churchgate Partners. https://esg.churchgatepartners.com/

EBA (2021). *EBA report on management and supervision of ESG risks for credit institutions investment firms.* https://www.eba.europa.eu/sites/default/files/document_library/Publications/Reports/2021/1015656/EBA%20Report%20on%20ESG%20risks%20management%20and%20supervision.pdf

Eccles, R. G., Ioannou, I., & Serafeim, G. (2014). The impact of corporate sustainability on organizational processes and performance. *Management Science, 60*(11), 2835–2857. https://doi.org/10.1287/mnsc.2014.1984

Emerick, D. (2021, October 21). *What is an ESG score?* https://www.esgthereport.com/what-is-an-esg-score/

Escrig-Olmedo, E., Fernández-Izquierdo, M., Ferrero-Ferrero, I., Rivera-Lirio, J., & Muñoz-Torres, M. (2019). Rating the raters: Evaluating how ESG rating agencies integrate sustainability principles. *Sustainability, 11*(3), 915. https://doi.org/10.3390/su11030915

Escrig-Olmedo, E., Rivera-Lirio, J. M., Muñoz-Torres, M. J., & Fernández-Izquierdo, M. Á. (2017). Integrating multiple ESG investors' preferences into sustainable investment: A fuzzy multicriteria methodological approach. *Journal of Cleaner Production, 162*, 1334–1345. https://doi.org/10.1016/j.jclepro.2017.06.143

European Banking Authority (2021). *Environmental social and governance disclosures.* Publication Office. https://data.europa.eu/doi/10.2853/808235

Farnham, K. (2023, November 29). ESG scores and ratings: What they are, why they matter. *ESG & Diversity.* https://www.diligent.com/resources/blog/esg-risk-scores

Friede, G., Busch, T., & Bassen, A. (2015). ESG and financial performance: Aggregated evidence from more than 2000 empirical studies. *Journal of Sustainable Finance & Investment, 5*(4), 210–233. https://doi.org/10.1080/20430795.2015.1118917

Gurol, B., & Lagasio, V. (2023). Women board members' impact on ESG disclosure with environment and social dimensions: Evidence from the European banking sector. *Social Responsibility Journal, 19*(1), 211–228. https://doi.org/10.1108/SRJ-08-2020-0308

Jayant, A., Gupta, P., Garg, S. K., & Khan, M. (2014). TOPSIS-AHP based approach for selection of reverse logistics service provider: A case study of mobile phone industry. *Procedia Engineering, 97*, 2147–2156. https://doi.org/10.1016/j.proeng.2014.12.458

Kaiser, L., & Welters, J. (2019). Risk-mitigating effect of ESG on momentum portfolios. *The Journal of Risk Finance, 20*(5), 542–555. https://doi.org/10.1108/JRF-05-2019-0075

Khemir, S. (2019). Perception of ESG criteria by mainstream investors: Evidence from Tunisia. *International Journal of Emerging Markets, 14*(5), 752–768. https://doi.org/10.1108/IJOEM-05-2017-0172

Kiron, D. (2012). Sustainability nears a tipping point. *Strategic Direction, 28*(7), 69–74. https://doi.org/10.1108/sd.2012.05628gaa.012

Lamanda, G., & Tamásné Vőneki, Z. (2024). Is ESG disclosure associated with bank performance? Evidence from the Visegrad Four countries. *Management of Environmental Quality: An International Journal, 35*(1), 201–219. https://doi.org/10.1108/MEQ-02-2023-0064

Lawson, B. (2023, January 17). ESG: Best practices for the energy industry. *Plante Moran.* https://www.plantemoran.com/explore-our-thinking/insight/2022/01/esg-best-practices-for-the-energy-industry

Li, T.-T., Wang, K., Sueyoshi, T., & Wang, D. D. (2021). ESG: Research progress and future prospects. *Sustainability, 13*(21), 11663. https://doi.org/10.3390/su132111663

Makridou, G., Doumpos, M., & Lemonakis, C. (2023). Relationship between ESG and corporate financial performance in the energy sector: Empirical evidence from European companies. *International Journal of Energy Sector Management, 18*(4), 873–895. https://doi.org/10.1108/IJESM-01-2023-0012

Menon, R. R., & Ravi, V. (2022). Using AHP-TOPSIS methodologies in the selection of sustainable suppliers in an electronics supply chain. *Cleaner Materials, 5*, 100130. https://doi.org/10.1016/j.clema.2022.100130

MSCI (2023). *ESG investing: ESG ratings.* MSCI. https://www.msci.com/our-solutions/esg-investing/esg-ratings

Nimani, A., Zeqiraj, V., & Spahija, D. (2022). The importance of corporate social responsibility for companies: The developing market study. *Journal of Governance and Regulation*, *11*(4, special issue), 314–320. https://doi.org/10.22495/jgrv11i4siart11

Ogonowski, P. (2022). Integrated AHP and TOPSIS method in the comparative analysis of the internet activities. *Procedia Computer Science*, *207*, 4409–4418. https://doi.org/10.1016/j.procs.2022.09.504

Paradowski, B., Bączkiewicz, A., & Watrąbski, J. (2021). Towards proper consumer choices—MCDM based product selection. *Procedia Computer Science*, *192*, 1347–1358. https://doi.org/10.1016/j.procs.2021.08.138

Parrado, E., Hoffman, B., & Jubert, T. A. i. (2020, July 25). *How ESG-focused investments can help transform Latin America*. World Economic Forum. https://www.weforum.org/agenda/2020/07/esg-investing-latin-america-covid-19-era/

Pfajfar, G., Shoham, A., Małecka, A., & Zalaznik, M. (2022). Value of corporate social responsibility for multiple stakeholders and social impact – Relationship marketing perspective. *Journal of Business Research*, *143*, 46–61. https://doi.org/10.1016/j.jbusres.2022.01.051

Popescu, I.-S., Hitaj, C., & Benetto, E. (2021). Measuring the sustainability of investment funds: A critical review of methods and frameworks in sustainable finance. *Journal of Cleaner Production*, *314*, 128016. https://doi.org/10.1016/j.jclepro.2021.128016

Rau, P. R., & Yu, T. (2024). A survey on ESG: Investors, institutions and firms. *China Finance Review International*, *14*(1), 3–33. https://doi.org/10.1108/CFRI-12-2022-0260

Refinitv (2022). *Environmental, social and governance (ESG) scores from Refinitv*. https://objects.scraper.bibcitation.com/user-pdfs/2023-04-12/79ebc5df-ed81-4edd-8ce4-7a962a6b4600.pdf

Sciarelli, M., Cosimato, S., Landi, G., & Iandolo, F. (2021). Socially responsible investment strategies for the transition towards sustainable development: The importance of integrating and communicating ESG. *The TQM Journal*, *33*(7), 39–56. https://doi.org/10.1108/TQM-08-2020-0180

Sevkli, M., Zaim, S., Turkyilmaz, A., & Satir, M. (2010). An application of fuzzy Topsis method for supplier selection. In *IEEE international conference on fuzzy systems* (pp. 1–7), Barcelona, Spain, 18–23 July, 2010. https://doi.org/10.1109/FUZZY.2010.5584006

SGA Knowledge Team (2022, September 15). *ESG score—Definition, process, implications & purpose*. SG Analytics. https://www.sganalytics.com/blog/what-is-esg-score-and-how-is-it-calculated/

Shafii, M., Rafiei, S., Abooee, F., Bahrami, M. A., Nouhi, M., Lotfi, F., & Khanjankhani, K. (2016). Assessment of service quality in teaching hospitals of Yazd University of Medical Sciences: Using multi-criteria decision making techniques. *Osong Public Health and Research Perspectives*, *7*(4), 239–247. https://doi.org/10.1016/j.phrp.2016.05.001

Shekhovtsov, A., & Sałabun, W. (2020). A comparative case study of the VIKOR and TOPSIS rankings similarity. *Procedia Computer Science*, *176*, 3730–3740. https://doi.org/10.1016/j.procs.2020.09.014

Sood, K., Pathak, P., Jain, J., & Gupta, S. (2023). How does an investor prioritize ESG factors in India? An assessment based on fuzzy AHP. *Managerial Finance*, *49*(1), 66–87. https://doi.org/10.1108/MF-04-2022-0162

Whelan, T., Atz, U., Holt, T. V., & Clark, C. (2021). *ESG and financial performance*. Rockefeller Capital Management. https://rcmbrand.rockco.com/wp-content/uploads/2021/02/NYU-RAM_ESG-Paper_2021_vfinal.pdf

World Economic Forum. (2021, September 20). *Explore the metrics*. World Economic Forum. https://www.weforum.org/stakeholdercapitalism/our-metrics

Yüksel, S., Kalyoncu, G., & Özdurak, C. (2023). Constructing an index for participation finance. *Borsa Istanbul Review*, *23*(4), 895–905. https://doi.org/10.1016/j.bir.2023.03.003

Zulqarnain, R. M., Saeed, M., Ahmad, N., Dayan, F., & Ahmad, B. (2020). *Application of TOPSIS Method for Decision Making*, *7*(2), 76–81.

APPENDIX

Table A1. Factors used for ESG ratings of ESG.factors

Factors	Definition	References
Energy Consumption	Energy consumption refers to the total energy used by the company in the process of power generation. It can be in the form of electricity, coal or any other fuel.	Li et al. (2021)
GHG Emission	Greenhouse gas emissions are categorised into three scopes; Scopes 1 and 2 are mandatory to report while Scope 3 is not. Direct emissions from the resources owned and controlled by the company come under Scope 1 emissions. Scope 2 emissions include indirect emissions from consumption of purchased electricity, steam, heat and cooling. Scope 3 emissions include indirect emissions like business travels that occur in the value chain of company.	Bernoville (2022)
Air Pollution	Amount of nitrogen oxides, sulphur oxides and the particulate matter in air.	Aich et al. (2021)
Water Consumption	Total amount of water consumed by the company (freshwater, seawater and water from other resources)	Lawson (2023)
Waste Generated	Includes the hazardous as well as the non-hazardous waste generated by the company.	Brunner and Rechberger (2015)
Incident Management Reporting	LTIFR or the lost time injury frequency rate is a safety measure which refers to the number of lost time injuries occurring per 1 million hours worked.	Lawson (2023)
Female Board Members	Percentage of women in the board of directors of the company.	Gurol and Lagasio (2023)
Female Senior Management	Percentage of women in the senior management of the company.	SGA Knowledge Team (2022)
Female Workforce	Percentage of women in the total workforce of the company.	MSCI (2023)
Differently Abled Workforce	Percentage of differently abled people in the total workforce of the company.	Churchgate (2023)
Employee Turnover	Percentage of employees that leave the company during a given time period.	(Eccles et al. (2014)
Pay Performance Gap (Highest to median ratio)	Ratio of the salary of the highest paid individual to the median salary of the company.	World Economic Forum (2021)
Donations/Philanthropy	Amount of money donated towards noble causes by the company	Rau and Yu (2024)

(Continued)

Table A1. (*Continued*)

Factors	Definition	References
Tax Paid Change	Percentage change in the tax paid by the company in the current financial year w.r.t to the previous year.	MSCI (2023)
Auditor fees Change	Percentage change in the fees paid to the auditor in the current financial year w.r.t to the previous year.	MSCI (2023)
Non-Executive Board Members	Percentage of non-executive members in the board of directors of the company.	SGA Knowledge Team (2022)
Independent Board Members	Percentage of members with no other links than being on board of directors of the company.	Gurol and Lagasio (2023)
Non-Executive Audit Committee Members	Percentage of non-executive members in the Audit Committee of the company.	SGA Knowledge Team (2022)
Non-Executive Remuneration Committee Members	Percentage of non-executive members in the Remuneration Committee of the company.	MSCI (2023)
Non-Executive Nomination Committee Members	Percentage of non-executive members in the Nomination Committee of the company.	MSCI (2023)
Non-Executive CSR Committee Members	Percentage of non-executive members in the CSR Committee of the company.	MSCI (2023)

Table A2. Impact & Units of ESG factors

ESG	Factors	Units	Variable	Impact
Environment	Energy Consumption	Giga Joules (GJ)	E1	Cost
	GHG Emission	Tonnes (t\CO2e)	E2	Cost
	Air Pollution	Metric Tonnes (MT)	E3	Cost
	Water Consumption	Kilolitres (KL)	E4	Cost
	Waste Generated	Metric Tonnes (MT)	E5	Cost
Social	Incident Management Reporting	Lost Time Injury Frequency Rate (LTIFR)	S1	Cost
	Female Board Members	Percentage	S2	Benefit
	Female Senior Management	Percentage	S3	Benefit
	Female Workforce	Percentage	S4	Benefit
	Differently Abled Workforce	Percentage	S5	Benefit
	Employee Turnover	Percentage	S6	Cost
	Pay Performance Gap (Highest to median ratio)	Ratio	S7	Cost
	Donations/ Philanthropy	Rupees	S8	Benefit
Governance	Tax Paid Change	Percentage	G1	Benefit
	Auditor fees Change	Percentage	G2	Benefit
	Non-Executive Board Members	Percentage	G3	Benefit
	Independent Board Members	Percentage	G4	Benefit
	Non-Executive Audit Committee Members	Percentage	G5	Benefit
	Non-Executive Remuneration Committee Members	Percentage	G6	Benefit
	Non-Executive Nomination Committee Members	Percentage	G7	Benefit
	Non-Executive CSR Committee Members	Percentage	G8	Benefit

Table A3. Data Collected

Variables	Company 1	Company 2	Company 3	Company 4
E1	278072239.00000	3385762610.00000	526920690.00000	92037470.31000
E2	27615000.00000	1149299.04000	50700446.10940	15119953.74000
E3	212897.00000	2138984.86364	329382.98000	55073.07000
E4	292258919.00000	997367000.00000	385607131.00000	90150249.00000
E5	6051993.00000	67265.64000	9747697.41500	1493616.77000
S1	0.15000	0.08000	0.03000	0.10000
S2	18.18182	8.33333	16.66667	11.11111
S3	0.00000	2.85714	0.00000	0.00000
S4	8.09762	7.90000	0.42980	4.36681
S5	0.15715	2.66237	0.00000	0.37430
S6	2.20000	7.57000	8.38000	4.76000
S7	54.55000	3.50000	0.95000	80.89000
S8	327700000.00000	125400000.00000	7220741.24000	171700000.00000
G1	38.43000	108.51219	142.20000	–96.01571
G2	44.46953	–5.30000	3.79723	16.91176
G3	81.81818	54.00000	83.33333	55.55000
G4	54.54545	31.00000	50.00000	55.55000
G5	100.00000	100.00000	66.66667	100.00000
G6	100.00000	100.00000	100.00000	100.00000
G7	100.00000	100.00000	100.00000	100.00000
G8	66.66667	66.66667	66.66667	66.66667

CHAPTER 7

FOSSIL-WASHING? THE FOSSIL FUEL INVESTMENT OF ESG FUNDS

Alain Naef[*]

ESSEC Business School and THEMA, France

ABSTRACT

Regulators are starting to question what it means for an investment vehicle to be labelled environmental, social, and corporate governance (ESG). Also, retail climate-conscious investors have a right to have clear information on their investments. Here I analysed all the large equity exchange traded funds labelled as ESG available at the two largest investors in the world: Blackrock and Vanguard. For Blackrock, out of 82 funds analysed, only 9% did not invest in fossil fuel companies. Blackrock ESG funds include investments in Saudi Aramco, Gazprom or Shell. But they exclude ExxonMobil or BP. This suggests a best-in-class approach by the fund manager, picking only certain fossil fuel companies that they see as generating less harm. But it is unclear what the criteria used are. For Vanguard, funds listed as ESG did not contain fossil fuel investment. Yet this needs to be nuanced as information provided by Vanguard on investments is less transparent and Vanguard offers fewer ESG funds.

Keywords: ESG investing; fossil fuel companies; exchange traded funds (ETF); financial regulation; fund management

JEL codes: G23; Q56; M14; G28; Q58

*Alain Naef, ESSEC Business School and THEMA, 3 Av. Bernard Hirsch, 95000 Cergy, France. E-mail: alain.naef@essec.edu.

Responsible Firms: CSR, ESG, and Global Sustainability
International Finance Review, Volume 23, 137–146
Copyright © 2025 by Alain Naef
Published under exclusive licence by Emerald Publishing Limited
ISSN: 1569-3767/doi:10.1108/S1569-376720240000023007

1. INTRODUCTION

Imagine buying a nice vegan sandwich with hummus, tomatoes and lettuce. It has a large label on it that reads 'Vegan'. And then, after eating it, finding out that it contains bacon on its ingredient list. This would be illegal. But also upsetting for customers. So, what about buying an investment fund labelled as ESG and finding out it contains fossil fuel investments? Here I ask: do all ESG-labelled funds contain investments in fossil fuel companies? And which fossil fuel companies do ESG funds choose?

Looking at investment exchange traded funds (ETFs) from Blackrock and Vanguard, the two largest asset managers in the world, I find that only 9% of Blackrock ESG funds are fossil-free. Vanguard has less transparency, but the disclosed data did not show fossil investment for the ESG ETFs in my sample. Looking into more details, Blackrock ESG funds shun some fossil fuel companies in all the 82 funds analysed. None of the 82 funds contains ExxonMobil or BP shares (see the detailed list in Appendix 1). They also exclude most coal companies. They do, however, contain Saudi Aramco, Gazprom or Shell shares. This suggests that as a fund manager, Blackrock has a best-in-class approach, shunning some stocks and including others.

This question is important as regulators today are starting to analyse what greenwashing means for large investors. In May 2022, German regulatory authorities did a sting police operation at Deutsche Bank's investment arm DWS. They were looking for evidence of misleading ESG labelling. In March 2022, Gary Gensler, the chair of the Securities and Exchange Commission (SEC), also made a food analogy: 'It is easy to tell if milk is fat free. It might be time to make it easier to tell whether a fund is really what they say they are'. The SEC has since proposed a rule to regulate ESG products, but it has not yet been passed into law. There is, therefore, interest in the (mis)labelling of ESG funds. The question here is not normative. I do not ask whether ESG funds should contain fossil fuel assets. I simply ask whether the largest investment funds invest in fossil assets and which fossil assets.

Investment funds could invest in fossil fuel companies and still have an ESG approach. They could do engagement, threat of divestment or activism (Kölbel et al., 2020; Naef & van't Klooster 2022). With engagement they could try to influence fossil fuel companies to change to a more sustainable mode of energy production in the future (Barko et al., 2022; Goodman et al., 2014). This as fossil fuel companies have started to show support for carbon taxes (Naef, 2024). Blackrock and Vanguard are also among the largest holders of fossil fuel companies overall (Dordi et al., 2022). Yet evidence of Blackrock engagement is limited (Belinga & Segrestin, 2023; Bédu et al., 2023; Sharfman, 2020; Tilba, 2022). The company announced in May 2022 (after the rise in oil prices following the invasion of Ukraine) that it was planning to vote against shareholder-led climate plans.[1] It also begs the question if ESG funds are doing enough. Can they have the same portfolio composition as non-ESG funds and simply promise engagement without clear accountability to their investors or regulators?

A whole strand of literature argues that ESG could use a best-in-class approach (Beisenbina et al., 2023). Best-in-class means picking stocks in every sector, including the fossil sector, but only investing in the "best" companies. Blackrock seems to be doing this as shown in this work, but there is no clear information on the selection criteria. Best-in-class is not immune to greenwashing concerns (In & Schumacher 2021). Recent research by the OECD also shows that ESG ratings are imperfect and ESG metrics from different providers are completely uncorrelated (Dimson et al., 2020; OECD. 2022). So depending on the rating chosen, just about any portfolio could become best-in-class ESG.

Here the question is whether ESG-rated funds do contain fossil fuel assets and which assets. Rompotis (2023) does a similar analysis, but does not investigate the composition of the products, and only looks at the market behaviour to see if ESG funds have similar returns and behaviours to non-ESG-labelled funds. The evidence suggests that they are indeed similar. The contribution here is to look inside the ETF packages for evidence of fossil fuel company shares. Reiser and Tucker (2019) also look at the questions of ETF funds but they do not offer a systematic review of fossil fuel investments as is done here.

BlackRock and Vanguard each present their ESG investing options distinctively, targeting different audiences with varying depths of information. BlackRock's approach, often described as 'best-in-class', aims to invest in companies demonstrating favourable ESG factors, including those within the fossil fuel industry that lead to sustainability. In contrast, Vanguard employs an 'exclusionary' or 'negative screening' approach, focusing on excluding stocks from specific industries like tobacco, weapons and fossil fuels outright. Both firms tailor their communications to appeal to their intended investors, with BlackRock addressing a more financially sophisticated audience and Vanguard emphasizing fundamental ESG principles and personal values alignment.

The analysis presented in this work comes with a series of limitations discussed further down. Despite these limitations, the findings are important at a time when regulators, intergovernmental bodies and society at large question the definition of ESG. This chapter offers systematic descriptive evidence to help the debate around these questions.

2. DATA AND METHODOLOGY

The data used here is all public data gathered from the websites of Blackrock and Vanguard. This is information a retail customer willing to invest in ETFs would have access to. I focus only on ETFs containing equities and labelled as ESG by investment managers. For Vanguard, this is done by filtering for 'ESG' labelled funds on its fund list. For Blackrock I focus on any fund with ESG in the fund name.

The Blackrock website has a section titled 'Explore all sustainable funds' which lists over 3,000 investment vehicles. Looking only at ETFs with equities reduces the sample to around 2,000 products. Looking for only products with ESG in the title reduces the list to 82 ETFs. For each ETF, I searched within the energy category investments if any fossil fuel companies were listed. Some products only list

the top 10 companies that the ETF invests in. In such cases, I looked at the sectorial breakdown of the fund to see if it includes energy stocks. All the Blackrock
funds that did not break down the individual shareholdings had investments in
energy stock. These could include fossil fuel companies, but this is impossible for
the public or investors to know for sure.

For Vanguard, I went on a page titled 'All mutual funds & ETFs'. There,
Vanguard lists only nine funds as ESG. This is because Vanguard has less of
a focus on ESG products as a recent report shows (Morningstar, 2023). Out of
the nine, eight contain equity and are analysed here (the ninth is bonds only).
Vanguard does not offer a single page with all the equity holdings of its ETFs
in one place. Nor does it offer a search function to look into the different ETFs.
Therefore, I only focused on the 100 largest investments of each fund to see if
they were fossil-free. When information was available, I also checked if the funds
invested in energy. This is all detailed in the results in Table 7.1. The information
provided by Vanguard is less transparent, making it unlikely for retail investors to
know whether the ESG EFTs are fossil-free or not.

3. LIMITATIONS

This study has many limitations. Data issues for investment by Vanguard are discussed above. The study only considers fossil fuel companies, while other heavy
industry companies might also negatively impact the environment but are not
listed here. Another big limitation of the approach taken here is that the website might display different information depending on the jurisdiction where the
website visitor is based. This does, therefore, not offer an exhaustive view of the
investment offering of the two largest firms. The goal here is just to understand
whether ESG-labelled investment vehicles can contain fossil fuel assets.

Finally, this study is limited as it only focuses on funds that are labelled ESG
by their emitters. Blackrock, for example, also offers a broader terminology. It
has one 'Paris-aligned' fund that does not have fossil fuel assets. And other low-
carbon funds that do. These are not analysed here, and the emphasis is exclusively
on ESG as this has been the focus of the recent move by regulators, and it allows
for a homogenous analysis. But this all calls for further research.

4. RESULTS

Out of the eight Vanguard funds analysed, I found no evidence of fossil fuel investments. Note that Vanguard in general offers less ESG products than Blackrock,
explaining the low number of funds found. The result of no fossil investment
could in part be due to data limitations as for three of the eight funds, Vanguard
does not offer easily accessible investment information. Most of these funds with
data issues however list a very small percentage of investment in the energy sector
(less than 0.2%) so it is unlikely that they have large fossil fuel positions and are
likely fossil-free. Table 7.1 below lists all the Vanguard funds, their identification,

Table 7.1. Top 10 Largest Blackrock and Vanguard ESG ETFs and
Their Investment in Fossil Fuels.

Fund Manager (Ticker)	AUM in Millions	Fossil-Free?	Nb of Equity Positions Disclosed on Website
Blackrock (CBUC)	12,826	No	573
Blackrock (EDMU)	12,826	No	573
Blackrock (EEDS)	12,826	No	573
Blackrock (SASU)	5,680	No	575
Blackrock (SAUA)	5,680	No	575
Blackrock (SDUS)	5,680	No	575
Blackrock (EDM2)	3,996	No	1066
Blackrock (EEDM)	3,996	No	1066
Blackrock (EDMW)	3,811	No	1350
Blackrock (EEWD)	3,811	No	1350
Vanguard (VFTAX)	15,700	Yes[a]	473
Vanguard (ESGV)	6,700	Yes[a]	997
Vanguard (VSGX)	3,400	Yes[b]	1394
Vanguard (VESGX)	984	Yes	37
Vanguard (VEIGX)	984	Yes	37
Vanguard (VBPIX)	248	Yes	30
Vanguard (VEOAX)	50	Yes	23
Vanguard (VEOIX)	50	Yes	24

Note: [a]Fossil-free for the 100 largest positions (and only 0.2% of stocks in the Energy sector). [b]Fossil-free for the 100 largest positions. AUM is asset under management for Blackrock and fund total net assets for Vanguard. It shows the size of the fund in million dollars. Vanguard only has 7 ESG-labelled equity funds, Blackrock has 82 and this table lists the 10 largest.

and the top 10 largest Blackrock ESG funds (the rest of the Blackrock funds and the detailed analysis are available in the Supplementary materials).

Out of the 82 Blackrock funds, only seven are completely fossil-free. In other words, 9% of Blackrock ESG ETFs are fossil-free. Fifty explicitly list fossil fuel investments. For 25 funds, they only list the top 10 companies that they have invested in. While these top-10 positions are not fossil fuel companies, the funds do contain energy investment in their sectorial breakdown. So these either contain fossil fuel investments or otherwise make it impossible for investors to know whether they contain fossil fuel investments. The online supplementary material offers the detail of each fund, the date of access and the URL for replication and updating purposes.

4.1 Blackrock's Best-in-Class Approach

The findings show that only Blackrock ETFs have fossil fuel positions. The next question is which fossil fuel investments. To understand the composition of Blackrock's fossil fuel companies, I compare their investments against the list of the 200 largest publicly listed fossil fuel companies by reserves.

Doing this I find that Blackrock ESG funds do not appear to invest in coal companies with one potential exception. Japanese market-focused ESG funds from Blackrock do invest in Idemitsu Kosan Ltd. This company partly operates coal mines in Australia, though its core business remains in oil and gas. So, with this exception, Blackrock ESG funds are coal-free.

Looking at oil and gas investments, the 82 Blackrock funds own shares of 29 out of the 100 largest oil and gas companies. The detailed list is available in Appendix 1. This means that Blackrock most likely follows a best-in-class approach, investing only in roughly a third of the oil and gas companies that they judge are the 'best' for the environment.

Two large companies are missing from Blackrock's list, BP and ExxonMobil. And Chevron, another large fossil fuel company, is absent from the 44 largest ESG funds and only appears in smaller funds.

Blackrock offers some limited explanation of its ESG strategy. It affirms on its website 'avoiding issuers or business activities with certain environmental, social and/or governance characteristics'. But it is unclear what the characteristics are. The formulation as 'and/or' makes it impossible to know if fossil investments are chosen on E, S or G grounds or a combination of the three. From the list of included investments, it is not easy to guess what the criteria are. Gazprom is unlikely to have advanced ESG reporting and so would Aramco. BP is excluded when it is one of the companies with the largest investments in renewable energy among oil majors (even if the war in Ukraine and the following increase in oil prices have somewhat slowed down investments). While the goal of the paper is not to offer normative judgement on which companies should and should not be included, it still questions the lack of transparency of the fund managers. Because of the nature of ESG, it could well be that these companies have been chosen on social or governance criteria, not the E criteria for Environmental. Maybe, all these firms have a separate chairperson and CEO and therefore display good governance. Or maybe they have advanced gender policies which score high on social issues. But there are no clear ways for investors to know why BP is excluded and Gazprom included.

5. CONCLUSION AND POLICY IMPLICATIONS

Climate-conscious investors should be weary when buying products by large asset managers labelled ESG. Only 9% of Blackrock's ESG-labelled equity ETFs are fossil-free. Most ESG products sold by Blackrock contain fossil fuel companies such as Saudi Aramco, Gazprom or Shell. It is unclear from the information provided by the fund manager how the fossil fuel companies are chosen, but it is likely that Blackrock takes a best-in-class approach. Yet, they are not disclosing their criteria and might also be relying on an outside ESG rating agency. They do however not invest in coal. Vanguard offers less ESG products and is less transparent in its reporting. But based on the analysis in this work, none of the Vanguard ESG products contain fossil fuel companies.

Including fossil fuel companies in ESG-labelled funds does not currently breach any laws, but it clearly raises some ethical concerns. While selling a product containing meat as vegan would be illegal, selling an ESG product with some of the companies causing the most harm to the environment is still acceptable. This might change if regulators such as the SEC manage to pass new laws regulating these issues. The stake for policymakers will be to understand how best-in-class approaches should be regulated. Another important question for policymakers will be to put clear guidelines on whether the companies are included in a portfolio for their Environmental, Social or Governance impact (or all three criteria). Clearly showing that the E, S and G contribution of each asset is important as research by the OECD has shown that the E criteria is not used in a consistent manner by the different rating providers. Regulators, such as the SEC, should urge fund managers to offer more transparency on their asset selection criteria. All ESG funds should list any products that are not traditionally considered as ESG, such as tobacco, weapons or fossil fuel.

NOTE

1. https://www.ft.com/content/4a538e2c-d4bb-4099-8f15-a28d0fefcea2

ACKNOWLEDGMENT

For feedback and comments, I am grateful to Monica Algarra and Simon Hinrichsen.

REFERENCES

Barko, T., Cremers, M., & Renneboog, L. (2022). Shareholder engagement on environmental, social, and governance performance. *Journal of Business Ethics, 180*(2), 777–812. https://doi.org/10.1007/s10551-021-04850-z

Bédu, N., Granier, C., & Revelli, C. (2023). Asset management and sustainability. Critical perspectives and reform issues. In T. Lagoarde-Segot (Ed.), *Ecological money and finance: Exploring sustainable monetary and financial systems* (pp. 683–725). Springer International Publishing. https://doi.org/10.1007/978-3-031-14232-1_22

Beisenbina, M., Fabregat-Aibar, L., Barberà-Mariné, M.-G., & Sorrosal-Forradellas, M.-T. (2023). The burgeoning field of sustainable investment: Past, present and future. *Sustainable Development 31*(2), 649–667. https://doi.org/10.1002/sd.2422

Belinga, R., & Segrestin, B. (2023). Responsibility, ownership, and the role of shareholders. In T. Lagoarde-Segot (Ed.), *Ecological money and finance: Exploring sustainable monetary and financial systems* (pp. 485–509). Springer International Publishing. https://doi.org/10.1007/978-3-031-14232-1_15

Dimson, E., Marsh, P., & Staunton, M. (2020). Divergent ESG ratings. *The Journal of Portfolio Management, 47*(1), 75–87. https://doi.org/10.3905/jpm.2020.1.175

Dordi, T., Gehricke, S. A., Naef, A., & Weber, O. (2022). Ten financial actors can accelerate a transition away from fossil fuels. *Environmental Innovation and Societal Transitions, 44* (September), 60–78. https://doi.org/10.1016/j.eist.2022.05.006

Goodman, J., Louche, C., van Cranenburgh, K. C., & Arenas, D. (2014). Social shareholder engagement: The dynamics of voice and exit. *Journal of Business Ethics, 125*(2), 193–210. https://doi.org/10.1007/s10551-013-1890-0

In, S. Y., & Schumacher, K. (2021). Carbonwashing: ESG data greenwashing in a post-Paris world. In T. Heller & A. Seiger (Eds.), *Settling climate accounts: Navigating the road to net zero* (pp. 39–58). Springer International Publishing. https://doi.org/10.1007/978-3-030-83650-4_3

Kölbel, J. F., Heeb, F., Paetzold, F., & Busch, T. (2020). Can sustainable investing save the world? Reviewing the mechanisms of investor impact. *Organization & Environment*, *33*(4), 554–574. https://doi.org/10.1177/1086026620919202

Morningstar (2023). *How BlackRock, State Street and Vanguard ESG proxy votes were cast.* Morningstar, Inc. Report. https://www.morningstar.com/sustainable-investing/how-blackrock-state-street-vanguard-cast-their-esg-proxy-votes

Naef, A. (2024, March). The impossible love of fossil fuel companies for carbon taxes. *Ecological Economics 217*, 108045. https://doi.org/10.1016/j.ecolecon.2023.108045

Naef, A., & van't Klooster, J. (2022). Responsibility for emissions: The case of the Swiss National Bank's foreign exchange reserves and the Norwegian oil fund. *Banque de France Working Paper.* https://entreprises.banque-france.fr/sites/default/files/medias/documents/wp_872_0.pdf

OECD. (2022). ESG ratings and climate transition: An assessment of the alignment of E pillar scores and metrics. *OECD Business and Finance Policy Papers.* OECD Publishing. https://doi.org/10.1787/2fa21143-en

Reiser, D. B., & Tucker, A. (2019). Buyer beware: Variation and opacity in ESG and ESG index funds. *Cardozo Law Review*, *41*, 1921.

Rompotis, G. G. (2023). Do ESG ETFs 'Greenwash'? Evidence from the US Market. *The Journal of Impact and ESG Investing*, April. https://doi.org/10.3905/jesg.2023.1.070

Sharfman, B. S. (2020). The conflict between BlackRock's shareholder activism and ERISA's fiduciary duties. *Case Western Reserve Law Review*, *71*, 1241.

Tilba, A. (2022). Appearance or substance of stewardship and ESG reporting? The challenges of translating "commitment" into tangible outcomes. *Sustainability Accounting, Management and Policy Journal*, *13*(5), 1015–1032. https://doi.org/10.1108/SAMPJ-03-2021-0091

APPENDIX 1

Table A1. Which of the Largest 100 Oil and Gas
Companies Do Blackrock ESG Funds Invest in?

Included by Blackrock = 1 Not included = 0	100 Largest Oil and Gas	Size Ranking (1–100)
1	Saudi Aramco	1
1	Gazprom	2
1	Novatek	9
1	Total energies	10
1	Chevron	11
1	Shell	13
1	ENI	15
1	ConocoPhillips	17
1	Equinor	20
1	Inpex	21
1	EOG Resources	22
1	EQT	23
1	Antero Resources	30
1	Pioneer Natural Resources	31
1	Ovintiv	34
1	Repsol	36
1	Devon Energy	40
1	Hess	44
1	OMV	45
1	PTT Exploration and Production	46
1	Marathon Oil	49
1	ARC Resources	52
1	Santos	53
1	Aker BP	67
1	Energean	69
1	Galp Energia SPGS	72
1	ENEOS Holdings	78
1	Advantage Energy	81
1	NuVista Energy	98
0	Rosneft	3
0	PetroChina	4
0	BP	5
0	ExxonMobil	6
0	Gazprom Neft	7
0	Lukoil	8
0	Petrobras	12
0	Tatneft	14
0	Canadian Natural	16
0	CNOOC	18
0	ONGC	19
0	Oxy	24
0	Sinopec	25
0	Southwestern Energy	26
0	Bashneft	27
0	Coterra	28
0	Range Resources	29
0	Cenovus Energy	32
0	Ecopetrol	33

(Continued)

Table A1. (*Continued*)

Included by Blackrock = 1 Not included = 0	100 Largest Oil and Gas	Size Ranking (1–100)
0	Diamondback Energy	35
0	Suncor Energy	37
0	Continental Resources	38
0	Tourmaline Oil	39
0	Chesapeake Energy	41
0	CNX Resources	42
0	Woodside Energy	43
0	Imperial Oil	47
0	YPF	48
0	Comstock Resources	50
0	APA Corporation	51
0	PDC Energy	54
0	Var Energi	55
0	SK Innovation	56
0	Murphy Oil	57
0	BHP	58
0	Sasol	59
0	National Fuel Gas	60
0	Gulfport Energy	61
0	Birchcliff Energy	62
0	California Resources	63
0	Whitecap Resources	64
0	Callon Petroleum	65
0	SM Energy	66
0	PGNiG	68
0	Mitsui	70
0	Peyto	71
0	Crescent Point Energy	73
0	MEG Energy	74
0	Origin Energy	75
0	Civitas Resources	76
0	Oil India	77
0	Matador Resources	79
0	Enerplus	80
0	Kosmos Energy	82
0	Reliance Industries	83
0	Permian Resources	84
0	Laredo Petroleum	85
0	Northern Oil & Gas	86
0	Pakistan Petroleum	87
0	JAPEX	88
0	Vermilion Energy	89
0	Chord Energy Corporation	90
0	MOL	91
0	Harbour Energy	92
0	Great Eastern Energy	93
0	Ranger Oil	94
0	Seplat Energy	95
0	Medco Energi	96
0	Paramount Resources	97
0	Baytex	99
0	PetroRio	100

CHAPTER 8

CLIMATE RISKS, SUSTAINABLE FINANCE, AND GREEN GROWTH: THE EVOLUTION OF FINTECH

Hai Hong Trinh[*a], Ilham Haouas[b] and Tien Thi Thuy Tran[a]

[a]Massey University, New Zealand
[b]Abu Dhabi University, United Arab Emirates

ABSTRACT

This study provides a bibliometric analysis of business literature on the inter-links of fintech, climate risks, and sustainable finance. Fintech growth promotes national environmental efficiency and green finance by decreasing carbon intensity toward the net-zero target. National fintech growth moderates the impact of environmental, social, and governance investment on bank efficiency. Fintech mitigates the loan bankruptcy risk imposed by climate risks with strict mortgage lending decisions due to climate concerns. Fintech applications in banking systems optimize financing costs and increase the accessibility of money for firms, decreasing corporate greenwashing behaviors and promoting green innovation. The existing literature leaves room for future studies on fintech to promote climate finance with important policies for climate action toward Sustainable Development Goals.

*Corresponding author: **Hai Hong Trinh** (Ph.D. Finance). The author is affiliated with the School of Economics and Finance, Massey University, 4442 New Zealand, and the British Accounting and Finance Association (BAFA-IPSIG), United Kingdom. For queries, please address them directly to: h.h.trinh@massey.ac.nz; hai.hong.trinh.confin@gmail.com; trinhhonghai95@gmail.com. ORCID record: https://orcid.org/0000-0003-0209-7259

Responsible Firms: CSR, ESG, and Global Sustainability
International Finance Review, Volume 23, 147–160
Copyright © 2025 by Hai Hong Trinh, Ilham Haouas and Tien Thi Thuy Tran
Published under exclusive licence by Emerald Publishing Limited
ISSN: 1569-3767/doi:10.1108/S1569-376720240000023008

Keywords: Fintech; climate risks; sustainable finance; green finance; climate finance

JEL codes: G1; G2; G3; F3

1. INTRODUCTION

Climate risks have imposed ultimate challenges on the stability of financial institutions and markets in the global economy (Trinh, 2023). Carbon dioxide concentration is the long-lasting root of economic conditions and policy uncertainty due to human-made processes in the market-based economy (Trinh, 2024). To cope with climate risks, technological innovations play diverse critical roles in promoting green growth (Trinh, 2021; Trinh et al., 2023). It is not an exceptional case for Fintech, an abbreviation for financial technology. Regarding McKinsey (2024), fintech refers to organizations that rely primarily on technology to perform essential financial services operations, such as storing, saving, borrowing, investing, moving, paying, and protecting money. Most fintech companies were founded after 2000, have raised funds since 2010, and have not yet attained maturity (McKinsey, 2024). Given the context, how has fintech contributed to climate change mitigation and sustainable finance for green growth? To what extent? So, what next? Based on the Scopus database (Scopus, 2024), this study answers such questions by analyzing the bibliometric literature in major business subjects, including business, management, and accounting; and economics, econometrics, and finance. Drawing the bibliometric data from Scopus shown in Fig. 8.1, Fintech studies started with a few articles in 2017 and have increased significantly, with an aggregate total of over 400 journal articles published as of 2023.

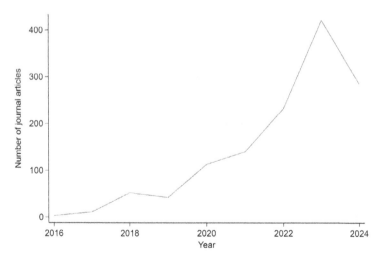

Fig. 8.1.   Number of Fintech-related articles. Authors' work.

Based on the journal quality list by **ABDC** (2024), we selectively present high-regarded journals that have published fintech-related studies for insightful but also concise discussions in Sub-sections 2 and 3. The bibliometric analysis shows that the applications of Fintech are favorable to the low-carbon transition of the economy by decreasing carbon intensity and overall greenhouse gas (GHG) emissions (Cheng et al., 2023; Pee & Pan, 2022; Tao et al., 2022), promoting green finance, and increasing carbon efficiency (Teng & Shen, 2023; Xu et al., 2023). For strictly mortgage lending decisions due to climate concerns (e.g., temperature anomalies and sea-level rise), Fintech helps lenders partially fill the climate-induced gap between the number and amount of approved loans and demanded mortgage lending applications (Duan & Li, 2024), with a higher loan default risk to farmers in particular (Gao et al., 2023). Fintech innovation facilitates corporate green transition (Wu et al., 2024), and digital enterprise supports low-carbon underdevelopment (Long et al., 2024), with its spillover effects documented by the literature (Abakah et al., 2023; Goodell et al., 2022; Huynh et al., 2020; Le et al., 2021; Tiwari et al., 2023).

The impacts of fintech on national green growth and environmental efficiency are affirmed but also divergent across regional economies (Coffie & Hongjiang, 2023; Muhammad et al., 2022; Zhou et al., 2022). Fintech adoption with rankings and green certificates drives firm value (Merello et al., 2022). A nation's money accessibility plays a crucial role in establishing the connection between fintech adoption, corporate environmental, social, and governance (ESG) incentives, and financial literacy (Ding et al., 2024), facilitating higher well-engaged business ESG standards and consequently attracting more attention from stakeholders to environmentally friendly firms. With better accessibility to finance, Fintech mitigates corporate tax avoidance specifically for firms located in lower Fintech-adopted regions and consequently fosters corporate green innovation (Jiang et al., 2024; Li et al., 2023, 2024) with lower financing costs and optimal expected returns (Atayah et al., 2024; Huang & Ma, 2024). Not limited to corporate green innovation and national environmental efficiency, fintech growth also contributes to banking systems as a result of banks' digital transformation and sizable green lending with fintech mergers and acquisitions (M&A) in certain conditions (Shang & Niu, 2023). Fintech structurally moderates the effects of ESG investment on bank efficiency (e.g., state-owned banks) and mitigates corporate greenwashing practices (Cao et al., 2024; Liu & Li, 2024; Xie et al., 2023), transforming the ways customers perceive digital banking services (Saif et al., 2024). With crowdfunding as a new avenue for entrepreneurs to access financial financing, green fintech innovation is crucial to crowdfunding success (Cumming et al., 2024; Tang et al., 2024).

The evolution of Fintech for green transition with evident roles in mitigating climate risks has been documented for a few markets like China (Cao et al., 2024; Cheng et al., 2023; Ding et al., 2024; Jiang et al., 2024; Long et al., 2024; Shang & Niu, 2023; Wu et al., 2024; Xie et al., 2023; Zhou et al., 2022), the United States (Duan & Li, 2024), and OECD economies (Cumming et al., 2024). Hence, the evolutionary adoption of fintech leaves enormous gaps for future studies on the rest of the world with uneven income distribution (Acemoglu & Ventura, 2002;

Jones, 1997). The heterogeneity of financial development, central banks, political risks, and economic policies are critical factors (Khan et al., 2023; Nghiem et al., 2023; Ngo et al., 2022; Phung et al., 2023; Trinh et al., 2022; Vo & Trinh, 2023), promoting the development of Fintech for green finance toward a net-zero target. The remaining parts of the study are structured as follows: Section 2 discusses fintech and climate risks. Section 3 discusses the interlinks between fintech and sustainable finance. Section 4 concludes the main implications and future directions.

2. FINTECH AND CLIMATE RISKS

Searching for the keywords "fintech" and "climate" or "carbon".[1] We selectively report the highly ranked published articles in the ABDC journal list. The interlinks between fintech and climate change mitigation are documented in the literature in our concise discussions as delineated in Table 8.1.

Cryptocurrency mining is gaining traction in the community, and fintech development helps economies achieve the low-energy transition (Tao et al., 2022). The study shows that fintech development minimizes GHG emissions. Policymakers

Table 8.1.   Fintech, climate change, and carbon risks.

Title	Year	Source title
Can Fintech development pave the way for a transition toward low-carbon economy: A global perspective	2022	Technological Forecasting and Social Change
Configuring the digital farmer: A nudge world in the making?	2021	Economy and Society
How does fintech influence carbon emissions: Evidence from China's prefecture-level cities	2023	International Review of Financial Analysis
Climate-intelligent cities and resilient urbanization: Challenges and opportunities for information research	2022	International Journal of Information Management
Financial technology stocks, green financial assets, and energy markets: A quantile causality and dependence analysis	2023	Energy Economics
Analysis of the carbon emission reduction effect of Fintech and the transmission channel of green finance	2023	Finance Research Letters
How Fintech and effective governance derive the greener energy transition: Evidence from panel-corrected standard errors approach	2023	Energy Economics
The impact of fintech on carbon efficiency: Evidence from Chinese cities	2023	Journal of Cleaner Production
Climate change concerns and mortgage lending	2024	Journal of Empirical Finance
Severe weather and peer-to-peer farmers' loan default predictions: Evidence from machine learning analysis	2023	Finance Research Letters
The color of FinTech: FinTech and corporate green transformation in China	2024	International Review of Financial Analysis
The effects of enterprise digital transformation on low-carbon urban development: Empirical evidence from China	2024	Technological Forecasting and Social Change

Note: The bibliometric data extracted by the corresponding author from Scopus as of 2024-04-25, using the licensed account offered by Massey University, Private Bag 11 222 Palmerston North, 4442, New Zealand.

should consider the costs and advantages of technological advancement. Brooks (2021) investigates the "digital farmer" ensemble as an instructive example of the behavioral turn in international development, in which smallholder farmers are digitally guided toward market-inclusion behaviors. Central to these interventions are digital platforms that act as human technologies, creating new types of market subjects that can be integrated into value chains and larger capital and data circuits. As such, they serve as both a continuation of the "long" Green Revolution and a departure point. The narrowing of options built into their design is expected to degrade key skilling processes in agricultural practice while weakening the social links of mutuality and reciprocity that underpin such processes, increasing vulnerability to climatic and market risks.

Cheng et al. (2023) use panel data from 253 prefecture-level cities in China from 2011 to 2019 to study the impact of fintech development on carbon emissions. The study shows that fintech significantly reduces carbon emissions, and this conclusion remains true even after accounting for potential endogeneity, the impact of resource endowment, alternative carbon emission measures, removing the impact of low-carbon pilot city policies, and winnowing treatment. The primary ways in which fintech influences carbon emissions are through industry structure, financial limitations, and green technology innovation. Fintech has a good impact on the actual economy, and there is optimism about its future expansion. Climate-first and climate-compatible cities are key to achieving a zero-carbon future (Pee & Pan, 2022). Resilience to both climatic and energy shocks is required for urban development. Information research can help optimize energy and resources. The climate-neutral digital economy and digital citizen involvement are also of interest. All major areas of information study can help with climate action.

Fintech and environmentally friendly financial instruments have been widely used for Industry 4.0 development and the aggressive transition to a low-carbon economy for their critical roles in restoring investor confidence in the financial services sector following the 2008 global financial crisis (Tiwari et al., 2023). They assist investors in diversifying their portfolios to hedge risks, maximize returns, and mitigate the detrimental effects of climate change. In the near term, fintech is extremely directionally predictable in all markets except green bonds in the lower quantile, and the predictability of all lag lengths is negative (Tiwari et al., 2023). Using provincial panel data from 2011 to 2020, this research by Xu et al. (2023) investigates the impact of fintech development on carbon emission intensity and the green finance transmission channel in China. Fintech development greatly reduces carbon emissions intensity. For the mechanism analysis of green finance as a transmission channel, Fintech reduces carbon emissions by encouraging the development of green financing. Fintech has a greater impact on higher quantiles of carbon emission intensity. Heterogeneity research reveals that the influence of Fintech on carbon emission reduction varies across the regions (e.g., Eastern, Central, and Western) in China.

Teng and Shen (2023) investigate the carbon efficiency and fintech of 276 Chinese cities from 2006 to 2019. Fintech has the potential to directly reduce carbon emissions. Fintech indirectly improves carbon efficiency by increasing government funding for science or green innovation. The impact of fintech on carbon efficiency is varied. Fintech can produce beneficial geographical spillover effects on urban carbon efficiency. Duan and Li (2024) investigate how loan officers' attitudes about climate change influence their mortgage lending decisions. The study found that extremely high local temperatures increase awareness of and belief in climate change in a place. During unusually warm weather, loan officers accept fewer mortgage applications and originate fewer loans. This effect is larger in counties with a high risk of sea-level rise, during periods of increased public awareness of climate change, and for loans issued by small lenders. The negative correlation between temperature and approval rate cannot be entirely explained by changes in local economic conditions, mortgage credit demand, or declining loan application quality. When the local temperature rises unusually, fintech lenders fill a portion of the demand gap created by traditional lenders.

Climate change affects farmers' loan default risk because extreme weather conditions reduce farmland productivity, farmers' income, and their ability to repay loans (Gao et al., 2023). Using farmers' loan data extracted from Lending Club and severe weather data from the United States, the three machine learning algorithms, including Artificial Neural Networks (ANNs), Gradient Boosting Trees, and Random Forest, are, respectively, successful at loan default predictions with accuracies of 70%, 74%, and 81%, according to Gao et al. (2023). The Shapley Additive Explanations results also show that severe weather and other explanatory variables are economically relevant.

Wu et al. (2024) use machine learning and text analysis approaches to create two major metrics: FinTech and corporate green transformation. Using data from Chinese listed enterprises from 2011 to 2020, the authors conclude that FinTech fosters corporate green transformation by reducing information asymmetry, relieving financial limitations, and enhancing risk-taking. The impact of FinTech on corporate green transformation is particularly pronounced in high-tech, non-state-owned, and polluting enterprises. Both intra- and inter-sector peer effects contribute to company green transformation. Enterprise digital transformation substantially promotes low-carbon urban development (Long et al., 2024). The authors document that enterprise digital transformation fosters low-carbon urban development through three key mechanisms: stimulating green technology innovation, expanding the size of green investment, and pushing industrial structure transformation. The impact of company digital transformation on low-carbon urban development is bolstered by government environmental concerns, environmental subsidies, and fintech innovation.

3. FINTECH AND SUSTAINABLE FINANCE

We search for the keywords "fintech" and "esg," or "csr," "green," and "sustainability."[2] We selectively present the published articles linking fintech with sustainable finance in Table 8.2.

For national green growth, Zhou et al. (2022) develop a comprehensive index to assess the green growth of the regional economy. Using Chinese

Table 8.2.   Fintech and sustainable finance

Title	Year	Source title
The impact of fintech innovation on green growth in China: Mediating effect of green finance	2022	Ecological Economics
Time and frequency domain connectedness and spill-over among fintech, green bonds and cryptocurrencies in the age of the fourth industrial revolution	2021	Technological Forecasting and Social Change
Diversification in the age of the 4th industrial revolution: The role of artificial intelligence, green bonds and cryptocurrencies	2020	Technological Forecasting and Social Change
Cooperative financial institutions: A review of the literature	2020	International Review of Financial Analysis
The fourth industrial revolution and environmental efficiency: The role of fintech industry	2022	Journal of Cleaner Production
Is the sustainability profile of FinTech companies a key driver of their value?	2022	Technological Forecasting and Social Change
Time and frequency connectedness of green equity indices: Uncovering a socially important link to Bitcoin	2022	International Review of Financial Analysis
Dynamic effect of Bitcoin, fintech and artificial intelligence stocks on eco-friendly assets, Islamic stocks and conventional financial markets: Another look using quantile-based approaches	2023	Technological Forecasting and Social Change
Do fintech adoption and financial literacy improve corporate sustainability performance? The mediating role of access to finance	2023	Journal of Cleaner Production
FinTech market development and financial inclusion in Ghana: The role of heterogeneous actors	2023	Technological Forecasting and Social Change
When do M&As with Fintech Firms Benefit Traditional Banks?	2024	British Journal of Management
Does fintech inhibit corporate greenwashing behavior? Evidence from China	2023	Finance Research Letters
ESG and crowdfunding platforms	2024	Journal of Business Venturing
FinTech and corporate green innovation: An external attention perspective	2023	Finance Research Letters
Initial coin offerings and ESG: Allies or enemies?	2023	Finance Research Letters
Sustainability, market performance and FinTech firms	2024	Meditari Accountancy Research
Does the digital transformation of banks affect green credit?	2023	Finance Research Letters
Fintech business and corporate social responsibility practices	2024	Emerging Markets Review
How does fintech prompt corporations toward ESG sustainable development? Evidence from China	2024	Energy Economics
Does ESG performance affect corporate tax avoidance? Evidence from China	2024	Finance Research Letters
Analyzing the determinant factors of the sustainability profile of Fintech and Insurtech companies	2023	Journal of Cleaner Production
ESG investment and bank efficiency: Evidence from China	2024	Energy Economics
The impact of bank fintech on ESG greenwashing	2024	Finance Research Letters

(Continued)

Table 8.2.   (*Continued*)

Title	Year	Source title
Substantive green innovation or symbolic green innovation: The impact of fintech on corporate green innovation	2024	Finance Research Letters
Does green matter for crowdfunding? International evidence	2024	Journal of International Financial Markets, Institutions and Money
The effects of enterprise digital transformation on low-carbon urban development: Empirical evidence from China	2024	Technological Forecasting and Social Change
Beyond conventions: Unraveling perceived value's role in shaping digital-only banks' adoption	2024	Technological Forecasting and Social Change

Note: The bibliometric data extracted by the corresponding author from Scopus as of 2024-04-25, using the licensed account offered by Massey University, Private Bag 11 222 Palmerston North, 4442, New Zealand.

province panel data from 2011 to 2018, the authors demonstrate that fintech innovation and green finance greatly support green economic growth. Fintech and green finance's impact on green growth varies by area. Fintech innovation primarily aids green economic growth by boosting green finance. The environmental efficiency of EU countries has improved over time (Muhammad et al., 2022). As signs of the fourth industrial revolution, the fintech and e-commerce industries have a positive impact and enhance environmental efficiency, whereas high-tech business has a negative impact. Economic growth and green finance investments improve environmental efficiency, whereas industrialization and R&D degrade it. Mobile phones, telcos, mobile money agents, customers, and traditional banks are the key actors in the market and are useful in the development of Ghana's fintech market and financial inclusion (Coffie & Hongjiang, 2023).

The connectedness among fintech and several markets has been documented in the literature. Le et al. (2021) investigate the time- and frequency-domain connectedness and spillover of fintech, green bonds, and cryptocurrencies. The authors argue that portfolios made up of assets have a high tail dependency and a higher short-term volatility transmission. Gold and oil, as well as the current-age asset, green bonds, prove to be effective hedges when compared to other assets. Fintech and general equity indices are ineffective hedging instruments. Huynh et al. (2020) emphasize the importance of AI and robotics stocks, green bonds, and Bitcoin for portfolio diversification. Portfolios containing these assets display high tail dependency. In the short term, volatility transmission is more prevalent. Bitcoin and gold are valuable assets for hedging, and gold may serve as a safe haven. NASDAQ AI and conventional stock indices are not suitable hedging tools for each other.

Furthermore, McKillop et al. (2020) discuss the benefits (and limitations) of FinTech as well as the role of financial cooperatives in the real economy, notably during times of crisis. Abakah et al. (2023) discover the causal asymmetry across quantiles and strong variability between markets regarding the distributional predictability of fintech, Bitcoin, and AI in relation to traditional markets, Islamic equities, renewable energy companies, and sustainable investments. The returns of fintech, Bitcoin, AI, and other markets indicate that Islamic stocks are a strong hedge against Bitcoin. The S&P Treasury Bond and S&P Green Bond are both excellent hedges for fintech stocks, while S&P Global Clean Energy is an excellent long-term hedge for AI stocks. Green indices are significantly connected with global stock market performance, as well as results in emerging markets, commodities markets, and FinTech (Goodell et al., 2022). The authors suggest that Bitcoin investors can use green funds to mitigate negative environmental effects.

For firm-level studies, rankings and green certificates drive the value of fintech firms, and sustainability efforts decline as market capitalization rises, posing an agency dilemma (Merello et al., 2022). Fintech adoption improves organizations' environmental and social sustainability (Siddik et al., 2023). Financial literacy improves an organization's economic sustainability. Access to money serves as a bridge between fintech adoption, financial literacy, and sustainable performance. Fintech growth enhances corporate ESG initiatives (Ding et al., 2024). Fintech growth improves business ESG standards by easing financial limitations. Fintech development attracts stakeholders' attention, motivating businesses to strategically engage in ESG activities.

Also, ESG performance considerably reduces the amount of company tax avoidance (Jiang et al., 2024). ESG performance discourages business tax avoidance by reducing finance restrictions, boosting internal control quality, and increasing external monitoring. ESG performance has a greater impact on tax avoidance in enterprises located in underdeveloped FinTech regions, as well as in firms with higher agency charges and poorer quality audits. Fintech company size has a beneficial impact on their sustainability profile (Merello et al., 2023). Fintech companies are more likely than insurance tech companies to perform responsibly and sustainably. The most profitable and least-indebted fintech companies exhibit more sustainable behavior. Older enterprises have a worse sustainability profile, notably in terms of the SDGs. The most important ESG factors are CSR reporting and the promotion of volunteerism. The growth of FinTech greatly encourages green corporate innovation (Li et al., 2023).

The influence of FinTech on boosting corporate green innovation is moderated by outside attention. The moderating effect of external attention is influenced by the corporate ownership structure and ESG performance. Fintech businesses provide a good contribution to firm CSR activities (Li et al., 2024). Political contacts, lower agency expenses, and internal control all help to increase the influence. Underlying aspects include bank loans, the internal capital market, public scrutiny, and strategic disparities. Fintech firms also reduce corporate social responsibility behavior. There is a direct correlation between stock performance and the Bloomberg ESG disclosure index, which makes it a reliable estimate of sustainability (Atayah et al., 2024). Furthermore, the results of this study indicate that, in terms of sustainability and stock performance, non-FinTech companies dominate FinTech companies. Stakeholder theory contends that more ESG disclosure will lessen the agency problem and safeguard the interests of shareholders. The results of this study corroborate this notion. Huang and Ma (2024) investigate the major enhancement of fintech in corporate green innovation from the standpoint of innovation motivation. Fintech can encourage corporate green innovation and is better suited for substantial green innovation. Fintech promotes green business innovation by lowering costs and improving expected returns.

For banking studies, Collevecchio et al. (2024) advance the scientific understanding of M&A contingency factors and, more broadly, open innovation in the context of fintech and banks. Furthermore, we provide early recommendations to managers and regulators on the effects of fintech M&A on traditional banks, demonstrating that they can be helpful under certain conditions. Banks' digital transformation improves the green credit scale (Shang & Niu, 2023). A higher level of bank management digitization is more beneficial to the expansion of green credit. Exogenous fintech and industry competitiveness drive banks' digital transformation, increasing the size of green lending. The enabling impact is particularly visible in the presence of state-owned banks, large banks, loose monetary policy, and strict financial supervision. Investing more in ESG increases bank efficiency (Cao et al., 2024). The impact of ESG investment on bank efficiency varies structurally depending on fintech moderation. The enabling effect of ESG investments is especially noticeable at state-owned banks. Also, banking fintech mitigates ESG greenwashing (Liu & Li, 2024). The effect is particularly evident in very contaminated industries and is more evident in non-state-owned companies. Fintech advancements are transforming how customers perceive value (Saif et al., 2024). The key motivator for digital bank adoption is the desire to maximize value. Customers' perceptions of value influence their willingness to adopt digital banking.

For the additional features of Fintech, Xie et al. (2023) investigate Fintech's impact on business greenwashing behavior as well as the mediating function of financial limitations. The study found that financial technology greatly reduces business greenwashing behavior and that financial limitations amplify this inhibitory effect. The findings have practical significance for preventing corporate greenwashing and fostering the high-quality development of corporate green ecological civilization. Cumming et al. (2024) hypothesize that ESG goals help crowdfunding platforms attract more investors and so survive longer. Using data from 508 security-based platforms formed in the 38 OECD nations between 2007 and 2020, the authors show that platforms with greater degrees of ESG selection criteria are more probable to survive over time. ESG standards are especially important for platforms that operate in nations with shorter power distances. When it comes to ESG, governance is the most important component of the three, but environmental requirements have grown in importance for platform survival in the past few years. As a disruptive force in fintech and crowdfunding developed as a new avenue for entrepreneurs to access financial financing, Tang et al. (2024) investigated the impact of the new variable "green" on crowdfunding success. This study examines the effects of COVID-19 and green on crowdfunding success. The influence of green on crowdfunding success varies across industrialized and underdeveloped countries. Green elements, along with other aspects, contribute to the success of crowdfunding.

In the FinTech industry, initial coin offerings, or ICOs, have drawn a lot of attention as a substitute for traditional financing methods for creative and avant-garde business concepts (Bitetto & Cerchiello, 2023). The authors attest to the connection between ESG and ICO success. The broad focus on sustainability-related issues appears to favor fundraising initiatives. Enterprise digital transformation substantially promotes low-carbon urban development (Long et al., 2024). Enterprise digital transformation fosters low-carbon urban development through three key mechanisms: stimulating green technology innovation, expanding the size of green investment, and pushing industrial structure transformation. The impact of company digital transformation on low-carbon growth in cities is bolstered by government environmental concerns, environmental subsidies, and fintech innovation.

4. POLICIES AND DIRECTIONS

Policies are the root of Fintech development: How do policy enablers design an adaptive framework for green Fintech adoption in the era of climate change? When extreme climate events become more frequent and severe all over the world, future studies are needed to investigate the roles of fintech in banking services for green finance. Given the impacts of climate risks on lending activities, the role of green fintech is specifically crucial to countries with a higher vulnerability to climate risks.[3] Furthermore, further works need to investigate the ways Fintech adoption would support financial resources and instruments for climate action such as multilateral funds, market-based and concessional loans from financial institutions, sovereign green bonds issued by national governments, and resources mobilized through carbon trading and carbon taxes. While investments in climate action can yield results that far outweigh the initial costs and a significant funding gap exists to advance the green transition and improve resilience in developing countries, future research may look into the roles of fintech in circulating international financial flows for climate change mitigation. To restrict global warming to 2°C or less and meet the Paris Agreement targets, the world must raise climate money at least threefold.[4]

NOTES

1. TITLE-ABS-KEY (fintech) AND TITLE-ABS-KEY (climate) OR TITLE-ABS-KEY (carbon)))) AND (LLIMIT-TO (SUBJAREA, "ECON") OR (LIMIT-TO (SUBJAREA, "BUSI") AND (LIMIT-TO (SRCTYPE, "j")) AND (LIMIT-TO (LANGUAGE, "English") AND (LIMIT-TO (DOCTYPE, "ar"))

2. (TITLE-ABS-KEY (fintech) AND TITLE-ABS-KEY (esg) OR TITLE-ABS-KEY (csr) OR TITLE-ABS-KEY (green) OR TITLE-ABS-KEY (sustainability)) AND (LLIMIT-TO (DOCTYPE, "ar") AND (LLIMIT-TO (SUBJAREA, "ECON") OR (LIMIT-TO (SUBJAREA, "BUSI") AND (LLIMIT-TO (SRCTYPE, "j")

3. Page 10 at Policy responses to fintech: a cross-country overview (bis.org)

4. What is climate finance and why do we need more of it? | Climate Promise (undp.org)

ACKNOWLEDGMENTS

We would like to thank Jongmoo Jay Choi, Laura H. Carnell, Professor Emeritus of Finance and International Business (Temple University, US, jjchoi@temple. edu), and Founding Editor, International Finance Review (Emerald, annual) for the invitation for our contribution to the edited book on "Responsible Firms: CSR, ESG, and Sustainability," International Finance Review (IFR), Volume 23, co-edited with Jimi Kim (University of New South Wales, Australia, jimi.kim@ unsw.edu.au).

REFERENCES

Abakah, E. J. A., Tiwari, A. K., Ghosh, S., & Doğan, B. (2023). Dynamic effect of Bitcoin, fintech and artificial intelligence stocks on eco-friendly assets, Islamic stocks and conventional financial markets: Another look using quantile-based approaches. *Technological Forecasting and Social Change, 192*, 122566. https://doi.org/10.1016/j.techfore.2023.122566

ABDC (2024). *ABDC Journal Quality List*. https://abdc.edu.au/abdc-journal-quality-list/

Acemoglu, D., & Ventura, J. (2002). The world income distribution*. *The Quarterly Journal of Economics, 117*(2), 659–694. https://doi.org/10.1162/003355302753650355

Atayah, O. F., Najaf, K., Ali, M. H., & Marashdeh, H. (2024). Sustainability, market performance and FinTech firms. *Meditari Accountancy Research, 32*(2), 317–345. https://doi.org/10.1108/MEDAR-08-2021-1405

Bitetto, A., & Cerchiello, P. (2023). Initial coin offerings and ESG: Allies or enemies? *Finance Research Letters, 57*, 104227. https://doi.org/10.1016/j.frl.2023.104227

Brooks, S. (2021). Configuring the digital farmer: A nudge world in the making? *Economy and Society, 50*(3), 374–396. https://doi.org/10.1080/03085147.2021.1876984

Cao, Q., Zhu, T., & Yu, W. (2024). ESG investment and bank efficiency: Evidence from China. *Energy Economics, 133*, 107516. https://doi.org/10.1016/j.eneco.2024.107516

Cheng, X., Yao, D., Qian, Y., Wang, B., & Zhang, D. (2023). How does fintech influence carbon emissions: Evidence from China's prefecture-level cities. *International Review of Financial Analysis, 87*, 102655. https://doi.org/10.1016/j.irfa.2023.102655

Coffie, C. P. K., & Hongjiang, Z. (2023). FinTech market development and financial inclusion in Ghana: The role of heterogeneous actors. *Technological Forecasting and Social Change, 186*, 122127. https://doi.org/10.1016/j.techfore.2022.122127

Collevecchio, F., Cappa, F., Peruffo, E., & Oriani, R. (2024). When do M&As with Fintech Firms Benefit Traditional Banks? *British Journal of Management, 35*(1), 192-209. https://doi.org/10.1111/1467-8551.12701

Cumming, D., Meoli, M., Rossi, A., & Vismara, S. (2024). ESG and crowdfunding platforms. *Journal of Business Venturing, 39*(1), 106362. https://doi.org/10.1016/j.jbusvent.2023.106362

Ding, J., Li, L., & Zhao, J. (2024). How does fintech prompt corporations toward ESG sustainable development? Evidence from China. *Energy Economics, 131*, 107387. https://doi.org/10.1016/j.eneco.2024.107387

Duan, T., & Li, F. W. (2024). Climate change concerns and mortgage lending. *Journal of Empirical Finance, 75*, 101445. https://doi.org/10.1016/j.jempfin.2023.101445

Gao, W., Ju, M., & Yang, T. (2023). Severe weather and peer-to-peer farmers' loan default predictions: Evidence from machine learning analysis. *Finance Research Letters, 58*, 104287. https://doi.org/10.1016/j.frl.2023.104287

Goodell, J. W., Corbet, S., Yadav, M. P., Kumar, S., Sharma, S., & Malik, K. (2022). Time and frequency connectedness of green equity indices: Uncovering a socially important link to Bitcoin. *International Review of Financial Analysis, 84*, 102379. https://doi.org/10.1016/j.irfa.2022.102379

Huang, J., & Ma, L. (2024). Substantive green innovation or symbolic green innovation: The impact of fintech on corporate green innovation. *Finance Research Letters, 63*, 105265. https://doi.org/10.1016/j.frl.2024.105265

Huynh, T. L. D., Hille, E., & Nasir, M. A. (2020). Diversification in the age of the 4th industrial revolution: The role of artificial intelligence, green bonds and cryptocurrencies. *Technological Forecasting and Social Change, 159*, 120188. https://doi.org/10.1016/j.techfore.2020.120188

Jiang, H., Hu, W., & Jiang, P. (2024). Does ESG performance affect corporate tax avoidance? Evidence from China. *Finance Research Letters, 61*, 105056. https://doi.org/10.1016/j.frl.2024.105056

Jones, C. I. (1997). On the Evolution of the World Income Distribution. *Journal of Economic Perspectives, 11*(3), 19–36. https://doi.org/10.1257/jep.11.3.19

Khan, Z., Haouas, I., Trinh, H. H., Badeeb, R. A., & Zhang, C. (2023). Financial inclusion and energy poverty nexus in the era of globalization: Role of composite risk index and energy investment in emerging economies. *Renewable Energy, 204*, 382-399. https://doi.org/10.1016/j.renene.2022.12.122

Le, T. N. L., Abakah, E. J. A., & Tiwari, A. K. (2021). Time and frequency domain connectedness and spill-over among fintech, green bonds and cryptocurrencies in the age of the fourth industrial revolution. *Technological Forecasting and Social Change, 162*, 120382. https://doi.org/10.1016/j.techfore.2020.120382

Li, B., Du, J., Yao, T., & Wang, Q. (2023). FinTech and corporate green innovation: An external attention perspective. *Finance Research Letters, 58*, 104661. https://doi.org/10.1016/j.frl.2023.104661

Li, B., Guo, F., Xu, L., & Meng, S. (2024). Fintech business and corporate social responsibility practices. *Emerging Markets Review, 59*, 101105. https://doi.org/10.1016/j.ememar.2023.101105

Liu, Z., & Li, X. (2024). The impact of bank fintech on ESG greenwashing. *Finance Research Letters, 62*, 105199. https://doi.org/10.1016/j.frl.2024.105199

Long, Y., Liu, L., & Yang, B. (2024). The effects of enterprise digital transformation on low-carbon urban development: Empirical evidence from China. *Technological Forecasting and Social Change, 201*, 123259. https://doi.org/10.1016/j.techfore.2024.123259

McKillop, D., French, D., Quinn, B., Sobiech, A. L., & Wilson, J. O. S. (2020). Cooperative financial institutions: A review of the literature. *International Review of Financial Analysis, 71*, 101520. https://doi.org/10.1016/j.irfa.2020.101520

McKinsey. (2024). *What is fintech?*

Merello, P., Barbera, A., & De la Poza, E. (2023). Analysing the determinant factors of the sustainability profile of Fintech and Insurtech companies. *Journal of Cleaner Production, 421*, 138437. https://doi.org/10.1016/j.jclepro.2023.138437

Merello, P., Barberá, A., & De la Poza, E. (2022). Is the sustainability profile of FinTech companies a key driver of their value? *Technological Forecasting and Social Change, 174*, 121290. https://doi.org/10.1016/j.techfore.2021.121290

Muhammad, S., Pan, Y., Magazzino, C., Luo, Y., & Waqas, M. (2022). The fourth industrial revolution and environmental efficiency: The role of fintech industry. *Journal of Cleaner Production, 381*, 135196. https://doi.org/10.1016/j.jclepro.2022.135196

Nghiem, X.-H., Trinh, H. H., & Khan, I. U. (2023). Can Central Banks go green? The interaction between monetary policy and climate change. In *Handbook of environmental and green finance* (Vol. 11, pp. 275–294). World Scientific (Europe). https://doi.org/10.1142/9781800614451_0009

Ngo, T., Trinh, H. H., Haouas, I., & Ullah, S. (2022). Examining the bidirectional nexus between financial development and green growth: International evidence through the roles of human capital and education expenditure. *Resources Policy, 79*, 102964. https://doi.org/10.1016/j.resourpol.2022.102964

Pee, L. G., & Pan, S. L. (2022). Climate-intelligent cities and resilient urbanisation: Challenges and opportunities for information research. *International Journal of Information Management, 63*, 102446. https://doi.org/10.1016/j.ijinfomgt.2021.102446

Phung, G., Truong, H., & Trinh, H. H. (2023). Determinants in the Development of Financial Centers: Evolution Around the World. In S.-J. Kim (Ed.), *Fintech, pandemic, and the financial system: challenges and opportunities* (Vol. 22, pp. 337–362). Emerald Publishing Limited. https://doi.org/10.1108/S1569-376720220000022015

Saif, M. A. M., Hussin, N., Husin, M. M., Muneer, A., & Alwadain, A. (2024). Beyond conventions: Unravelling perceived value's role in shaping digital-only banks' adoption. *Technological Forecasting and Social Change, 203*, 123337. https://doi.org/10.1016/j.techfore.2024.123337

Scopus. (2024). https://www.scopus.com/

Shang, X., & Niu, H. (2023). Does the digital transformation of banks affect green credit? *Finance Research Letters, 58*, 104394. https://doi.org/10.1016/j.frl.2023.104394

Siddik, A. B., Rahman, M. N., & Yong, L. (2023). Do fintech adoption and financial literacy improve corporate sustainability performance? The mediating role of access to finance. *Journal of Cleaner Production, 421*, 137658. https://doi.org/10.1016/j.jclepro.2023.137658

Tang, X., Yao, X., Dai, R., & Wang, Q. (2024). Does green matter for crowdfunding? International evidence. *Journal of International Financial Markets, Institutions and Money, 92*, 101950. https://doi.org/10.1016/j.intfin.2024.101950

Tao, R., Su, C.-W., Naqvi, B., & Rizvi, S. K. A. (2022). Can Fintech development pave the way for a transition towards low-carbon economy: A global perspective. *Technological Forecasting and Social Change, 174*, 121278. https://doi.org/10.1016/j.techfore.2021.121278

Teng, M., & Shen, M. (2023). The impact of fintech on carbon efficiency: Evidence from Chinese cities. *Journal of Cleaner Production, 425*, 138984. https://doi.org/10.1016/j.jclepro.2023.138984

Tiwari, A. K., Abakah, E. J. A., Shao, X., Le, T. N. L., & Gyamfi, M. N. (2023). Financial technology stocks, green financial assets, and energy markets: A quantile causality and dependence analysis. *Energy Economics, 118*, 106498. https://doi.org/10.1016/j.eneco.2022.106498

Trinh, H. H. (2021). Energy technology RD&D budgets, environmental sustainability, and energy transition: A review of emerging trends, policies, and pathways. In M. Fathi, E. Zio, & P. M. Pardalos (Eds.), *Handbook of smart energy systems* (pp. 1–23). Springer International Publishing. https://doi.org/10.1007/978-3-030-72322-4_186-1

Trinh, H. H. (2023). Climate finance, policy uncertainty, and global financial stability: A systematic review through bibliometric analysis. In *Banking resilience* (Vol. 9, pp. 209–225). World Scientific (Europe). https://doi.org/doi:10.1142/9781800614291_0006

Trinh, H. H. (2024). *Climate change, policy uncertainty, and economic conditions: US state-level evidence*. SSRN. https://doi.org/https://dx.doi.org/10.2139/ssrn.4581860

Trinh, H. H., McCord, M., Lo, D., & Squires, G. (2023). Do green growth and technological innovation matter to infrastructure investments in the era of climate change? Global evidence. *Applied Economics, 55*(35), 4108–4129. https://doi.org/10.1080/00036846.2022.2125493

Trinh, H. H., Sharma, G. D., Tiwari, A. K., & Vo, D. T. H. (2022). Examining the heterogeneity of financial development in the energy-environment nexus in the era of climate change: Novel evidence around the world. *Energy Economics, 116*, 106415. https://doi.org/10.1016/j.eneco.2022.106415

Vo, D. T. H., & Trinh, H. H. (2023). Financing renewable energy transition toward sustainable development goals: policies and economic implications in the era of climate change. In *Green finance and sustainable development goals* (Vol. 12, pp. 269–297). World Scientific (Europe). https://doi.org/doi:10.1142/9781800614482_0010

Wu, F., Hu, Y., & Shen, M. (2024). The color of FinTech: FinTech and corporate green transformation in China. *International Review of Financial Analysis, 94*, 103254. https://doi.org/10.1016/j.irfa.2024.103254

Xie, J., Chen, L., Liu, Y., & Wang, S. (2023). Does fintech inhibit corporate greenwashing behavior? Evidence from China. *Finance Research Letters, 55*, 104002. https://doi.org/10.1016/j.frl.2023.104002

Xu, J., Chen, F., Zhang, W., Liu, Y., & Li, T. (2023). Analysis of the carbon emission reduction effect of Fintech and the transmission channel of green finance. *Finance Research Letters, 56*, 104127. https://doi.org/10.1016/j.frl.2023.104127

Zhou, G., Zhu, J., & Luo, S. (2022). The impact of fintech innovation on green growth in China: Mediating effect of green finance. *Ecological Economics, 193*, 107308. https://doi.org/10.1016/j.ecolecon.2021.107308

CHAPTER 9

THE ESG BACKLASH: POLITICS, IDEOLOGY, AND THE FUTURE OF SUSTAINABLE BUSINESS

Henrik Skaug Sætra

University of Oslo, Norway

ABSTRACT

This article critically examines the recent opposition to environmental, social, and governance (ESG) initiatives, which have been increasingly scrutinized and politicized, particularly in the US. The article deals with the inherent political and economic tensions that challenge the adoption and effectiveness of ESG initiatives, highlighting the debate over shareholder versus stakeholder priorities and the broader implications for corporate social responsibility. The criticism of ESG is deeply rooted in the concerns over its impact on financial performance and perceived regulatory overreach, leading to a preference for maximizing shareholder value at the expense of broader societal goals. This chapter explores the potential future scenarios for ESG, considering the shifting landscape of sustainability in business practices amidst growing conservative resistance. This analysis is crucial for understanding the trajectory of sustainable finance and corporate contributions to environmental and social objectives in a polarized socio-political context.

Keywords: ESG backlash; ESG pushback; anti-ESG; greenhushing; greenwashing

JEL codes: G30; Q01; Q56; M14

Responsible Firms: CSR, ESG, and Global Sustainability
International Finance Review, Volume 23, 161–167
Copyright © 2025 by Henrik Skaug Sætra
Published under exclusive licence by Emerald Publishing Limited
ISSN: 1569-3767/doi:10.1108/S1569-376720240000023009

INTRODUCTION

The illusion of universal consensus around sustainable development is tempting. Some might, for example, believe that all share a desire to combat climate change, preserve natural environments and ensure inclusive economic growth. However, there are deep and emerging conflicts surrounding the corporate sustainability space, connected both to challenging economic times and the growth of conservative political movements. More concretely, corporate sustainability is now under heavy fire in major regions – particularly in the US.

ESG is a popular target of forces actively undermining efforts to promote sustainable development. However, the criticism is more fundamental and would not be resolved by replacing ESG with similar frameworks, as the core of the criticism relates to perennial issues in political economy related to, for example, shareholder vs. stakeholder capitalism, the social responsibility of corporations, diverging opinions on short- vs. long-term trade-offs, the consequences of trying to implement social justice concerns in markets, controversy over evidence related to whether ESG metrics positively correlates with market performance, etc. In this article I sift through these various categories of arguments that all play into what is referred to as an ongoing *ESG backlash, ESG pushback*, or *anti-ESG efforts* (Masters & Temple-West, 2023).

ESG AND THE CHANNELING OF PRIVATE CAPITAL TOWARD SUSTAINABILITY-RELATED EFFORTS

In recent years, a growing consensus on the need to pursue sustainable development has emerged. This consensus refers to increasing *global* coordination and tighter linkages and alignment of *public and private* initiatives related to sustainable development. The concept of sustainability and sustainable development is still largely based on the Brundtland commission's report *Our Common Future* from 1987, which stated that we have "the ability to make development sustainable to ensure that it meets the needs of the present without compromising the ability of future generations to meet their own needs" (Brundtland et al., 1987).

The United Nation's Sustainable Development Goals (SDGs), with a goal period from 2015 to 2030, serves as the most prominent operationalization of sustainable development today (United Nations, 2015). The colorful squares reflecting a seeming desire to do all kinds of good are promoted by politicians, civil society actors, *and* businesses. And these stakeholders are not only promoting the SDGs in their own silos. Much effort has focused on the need to funnel private capital into the green and just transition – in part because of the so-called "finance gap" (Dhanani, 2023). Furthermore, there is increased focus on public–private partnerships, as illustrated by the focus on partnerships in the SDGs with the 17th goal "Partnerships for the goals."

ESG is another popular framework for operationalizing sustainable development, particularly in the world of business and finance. While many stakeholders have only recently become preoccupied with ESG, it is an old concept with roots in the socially responsible investment movement that emerged in the 1960s (Crona & Sunsdström, 2023). In short, ESG looks at a company's impact on, and vulnerability to, a range of sustainability issues. Examples of topics covered are GHG emissions, diversity, equity, and inclusion status and efforts, and routines related to sustainability, board diversity, etc.

ESG performance has been linked both to financial performance and company valuation (Fafaliou et al., 2022; Friede et al., 2015), and it has been argued that good performance on relevant indicators also correlates positively with innovation capacity (Ambec et al., 2013; Fafaliou et al., 2022; Porter & Van der Linde, 1995). One early criticism of ESG was that it was hard to quantify ESG factors, something showing in the broad variation between different ESG ranking agencies (Berg et al., 2022). However, with the motto "don't let perfect be the enemy of good," many have tended to proceed despite a lack of quality data, while attempting to improve both data sources and ways to disclose it. Other challenges relate to a proliferation of frameworks and standards (Dimson et al., 2020; Esty & Cort, 2020; Sætra, 2021) and the resulting challenge of getting standardized and comparable ESG performance data for investors and other stakeholders interested in evaluating company ESG performance (Berg et al., 2022; Dimson et al., 2020; Eng et al., 2021).

Another conflict, however, has been brewing for some time and has led to a quite drastic and radical shift in both communication and action related to sustainability-related efforts previously associated with the ESG label. And this stems not from the limitations related to data or strong action, but from the idea that ESG – and in essence sustainability more broadly – is not necessarily good, and at least not something corporations should pursue.

DON'T BE "GOOD" – GREED IS GOOD

The last conflict is partly fueled by what is referred to as the *ESG backlash, ESG pushback*, or *anti-ESG efforts* (Masters & Temple-West, 2023). This backlash has gained significant traction recently, with incidents such as Elon Musk in 2023 proclaiming that ESG is both a "scam" and "the devil" (Gordon, 2023). However, the pushback is not a completely new phenomenon. A primary historical root of this movement is Friedman's famous criticism of corporate social responsibility from the 1950s onwards (Smith, 2024). More recently, vocal critics started pushing back against what they label "ESG activism" from investors and asset managers (Barzuza et al., 2019), and US legislators have introduced "anti-ESG" laws barring public entities from, for example, using banks with certain ESG policies (Garrett & Ivanov, 2022).

The conflict over ESG clearly demonstrates that what is sometimes perceived as a consensus related to, for example, the SDGs, is illusory. While many have played along for a while now, the idea of sustainable development and the operationalization of it seen in the SDGs is, in fact, highly controversial in certain circles. While stakeholders in UN processes reached agreement on the SDGs, conservative forces are fighting back in the world of finance. And this goes beyond details related to, for example, diverging opinions on LGBTQ+ people and democracy, as such globally controversial issues are already largely left out of the SDG framework (Sætra & Ese, 2023). Those behind the ESG backlash represent a more fundamental opposition to the core ideas that form the basis of sustainable development.

A clear example of what has happened is Blackrock, which lent considerable support to the ESG movement (if we can call it that) by supporting it in annual letters and speeches by CEO Larry Fink (King, 2016). Now, almost 10 years later, Blackrock has abandoned the ESG label and instead speak of "transition investing," something more clearly environmentally focused and less contentious (Pitcher & Ramkumar, 2024).

But how and why did ESG issues become contentious? It boils down to the idea that what some consider common sense and unequivocally good initiatives related to social good and diversity, for example, is by others conceived as a part of a political and activist progressive agenda. An agenda that is portrayed as deeply inimical to the core values some hold dear, which often have their basis in conservative, capitalist, and American conceptions of the good. For example, The Heritage Foundation exemplifies this opposition, fearing ESG diverts shareholder capital and calling it "woke corporate capitalism" (The Heritage Foundation, 2021b). This is also personal for investors who fear that their capital "is now being diverted to causes and purposes that you never intended to support" (The Heritage Foundation, 2021a). The core arguments of recent anti-ESG efforts tend to focus on the following points:

1. Political and Ideological Bias: Critics argue that ESG introduces political and ideological biases into business decisions, aligning with a progressive agenda.
2. Impact on Financial Performance: There's concern that prioritizing ESG criteria could detract from a company's financial performance.
3. Regulatory and Economic Concerns: The emphasis on ESG is feared to lead to overregulation, burdening businesses with excessive mandates.
4. Undermines Shareholder Value: It's argued that ESG initiatives detract from maximizing shareholder value, suggesting companies should prioritize profits over broader social or environmental goals.

WHAT'S NEXT FOR ESG? FOUR SCENARIOS

So, where does that leave us? As organizations shy away from the ESG label because they fear the wrath of conservative crowds, we are suddenly in a situation in which "greenhushing" (Keter, 2024) has become a thing, and where it is now quite ok – even *good* – to talk about maximizing shareholder profits in the short-term rather than engaging in what critics perceive as progressive do-goodism aimed at social justice, just transitions, peace, and other fluffy things.

There are now several options on the table, and two key choices worth noting. The first is whether one sticks to the concept ESG or seeks alternative labels or frameworks. The second is to what degree businesses actively contribute to the

	Focus on short-term shareholder profit	Promotion of sustainable development
Abandon ESG	(1) Greed is allowed to be good	(3) "Greenhushing" and the quest for alternative frameworks and methods for effective sustainable finance
Keep ESG	(2) "Greenwashing"	(4) Effective action through continuous improvement of ESG reporting and monitoring frameworks

Fig. 9.1. Two Strategies and Four Potential Scenarios Related to ESG.

promotion of sustainable development in the ESG dimensions. This leaves us with the four scenarios – or outcomes – shown in Fig. 9.1.

The four scenarios have significant consequences for how the world of sustainable finance, and thus also business contributions aimed directly at promoting sustainable development, develop in the near future.

Scenario 1 entails reverting to the motto that greed is good, and that short-term shareholder value is not just accepted but the *proper* goal of corporations. This approach would likely be favored by those who view the push for sustainability as fundamentally incompatible with their business model or ideology. However, it represents a significant retreat from the progress made in recent years toward integrating environmental and social considerations into business practices.

Scenario 2 will according to some be where we're at today – where ESG is pursued on paper, but largely in greenwashing efforts not coupled with strong action. This is a situation that neither those who push back against ESG *nor* those wanting effective action would be satisfied with. The challenge here is balancing genuine sustainability efforts with the market and political pressures that promote a focus on short-term financial gains over long-term environmental and social objectives.

Scenario 3 occurs if corporations shun the ESG label out of fear for reactions from the anti-ESG actors and pursue "greenhushing" by continuing and developing their efforts aimed at promoting ESG-related initiatives through other labels. The difficulty lies in crafting a new approach that is both genuinely committed to sustainability and capable of gaining traction in a skeptical or hostile environment. This could involve rebranding efforts, developing new metrics for success, or even pioneering innovative finance mechanisms that align with, for example, the SDGs without explicitly invoking the ESG label.

Scenario 4 is one where there is strong pushback against the pushback, so to speak, and corporations and regulators fight to preserve and further develop ESG frameworks and regulations. In the current situation, particularly in the US, this seems like an unlikely outcome, as significant actors have already abandoned the term – making the fight for ESG preservation an uphill battle. Proponents would need to engage in advocacy, education, and perhaps most challenging, confrontation with deeply entrenched interests that view ESG as antithetical to their principles and financial interests. While it may appear futile given the current backlash, this approach relies on the belief that sustained effort can change perceptions and eventually lead to broader acceptance.

CONCLUSION AND RECOMMENDATIONS FOR STAKEHOLDERS

The way forward in addressing the ESG backlash and the politicization of sustainable development requires a multifaceted approach that embraces collaboration, consensus-building, compromise, and an unwavering commitment to sustainable development. To effectively tackle the challenges of climate change, inequality, and resource depletion, it is imperative that businesses, governments, and civil societies integrate sustainable practices. ESG has taken us some way, and if it is abandoned now, there is an urgent need for an alternative.

The journey toward a sustainable future necessitates collective efforts across sectors, highlighting partnerships and fostering innovation. Achieving consensus in today's polarized discourse arenas is critical, and it calls for recognizing that sacrifices are necessary for the greater good. Compromise is essential, allowing for different priorities and strategies to coalesce around common goals for the long-term viability of our planet and the beings inhabiting it.

As we strive for a more sustainable and equitable future, it is crucial to remain patient, persistent, and to actively fight for our common future. The urgency to act is clear, and by standing strong in face of the pushback, we can navigate the complexities of sustainable development and overcome the challenges posed by the ESG backlash.

REFERENCES

Ambec, S., Cohen, M. A., Elgie, S., & Lanoie, P. (2013). The Porter hypothesis at 20: Can environmental regulation enhance innovation and competitiveness? *Review of Environmental Economics and Policy*, 7(1), 2–22.

Barzuza, M., Curtis, Q., & Webber, D. H. (2019). Shareholder value (s): Index fund ESG activism and the new millennial corporate governance. *Southern California Law Review*, 93, 1243.

Berg, F., Koelbel, J. F., & Rigobon, R. (2022). Aggregate confusion: The divergence of ESG ratings. *Review of Finance*. https://doi.org/10.1093/rof/rfac033

Brundtland, G. H., Khalid, M., Agnelli, S., Al-Athel, S., & Chidzero, B. (1987). Our common future. *New York*, 8.

Crona, B., & Sunsdström, E. (2023). Sweet spots or dark corners? An environmental sustainability examination of Big Data and AI in ESG. In T. Rana, A. Lowe, & J. Svanberg (Eds.), *Handbook of big data and analytics in accounting and auditing*. Springer.

Dhanani, Q. (2023, Sep 11, 2023). *Closing the SDG financing gap requires collective creativity*. Boston Consulting Group. Retrieved March 27, 2023, from https://www.bcg.com/capabilities/social-impact/expert-insights/qahir-dhanani

Dimson, E., Marsh, P., & Staunton, M. (2020). Divergent ESG ratings. *The Journal of Portfolio Management, 47*(1), 75–87. https://doi.org/10.3905/jpm.2020.1.175

Eng, L. L., Fikru, M., & Vichitsarawong, T. (2021). Comparing the informativeness of sustainability disclosures versus ESG disclosure ratings. *Sustainability Accounting, Management and Policy Journal.* https://doi.org/10.1108/SAMPJ-03-2021-0095

Esty, D. C., & Cort, T. (Eds.). (2020). *Values at work: Sustainable investing and ESG reporting.* Palgrave McMillan.

Fafaliou, I., Giaka, M., Konstantios, D., & Polemis, M. (2022). Firms' ESG reputational risk and market longevity: A firm-level analysis for the United States. *Journal of Business Research, 149,* 161–177. https://doi.org/10.1016/j.jbusres.2022.05.010

Friede, G., Busch, T., & Bassen, A. (2015). ESG and financial performance: Aggregated evidence from more than 2000 empirical studies. *Journal of Sustainable Finance & Investment, 5*(4), 210–233. https://doi.org/10.1080/20430795.2015.1118917

Garrett, D., & Ivanov, I. (2022). Gas, guns, and governments: Financial costs of anti-ESG policies. *Jacobs Levy Equity Management Center for Quantitative Financial Research Paper.*

Gordon, J. (2023, June 16). ETF wrap: Musk says 'ESG is the devil'. *ETF Stream.*

Keter. (2024). *Green hushing & the anti-ESG movement.* Keter. Retrieved March 27, 2024, from https://www.keteres.com/resource/green-hushing-the-anti-esg-movement

King, E. (2016, Feb 5). Blackrock: World's largest investor flags up climate risk. *Climate Home News.* https://www.climatechangenews.com/2016/02/05/blackrock-worlds-largest-investor-flags-up-climate-risk/

Masters, B., & Temple-West, P. (2023, Dec 4, 2023). The real impact of the ESG backlash. *Financial Times.* https://www.ft.com/content/a76c7feb-7fa5-43d6-8e20-b4e4967991e7

Pitcher, J., & Ramkumar, A. (2024, March 3). Step aside, ESG. BlackRock is doing 'Transition Investing' now. *The Wall Street Journal.* https://www.wsj.com/finance/investing/step-aside-esg-blackrock-is-doing-transition-investing-now-59df3908

Porter, M. E., & Van der Linde, C. (1995, September–October). Green and competitive: Ending the stalemate. *Harvard Business Review.* https://hbr.org/1995/09/green-and-competitive-ending-the-stalemate

Sætra, H. S. (2021). A framework for evaluating and disclosing the ESG related impacts of AI with the SDGs. *Sustainability, 13*(15). https://doi.org/10.3390/su13158503

Sætra, H. S., & Ese, J. (2023). Shinigami eyes and social media labeling as a technology for self-care. In H. S. Sætra (Ed.), *Technology and sustainable development: The promise and pitfalls of techno-solutionism* (pp. 53–69). Routledge. https://doi.org/10.1201/9781003325086-2

Smith, D. C. (2024). The intellectual history of Milton Friedman's criticism of corporate social responsibility. *Modern Intellectual History,* 1–27.

The Heritage Foundation. (2021a, 16 May 2022). *Heritage explains: The ESG pushback.* Retrieved March 27, 2022, from https://www.heritage.org/progressivism/heritage-explains/woke-corporate-capitalism

The Heritage Foundation. (2021b). *Heritage explains: Woke corporate capitalism.* Retrieved March 27, 2021, from https://www.heritage.org/progressivism/heritage-explains/woke-corporate-capitalism

United Nations. (2015). Transforming our world: The 2030 Agenda for Sustainable Development. *Division for Sustainable Development Goals,* New York, NY, USA.

PART IV

MNE, AI, AND GLOBAL SUSTAINABILITY

CHAPTER 10

SUSTAINABILITY AS STRATEGY: THE FINANCIAL PERFORMANCE OF UN GLOBAL COMPACT NETWORK AUSTRALIA (UNGCNA) MEMBER FIRMS ON THE AUSTRALIAN SECURITIES EXCHANGE (ASX)

Paul X. McCarthy[a], Michael Parker[b] and Xian Gong[c]

[a]*University of New South Wales, Sydney, Australia*
[b]*Praxis Comm./ University of Technology Sydney, Australia*
[c]*University of Technology Sydney, Australia*

ABSTRACT

This study assesses the impact of corporate engagement in sustainability and ethical practices on shareholder returns as defined by participation in the UN Global Compact Network Australia (UNGCNA). A dataset of 60 UNGCNA participating companies was compared to a similar set of 60 non-participating companies from the Australian Securities Exchange. The UNGCNA participating companies are also considered against the All-Ordinaries Index, which includes the top 500 listed companies in Australia, which is the country's oldest market index and is often used as a benchmark. We analyse the growth in

Responsible Firms: CSR, ESG, and Global Sustainability
International Finance Review, Volume 23, 171–176
Copyright © 2025 by Paul X. McCarthy, Michael Parker, and Xian Gong
Published under exclusive licence by Emerald Publishing Limited
ISSN: 1569-3767/doi:10.1108/S1569-376720240000023010

total enterprise value or market capitalization over three years. The findings reveal a significant positive differential in shareholder returns for UNGCNA participants against both comparison groups. Sustainable business practices may explain the differential or, more likely, these companies have an overarching management approach or style that sets them apart, and this approach includes the pursuit of sustainable performance.

Keywords: Sustainability; UN global compact; shareholder returns; financial performance; corporate governance; corporate culture; social responsibility

JEL Codes: G34; M14; Q56

INTRODUCTION

The UNGCNA, the local branch of the world's largest corporate sustainability initiative, aligns Australian businesses, non-profits, and universities with the Ten Principles of the UN Global Compact. These principles encompass human rights, labour, environmental stewardship, and anti-corruption, providing a framework for companies to integrate ethical and sustainable practices into their strategies and operations. By encouraging greater transparency, accountability, and identifying opportunities that deliver positive outcomes, the UNGCNA enables participants to collectively contribute to the UN Sustainable Development Goals (SDGs).

In Australia there are approximately 330 companies participating in the UNGCNA. Of these 68 (20.6%) are listed on the Australian Stock Exchange (ASX).

The motivation for this study stems from the growing importance of sustainability as a strategic imperative for businesses. As the world faces unprecedented environmental and social challenges, such as climate change, poverty, and inequality, corporations are expected to play a positive role in addressing these issues. Moreover, consumers, investors, and regulators are increasingly scrutinizing the environmental, social, and governance (ESG) performance of companies, creating both opportunities and risks for businesses. Therefore, it is essential to understand how sustainability initiatives affect the financial outcomes of firms, and whether there is a business case for adopting the UN Global Compact's Ten Principles and the UN's Sustainable Development Goals.

The contribution of this study is twofold. First, it provides empirical evidence on the relationship between UNGCNA membership and shareholder returns, using a unique dataset of ASX-listed companies. Second, it offers insights into the potential mechanisms and drivers behind this relationship, such as enhanced reputation, innovation, risk management, and stakeholder engagement. The study also discusses the implications and limitations of the findings, as well as directions for future research.

METHODOLOGY
Research Design

This study adopts a comparative analysis framework to evaluate the financial performance of UNGCNA participants and non-participants listed on the ASX. Our approach is grounded in a matched-pair design, where each UNGCNA participant is paired with a non-participant firm that is similar in size, industry, and other relevant characteristics. This design minimizes the impact of confounding variables, allowing for a clearer assessment of the relationship between UNGCNA participation and financial performance.

Sample Selection and Matching Criteria

At the time of publication there were approximately 330 companies participating in the UNGCA and 68 (20.6%) of these are ASX listed. While this is a small percentage (4%) of all the 2,000 companies ($n = 2,005$) listed on the ASX they represent 27% of the Top200 companies and 39% of the Top100 companies by market capitalization.

The selection of the 120 companies used in the analysis involved a systematic process, starting with the identification of all ASX-listed companies that are UNGCNA participants as of the study's commencement date. Non-participant companies were then identified, ensuring a wide representation of industries to match the diversity within the UNGCNA participant base.

The matching process employed several criteria to ensure comparability between the two groups:

- Size: Measured by total assets and market capitalization, ensuring that companies are of similar financial scale.
- Industry: Companies were matched within the same industry classification, based on the Global Industry Classification Standard, to account for sector-specific factors that might influence financial performance.
- Operating History: Preference was given to companies with a similar length of operation, to control for lifecycle effects.

Data Collection

Data on market capitalization, shareholder returns, and other financial indicators were collected from verified financial databases and company reports. Participation in the UNGCNA was verified through the official UNGCNA participants list. Additional data on ESG practices were collected to explore potential mediators in the relationship between UNGCNA participation and financial performance.

Analytical Techniques

The study employed a range of statistical techniques to analyse the data including descriptive statistics to provide an overview of the characteristics of the two groups of companies and regression analysis: to test the hypothesis that

UNGCNA participation is associated with higher shareholder returns, controlling for potential confounding factors such as size, industry, and ESG practices.

RESULTS

The analysis conducted in this study demonstrates a significant performance differential between the two portfolios. Specifically, the UNGCNA participant portfolio exhibited an 18% growth in enterprise value over the study period, compared to a 3% growth for the non-member portfolio and 2.8% for the All Ordinaries, a composite of the largest 500 ASX listed companies. This remarkable difference underscores the financial advantage of sustainable business practices, translating to an average annual share market return difference of 4.93% in favour of UNGCNA participants.

To visually represent these findings, Fig. 1 illustrates the annual performance comparison between UNGCNA participant and non-participant companies for the years 2022, 2023, and 2024. This graphical representation clearly shows that UNGCNA-aligned firms have consistently outperformed their non-participant counterparts, reinforcing the quantitative analysis results.

Fig. 10.1 illustrates the annual shareholder returns, measured by the growth in enterprise value, for companies participating in the UNGCNA compared to non-participating companies. The data reveals that UNGCNA-aligned firms consistently outperform their non-participating counterparts, with an 18% growth in enterprise value over the study period, compared to 3% for non-members and 2.8% for the All Ordinaries Index. This highlights the financial advantages of sustainable business practices for shareholders.

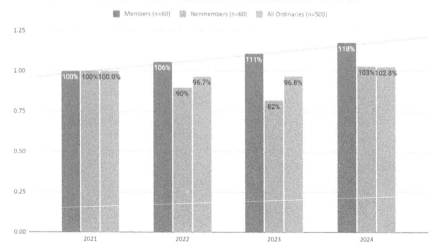

Fig. 10.1.   Annual Shareholder Returns Comparison Between UNGCNA
Participant and Non-Participant Companies (2022–2024).

DISCUSSION

Our findings resonate with a substantial and growing corpus of research underscoring the connection between sustainable practices and superior financial performance. The comprehensive analysis by Friede et al. (2015) unveils a consistent positive link between ESG factors and financial outcomes across a vast array of studies, reinforcing the financial merit of sustainable business conduct. Similarly, Khan et al. (2016) highlight the significant financial implications of sustainability practices, further substantiating the material benefits of such initiatives. Moreover, Eccles and Krzus (2010) emphasize the strategic importance of integrated reporting for sustainability, suggesting that transparent communication about sustainability efforts is critical for realizing their financial benefits. Edmans (2011) further expands on this perspective by illustrating how intangible assets, such as employee satisfaction – a key component of ESG – can lead to enhanced equity prices, indicating a market appreciation for firms that invest in their social capital. Furthermore, the research by George Serafeim (2020) introduces an important dimension to the sustainability-financial performance discourse: public sentiment. Serafeim's findings suggest that public sentiment significantly influences the valuation of a firm's sustainability activities.

Our research builds upon these foundational studies, situating the benefits of UNGCNA participation within this broader discourse. By aligning with UNGCNA principles, firms not only adhere to global sustainability standards but also strategically position themselves for financial outperformance, illustrating the dual moral and economic rationale for embracing sustainable practices.

So, while sustainable practices in their own right may not fully explain strong financial performance, it does appear that there is an overarching approach to management within UNGCNA participants that is achieving superior performance and that approach includes the adoption of sustainable practices.

CONCLUSION

This study provides clear empirical evidence that aligning with the UNGCNA offers strategic and financial benefits for companies listed on the ASX. Our findings build on the research of scholars such as Friede et al. (2015), Khan et al. (2016), Eccles and Krzus (2010), and Edmans (2011), highlighting the real-world advantages of incorporating sustainability practices into the core strategies of businesses. Moreover, the influence of public sentiment on how sustainability efforts are valued financially, as discussed by George Serafeim (2020), adds a layer of complexity to these benefits. Specifically, Serafeim's work suggests that the financial valuation of a company's sustainability activities can significantly vary based on public perception. This emphasizes that, beyond the inherent advantages of UNGCNA alignment, how these sustainability efforts are perceived externally can further impact a company's financial outcomes.

The positive relationship between ESG engagement and financial performance not only validates the ethical imperatives of sustainability but also highlights its role as a catalyst for financial success. UN Global Compact participation, therefore, emerges as a strategic asset that can propel companies towards both achieving global sustainability standards and enhancing shareholder returns. This confluence of ethical commitment and financial strategy enriches the narrative for corporate participation in sustainability initiatives, offering compelling evidence for the business case of joining the UN Global Compact.

Ultimately, this study contributes to the growing body of literature advocating for sustainability as an integral component of strategic business planning, urging corporations to embrace global sustainability initiatives like the UN Global Compact as a pathway to financial and ethical excellence.

REFERENCES

Friede, G., Busch, T., & Bassen, A. (2015). ESG and financial performance: Aggregated evidence from more than 2000 empirical studies. *Journal of Sustainable Finance & Investment, 5*(4), 210–233.

Khan, M., Serafeim, G., & Yoon, A. (2016). Corporate sustainability: First evidence on materiality. *The Accounting Review, 91*(6), 1697–1724.

Eccles, R. G., & Krzus, M. P. (2010). Integrated reporting for a sustainable strategy. *Financial Executive, 26*(2), 28–32.

Edmans, A. (2011). Does the stock market fully value intangibles? Employee satisfaction and equity prices. *Journal of Financial Economics, 101*(3), 621–640.

Serafeim, G. (2020). Public sentiment and the price of corporate sustainability. *Financial Analysts Journal, 76*(2), 26–46.

CHAPTER 11

BUSINESS ENGAGEMENT WITH THE SUSTAINABLE DEVELOPMENT AGENDA: EVIDENCE FROM TÜRKIYE

Burcin Hatipoglu[a] and Bengi Ertuna[b]

[a]University of New South Wales, Canberra, Australia
[b]Bogazici University, Istanbul, Türkiye

ABSTRACT

In this chapter, we analyze the interplay between the traditional conception of corporate social responsibility (CSR) and international norms and initiatives to understand business engagement with the development agenda. Drawing on empirical evidence from 50 publicly listed companies, this article delineates the conditions under which CSR can play a constructive role in engaging with grand challenges, addressing development agenda and public policy gaps in a developing country, Türkiye. We defined and used four CSR dimensions to portray the companies' response to the development agenda: integration with the core business, the extent of reach, instruments for implementation, and collaboration with external partners. Findings indicate that companies acting in line with the local conception of CSR by adopting a social mission beyond business display alignment of their CSR strategy with the global sustainable development agenda by adopting international norms and initiatives.

Responsible Firms: CSR, ESG, and Global Sustainability
International Finance Review, Volume 23, 177–201
Copyright © 2025 by Burcin Hatipoglu and Bengi Ertuna
Published under exclusive licence by Emerald Publishing Limited
ISSN: 1569-3767/doi:10.1108/S1569-376720240000023011

Keywords: Corporate social responsibility; institutional theory; sustainable development; Türkiye; development agenda

JEL Codes: M14; O17; Q01; O52

Grand challenges are complex, multidimensional, global problems that require coordinated action and collaboration from multiple stakeholders in diverse fields at several levels (George et al., 2016). They include systemic issues related to climate change, poverty and inequality, justice and human rights, and gender equality (United Nations, 2020), all of which became more pronounced after the COVID-19 pandemic. There is a growing consensus that business has a role in addressing grand challenges and can effectively deal with at least some of them (Howard-Grenville et al., 2019; Smith et al., 2010).

While CSR is acknowledged as an important construct for engaging business as a partner in solving grand challenges, there is a critical inquiry into its contribution to the development agenda (Frynas & Yamahaki, 2016; McGahan, 2020; Wright & Nyberg, 2017). For instance, Frynas (2008) argues that mainstream CSR is ineffective in addressing global development challenges, citing a lack of empirical evidence that CSR initiatives impact the societal good. Empirical evidence would contribute to a nuanced understanding of the role of business in the global development agenda, which is particularly urgent in developing countries. Developing countries manifest different CSR conceptions that reflect the heterogeneity and multiplicity of their institutional orders and their results (Jamali et al., 2017; Miska et al., 2016). Using Western frames of reference to evaluate CSR programs in developing countries is, therefore, a questionable practice, so it behooves us to develop alternative methodologies for analyzing business responses to grand challenges, and these methodologies need to account for the idiosyncrasies of the developing country.

To address this need, our chapter analyzes how businesses in a developing country respond to grand challenges. To examine CSR's context-laden and institutionally bound nature, we adopted an institutional perspective, focusing on the dynamics of the historically rooted traditional understanding of CSR and global CSR norms and its initiatives diffusing into the local context. We developed a framework to identify distinct types that reflect company responses to the competing conceptions of CSR in the local context: one is rooted in the local conception of business purpose in a state-dependent context (Fainshmidt et al., 2018; La Porta et al., 2008) and the other is dictated by the global CSR norm (Jamali et al., 2017; Mühle, 2010). In the foreground of the dynamics of these two competing forces, we used a set of CSR dimensions from the extant literature (integration with the core business, extent of reach, instruments for implementation, and external partnerships) to analyze mechanisms business use to engage with the development agenda (Agarwal et al., 2017; Jamali et al., 2017; Mühle, 2010; Nelson et al., 2015; Torres-Rahman et al., 2015).

Türkiye provides a suitable setting for exploring the business response to competing CSR conceptions. It has a long tradition of business–society relations and recent exposure to global CSR norms (Ararat et al., 2018; Ertuna & Tukel, 2010; Özen & Küskü, 2009). Historical patterns of business–society relations in the country's state-led market economy have entailed filling social policy gaps and primacy to the development goals of the state. Regarding its supporting public good, business involvement with CSR in Türkiye resembles the involvement reported for other developing nations like China, India, and Brazil (Fainshmidt et al., 2018; Kang & Moon, 2012). On the other hand, with the recent introduction of global CSR norms, a competing conception collides with the local conception, introducing a new set of initiatives, conventions, and mechanisms to the business agenda. As a result of this collision, contextualized CSR manifestations have emerged, creating "dynamic variations," some of which are comparable to those in other non-Western countries (Jamali et al., 2017, p. 344). Analyzing the translation and adaptation of global CSR conceptions in non-Western settings using mainstream frameworks is not meaningful, as they lack "local relevance" (Jamali et al., 2017, p. 346). Hence, we offer an alternative framework for analyzing business responses to development challenges.

Our sample consisted of 50 companies listed on the Borsa Istanbul Stock Exchange (BIST-50 Index companies). Based on companies' responses to the two competing conceptions in the context (local and global CSR), we defined four types reflecting CSR orientations. We identified the CSR attributes for each type and explained that companies that blend two competing conceptions display broader engagement with grand challenges, as these companies both embrace a locally embedded social mission beyond business purposes (social objectives) and combine elements of local CSR instruments with international ones.

Our contribution is twofold. First, we develop a framework to systematically analyze business engagement with the global development agenda. In doing so, we "simplify and distill" CSR orientations and their attributes in response to two competing conceptions influencing business–society relationships: one based on the local conception of business purpose and the other determined by the global CSR norm. Our framework can be adapted to different settings by identifying local conception of CSR and the diffusion of global CSR norm in each institutional context. Second, we respond to the call for empirical evidence on the impact of CSR initiatives on the public good (Frynas, 2008) and provide evidence on companies' engagement with grand challenges using non-Western frames of reference. We contribute to the literature on business engagement with grand challenges by identifying a variant of CSR orientation in the Turkish business context and explaining how this variant translates and localizes grand challenges. Attuned to the orders of both the state and the global CSR conceptions, this variant offers a model for bringing development challenges espoused by the government to the corporate level and acts as a facilitator for grand challenge engagement through CSR, thus offering possibilities for crossbreeding in different contexts.

The rest of this chapter proceeds as follows: We first introduce the relationship between business and the development agenda, the literature on the institutional theory perspective, and the competing CSR conceptions in developing countries in general and Türkiye in particular. Then, we explain our research methods and present our findings, highlighting the different types of CSR attributes that emerge from our data. We conclude with theoretical implications and recommendations for management.

THE DEVELOPMENT AGENDA AND BUSINESS

While business is widely accepted as a partner for working with grand challenges, scholars and international organizations are working on effective business engagement mechanisms with the global development agenda. Different platforms, tools, and mechanisms have been developed to increase the effectiveness of business involvement in development challenges worldwide (e.g., Business Charter for Sustainable Development and Business for 2030). An active community of consultants publishes guidelines to help companies step in. The Global Reporting Initiative (GRI) and the United Nations Global Compact (UNGC) launched guidelines in July 2018 for defining priorities and business reporting on the challenges (GRI & UN Global Compact, 2018). With a growing international agenda that encourages businesses to engage in development, an emerging scholarly interest in development-oriented CSR complements this international action by extending the boundaries of the dominant paradigm to include new perspectives. These include human development as corporate responsibility, development-oriented CSR, and political CSR for analyzing how companies can contribute to the global development agenda (Renouard & Ezvan, 2018; Van Zanten & Van Tulder, 2018).

Despite the important role ascribed to business as a partner for addressing grand challenges, scholarly work on the role of CSR in addressing those challenges is scarce; what exists usually originates in Western countries that have strong market mechanisms and institutions. Even in such settings, there is skepticism about CSR's positive contribution to the global development agenda and goals (Frynas, 2008). Business appears to focus on goals that are relatively easy to attain rather than on urgent issues that require systemic change. The result is a disjuncture between rhetoric and action (GlobeScan-SustainAbility. 2019). Moreover, grand challenges and CSR are complex, context-dependent constructs with different expressions in different settings and times. More profound ones require immediate action in developing countries. Solutions to these problems usually entail changes in institutional structures deeply rooted in society (George et al., 2016). Deciphering the institutional system's organizing principles can facilitate our understanding of how businesses perceive and respond to grand challenges through their CSR.

Institutional Theory and CSR

Various theoretical lenses have been borrowed from various disciplines to understand CSR's complexities. Institutional theory has been widely applied to decipher the different guises that CSR assumes in different contexts and time periods, acknowledging that CSR cannot be decoupled from its institutional context (Aguinis & Glavas, 2012; Jamali & Carroll, 2017; Matten & Moon, 2020).

In Scandinavia, Hovring's (2017) description of CSR manifestations is based on how multiple and contradictory institutional logics (such as ethics and development) are reconciled and translated into practice at the organizational and individual levels. Jamali et al. (2017) present a framework for understanding different CSR manifestations in developing countries. They suggest the presence of a global Western-centric norm, and using a sample of four developing countries, they demonstrate how the global assumptive conception is translated and adapted at the local level through its interaction with an institutionally embedded array of CSR conceptions.

A global CSR conception is also acknowledged in studies examining the worldwide diffusion of CSR (Kaplan & Kinderman, 2020). Mühle (2010) suggests that CSR has become a global business norm, along with its values (e.g., Universal Declaration of Human Rights), principles (e.g., principles of the UNGC), initiatives (e.g., CEO Water Mandate), and mechanisms (e.g., GRI Reporting). The emergence of a global CSR conception coincided with changes in expectations relating to the role of companies in addressing grand challenges, which led to a recognition of a purpose beyond profit maximization.

CSR Dimensions for Engagement with Grand Challenges

The literature on business engagement with the grand challenges identifies CSR dimensions that facilitate the generation of impact and the pursuit of social and financial goals. The global CSR norm originated in Anglo-Saxon countries and aligns closely with the instrumental approach (Garriga & Melé, 2004; Matten & Moon, 2020), which views CSR as a strategic tool for company value maximization. Societal demands are embedded in the business model if they serve these societal interests and contribute to maximizing company value (Kolk & Pinkse, 2006). Accordingly, implementation guidelines are embedded in the instrumental approach to CSR, which suggests alignment with core business activities. In a report by the SDG Fund, a framework for action is developed for better business engagement with development challenges (Torres-Rahman et al., 2015). One of the framework's key dimensions is alignment with core business products, processes, and competencies, even in alternatives to commercially driven CSR initiatives (e.g., hybrid and philanthropic). Alignment with a company's core business reportedly increases scale and sustainability. Transformative, scalable, and sustainable business engagement with the development agenda can be achieved if CSR initiatives are embedded in core operations and competencies (Nelson et al., 2015). Alignment with the core business supports the business case for CSR, thereby contributing to the legitimacy of development-oriented business action for the shareholders (Hengst et al., 2020; Kaplan & Kinderman, 2020).

Better engagement with sustainable development is also associated with the extended reach of CSR initiatives through the supply chain (Nelson et al., 2015). In that way, companies can assume broader responsibilities and address their impacts through their value chain (Matten & Moon, 2020). The monitoring and reporting of CSR initiatives facilitates companies' engagement with grand challenges (GRI, 2018). Drawing on examples from reporting schemes, companies should communicate the societal changes they achieve through their CSR initiatives (Torres-Rahman et al., 2015).

Multi-stakeholder partnerships and collaborations for CSR initiatives facilitate business engagement with grand challenges and offer the possibility of increasing impact and scalability (Agarwal et al., 2017; Grayson & Nelson, 2013; Mühle, 2010; Torres-Rahman et al., 2015). By leveraging each sector's competencies for transformative change, multi-sector partnerships can help tackle grand challenges.

Developing Country Contexts and Turkiye

Developing countries are characterized by high political and economic uncertainties coupled with weaknesses in their institutional systems – e.g., discretionary enforcement of laws and regulations, violation of rights, immature welfare policies, and state involvement in economic allocation – all of which lead to institutional voids and necessities. Companies operating in weak institutional settings might adopt strategic partnerships to deal with governance issues as an alternative nonmarket strategy (Dorobantu et al., 2017). Staying close to the state, diversifying across industries through business groups of companies, and forming partnerships with nonmarket stakeholders are strategies that companies adopt to create value in weak institutional settings. Furthermore, when a group firm is involved in CSR, the benefits can accrue to all firms in the group (Choi et al., 2018). Consequently, CSR can act as an adaptive nonmarket strategy both to complement the development goals of the state (Dorobantu et al., 2017) and to fill institutional voids, given that society expects private actors, such as families, clans, and companies, to assume responsibility (Forcadell & Aracil, 2017). In developing countries, there is a greater demand for businesses to engage in welfare issues (Marquis & Raynard, 2015). CSR strategy is primarily determined by societal expectations, shaped by interactive effects of the state's development goals and business perceptions of social policy gaps.

As a middle-income developing country (Hoskisson et al., 2013), Türkiye exhibits the institutional characteristics of many other developing countries. The Turkish business system is state-dependent, so the state allocates resources, not market-based mechanisms (Fainshmidt et al., 2018; La Porta et al., 2008). Thus, maintaining relations with the state is a significant factor in business success (Yamak & Ertuna, 2012). According to Fainshmidt et al. (2018), Türkiye is also similar to hierarchically coordinated countries like South Korea, Jordan, Lebanon, and Taiwan, where the state pursues development goals and coordinates the system with concentrated owners (e.g., business groups) and state-led agencies. In Türkiye, CSR is one way to maintain relations with the government, and companies prioritize development-related issues and contribute to public value creation (Jamali et al., 2018; Kang & Moon, 2012). In this way, companies, supported by values of solidarity and sharing prevalent in society, aim to fill the social policy gaps (Buğra, 2008).

In the Turkish business context, where family-owned business groups dominate, it is common for companies to address development challenges and to have locally embedded non-commercial objectives (social objectives), which are usually in the form of philanthropic activities of the founding family members (OECD, 2006). Given a historical pattern of business–society relationships, CSR initiatives focus on non-commercial, development-oriented objectives that contribute to community good and complement the public policy gaps of the state. Uyan-Atay and Tuncay-Celikel (2015) document the constructive role that Turkish business groups play in the development and governance of the country by assisting the welfare state through philanthropy. Often, building on the values of their founding members, family business groups display corporate philanthropy and employ mechanisms such as charitable foundations, employ group-wide CSR strategies (Yamak et al., 2019), and engage in "corporate responsibility for the public good" in areas that are most needed; for instance education and health (Ararat et al., 2018, p. 912). In this respect, Türkiye shares similarities with some of the attributes of business groups reported for South Korea (Choi et al., 2018; Oh et al., 2018).

Scholars note the multiple manifestations of CSR in Türkiye. Özen and Küskü (2009, p. 306) observe how some "model organizations" choose to set nonmarket objectives, aiming to contribute to the modernization goals of the Turkish Republic, whereas others choose to fulfill only their economic and regulatory obligations. Özen and Küskü (2009) suggest that these "model organizations" are more likely to transfer voluntary practices like environmental citizenship from developed nations and promote them at home. Ertuna and Tukel (2010) show how long-standing traditional values influence CSR behavior while international initiatives penetrate the country using market-driven mechanisms. Ozdora-Aksak and Atakan-Duman (2016) identify core business-focused CSR initiatives, discretionary initiatives, and a blend of traditional and international approaches to CSR in Türkiye.

The above studies imply the existence of competing conceptions surrounding CSR in the Turkish business context, reflected by the colliding dynamics of business–society–state relations and global CSR norms. We focus on these two competing conceptions of CSR to develop a framework for identifying different CSR orientations and answering our first research question.

- *RQ1: How do companies respond to competing CSR conceptions in the context?*

Using the framework we have developed – one based on the two main competing institutional forces surrounding CSR in Türkiye, we aim to analyze how companies with different CSR orientations (i.e., different types) articulate and address grand challenges. In doing so, we use a set of CSR dimensions associated with business engagement in grand challenges. To realize our aim, we focus on the following research question:

- *RQ2: How do companies with different responses to competing conceptions articulate and address development challenges through their CSR?*

Conceptual Model and the Variables

The present study considers two competing conceptions surrounding CSR: one is historically rooted in the understanding of social responsibility in the local context; the other, more recent, is based on international influences. The study assumes that different interpretations of CSR will result from the collision of competing institutional orders of CSR. We operationalize different CSR orientations based on two competing CSR conceptions: Embracing non-commercial and locally embedded societal objectives is a business' response to the institutional orders of the local CSR conception to build legitimacy with the state and society. Accepting the guidance of international norms and initiatives denotes a response to global CSR conception. The two conceptions of CSR we focus on in this study are

Local Conception of CSR: Identified by the objective underlying the CSR strategy. If a company establishes a locally embedded social objective (e.g., a social development goal that lies outside its core business model that fills a gap in public policy and thereby complements the social and development goals of the state) in addition to its commercial objectives, it is assumed to respond to the orders of local conception.

Global Conception of CSR: Denotes the sources of the norms for CSR. If a company voluntarily adopts international initiatives and its CSR policies and practices are shaped by international norms, conventions, and initiatives in addition to mandatory regulations, it is assumed to respond to the orders of global CSR conception.

We then identified four (2 × 2) types based on the two competing conceptions surrounding CSR in the context (Fig. 11.1). These types illustrate how companies respond to competing conceptions and denote companies' CSR orientations.

To identify how businesses with different CSR orientations articulate and address development challenges, we used a set of dimensions from the literature on business engagement with the development agenda (Agarwal et al., 2017; Jamali et al., 2017; Mühle, 2010; Nelson et al., 2015; Torres-Rahman et al., 2015) and defined four CSR dimensions to answer our first research question.

Integration with core business denotes whether the company incorporates CSR into its business model.

Extent of reach indicates whether the CSR programs are executed through the value chain, such as dealers, suppliers, group companies, foundations, and other institutions (e.g., museums, universities, and hospitals).

Instruments for implementation indicate whether the company reports CSR policies, programs, and progress.

Collaboration with external partners denotes whether a company collaborates with multiple stakeholders, e.g., the government, civil society organizations, universities, and research institutions for CSR programs.

Our conceptual model is presented in Fig. 11.1.

METHODOLOGY

Study Design

We used qualitative methodology in our research design. First, we developed a framework based on the institutional orders surrounding CSR in Türkiye. Using

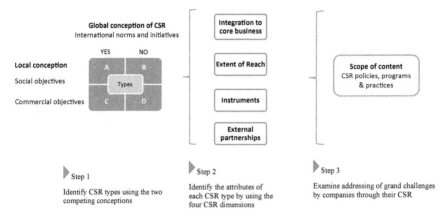

Fig. 11.1. Conceptual Model.

this framework, we conducted a content analysis on company documents to identify CSR orientations (types) (Step 1) and type attributes using CSR dimensions (Step 2). Then, we analyzed the companies' CSR policies, programs, and practices to assess their engagement with development (Step 3) and matched these assessments with type attributes to determine how companies address and articulate development challenges through their CSR programs. As new themes emerged, they were employed to detect patterns in the data (Gioia et al., 2013). This step-by-step research design allowed us to explain how companies translate a grand challenge into practice through their CSR initiatives.

Sample Companies and the Data Collection

Our sample included 50 companies listed on Borsa Istanbul (BIST-50 index companies in 2015, Appendix 1). All companies are locally founded, yet some are involved in strategic partnerships with multinational enterprises (MNEs) (e.g., Ford Otosan or Coca-Cola Beverages). The market value of the companies in the BIST-50 index represents 70% of the market value of all publicly traded companies in Borsa Istanbul. The BIST-50 companies included 22 companies in the manufacturing sector, 11 holding companies, 8 banking companies, and 9 other wholesale, retail, air transport, mining, and telecommunications companies (see Appendix 1 for a complete list). Holding companies that manage a portfolio were purposefully included in the sample because they are the key actors in orchestrating their group of companies' CSR efforts in the Turkish business context, dominated by family groups. The average market capitalization of companies in our sample was 7.8 billion Turkish Liras as of the end of 2016. Concerning ownership, the average share of controlling owners was 51.9%, while the average size of free float was 35.4%. The average share of foreign ownership was 35.4%.

Companies typically communicate information about their CSR initiatives via their websites and public disclosures. Self-disclosures by companies are criticized for public relations and greenwashing (Jain et al., 2017), but researchers frequently use them for studying CSR (Mahoney et al., 2013; Ozdora-Aksak &

Atakan-Duman, 2016). To examine CSR programs and practices, we collected data from company websites (2015–2016): CSR/sustainability reports, annual reports including mandatory Corporate Governance Compliance Reports, and the specific sections of company websites, such as "History," "Mission and Vision," "About Us," "Social Responsibility," and "Sustainability" pages. Our combined CSR-related research experience has made us knowledgeable about the ongoing CSR programs in our country, like Jamali et al. (2017). The data were triangulated from Carbon Disclosure Project reports, the Women Empowerment Principles (UN-WEP) pages, and the websites of company foundations, partnering NGOs, universities, and other local organizations, thus satisfying Lincoln and Guba's (1985) credibility criterion for qualitative rigor.

Coding and Data Analysis

We analyzed the documents in three steps using content analysis. First, we systematically read the documents and coded the sentences to capture the *local and global conceptions* of CSR. This coding resulted in rich content reflecting different company responses to the competing conceptions, which were then categorized according to the definition of the two variables to construct an evaluation grid (Cloutier & Ravasi, 2021). In other words, we identified and coded for the presence of nonmarket objectives (i.e., explicit social mission) and the guidance of international initiatives and conventions as basis of CSR strategies and the basis of norms and initiatives, respectively, for local and global conception, for all companies (Appendix 1). In addition, nonmarket objectives and international initiatives and conventions were extracted from the rich content and compiled for illustration. We used multiple coders throughout data analysis to ensure inter-rater reliability (Gioia et al., 2013). Although there was not a high discrepancy between researchers, the categorization of two companies was reassessed (Vestel and THY) in Step 1 (inter-rater reliability was 0.94, calculated by using the entire sample and categorizations).

Furthermore, we worked separately to overcome cognitive inertia, so while one of us coded the documents manually, the other used qualitative data analysis software (NVivo 12). To maintain Lincoln and Guba's (1985) criteria of dependability and conformability, these two sets of workbooks, together with tables created on Excel sheets, assured an audit trail (Cloutier & Ravasi, 2021). After completing the coding and evaluation analysis phase, four types were identified (A, B, C, and D) using two elemental categories of competing conceptions as variables (Fig. 11.1).

To identify patterns within and across different CSR orientations and define each configuration's attributes, the documents were coded in Step 2 using the four CSR dimensions (*integration to core business, reach, instruments for implementation, and collaboration with external partners*). Once again, the resulting qualitative content was compiled for each type and then coded as present (1) or not (0), using the definition of the four variables of CSR dimensions. The resulting tables are presented in Appendix 1 and used to summarize the shared attributes of the four types.

RESULTS

CSR Orientations

An analysis of company documents using the first two variables – *local and global conceptions of CSR* – revealed that of the 50 sample companies, 24 maintained social objectives, and 24 joined international initiatives to guide their CSR policies, practices, programs, and partnerships. These sets had intersecting companies. The companies with social objectives supported development challenges according to their perception of the state's social policy gaps and the community's expectations. As shown in Table 11.1, these companies aim to "advance society" (İşbank) and "modernize society" (Doğan Holding); they see themselves as leaders in society by taking a "pioneering role" (Sabancı Holding) and strive to "set an example" (Garanti). They state that going beyond economic goals is a moral obligation, a "primary responsibility" (Arçelik), and they have "a mission to improve the well-being of the society" (Eczacıbaşı Holding). Since almost half of the companies base their CSR strategy on social objectives, local CSR conception continues to influence their engagement with the global development agenda. Perceptions of public policy gaps and the need for local legitimacy with the state and society direct companies to social objectives and development-oriented missions per the orders of the culturally ingrained local CSR conception supported by the values of the founding owners. Illustrative quotes on social objectives are presented in Table 11.1.

Table 11.1. Illustrative Quotes.

Company and Source	Social Objectives in Line with Local Conception of CSR
Sabancı Holding **Annual Report 2015,** **p. 96.**	"We do not regard the scope of our social responsibility as being limited to just our business operations. We determine our level of social responsibility and focus on what is good for society and the environment as a whole. We pursue a pioneering role in our actions that protect democracy, human rights, and the environment.".
İşbank, Corporate **Governance** **Compliance Report,** **2015, p. 7.**	"Since its establishment, focusing seriously on the issues, which are the basic needs of the modern society and which are directly related to the country's future, İşbank supports ..., the social responsibility projects in education, environment, culture and arts, which are qualified to be long-lasting, being able to advance the society, far-reaching, sustainable and extendable."
Arçelik Sustainability **Report, 2015, p. 47.**	"Arçelik regards devising and implementing sustainable projects devoted to the development of social standards and the solution of social problems to be among its primary responsibilities, in light of its corporate values and culture."
Doğan Group Social **Responsibility Policy,** **2015, p. 2.**	"Our Group believes that a strong and contemporary society would come into existence through raising modern generations that would respect universal values and contribute to the solution of social and economic problems...."
Garanti Bank Annual **Report 2015, p. 9**	"We believe the environmental and social values Garanti creates for its stakeholders will set an example not only for the banking sector but also for the entire economy and provide significant contributions to our national development."
Eczacıbaşı Holding **Website, Social** **Responsibility.**	"In line with its mission of improving the well-being of the society, the Eczacıbaşı Group is committed to promoting social and economic development, encouraging cultural and scientific activity, and preserving scarce natural resources through responsible business practices and sponsorship."

Twenty-four companies committed to international conventions, such as the United Nations Declaration on Human Rights and the International Labor Organization; more than half signed the UNGC. Several hold memberships in industry-specific international organizations, such as the European Committee of Domestic Equipment Manufacturers (Arçelik) and the World Steel Association (Erdemir). Some are involved in issue-specific organizations, such as the Global Ethics Network (Migros), the CEO Water Mandate (Anadolu Efes), and the United Nations Women Empowerment Principles (Garanti). Şişecam, Türkiye's largest glass manufacturer, explained its commitment as follows: "As a multinational company, we find adherence to international standards to be critical, and we adopt international standards on quality, environment, energy, and OH&S" (Şişecam, 2014, p. 7). These findings confirmed the locally founded companies' acceptance of global CSR norms, thereby espousing a global CSR conception supported by universal norms, principles, and initiatives. Companies involved in strategic partnerships with MNEs are likely to be influenced by their partners' CSR practices. Similar to other contexts (Choi et al., 2018), large-sized business groups such as Koc Holding, Sabanci Holding, or the Anadolu Group have foreign partners, are involved in international markets, and are likely to mimic the global CSR practices of their partners. For example, Coca-Cola beverages in Türkiye (a partnership of Anadolu Group) support women empowerment initiatives, like the global Coca-Cola company.

Using the framework, we identified four types of CSR orientation in Türkiye; the attributes of each are shown in Table 11.2.

Table 11.2.   A Typology of CSR Orientations.

Global Conception ➲ Local Conception ➒	International Norms and Initiatives	No International Norms and Initiatives
Social Objectives	**A-HYBRID** CSR Operationalization: Beyond compliance, CSR is integrated into the core business and multi-stakeholder partnerships for CSR, transparency through CSR reports, and philanthropy using group mechanisms.	**B-TRADITIONAL** CSR Operationalization: Compliance with the law, public–private and business-NGO partnerships for philanthropy, using group mechanisms when available, and low CSR transparency.
Commercial Objectives	**C-STRATEGIC** CSR Operationalization: Beyond compliance, CSR is integrated into the core business, multi-stakeholder partnerships for CSR, and transparency through CSR reports.	**D-NON-RESPONSIVE** CSR Operationalization: Compliance with the law, philanthropy in the form of donations, no partnerships or transparency.

CSR Attributes and Grand Challenges

Type *A-Hybrid* refers to those 15 companies with social objectives that follow international norms and initiatives in their CSR (Appendix 1). This group, responding to the competing conceptions of the context by attending to both global and local conceptions, blends elements of both and adapts them to the local environment. A *hybrid company aligns CSR practices and programs with its core business and aims for social goals beyond its core business that align* with its social objectives. It operationalizes CSR through (i) its core business, (ii) multi-stakeholder partnerships, (iii) CSR reports, and (iv) philanthropy through group mechanisms. For instance, Eczacıbaşı Holding (a conglomerate including bathroom fittings, health products, and pharmaceuticals) renewed the bathrooms of boarding schools and provided hygiene education to youth in cooperation with the Association for Supporting Contemporary Life, the Ministry of National Education, and employee volunteers. Aside from developing core business-aligned CSR initiatives, the company continued its philanthropy through the Eczacıbaşı Foundation to support music, art, and other cultural events nationwide.

Employing numerous mechanisms, *Hybrid* companies can address diverse development challenges. They achieve localization by aligning their social objectives with social policy gaps. As such, the results confirm that these companies are more attuned to local issues, such as gender equality and quality education. Garanti and IşBank, for instance, have addressed local needs and complemented the government's social goals when taking part in the program "Finance and Advice for Women in Business," run by the European Bank for Reconstruction and Development, the European Union, and the Turkish government. They have extended their activities beyond commercial goals to provide technical mentorship to women entrepreneurs while adopting and blending the values and principles of global CSR conception. Similarly, Yapı Kredi Bank, in collaboration with the Volunteers Foundation of Turkiye (TEGV), focused on helping children who do not have access to "contemporary education" to develop good reading habits.

It is worth noting that, of the nine holding companies in our sample, four are of this type. Holding companies in our sample show similarities to business groups in South Korea, in that they display cross control of their group companies (Choi et al., 2018) and orchestrate their CSR practices and programs. Koc Holding and group companies such as Aygaz, Tofaş, Ford Otosan, and Tupras are all in the *Hybrid* group. Our findings show that holding companies that blend the two competing conceptions address a more comprehensive range of grand challenges and engage with salient systemic challenges of the context. They combine elements of both global and local CSR. For example, Koc Holding integrates into the core business of its managing group companies "For My Country." Development challenges are selected as a new theme for the group every three years. In addressing the gender equality theme, Koç Holding adopted international principles from UN Women, extending the scope of its reach to its suppliers and dealers, utilizing various group institutions and mechanisms, and forming partnerships with various ministries and prominent local NGOs.

Type *B-Traditional* refers to those companies with social objectives but without reference to international initiatives and conventions. This type includes nine companies (Appendix 1) that respond to local social policy gaps, promoting issues such as healthy living and sports for Turkish youth (Enka Holding), health and education (İhlas Holding), and support social services of the state and contribute to the country's social development (Park Holding). This category also includes themes of national interest, such as "raising national pride as an international company" (Vestel) and "maintaining the country's international visibility" (Turkish Airlines). As such, *Traditional* companies employ CSR to complement the development goals of the state rather than strategic purposes. Even if they claim to have social development goals, they address a broad development agenda where specific local needs are addressed only at a low level. Their CSR engagement is at the philanthropy level, making donations to schools (İhlas Holding, Park Elektrik, and Turkish Airlines), providing scholarships (Alarko Holding), supporting sports (Enka), and donating to organizations that help disabled people (Vestel). As in other contexts with strong business groups (e.g., Choi et al. (2018) cite South Korea), three of the four holding companies of this type extend their reach in their philanthropic activities using group mechanisms, such as foundations and group companies.

Type *C-Strategic* indicates companies with market objectives and refers to international conventions for guidance (Appendix 1). The nine companies in this type approach CSR strategically, integrating it into their core business, forming multi-stakeholder partnerships, and reporting their CSR activities using international reporting guidelines. For instance, the Industrial Development Bank of Turkiye (TSKB), an investment bank, prioritizes material issues and offers loans for projects in renewable energies, resource efficiency, and sustainable tourism. The capacity of *Strategic* companies to meet local needs is moderate, as their engagement with development issues remains within the scope of their core operations. Their localization strategies, therefore, derive from their strategic business models.

Type *D-Non-responsive* refers to organizations without social objectives and does not refer to international conventions for guidance (Appendix 1). These companies interpret CSR as complying with legal requirements and performing philanthropic activities. Of the 50 companies in our sample, 17 fell into this category. Their "compliance approach" to CSR might be due to the temporality and newness of the global development agenda. For example, Petkim, a leading petrochemical holding, was previously state-owned. This may explain its continued use of adaptive social strategies and sensitivity to social policy gaps. Many other companies in this group are unaware of local issues. For example, the locally salient issue of gender equality is typically ignored by companies in the *D-Non-responsive* group.

Engagement with Development Challenges

The companies in our sample addressed a wide array of development challenges through their CSR programs and practices. Our analysis's first and second steps established important conditions for addressing grand challenges. When companies do not respond to dominant CSR conceptions (e.g., *D-Non-responsive*), their ability to address grand challenges is limited. Adopting social objectives or a development-oriented mission does not change this result (*B-Traditional*).

However, when companies start following international initiatives (*C-Strategic*), they also start addressing more development challenges, but only those that can be embedded into the core business. The broadest grand challenges addressed are when companies respond to both the local conception of CSR in the context and blend them with the global CSR conception (*A-Hybrid*). The grand challenges that are most frequently tackled through CSR activities are related to affordable and clean energy (39 companies), climate change (35 companies), and education (32 companies).

We observe that standards for water (20 companies), energy (39 companies), climate change (35 companies), and the environment (22 companies) are entering the country through the global CSR conception, and when they do, they interface with resource efficiency and the growth concerns of the state, making energy and climate action the most frequently targeted goals of CSR practices and programs. As such, they are translated and take on a new meaning by blending with local concerns: "efficiency gains for the company and the economy through improvements in operations." We found similar statements in many of the reports we examined: "Dependence on foreign energy plays a significant role in the magnitude of the country's account deficit...Akbank develops unique financing solutions for solar energy and geothermal energy projects" (Akbank, 2015, p. 57) and "We (Arçelik) continued contributing to Market Transformation of Energy Efficiency Products Project, which encourages the use of energy-efficient electronic appliances in Türkiye" (Arçelik, 2014, p. 2). Through this new meaning, the companies aim to level with the global norms and support the explicit government position on national economic growth and resource efficiency.

Grand challenges are not equally salient in every context. As the analysis we conducted in the third step of our study reveals, companies are not ignorant of local pressing issues. They address education (32 companies), gender equality (24 companies), health (24 companies), industry and innovation (24 companies), and decent work and economic growth (18 companies). It is worth noting that companies engaging with these issues are predominantly *A-Hybrid* companies, especially concerning gender equality, decent work, and economic growth.

As the literature shows (Ertuna & Tukel, 2010; Turker & Altuntas, 2015), philanthropy is a long-established form of CSR. However, with the more recent CSR interpretations in the context, we also observe initiatives that align with the company's core businesses. For instance, Turkcell (*C-Strategic* type) financially supports a project (Snowdrops) that provides equal opportunities in education for underprivileged girls (*philanthropic*); it has also developed a project in partnership with the Ministry of National Education for designing and building vocational education and technology classes for disabled students (*integration with core business*). Likewise, Doğuş Otomotiv (*C-Strategic* type) runs a project to raise awareness about cell phone use during driving (Traffic is Life!) (*integration with core business*), and the Sabancı Group (*A-Hybrid* type) company CarrefourSa implements a project (From Farm to School) in partnership with UNICEF to raise awareness of child labor in agriculture (*integration with core business*).

DISCUSSION AND CONCLUSION

Engaging business with grand challenges is an intriguing issue in developing countries with historically and culturally ingrained systemic development challenges. These countries embody unique understandings of business–society relations with multiple manifestations, symbols, and practices of CSR. Motivated by the multiplicity of developing countries' characteristics, we offer a framework to systematically analyze business engagement with grand challenges using an institutional theory perspective. In this framework, we use two competing conceptions of CSR to identify CSR orientations (types) and define a set of CSR dimensions to assess ways to engage with grand challenges in different orientations. We chose Türkiye as our context to apply our framework, and we believe that this setting provides a fertile ground for understanding the influence of an explicit social mission beyond business to guide companies' CSR. Our findings corroborate the study of Gümüsay et al. (2020), pointing to the strengths of the institutional theory lens for tackling development issues such as grand challenges.

The findings on the grand challenges engagement of companies that adopt social objectives as dictated by the local CSR conception may contribute to the developing literature on company purpose and the role of purposeful companies in addressing global systemic challenges (Henderson & Serafeim, 2020). Companies of the *A-Hybrid* type, typically large commercial companies, traditionally apply locally embedded social objectives; they are similar to B-corporations in their approach to CSR, but they also adopt the norms and initiatives of global CSR conception. *A-Hybrid* type acts as a facilitator for bringing grand challenges from the state to the corporate level, thus offering possibilities for crossbreeding across different contexts. Research has shown that Türkiye shows similarities to hierarchically coordinated countries like South Korea, Jordan, Lebanon, and Taiwan (Choi et al., 2018; Fainshmidt et al., 2018; Oh et al., 2018). Thus, we propose using our framework in such contexts to assess companies' responses to development challenges. Our framework can also be adapted to other contexts based on future researchers' assessment of the company-level CSR strategies, norms, and attributes in conjunction with the macro-level institutional orders surrounding CSR in each context.

Türkiye is a developing country with a state-dependent business system that exhibits most of the institutional weaknesses and deficiencies that typify developing countries (Kang & Moon, 2012). Its traditional business–society relations indicate the presence of a local CSR conception that is shaped primarily by the institutional orders of the "state," together with a global CSR conception. We provided evidence for four (2 × 2) CSR orientations (types), grounded in two competing CSR conceptions and operationalized by combining the two elemental categories at the company level. We identified how companies articulate and address grand challenges through their CSR. Companies of the same CSR type display similar responses to multiple conceptions but utilize distinct instruments for addressing grand challenges.

We found that companies that blend global CSR conception with local institutional basis (type A-*Hybrid*) are generally better able to address grand challenges (as evidenced by their wide grand challenge coverage) and attend to salient local development challenges. Thus, translating the global CSR conception (types A-*Hybrid* and C-*Strategic*), following international conventions, and adopting internally advocated mechanisms, integrating with the core business and using international reporting guidelines facilitate identification with the global development agenda and offer instruments for engagement. This conclusion complements the finding of Miska et al. (2016), who suggested the influence of the state and global CSR association on the companies' global CSR integration in China. In Türkiye's case, however, blending global CSR conception with a local institutional basis (type A-*Hybrid*) extends engagement with salient development challenges of the context. In adapting to the global CSR conception, these companies align their non-commercial, social objectives with social policy gaps, and they utilize historical mechanisms to engage with issues diffusing from the global CSR discourse. They also activate group-wide resources and collaborate with the state to initiate collective action. As Choi et al. (2018) suggested it is to the advantage of the group firms to act collectively since CSR initiatives can impact group firms positively and vice versa.

CSR also lends itself as a platform for businesses to build relations with the state and other constituencies to encourage collective action toward grand challenges *(Traditional* and *Hybrid* types). Leveraging their corporate know-how, companies collaborate with the government, public agencies, and NGOs in policymaking and implementation, using CSR as a tool for lobbying and dialoguing with the state. In this manner, how CSR conceptions are translated and adapted at the local level by aiming to fill the policy gaps and how these reinforce bargaining power with the state match with the basis that is operational in another country from the Middle East, that is, Lebanon (Jamali et al., 2017).

Having social objectives seems to facilitate articulating and addressing the global development agenda, and combining social objectives with instruments of the global CSR conception enhances engagement. On the other hand, responding only to local CSR conception without adopting global conception does not support engagement, as indicated by our findings on type B *(Traditional)* companies, which had the lowest grand challenge coverage. Without a global CSR conception, the development-oriented, social objectives often reflect the state's goals and social policies. Type D *(Non-responsive)* companies share similar results with those in type B in that they lack guidance from institutional orders of both local and global CSR conception; they opt instead for legal compliance and efficiency-based sustainability objectives for CSR. Thus, our findings indicate that a CSR orientation that blends the competing conceptions in a given context (type A) results in a more balanced grand challenge coverage. Factors differentiating companies' engagement with development challenges via CSR include initiatives targeting society, partnerships with companies in other sectors (and the state), employee engagement, and in-house programs. Hybrid CSR orientations in Türkiye and how objectives and norms are paired through translating, blending, and adapting resemble those in other countries in the Middle East (see Jamali et al., 2017, 2018), but they differ dramatically from the ones in developed nations. We, therefore, confirm the importance of context in CSR research and recommend utilizing context-sensitive analysis methods and frameworks.

A theoretical implication of our research is that any study exploring CSR programs and research in developing countries can contribute to debates surrounding the purpose of companies in those settings and offer frames of reference for better engagement with the development agenda. Because CSR in developing countries is an emerging field of study, there is an urgent need to find relevant analytical tools. The multilevel factors in developing nations create complex CSR expression systems that are difficult for researchers to portray.

We contribute to the institutional theory literature by distilling CSR orientations and their attributes in the way they respond to two competing conceptions, one based on the historical conception of business purpose and the other dictated by the global CSR norm (Thornton et al., 2012, p. 59). Based on competing CSR conceptions in Türkiye, we developed a framework that illustrates the application of the institutional theory perspective to CSR and offers an opportunity to integrate macro-level institutional orders with company-level CSR implementations. By adopting a context-sensitive approach to CSR, the framework offers a systematic approach to evaluating different strategies and mechanisms companies employ to reconcile the multiple and often contradictory institutional orders surrounding CSR. This framework can also be adapted to accommodate other research questions and researchers' evaluations of relevant institutional orders surrounding CSR conceptions in the context.

We have provided context-specific evidence on how businesses engage with grand challenges by approaching CSR through the institutional theory perspective. The literature has widely examined the link between CSR and financial results. The social development effects of CSR, however, are understudied. Our study confirmed the significance of a company's integrating its core business, multi-stakeholder partnerships, and international guidelines in engaging with sustainable development.

The chapter has practical implications, particularly for managers operating in non-Western countries that possess multiple and competing conceptions of CSR. Our findings on companies that display strong engagement with the development agenda indicate the importance of blending international and local conceptions and recognizing the state's role in raising awareness and initiating action. As outlined by Jamali et al. (2017), managers should be attuned to the changes in the social issues (the institutional voids) while developing their managerial capabilities to translate and adapt grand challenges and global guidelines at the local level. They will make many iterations to find the best fit for their organizations while facing multiple conceptions of CSR. Furthermore, the managers should expect to be challenged by the changing regulations and expectations of the state for CSR. By using formal and informal mechanisms (e.g., partnerships in CSR programs), advocacy by the state may induce businesses to address culturally rooted and complex social issues.

Further studies should unravel why development challenges remain unaddressed by companies and encourage businesses to generate innovative solutions to the development agenda. A society's norms and values are culturally ingrained, and developmental challenges are complex and require systematic solutions. Genuine solutions, therefore, require a multi-dimensional approach that works with the various layers of society. This raises questions about the effectiveness of business engagement with grand challenges, especially regarding its ability to induce widespread structural and institutional transformations. Consequently, there is a clear need for studies that analyze the depth of coverage that companies exhibit on a single challenge, such as gender equality, to gain insights about the feasibility of and mechanisms of structural transformations.

Our findings about companies with strong engagement also hint at the importance of founding owners' values. Most companies in type-A are family-owned holdings whose business values are handed down from their founding owners, e.g., Koç and Sabancı Holding companies. They also assume a leading role in long-established business–society relations. Thus, further studies on how multiple and competing conceptions are reconciled at the individual level can provide insights for developing strong engagement with grand challenges.

The chapter has limitations. Our empirical research was exploratory, and we gleaned insights from a set of large publicly listed companies. The results can differ for medium- and small-sized private companies. Our framework can be adapted to the dynamic, changing institutional orders, so it is also highly likely that some of our sample companies may have discovered new ways to address grand challenges through mimetic isomorphism, that is, by imitating global best practices or through normative isomorphism, by joining local initiatives (Frynas & Yamahaki, 2016; Miska et al., 2016). Future studies could follow how CSR orientations have changed over the years. We acknowledge that our research comes from company-originated documents, and actual company CSR practices can differ from the rhetoric (GlobeScan-SustainAbility. 2019). To overcome this limitation, our research could have benefited from interviews with company founders, leaders, and managers of partnering institutions, especially concerning the orientations and attributes identified in this research, enablers, and challenges for genuine engagement with the development challenges. Finally, the research was conducted in a single country with a particular mix of CSR orientations, yet grand challenges and CSR are context-dependent constructs, so adaptations will be necessary in other developing nations.

REFERENCES

Agarwal, N., Gneiting, U., & Mhlanga, R. (2017). *Raising the bar: Rethinking the role of business in the Sustainable Development Goal.* Oxfam Discussion Papers.

Aguinis, H., & Glavas, A. (2012). What we know and do not know about corporate social responsibility: A review and research agenda. *Journal of Management, 38*(4), 932–968.

Akbank. (2015). *Akbank sustainability report.* https://www.akbankinvestorrelations.com/en/images/pdf/2015_akbank_sustainability_report.pdf

Ararat, M., Colpan, A. M., & Matten, D. (2018). Business groups and corporate responsibility for the public good. *Journal of Business Ethics, 153*(4), 911–929.

Arçelik. (2014). *Arçelik sustainability report.* https://www.arcelikglobal.com/media/ayypa5g3/sustainability_report_2014.pdf

Buğra, A. (2008). *Kapitalizm, yoksulluk ve Türkiye'de sosyal politika (Capitalism, poverty and social politics in Turkey).* Iletisim yayınları.

Choi, J. J., Jo, H., Kim, J., & Kim, M. S. (2018). Business groups and corporate social responsibility. *Journal of Business Ethics, 153*, 931–954.

Cloutier, C., & Ravasi, D. J. S. O. (2021). Using tables to enhance trustworthiness in qualitative research. *Strategic Organization, 19*(1), 113–133.

Dorobantu, S., Kaul, A., & Zelner, B. (2017). Nonmarket strategy research through the lens of new institutional economics: An integrative review and future directions. *Strategic Management Journal*, *38*(1), 114–140.

Ertuna, B., & Tukel, A. (2010). Traditional versus international influences: CSR disclosures in Turkey. *European Journal of International Management*, *24*(3), 273.

Fainshmidt, S., Judge, W. Q., Aguilera, R. V., & Smith, A. (2018). Varieties of institutional systems: A contextual taxonomy of understudied countries. *Journal of World Business*, *53*(3), 307–322.

Forcadell, F. J., & Aracil, E. (2017). Sustainable banking in Latin American developing countries: Leading to (mutual) prosperity. *Business Ethics*, *26*(4), 382–395.

Frynas, J. G. (2008). Corporate social responsibility and international development: Critical assessment. *Corporate Governance*, *16*(4), 274–281.

Frynas, J. G., & Yamahaki, C. (2016). Corporate social responsibility: Review and roadmap of theoretical perspectives. *Business Ethics: A European Review*, *25*(3), 258–285.

Garriga, E., & Melé, D. (2004). Corporate social responsibility theories: Mapping the territory. *Journal of Business Ethics*, *53*(1), 51–71.

George, G., Howard-Grenville, J., Joshi, A., & Tihanyi, L. (2016). Understanding and tackling societal grand challenges through management research. *Academy of Management Journal*, *59*(6), 1880–1895.

Gioia, D. A., Corley, K. G., & Hamilton, A. L. (2013). Seeking qualitative rigor in inductive research: Notes on the Gioia methodology. *Organizational Research Methods*, *16*(1), 15–31.

GlobeScan-SustainAbility. (2019). *The GlobeScan-SustainAbility Survey 2019*. Retrieved September 1, 2019, from https://globescan.com/wp-content/uploads/2019/07/GlobeScan-SustainAbility-Leaders-Survey-2019-Report.pdf

Grayson, D., & Nelson, J. (2013). *Corporate responsibility coalitions: The past, present and future of alliances for sustainable capitalism*. Stanford University Press.

GRI (2018). *The SDG compass: New indicators available for more meaningful sustainability reporting.*

GRI, & UN Global Compact (2018). *Business reporting on the SDGs: An analysis of the goals and targets.*

Gümüsay, A. A., Claus, L., & Amis, J. (2020). Engaging with grand challenges: An institutional logics perspective. *Organization Theory*, *1*(3), 2631787720960487.

Henderson, R., & Serafeim, G. (2020). Tackling climate change requires organizational purpose. In *AEA Papers and Proceedings*, *110*, 177–180.

Hengst, I.-A., Jarzabkowski, P., Hoegl, M., & Muethel, M. (2020). Toward a process theory of making sustainability strategies legitimate in action. *Academy of Management Journal*, *63*(1), 246–271.

Hoskisson, R. E., Wright, M., Filatotchev, I., & Peng, M. W. (2013). Emerging multinationals from mid-range economies: The influence of institutions and factor markets. *Journal of Management Studies*, *50*(7), 1295–1321.

Høvring, C. M. (2017). Caught in a communicative catch-22? Translating the notion of CSR as shared value creation in a Danish CSR frontrunner. *Business Ethics: A European Review*, *26*(4), 369–381.

Howard-Grenville, J., Davis, G. F., Dyllick, T., Miller, C. C., Thau, S., & Tsui, A. S. (2019). Sustainable development for a better world: Contributions of leadership, management, and organizations. *Academy of Management Discoveries*, *5*(4), 255–366.

Jain, T., Aguilera, R. V., & Jamali, D. (2017). Corporate stakeholder orientation in an emerging country. *Journal of Business Ethics*, *143*(4), 701–719.

Jamali, D., & Carroll, A. (2017). Capturing advances in CSR: Developed versus developing country perspectives. *Business Ethics: A European Review*, *26*(4), 321–325.

Jamali, D., Jain, T., & Samara, G. (2018). Understanding CSR behaviours across the Middle East: A review and research agenda. *Academy of Management Proceedings*, *18*(1), 14485.

Jamali, D., Karam, C., Yin, J., & Soundararajan, V. (2017). CSR logics in developing countries: Translation, adaptation and stalled development. *Journal of World Business*, *52*(3), 343–359.

Kang, N., & Moon, J. (2012). Institutional complementarity between corporate governance and corporate social responsibility: A comparative institutional analysis of three capitalisms. *Socio-Economic Review*, *10*(1), 85–108.

Kaplan, R., & Kinderman, D. J. B. (2020). The business-led globalization of CSR: Channels of diffusion from the United States into Venezuela and Britain, 1962-1981. *Business & Society*, *59*(3), 439–488.

Kolk, A., & Pinkse, J. (2006). Stakeholder mismanagement and corporate social responsibility crises. *European Management Journal*, *24*(1), 59–72.

La Porta, R., Lopez-De-Silanes, F., & Shleifer, A. (2008). The economic consequences of legal origin. *Journal of Economic Literature, 46*(2), 285–332.

Lincoln, Y. S., & Guba, E. G. (1985). *Naturalistic inquiry*. Sage.

Mahoney, L. S., Thorne, L., Cecil, L., & LaGore, W. (2013). A research note on standalone corporate social responsibility reports: Signaling or greenwashing? *Critical Perspectives on Accounting, 24*(5), 350–359.

Marquis, C., & Raynard, M. (2015). Institutional strategies in emerging market. *The Academy of Management Annals, 9*(1), 291–335.

Matten, D., & Moon, J. (2020). Reflections on the 2018 decade award: The meaning and dynamics of corporate social responsibility. *Academy of Management Review, 45*(1), 7–28.

McGahan, A. M. (2020). Where does an organization's responsibility end? Identifying the boundaries on stakeholder claims. *Academy of Management Discoveries, 6*(1), 8–11.

Miska, C., Witt, M. A., & Stahl, G. K. (2016). Drivers of Global CSR Integration and Local CSR Responsiveness: Evidence from Chinese MNEs. *Business Ethics Quarterly, 26*(3), 317–345.

Mühle, U. (2010). *The politics of corporate social responsibility: The rise of a global business norm*. Campus Verlag.

Nelson, J., Porth, M., Valikai, K., & McGee, H. (2015). *A path to empowerment: The role of corporations in supporting women's economic progress*. Corporate Social Responsibility Initiative at the Harvard Kennedy School and the US Chamber of Commerce Foundation.

Oh, W. Y., Chang, Y. K., Lee, G., & Seo, J. (2018). Intragroup transactions, corporate governance, and corporate philanthropy in Korean business groups. *Journal of Business Ethics, 153*(4), 1031–1049.

OECD (2006). *Corporate governance in Turkey: A pilot study*. OECD Publishing.

Ozdora-Aksak, E., & Atakan-Duman, S. (2016). Gaining legitimacy through CSR: An analysis of Turkey's 30 largest corporations. *Business Ethics: A European Review, 25*(3), 238–257.

Özen, Ş., & Küskü, F. (2009). Corporate environmental citizenship variation in developing countries: An institutional framework. *Journal of Business Ethics, 89*(2), 297–313.

Renouard, C., & Ezvan, C. (2018). Corporate social responsibility towards human development: A capabilities framework. *Business Ethics: A European Review, 27*(2), 144–155.

Şişecam. (2014). *Şişecam 2014 sustainability report*. https://www.sisecam.com.tr/en/Documents/sustainability/archive/pasabahce/Pasabahce_2014_Sustainability_Report.pdf

Smith, N. C., Bhattacharya, C. B., Vogel, D., & Levine, D. I. (2010). *Global challenges in responsible business*. Cambridge University Press.

Thornton, P. H., Ocasio, W., & Lounsbury, M. (2012). *The institutional logics perspective: A new approach to culture, structure, and process*. Oxford University Press.

Torres-Rahman, Z., Baxter, G., Rivera, A., & Nelson, J. (2015). *Business and the United Nations: Working together towards the sustainable development goals: A framework for action*. Harvard Kennedy School CSR Initiative and Inspiris Limited.

Turker, D., & Altuntas, C. (2015). Sustainable supply chain management in the fast fashion industry: An analysis of corporate reports. *European Management Journal, 32*(5), 837–849.

United Nations. (2020, Sep 19). *Nations United: Urgent solutions for urgent times | Presented by Thandie Newton*. https://www.youtube.com/watch?v=xVWHuJOmaEk&vl=en

Uyan-Atay, B., & Tuncay-Celikel, A. (2015). CSR practices in Turkey: Examining CSR reports. In M. Blowfield, C. Karam, & D. Jamali (Eds.), *Development-oriented corporate social responsibility* (pp. 167–188). Greenleaf Publishing.

Van Zanten, J. A., & Van Tulder, R. (2018). Multinational enterprises and the Sustainable Development Goals: An institutional approach to corporate engagement. *Journal of International Business Policy, 1*(3), 208–233.

Wright, C., & Nyberg, D. (2017). An inconvenient truth: How organizations translate climate change into business as usual. *Academy of Management Journal, 60*(5), 1633–1661.

Yamak, S., & Ertuna, B. (2012). Corporate governance and initial public offerings in Turkey. In A. Zattoni & W. Judge (Eds.), *Global perspectives on governance and initial public offerings* (pp. 470–498). Cambridge University Press.

Yamak, S., Ergur, A., Karatas-Ozkan, M., & Tatli, A. (2019). CSR and leadership approaches and practices: A comparative inquiry of owners and professional executives. *European Management Review, 16*(4), 1097–1114.

Appendix 1. Dataset-Companies from BIST Istanbul Stock Exchange Sorted According to their CSR Orientation (Types).

Type A-Hybrid

Company	Industry	Ownership (%)				Step 1: Competing Conceptions			Step 2: CSR Dimensions			
		Market Cap (million TL-2016)	Controlling Owners	Foreign Ownership	Freefloat	Nonmarket Objectives	Int. Initiatives	Type	Integration to Core-Business	Extent of Reach	CSR Reporting	External Partnerships
Akbank	Banking	26,800.0	40.8	–	51.3	√	√	A	√	√	√	√
Anadolu Efes	Beverages	11,184.9	43.0	24.0	32.2	√	√	A	√	√	√	√
Arçelik	Domestic appliances	94,399.2	63.3	–	25.0	√	√	A	√	√	√	√
Aygaz	LPG gas	3,030.0	46.5	24.5	24.1	√	√	A	√	√	√	
Doğan Holding	Holding company	1,491.7	57.8	–	35.9	√	√	A	√	√		√
Eczacıbaşı İlaç	Holding company	1,452.8	79.8	–	20.9	√	√	A	√		√	√
Ford Otosan	Motor vehicles	10,625.6	38.5	41.0	17.8	√	√	A	√	√	√	√
Garanti	Banking	29,904.0	6.2	39.9	50.0	√	√	A	√	√	√	√
İşbank	Banking	20,699.9	40.1	–	30.8	√	√	A	√	√	√	√
Koç Holding	Holding company	27,717.4	62.1	–	22.2	√	√	A	√	√	√	√
Sabancı Holding	Holding company	16,894.5	35.2	–	44.1	√	√	A	√	√	√	√
Şekerbank	Banking	1,945.4	60.9	25.4	24.0	√	√	A	√		√	
Tofaş	Motor vehicles	9,475.0	37.6	37.9	24.1	√	√	A	√	√	√	√
Tupras	Energy	17,429.2	51.0	–	48.9	√	√	A	√	√	√	√
Yapı Kredi Bank	Banking	14,301.8	40.9	40.9	17.8	√	√	A	√	√	√	√

| Type B-Traditional | | | Ownership (%) | | | Competing Conceptions | | | CSR Dimensions | | | |
Company	Industry	Market Cap (million TL-2016)	Controlling Owners	Foreign Ownership	Freefloat	Social Objectives	Int. Initiatives	Type	Integration to Core-Business	Extent of Reach	CSR Reporting	External Partnerships
Alarko Holding	Holding company	681.6	67.3	–	28.4	✓		B		✓		
Enka Insaat	Holding company	18,080.0	69.7	–	12.4	✓		B		✓		
İhlas Holding	Holding company	173.9	10.6	–	86.3	✓		B				
Park Elektrik	Mining	436.2	68.0	–	31.5	✓		B				
Turkish Airlines	Air transport	10,198.2	49.1	–	50.3	✓		B			✓	
Vestel	Consumer electronics	1,714.2	77.5	–	21.0	✓		B		✓		
Aselsan	Defense technology	8,435.0	84.6	–	15.3	✓		B			✓	
Tekfen Holding	Holding company	1,494.8	56.7	–	43.3	✓		B	✓	✓		
Tat Gida	Food and beverage	753.4	47.0	5.2	41.3	✓		B	✓	✓		

(Continued)

Appendix 1. *(Continued)*

Type C-Strategic			Ownership (%)				Competing Conceptions			CSR Dimensions			
Company	Industry	Market Cap (million TL-2016)	Controlling Owners	Foreign Ownership	Freefloat	Social Objectives	Int. Initiatives	Type	Integration to Core-business	Extent of Reach	CSR Reporting	External Partnerships
Doğuş Otomotiv	Motor vehicles	2,424.4	85.3	–	24.8		✓	C	✓	✓	✓	✓
TSKB	Banking	2,660.0	46.9	–	39.6		✓	C	✓		✓	✓
Turkcell	telecommunications	21,780.0	51.0	20.9	34.8		✓	C	✓		✓	✓
Ülker	Food and beverage	6,019.2	28.9	21.0	42.7		✓	C	✓		✓	
Aksa Energy	Energy	1,935.1	62.0	16.6	21.4		✓	C	✓		✓	
Coca Cola Beverages	Beverages	9,447.3	54.0	20.1	26.0		✓	C	✓	✓	✓	✓
TAV Airport Holding	Holding company	6,608.1	18.2	38.0	40.6		✓	C	✓		✓	
Otokar	Motor vehicles	2,155.2	70.0	–	27.5		✓	C	✓	✓	✓	
Çimsa	Cement	2,066.8	59.7	–	40.4		✓	C	✓	✓	✓	

Type D-Non-Responsive

Company	Industry	Market Cap (million TL-2016)	Controlling Owners	Foreign Ownership	Freefloat	Social Objectives	Int. Initiatives	Type	Integration to Core-Business	Extent of Reach	CSR Reporting	External Partnerships
			Ownership (%)			Competing Conceptions			CSR Dimensions			
Erdemir	Metals	10,640.0	49.3	12.1	47.5			D	✓		✓	✓
Migros	Retail	3,106.6	50.0	30.5	19.4			D	✓		✓	✓
Sişecam	Holding company	6,061.0	74.2	–	34.5			D	✓		✓	✓
Vakıfbank	Banking	9,575.0	74.6	–	25.1			D	✓		✓	
GSD Holding	Holding company	260.0	44.5	9.9	59.7			D				
İzmir Demir Çelik	Metals	750.0	78.4	–	16.0			D				
Kardemir	Metals	850.4	9.8	–	94.0			D				
Kartonsan	Cardboard	863.3	75.2	–	24.5			D				
Petkim	Chemicals	4,590.0	–	51.0	39.7			D	✓			
Trakya Cam	Glass	1,619.9	69.0	–	30.6			D			✓	
Afyon Cement	Cement	614.0	51.0	–	47.6			D				
Bağfaş	Chemicals	578.3	40.4	–	57.9			D		✓		
BIM Stores	Retail	15,589.9	35.2	–	64.8			D				
Ege Endüstri	Metals	989.7	65.4	–	34.6			D				
Halkbank	Banking	12,987.5	51.1	–	48.9			D	✓		✓	
Soda Sanayi	Metals minerals	2,791,8	61.0	–	16.4			D		✓	✓	

CHAPTER 12

THE TRANSFORMATIVE IMPACT OF AI ON CSR, ESG, AND SUSTAINABILITY: CRITICAL REVIEW AND CASE STUDIES

Bora Ozkan

Temple University, PA, USA

ABSTRACT

In this chapter, the utilization of Artificial Intelligence (AI) and Machine Learning (ML) tools, improved by human expertise, offers a detailed investigation into their transformative effects on Corporate Social Responsibility (CSR), Environmental, Social, and Governance (ESG) standards, and sustainability. Initial insights and structural foundations were developed using AI, specifically utilizing ChatGPT-4, with the author significantly enhancing the content through in-depth academic research and analysis. This synergistic approach provides a holistic view of AI and ML's role in promoting ethical business practices, improving sustainability reporting efficiency, and facilitating informed decision-making within CSR and ESG frameworks. Incorporating extensively verified and expanded real-world examples, the work delves into the practical applications of these technologies and addresses the ethical considerations they raise. This collaboration highlights the evolving role of AI in research and emphasizes the critical importance of integrating AI-generated insights with scholarly research to drive forward sustainable and socially responsible corporate strategies and policies.

Responsible Firms: CSR, ESG, and Global Sustainability
International Finance Review, Volume 23, 203–218
Copyright © 2025 by Bora Ozkan
Published under exclusive licence by Emerald Publishing Limited
ISSN: 1569-3767/doi:10.1108/S1569-376720240000023012

Keywords: Artificial Intelligence; Machine Learning; Corporate Social
Responsibility; Environmental; Social; and Governance; Global
Sustainability; ethical AI; ChatGPT; academic research;

JEL Classifications: M14; Q01; O33; Q56

INTRODUCTION

Disruptive digital technological innovation can alter the corporate landscape
(Choi & Ozkan, 2019). In an era where corporate responsibility extends beyond
profit margins to encompass social, environmental, and governance (ESG) concerns, the concept of Corporate Social Responsibility (CSR), ESG standards,
and global sustainability have become pivotal in shaping the character of modern businesses. This chapter, nestled within the special issue of the International
Finance Review on "Responsible Firms," is dedicated to unraveling the profound
impact of AI and ML on these crucial areas. Significantly, this work has been
crafted with the assistance of ChatGPT-4, an AI language model, exemplifying
the very essence of our topic – the integration of AI into the realms of CSR, ESG,
and global sustainability.

Before the arrival of Artificial Intelligence (AI) and Machine Learning (ML)
technologies, the domains of CSR, ESG standards, and global sustainability
largely relied on traditional methodologies for data gathering, analysis, and strategic implementation (Napier, 2019). In this pre-digital era, as detailed by Carroll
and Shabana (2010), CSR was predominantly viewed through a philanthropic
lens, with companies focusing on compliance and ethical obligations without the
advanced analytical capabilities to integrate CSR deeply into business strategies.
The assessment and integration of ESG factors into corporate decision-making
were similarly constrained, often based on qualitative data and manual reporting, limiting the ability to measure impact accurately or predict future trends
(Schaltegger & Wagner, 2011). The introduction of AI and ML is revolutionizing
these fields, offering new ways to analyze vast datasets, enhance decision-making,
and embed CSR, ESG, and sustainability more deeply into the fabric of corporate strategies.

The goal of this work is to provide a comprehensive platform for researchers,
practitioners, and policymakers to converge, sharing their latest findings, insights,
and experiences. We delve into the measurement, management, and impact of
CSR, ESG, and sustainability initiatives, particularly under the transformative
lens of AI and ML technologies. As we explore these themes, we will uncover how
AI and ML are not just tools for efficiency and innovation but also catalysts for
ethical, sustainable, and socially responsible business practices.

The advent of AI and ML has opened new frontiers in various sectors, including finance, healthcare, and manufacturing.[1] In the context of CSR and sustainability, these technologies offer unprecedented capabilities in data processing,
predictive analytics, and decision-making, enabling firms to achieve their sustainability goals with greater precision and insight (Kumar et al., 2022). ESG

projects faced serious challenges in the fast-changing organizational environment generated by COVID-19, which induced board intervention regarding innovation, networks, and organizational changes (Csedő et al., 2022). From enhancing environmental management through intelligent resource allocation to fostering social governance with data-driven strategies, AI and ML stand at the forefront of a new era in corporate responsibility.

Moreover, as we journey through this work, we will present real-world case studies that illustrate the tangible impacts of AI and ML in actualizing CSR, ESG, and sustainability objectives. These examples will not only demonstrate the current applications but also inspire future innovations in this rapidly evolving field.

In crafting this work, the input from ChatGPT-4 has been instrumental, showcasing the practical utility of AI in academic and research endeavors. This collaboration symbolizes a broader shift in how AI tools are becoming integral to our professional and intellectual landscapes, reshaping how knowledge is created, shared, and applied. As we embark on this exploratory journey, our aim is to offer a nuanced understanding of the dynamic interplay between AI, ML, and responsible corporate practices. We aspire to provide a thought-provoking and enlightening discourse that spurs further research and action in leveraging AI and ML for a more sustainable and socially responsible future.

SECTION 1: THEORETICAL BACKGROUND

The concepts of CSR, ESG criteria, and global sustainability form the cornerstone of modern corporate culture. CSR is characterized by voluntary corporate actions aimed at social consciousness and responsibility beyond what legal mandates require, suggesting that such initiatives hold significant strategic implications for businesses (Carroll, 1979; McWilliams & Siegel, 2001; McWilliams et al., 2006). This approach to CSR underscores the evolving expectations placed on corporations to not only comply with legal requirements but to actively contribute to social, environmental, and economic well-being in a way that aligns with broader societal values.

ESG criteria, as an extension of CSR, serve as crucial benchmarks for assessing a company's commitment to operating in an ethically, socially, and environmentally responsible manner. ESG activities, coupled with transparent reporting, offer a pathway for companies to tackle social issues while enhancing corporate value (Gerged et al., 2023). Effective ESG efforts necessitate concrete actions starting with the development of a robust ESG model that resonates with diverse stakeholders. Such a model should be tailored to accommodate the specific economic and social contexts of different countries, highlighting the importance of a localized approach to ESG criteria implementation. To foster a sustainable society, it is imperative to establish country-specific ESG models that reflect the unique economic and social landscapes of each country, thus ensuring the relevance and effectiveness of ESG initiatives (Park & Jang, 2021).

Global sustainability, in its broadest sense, encompasses efforts to meet the needs of the present without compromising the ability of future generations to meet their own needs, particularly concerning the natural environment and the use of resources. This foundational understanding of CSR, ESG, and sustainability highlights the increasing importance of ethical, responsible business practices and the role of corporations in contributing to a sustainable future, prior to the widespread integration of AI and ML systems in these domains (Chang & Ke, 2024).

The concepts of CSR, ESG criteria, and global sustainability form the cornerstone of modern corporate culture. CSR refers to a company's commitment to manage the social, environmental, and economic effects of its operations responsibly and in alignment with public expectations. ESG criteria, meanwhile, are a set of standards for a company's operations that socially conscious investors use to screen potential investments (Fulton et al., 2012). These criteria focus on how a company safeguards the environment, manages relationships with employees, suppliers, customers, and the communities where it operates, and practices governance, including leadership, executive pay, audits, internal controls, and shareholder rights. Global sustainability, in its broadest sense, encompasses efforts to meet the needs of the present without compromising the ability of future generations to meet their own needs, particularly concerning the natural environment and the use of resources.

To further enrich the discussion on CSR, it's instrumental to consider the relationship between temporal orientation and corporate responsibility on a global scale (Choi et al., 2023). Their research underscores the significance of how companies' future-oriented perspectives influence their commitment to CSR practices. This temporal orientation fosters a proactive approach toward CSR, embedding it as a strategic imperative within the corporate culture rather than a reactive or compliance-driven effort. This perspective is pivotal for understanding the depth and breadth of CSR's impact on global sustainability and ethical business practices.

AI is a field of computer science dedicated to creating systems capable of performing tasks that normally require human intelligence. These tasks include learning, reasoning, problem-solving, perception, and language understanding. ML, a subset of AI, is the study of computer algorithms that improve automatically through experience and using data. It is seen as a crucial element in the development of AI.

AI and ML technologies are increasingly intersecting with CSR, ESG, and sustainability efforts. These technologies provide powerful tools for analyzing large datasets, predicting outcomes, optimizing operations, and making more informed decisions (Kumar et al., 2022). In the context of CSR, AI can aid in identifying and managing ethical risks, enhancing stakeholder engagement, and streamlining sustainability reporting. Adoption of AI technologies in business is changing almost all aspects of doing business in socially responsible ways since AI technologies have three distinct and interrelated facets namely autonomy, learning, and inscrutability (Berente et al., 2021). For ESG, AI can be used to monitor compliance, assess risks, and provide transparency to investors and other stakeholders. AI has the potential to revolutionize the integration of ESG factors into investment decision-making processes. By leveraging advanced algorithms, ML, and data analytics, AI can analyze large volumes of data and identify patterns, trends, and correlations that may not be visible to human analysts. This can enable more accurate and comprehensive assessments of a company's ESG performance, including its environmental impact, social responsibility, and corporate governance practices (Salampasis, 2017). AI can play a crucial role in addressing environmental sustainability challenges by minimizing energy costs, reducing energy consumption, reducing pollution and waste, and supporting circular economy strategies (Enholm et al., 2021). In terms of global sustainability, AI and ML offer solutions for efficient resource use, reducing environmental impact, and contributing to sustainable development goals (SDGs). Van Wynsberghe (2021) posits that "Sustainable AI is focused on more than AI applications; rather, it addresses the whole sociotechnical system of AI," suggesting that the essence of Sustainable AI transcends merely sustaining AI's development. Instead, it revolves around developing AI in a manner that supports the sustainability of environmental resources for present and future generations, upholds economic models beneficial for societies, and respects societal values crucial to specific communities.

This intersection is not without challenges. The ethical use of AI and ML in these domains raises questions about bias, privacy, and accountability. Companies venturing into this space must navigate these challenges thoughtfully, ensuring that the deployment of these technologies aligns with broader societal values and corporate responsibility goals (Lescrauwaet et al., 2022).

This work is particularly relevant in today's context, where there is an increasing push for companies to operate responsibly and sustainably. With the advent of AI and ML, there are new opportunities and challenges in achieving these objectives. The integration of AI and ML in CSR, ESG, and sustainability initiatives represents a frontier in corporate innovation and responsibility. By exploring this integration, this chapter aims to shed light on the potential of these technologies to transform corporate practices for the better, while also addressing the complexities and ethical considerations that come with it.

Through this exploration, the work aims to contribute to the broader discourse on corporate responsibility, offering insights and guidance for businesses, policymakers, and stakeholders on harnessing the power of AI and ML for the greater good.

SECTION 2: AI AND ML IN CORPORATE SOCIAL RESPONSIBILITY

The integration of AI in ethical business practices marks a significant stride in CSR. AI can play a pivotal role in identifying and mitigating ethical risks, ensuring compliance with regulations, and even in decision-making processes that consider ethical implications (Walz & Firth-Butterfield, 2019–2020). For instance, AI algorithms can analyze vast amounts of data to detect patterns indicative of unethical practices such as corruption, fraud, or labor violations. This capability enables companies to take proactive measures in maintaining ethical standards. Having a full scope of AI to capture the connections among all the major dimensions is the key to Socially Responsible AI Algorithms (SRAs) (Cheng et al., 2021). They define Social Responsibility of AI inclusively, highlighting principles such as Fairness and Inclusiveness, means like SRAs, and objectives aimed at improving humanity.

Responsible AI is a critical governance structure for managing, implementing, assessing, and overseeing AI systems to enhance service delivery (Wang et al., 2020). It emphasizes the creation and application of AI solutions that are ethical, transparent, and accountable, which helps in building trust and minimizing privacy breaches.

AI can automate the collection and analysis of data related to CSR activities, making the reporting process more efficient and accurate (Bonsón et al., 2021). ML algorithms can analyze trends over time, providing insights into the effectiveness of CSR initiatives and areas for improvement. These technologies also enable real-time monitoring of CSR initiatives, allowing companies to quickly identify and address any issues that arise.

Case Study: Company Using AI in CSR Initiatives

A notable example of a company leveraging AI in CSR initiatives is IBM,[2] which uses AI to help companies meet their sustainability goals. AI tools are used for various use cases such as asset management, inventory management, schedule optimization, anomaly detection, and ESG reporting. As companies adopt generative AI in these new use cases, they also need to pay attention to a new set of risks that are emerging ranging from potential privacy concerns to a lack of factuality. A Responsible AI approach and an AI Governance framework are both needed to ensure that guardrails are in place for the responsible use of both Classic and generative AI. Sustainability goals and other business goals go hand in hand. For many of these use cases, there is a close relationship between sustainability and cost. Reducing energy, avoiding waste, and optimizing resources have financial benefits as well as environmental advantages. Using new sustainability applications powered by AI, companies will find it easier to make decisions that are aligned with their sustainability goals.

AI's impact on social responsibility extends beyond individual corporate actions. It can contribute to broader societal benefits, such as improving community welfare and supporting social causes. For example, AI-driven platforms can connect businesses with local communities, facilitating partnerships that address social issues like education, healthcare, and poverty. This broader view of social responsibility underscores the potential of AI to foster a more interconnected and mutually supportive business-community relationship.

The 2019 report by McKinsey Global Institute titled "Tech for Good: Smoothing disruption, improving well-being"[3] discusses the potential of advanced technologies, including smart automation and AI, to not only raise productivity and GDP growth but also to improve well-being more broadly, including through healthier life and longevity and more leisure. The report suggests that good outcomes for the economy overall and for individual well-being come about when technology adoption is focused on innovation-led growth rather than purely on labor reduction and cost savings through automation. This needs to be accompanied by proactive transition management that increases labor market fluidity and equips workers with new skills.

As companies integrate AI into their operations, ensuring the ethical development and use of AI itself becomes a CSR goal. This involves addressing issues related to data privacy, bias in AI algorithms, and the transparency of AI systems. Companies leading in CSR are those that not only use AI responsibly but also contribute to the development of ethical AI standards and practices. By doing so, they not only protect their stakeholders but also set a precedent in the responsible use of technology. Eitel-Porter (2020) recommends developing ethical and technical frameworks that can be clearly represented in AI. These frameworks should be tested and measured all the time to ensure that the system remains ethical and effective throughout its lifecycle.

The integration of AI and ML in CSR represents a significant shift in how companies approach their social responsibilities. By enhancing ethical business practices, improving monitoring, and reporting mechanisms, and extending the reach of social responsibility initiatives, AI has the potential to greatly amplify the impact of CSR efforts. However, it is essential for companies to navigate this integration with an eye toward the ethical implications of AI, ensuring that these powerful technologies are used in a manner that aligns with the core values of CSR. This exploration of AI and ML in CSR not only highlights the current applications but also sets the stage for future innovations and ethical considerations in this rapidly evolving field.

SECTION 3: AI-DRIVEN APPROACHES TO ESG

The application of AI in environmental management is revolutionizing how companies approach their environmental responsibilities. Using predictive analytics and ML, businesses can better anticipate environmental risks and optimize their resource use. AI systems can forecast environmental impacts of various actions, enabling companies to make more sustainable choices. For instance, AI can optimize energy consumption in manufacturing processes or predict the environmental impact of supply chain decisions. This proactive approach not only aids in reducing a company's ecological footprint but also aligns with the environmental aspect of ESG criteria. AI design technology significantly improves environmental planning and urban management by adapting different approaches to meet the needs of specific interest groups (Yu et al., 2021). This adaptation, facilitated by gathering unique information from these groups, greatly enhances the performance, accuracy, and efficiency of these processes.

Social governance within ESG frameworks is greatly enhanced by AI technologies. AI can analyze employee feedback in real-time, helping companies to better understand and respond to employee needs, thus improving workplace conditions and employee satisfaction. Additionally, AI-driven analytics can provide insights into customer behavior and preferences, enabling companies to align their products and services more closely with societal values and needs. This aspect of AI application demonstrates its potential in strengthening stakeholder relationships and fostering a more inclusive approach to business operations. AI has the power to analyze large datasets from various sources, providing boards and executives with essential insights (Hilb, 2020). This data-driven decision-making approach helps in identifying potential opportunities, risks, and trends that could go unnoticed.

Case Study: Google Utilizing AI for ESG Improvement

An exemplary case of an organization leveraging AI to enhance its ESG performance is Google. This organization has implemented AI systems to manage its energy consumption and reduce carbon emissions. Google implemented DeepMind's AI to optimize energy usage in its data centers. This AI system analyzes various data points – like temperature, power usage, and server capacity – to predict and minimize energy needs. The AI system dynamically adjusts cooling systems, which are major energy consumers, in real-time. This has led to a significant reduction in the amount of energy used for cooling, which Google reported as a 40% reduction in energy consumption for cooling and a 15% overall reduction in data center power usage effectiveness.[4] Google also developed a platform that shifts the timing of numerous computing tasks to when renewable energy sources, like wind and solar, are most plentiful. This AI-driven approach allows Google to match energy-intensive tasks with times when low-carbon power sources are more available, effectively reducing the carbon footprint of these operations.[5] Google's use of AI in managing energy consumption and reducing carbon emissions stands as a testament to the potential of technology in enhancing ESG performance. Their approach illustrates how AI can be a powerful tool not only for operational efficiency but also for achieving significant environmental impacts, aligning technological innovation with sustainability goals. This case exemplifies how organizations can leverage AI to make substantial contributions to their ESG initiatives, particularly in the realms of environmental stewardship and responsible resource management.

As with any AI application, ethical considerations are paramount, especially in the context of ESG. Ensuring the fairness and transparency of AI algorithms, protecting data privacy, and mitigating any potential biases are essential to maintain the integrity of ESG initiatives. Companies must establish robust ethical guidelines and governance structures to oversee the implementation of AI in their ESG strategies, ensuring that these technologies are used responsibly and in alignment with broader societal values. Various systemic risks posed by AI are explained, including algorithmic biases causing allocation-related harms, disparities in access and benefits, the likelihood of cascading failures and external disruptions, and the challenge of balancing efficiency with resilience (Galaz et al., 2021). They scrutinize these emerging risks, raise critical questions, and critique the inadequacies of current governance frameworks in addressing AI-related sustainability risks. Concurrently, the urgency for lagging governments to enact and implement regulations ensuring the safety of individuals and organizations utilizing AI systems for personal, educational, or commercial endeavors is underscored (Camilleri, 2023).

AI-driven approaches offer transformative potential for companies looking to enhance their performance in ESG aspects. By harnessing the power of AI in environmental management, social governance, and corporate governance, businesses can achieve more sustainable, ethical, and efficient operations. However, the successful integration of AI into ESG initiatives requires a careful balance between technological innovation and ethical responsibility. As AI continues to evolve, its role in shaping the future of ESG in the corporate world will undoubtedly expand, offering new opportunities and challenges for companies committed to responsible and sustainable business practices.

SECTION 4: GLOBAL SUSTAINABILITY AND AI

The intersection of AI with global sustainability is creating new pathways for addressing some of the world's most pressing environmental challenges. AI technologies, through their advanced data processing and predictive analytics capabilities, are instrumental in climate change mitigation, biodiversity conservation, and renewable energy optimization. For instance, AI can be used to model climate change scenarios, helping policymakers and companies to develop more effective strategies for reducing carbon footprints and adapting to changing environmental conditions. AI-driven models are also being used to predict and mitigate the impacts of extreme weather events, contributing to more resilient communities and ecosystems. Compelling evidence of AI's potential to tackle major socio-environmental challenges is provided through two case studies in a recent book (Taghikhah et al., 2022). The first case explores how machine intelligence supports the formulation and implementation of strategies promoting pro-environmental behavior among communities. The subsequent section examines AI's application in wildfire management and the optimization of renewable energy production. The integration of ML methods within supply chain management is examined, underscoring current applications and pinpointing future research directions (Mohamed-Iliase et al., 2020). Their study evaluates the employment of ML techniques in supply chain environments, aiming to investigate their utility as tools for supply chain decision-makers. By harnessing the increasing amount of available data and using specialized tools for analysis, the research seeks to enhance decision-making processes within supply chains.

ML is revolutionizing sustainable supply chain management by enabling more efficient and transparent operations. By analyzing data from various stages of the supply chain, ML algorithms can identify inefficiencies, predict demand patterns, and optimize logistics for reduced environmental impact. This includes minimizing waste, optimizing routes for transportation to reduce fuel consumption, and predicting maintenance needs to prevent breakdowns and excessive energy usage. Such applications not only contribute to environmental sustainability but also improve the economic efficiency of supply chains.

Case Study: International Efforts Where AI Has Contributed to Sustainability Goals

The United Nations Industrial Development Organization (UNIDO) engaged in a series of high-level expert sessions during the AI for Good Global Summit

2023. This summit focused on harnessing AI for sustainable industrialization. UNIDO's AIM-Global initiative, launched in 2023, aims to promote responsible, sustainable, and inclusive use of AI in the industrial sector. The summit brought together international leaders and experts to identify practical AI solutions contributing to advancing the SDGs of the 2030 Agenda.[6] During the AI for Good Global Summit, UNIDO highlighted successful practices derived from technical assistance projects implemented in countries like Belarus, Jordan, Namibia, Tanzania, and Venezuela. These projects explored applications of AI in product lifecycle management, smart factories, and supply chain management, showcasing AI's impact on manufacturing sustainability, efficiency, and competitiveness.

The sustainable application of AI models plays an important role in facilitating the implementation of the 2030 Agenda for Sustainable Development (Perucica & Andjelkovic, 2022). Similarly, AI technologies have the potential to support 79% of the SDGs, especially impacting environmental objectives (SDGs 13, 14, and 15) (Vinuesa et al., 2020). AI applications in this regard span natural language processing, image recognition, data analytics, and pattern recognition, serving various purposes such as identifying endangered species, promoting smart energy solutions, and optimizing energy usage.

AI's application extends to environmental conservation and biodiversity protection. For example, AI-powered drones and sensors are being used for wildlife monitoring and habitat protection, providing data that is critical for conservation efforts. For example, in the Masai Mara National Reserve, southwest Kenya, drones equipped with AI are used to track and monitor elephant populations.[7] This technology helps to identify individual elephants by analyzing unique characteristics such as tears in ears, head size, and tusk shape. This non-invasive approach is more humane than other methods like attaching radio collars and provides real-time data for conservation efforts. Drones, also known as unmanned aerial vehicles, are increasingly being used in wildlife conservation.[8] They offer several advantages over traditional methods, such as covering large areas quickly, accessing remote locations, and collecting data with minimal disturbance to animals. AI plays a crucial role in analyzing the vast amounts of data collected by drones, enabling faster and more accurate insights for conservationists. This combination of drones and AI is used for population monitoring, anti-poaching surveillance, habitat assessment, and disaster response in wildlife conservation.

AI algorithms can also analyze satellite imagery to track deforestation or illegal fishing activities, enabling quicker responses to environmental threats. Microsoft has developed PrevisIA, an AI tool that forecasts deforestation and forest fires in the Amazon before they occur. This tool uses intelligent algorithms in the cloud to predict environmental changes. It is part of a coordinated effort involving corporations, nonprofits, and governments to protect the Amazon.[9] Planet, a satellite imagery company, has partnered with the Norwegian government and Kongsberg Satellite Services to provide high-resolution satellite imagery of tropical regions. This initiative aims to combat deforestation and is in collaboration with the United Nations Food and Agriculture Organization (FAO). The satellite data is integrated into SEPAL, a cloud-based analysis platform developed by the FAO, to better track deforestation and land use.[10] These applications demonstrate AI's potential in preserving natural ecosystems and promoting biodiversity.

While AI holds great promise for advancing global sustainability, the technology itself needs to be sustainable. The energy consumption of training large AI models and the environmental impact of data centers are concerns that need addressing. Sustainable AI involves developing more energy-efficient algorithms and using renewable energy sources for data processing. This aspect of AI sustainability is crucial for ensuring that the technology's deployment does not counteract its environmental benefits. A comprehensive analysis of the carbon footprint associated with AI computing, which examines the entire development cycle of ML models, especially in large-scale industrial applications, and the life cycle of system hardware was conducted by Wu et al. (2022). Their study also assessed the operational and manufacturing carbon footprints of AI computing, offering an end-to-end analysis that underscores the significance of hardware-software design choices and optimizations at scale in reducing the overall carbon emissions of AI technologies.

AI and ML are proving to be indispensable tools in the pursuit of global sustainability. From optimizing resource use in industrial processes to protecting ecosystems and biodiversity, AI's applications are diverse and impactful. However, the journey toward sustainable AI involves continuous evaluation and improvement of the technologies themselves, ensuring that their implementation is in harmony with the broader goals of environmental conservation and sustainability. As the world grapples with environmental challenges, the innovative use of AI and ML offers a hopeful avenue for creating a more sustainable and resilient future.

Section 5: Ethical Considerations and Challenges in AI and ML Applications

Incorporating AI and ML into CSR and ESG initiatives presents not just opportunities but also significant ethical challenges. This section explores the ethical considerations and challenges inherent in deploying AI and ML technologies in the context of CSR and ESG standards.

Mehrabi et al. (2021) investigated the main sources of unfairness in ML outcomes, emphasizing biases present in the data and arising from the algorithms themselves. Their research underscores the impact of data biases on the learning processes of algorithms and scrutinizes how algorithmic functions might lead to unfair decisions independently. Moreover, the study noted the adverse effects of biased algorithmic outcomes on user experience, which contributes to a feedback loop involving data, algorithms, and users that not only perpetuates but could also intensify existing biases. This phenomenon highlights the intricate relationship among data, algorithms, and users, pointing out the obstacles in attaining fairness within ML (Mehrabi et al., 2021).

In the context of CSR and ESG, such biases could lead to unfair practices or discriminatory outcomes, undermining the core objectives of these initiatives. Companies must ensure that their AI systems are developed and implemented with an eye toward fairness, with regular audits to identify and mitigate any biases. Minkkinen et al. (2022) explore the challenges facing AI auditing practices, highlighting issues such as imprecise definitions, limited scope, the difficulty of assessing external influences, and a shortage of essential information for accurate evaluations of AI systems. The study points to a broad agreement on the significance of ethical principles in AI, such as transparency, fairness, non-maleficence, responsibility, and privacy, but it also underscores the hindrances to effective auditing due to the absence of standardized metrics for these principles. This lack of clarity in standards leads to ambiguity in AI auditing, prompting critiques about the cursory and inaccurate use of the term "audit," especially by AI consultancy firms. The need for developing more detailed and well-defined auditing practices in the AI industry is emphasized (Minkkinen et al., 2022).

Transparency and accountability are crucial for building trust in AI systems, especially when they are used in areas impacting CSR and ESG. Companies need to be transparent about how AI and ML are being used, the nature of the data being processed, and the decision-making processes involved. This transparency is essential not only for ethical compliance but also for maintaining stakeholder trust. Furthermore, there must be clear accountability mechanisms in place for the outcomes of AI and ML applications, ensuring that companies can be held responsible for their AI-driven actions. Fritz-Morgenthal et al. (2022) emphasize the critical need for precise definitions of fairness in AI models and a thorough comprehension of the sources and impacts of bias. Their research stresses the importance of developing AI systems that are ethically sound and socially fair, with the goal of minimizing the perpetuation of existing inequalities. They advocate for the necessity of explainability in AI models, arguing that ensuring AI decisions are transparent, accountable, and subject to scrutiny is crucial for addressing the ethical dilemmas presented by AI and promoting its responsible application.

Data privacy is a significant concern in AI and ML applications. Companies collecting and analyzing large volumes of data must ensure that they are doing so in a way that respects individual privacy rights and complies with data protection regulations. This is particularly relevant in CSR and ESG initiatives, where sensitive environmental, employee, or community data may be involved. Robust data security measures and ethical data handling practices are critical for protecting privacy and maintaining the integrity of AI and ML applications. Bonsón and Bednárová (2022) address privacy concerns within the realm of AI, pointing out the potential threats to human rights, data security, and privacy stemming from unregulated AI usage. They suggest that enhancing corporate transparency regarding AI usage and establishing precise reporting guidelines can mitigate these risks. The significance of privacy, particularly in the context of AI systems handling personal information, is underscored, highlighting its status as a fundamental human right.

To effectively navigate these ethical challenges, companies should adopt comprehensive strategies for the responsible implementation of AI and ML. This process includes establishing ethical guidelines for AI use, conducting impact assessments to understand the potential ethical implications of AI initiatives, and engaging with stakeholders to address their concerns and expectations. Continuous learning and adaptation are essential, as the ethical landscape of AI is constantly evolving. Lobschat et al. (2021) focus on developing a foundational comprehension of Corporate Digital Responsibility (CDR) to foster academic research and practical engagement in this field. They pinpoint several critical research domains within CDR, such as analyzing digital behavior, harmonizing ethical considerations with operational efficiency, evaluating organizational preparedness for CDR, and the effective dissemination and adoption of a CDR ethos within organizations. The potential benefits of CDR for enhancing an organization's competitive edge and financial success are emphasized, advocating for the creation of conceptual and analytical frameworks to thoroughly evaluate these effects. This requires the formulation of comprehensive scales and metrics, both financial and non-financial, for the assessment of CDR efforts (Lobschat et al., 2021).

As we conclude this exploration of ethical considerations and challenges in AI and ML applications within CSR and ESG contexts, it becomes clear that the journey toward ethical AI is both complex and critical. The interplay of biases in data and algorithms, coupled with the need for transparency and accountability, underscores the intricate challenges that organizations face. Ensuring fairness and avoiding discriminatory outcomes is not just a technical issue but a moral imperative, requiring a deep understanding of the nuances of AI behavior and decision-making processes.

Moreover, the sanctity of data privacy and security stands as a pillar in this ethical landscape. As AI systems increasingly rely on personal information, organizations must navigate the delicate balance between leveraging data for beneficial outcomes and upholding the privacy rights of individuals. This responsibility extends beyond mere compliance with regulations, embedding itself into the very fabric of organizational culture and practice.

The implementation of responsible AI and ML demands a proactive approach, where ethical guidelines are not just established but also dynamically adapted to the evolving technological and societal landscape. Engaging with stakeholders, conducting thorough impact assessments, and fostering an environment of continuous learning and adaptation are essential steps in this journey.

In essence, the path toward ethical AI and ML in the context of CSR and ESG is not a static one but an evolving narrative that demands constant vigilance, reflection, and action. It is a path that requires organizations to not only harness the power of AI and ML for competitive advantage but also to wield these technologies with a deep sense of responsibility toward society and the environment.

SECTION 6: FUTURE DIRECTIONS AND RECOMMENDATIONS

The evolving landscape of AI and ML signals a new era in CSR, ESG standards, and global sustainability. Innovations in natural language processing, reinforcement learning, and predictive analytics are poised to revolutionize how businesses manage their social and environmental impacts, embedding AI and ML as central components of sustainable business practices. This shift toward technological integration signifies a future where AI and ML are not just facilitators of efficiency and innovation but are essential for achieving societal and environmental objectives (Kaplan & Haenlein, 2020; Wamba et al., 2024).

As AI and ML technologies advance, their role in CSR, ESG, and sustainability becomes increasingly critical. The availability of vast datasets and the refinement of AI algorithms provide companies with unprecedented tools to measure, manage, and enhance their sustainability efforts. Furthermore, AI's ability to adapt to changing regulations and societal expectations underscores its potential as a cornerstone of organizational strategy, driving not only economic benefits but also contributing significantly to environmental stewardship and social well-being (Daugherty & Wilson, 2018).

The synergy between AI and emerging technologies such as the Internet of Things (IoT), blockchain, and edge computing offers innovative solutions to CSR and sustainability challenges. For instance, integrating AI with IoT promises more effective environmental monitoring systems, while blockchain technology can enhance supply chain transparency and traceability. Such integrations represent a leap toward smarter, more sustainable systems that address pressing societal and industry challenges (Kshetri, 2017; Tschorsch & Scheuermann, 2016).

For practitioners and policymakers alike, staying well-informed of these technological developments is crucial. Practitioners must invest in the necessary skills and infrastructure to leverage AI and ML effectively, while policymakers should foster an environment that encourages ethical AI use in CSR and ESG initiatives through appropriate frameworks and incentives.

In conclusion, AI and ML are set to play a pivotal role in the next wave of CSR, ESG, and global sustainability innovation. However, navigating this journey requires a balanced approach that considers technological advancements alongside ethical and societal impacts. By responsibly integrating these technologies, companies can enhance their sustainability performance and contribute to broader societal goals, marking a significant step toward a more sustainable and equitable future.

NOTES

1. For more detailed information check out McKinsey Global Institute 2017 discussion paper.
2. IBM is using AI to help companies, visit their blog post on sustainability.
3. For more detailed information check out McKinsey Global Institute 2019 discussion paper.
4. Google is using AI to reduce data center cooling bill, visit their impact blog post.
5. Google developed a new way to reduce their data centers' electricity consumption when there is high stress on the local grid, visit their infrastructure blog post.
6. UNIDO engaged in a series of high-level expert session during the AI for Good Global Summit 2023.
7. New AI-powered drone technology aids elephant conservation.
8. The future of wildlife conservation: how drones and AI are revolutionizing the field.
9. New AI tool helps forecast Amazon deforestation.
10. How better access to satellite imagery is helping.

REFERENCES

Berente, N., Gu, B., Recker, J., & Santhanam, R. (2021). Managing artificial intelligence. *MIS Quarterly*, 45(3), 1433–1450.

Bonsón, E., & Bednárová, M. (2022). Artificial Intelligence disclosures in sustainability reports: Towards an Artificial Intelligence reporting framework. In V. Kumar, J. Leng, V. Akberdina, & E. Kuzmin (Eds.), *Digital transformation in industry* (Lecture Notes in Information Systems and Organisation, Vol. 54). Springer. https://doi.org/10.1007/978-3-030-94617-3_27

Bonsón, E., Lavorato, D., Lamboglia, R., & Mancini, D. (2021). Artificial intelligence activities and ethical approaches in leading listed companies in the European Union. *International Journal of Accounting Information Systems, 43*, 100535. https://doi.org/10.1016/j.accinf.2021.100535

Camilleri, M. A. (2023). Artificial intelligence governance: Ethical considerations and implications for social responsibility. *Expert Systems*, e13406. https://doi.org/10.1111/exsy.13406

Carroll, A. B. (1979). A three-dimensional conceptual model of corporate performance. *Academy of Management Review, 4*(4), 497–505.

Carroll, A. B., & Shabana, K. M. (2010). The business case for corporate social responsibility: A review of concepts, research and practice. *International Journal of Management Reviews, 12*(1), 85–105.

Cheng, L., Varshney, K. R., & Liu, H. (2021). Socially responsible AI algorithms: Issues, purposes, and challenges. *Journal of Artificial Intelligence Research, 71*, 1137–1181.

Chang, Y.-L., & Ke, J. (2024). Socially responsible artificial intelligence empowered people analytics: A novel framework towards sustainability. *Human Resource Development Review, 23*(1), 88–120. https://doi.org/10.1177/15344843231200930

Choi, J. J., Kim, J., & Shenkar, O. (2023). Temporal orientation and corporate responsibility: Global evidence. *Journal of Management Studies, 60*(1), 82–119.

Choi, J. J., & Ozkan, B. (2019). Innovation and disruption: Industry practices and conceptual bases. In J. J. Choi & B. Ozkan (Eds.), *Disruptive innovation in business and finance in the digital world (International Finance Review*, Vol. 20). Emerald Publishing Limited.

Csedő, Z., Magyari, J., & Zavarkó, M. (2022). Dynamic corporate governance, innovation, and sustainability: Post-COVID period. *Sustainability, 14*(6), 3189. https://doi.org/10.3390/su14063189

Daugherty, P. R., & Wilson, H. J. (2018). *Human + machine: Reimagining work in the age of AI.* Harvard Business Review Press.

Eitel-Porter, R. (2021). Beyond the promise: Implementing ethical AI. *AI and Ethics, 1*, 73–80.

Enholm, I. M., Papagiannidis, E., Mikalef, P., et al. (2022). Artificial intelligence and business value: A literature review. *Information Systems Frontiers, 24*, 1709–1734. https://doi.org/10.1007/s10796-021-10186-w

Fritz-Morgenthal, S., Hein, B., & Papenbrock, J. (2022). Financial risk management and explainable, trustworthy, responsible AI. *Frontiers in Artificial Intelligence, 5*, 779799.

Fulton, M., Kahn, B. M., & Sharples, C. (2012, June 12). Sustainable investing: Establishing long-term value and performance. *Deutsche Bank.* https://dx.doi.org/10.2139/ssrn.2222740

Galaz, V., Centeno, M. A., Callahan, P. W., Causevic, A., Patterson, T., Brass, I., Baum, S., Farber, D., Fischer, J., Garcia, D., McPhearson, T., Jimenez, D., King, B., Larcey, P., & Levy, K. (2021). Artificial intelligence, systemic risks, and sustainability. *Technology in Society, 67*, 101741. https://doi.org/10.1016/j.techsoc.2021.101741

Gerged, A. M., Salem, R., & Beddewela, E. (2023). How does transparency into global sustainability initiatives influence firm value? Insights from Anglo-American countries. *Business Strategy and the Environment, 32*(7), 4519–4547. https://doi.org/10.1002/bse.3379

Hilb, M. (2020). Toward artificial governance? The role of artificial intelligence in shaping the future of corporate governance. *Journal of Management Governance, 24*, 851–870. https://doi.org/10.1007/s10997-020-09519-9

Kaplan, A., & Haenlein, M. (2020). Rulers of the world, unite! The challenges and opportunities of artificial intelligence. *Business Horizons, 63*(1), 37–50. https://doi.org/10.1016/j.bushor.2019.09.003

Kshetri, N. (2017). Blockchain's roles in meeting key supply chain management objectives. *International Journal of Information Management, 39*, 80–89. https://doi.org/10.1016/j.ijinfomgt.2017.12.005

Kumar, S., Sharma, D., Rao, S. et al. (2022). Past, present, and future of sustainable finance: insights from big data analytics through machine learning of scholarly research. *Annals of Operations Research.* https://doi.org/10.1007/s10479-021-04410-8

Lescrauwaet, L., Wagner, H., Yoon, C., & Shukla, S. (2022). Adaptive legal frameworks and economic dynamics in emerging technologies: Navigating the intersection for responsible innovation. *Law and Economics, 16*(3), 202–220. https://doi.org/10.35335/laweco.v16i3.61

Lobschat, L., Mueller, B., Eggers, F., Brandimarte, L., Diefenbach, S., Kroschke, M., & Wirtz, J. (2021). Corporate digital responsibility. *Journal of Business Research, 122*, 875–888. https://doi.org/10.1016/j.jbusres.2019.10.006

McWilliams, A., & Siegel, D. (2001). Corporate social responsibility: A theory of the firm perspective. *Academy of Management Review, 26*(1), 117–127.

McWilliams, A., Siegel, D. S., & Wright, P. M. (2006). Corporate social responsibility: Strategic implications. *Journal of Management Studies*, *43*(1), 1–18.

Mehrabi, N., Morstatter, F., Saxena, N., Lerman, K., & Galstyan, A. (2021). A survey on bias and fairness in machine learning. *ACM Computing Surveys*, *54*(6), Article 115. https://doi.org/10.1145/3457607

Minkkinen, M., Niukkanen, A., & Mäntymäki, M. (2022). What about investors? ESG analyses as tools for ethics-based AI auditing. *AI & Society*, *39*, 329–343 (2024). https://doi.org/10.1007/s00146-022-01415-0

Mohamed-Iliasse, M., Loubna, B., & Abdelaziz, B. (2020). Is machine learning revolutionizing supply chain? In *2020 5th international conference on logistics operations management (GOL)*, Rabat, Morocco. https://doi.org/10.1109/GOL49479.2020.9314713

Napier, E. (2019). Technology enabled social responsibility projects and an empirical test of CSR's impact on firm performance. https://doi.org/10.57709/14263139

Park, S. R., & Jang, J. Y. (2021). The impact of ESG management on investment decision: Institutional investors' perceptions of country-specific ESG criteria. *International Journal of Financial Studies*, *9*(3), 48. https://doi.org/10.3390/ijfs9030048

Perucica, N., & Andjelkovic, K. (2022). Is the future of AI sustainable? A case study of the European Union. *Transforming Government: People, Process and Policy*, *16*(3), 347–358.

Salampasis, D. (2017). Leveraging robo-advisors to fill the gap within the sri marketplace. *Journal of Innovation Management*, *5*(3), 6–13. https://doi.org/10.24840/2183-0606_005.003_0002

Schaltegger, S., & Wagner, M. (2011). Sustainable entrepreneurship and sustainability innovation: Categories and interactions. *Business Strategy and the Environment*, *20*(4), 222–237.

Taghikhah, F., Erfani, E., Bakhshayeshi, I., Tayari, S., Karatopouzis, A., & Hanna, B. (2022). Artificial intelligence and sustainability: Solutions to social and environmental challenges. In *Artificial intelligence and data science in environmental sensing* (pp. 93–108). Academic Press.

Tschorsch, F., & Scheuermann, B. (2016). Bitcoin and beyond: A technical survey on decentralized digital currencies. *IEEE Communications Surveys & Tutorials*, *18*(3), 2084–2123. https://doi.org/10.1109/COMST.2016.2535718

van Wynsberghe, A. (2021). Sustainable AI: AI for sustainability and the sustainability of AI. *AI Ethics*, *1*, 213–218. https://doi.org/10.1007/s43681-021-00043-6

Vinuesa, R., Azizpour, H., Leite, I., Balaam, M., Dignum, V., Domisch, S., Felländer, A., Langhans, S. D., Tegmark, M., & Nerini, F. F. (2020). The role of artificial intelligence in achieving the sustainable development goals. *Nature Communications*, *11*(1). 233. https://doi.org/10.1038/s41467-019-14108-y

Walz, A., & Firth-Butterfield, K. (2019-2020). Implementing ethics into artificial intelligence: Contribution, from legal perspective, to the development of an AI governance regime. *Duke Law & Technology Review*, *18*, 176–231. https://heinonline.org/HOL/P?h=hein.journals/dltr18&i=176

Wamba, S. F., Queiroz, M. M., Pappas, I. O., & Sullivan, Y. (2024). Artificial intelligence capability and firm performance: A sustainable development perspective by the mediating role of data-driven culture. *Information Systems Frontiers*, *67*, 101741. https://doi.org/10.1007/s10796-023-10460-z

Wang, Y., Xiong, M., & Olya, H. (2020). Toward an understanding of responsible artificial intelligence practices. In T. X. Bui (Ed.), *Proceedings of the 53rd Hawaii international conference on system sciences* (HICSS 2020), Maui, Hawaii, USA (pp. 4962–4971). Hawaii International Conference on System Sciences (HICSS).

Wu, C. J., Raghavendra, R., Gupta, U., Acun, B., Ardalani, N., Maeng, K., Chang, G., Aga, F., Huang, J., Bai, C., & Gschwind, M. (2022). Sustainable AI: Environmental implications, challenges, and opportunities. *Proceedings of Machine Learning and Systems*, *4*, 795–813.

Yu, K. H., Zhang, Y., Li, D., Montenegro-Marin, C. E., & Kumar, P. M. (2021). Environmental planning based on reduce, reuse, recycle and recover using artificial intelligence. *Environmental Impact Assessment Review*, *86*, 106492. https://doi.org/10.1016/j.eiar.2020.106492

CHAPTER 13

HOW DO CONSUMER GOODS MULTINATIONALS ENGAGE WITH CORPORATE SUSTAINABILITY? A CROSS-COMPANY CASE STUDY ANALYSIS

Marco Simões-Coelho, Ariane Roder Figueira[a] and Eduardo Russo[b]

[a]Federal University of Rio de Janeiro, Brazil
[b]Tecnológico de Monterrey, Mexico

ABSTRACT

Motivated by the advancements in the discussions of environmental, social, and governance globally, this study aims to improve the knowledge of corporate sustainability motivations and engagement through a qualitative cross-company case study analysis of two consumer goods multinationals, Natura & Co. headquartered in Brazil, and The Coca-Cola Company, headquartered in the USA. The cases were chosen to compare the two companies' corporate sustainable development (SD) motivations, one headquartered in an emerging and the other in a developed country. This study also assesses the balance between these corporations' global and local sustainability agendas, comparing their worldwide engagement promises to their actual deliveries vis-à-vis national-institutional arrangements. As contributions to the field, comparing the cases surfaced valuable insights and additional theoretical abstractions on corporate sustainability, including proposing a new SD-engagement typology.

Responsible Firms: CSR, ESG, and Global Sustainability
International Finance Review, Volume 23, 219–243
Copyright © 2025 by Marco Simões-Coelho, Ariane Roder Figueira and Eduardo Russo
Published under exclusive licence by Emerald Publishing Limited
ISSN: 1569-3767/doi:10.1108/S1569-376720240000023013

Keywords: ESG; sustainability; corporate social responsibility; consumer goods multinationals; corporate engagement

JEL codes: M14; F23

1. INTRODUCTION

The role of corporations in SD seems like an anomaly in the age of internationalism. It is one area where companies still need to take the global lead, even though business leaders seem to increasingly accept their responsibility in this arena (Pless et al., 2012). The many examples that compose the United Nations (UN) industry books (UN and KPMG. 2016) or the findings on corporate sustainability research (Schneider, 2015) show that their engagement depends on both internal and external conditions and drivers to move the organization (Lozano, 2015).

It has been argued that political, economic, and cultural local contexts deeply affect how corporate responsibility is viewed and implemented (Gjølberg, 2010), indicating a pattern for corporate engagement in sustainability and how motivation turns into engagement. The institutional environment seems like one of the critical forces shaping corporate social responsibility in different countries (Fransen, 2013), while there is a continuous gap in the knowledge between the interaction between national-institutional policies and the social and environmental outcomes, especially if we consider the different institutions, regulations, and consumer tastes that exist in developed and emerging nations (Fransen, et al., 2019), and the necessary strategies adaptations derived from these arrangements.

The present research aims to investigate corporate motives for the engagement of consumer goods multinational enterprises (CG-MNEs) with sustainable development (SD) and how the regional arrangements implicate the implementation of their environmental, social, and governance (ESG) agenda. To that end, this study assesses whether corporate origin, as well as regional motivations, influence the implementation of sustainability activities by these CG-MNEs. It also compares two companies with operations in every macro-region of the world, one headquartered in a developed and the other in an emerging economy, to observe if and how the corporate SD strategy's implementation differs in their global operations and subsidiaries depending on local conditions and corporate history.

ESG and corporate SD are understood as interchangeable terms throughout this chapter, as previously applied in the literature (Garcia et al., 2019). The concept of macro-regions and their subdivisions, developed by the United Nations (UN) (United Nations Statistics Division, 2012), is used to delimit regions and countries' areas. The macro-regions follow not only continental borders but also aim to segregate by economic development as far as possible. There is also an indication that the level of commitment to social responsibility and sustainability depends on a company's country or regional origin (Sotorrío & Sánchez, 2008), influencing performance and directly impacting competitive success (Gallardo-Vázquez & Sanchez-Hernandez, 2014).

Thus, it is possible to propose that the engagement with sustainability changes for multinational companies according to both their commitment to the ESG agenda and the institutional arrangements of the locations where they conduct their business. Different authors have discussed these topics, as demonstrated by the literature throughout this study. However, the crossing of two authors' work inspires this study: Anselm Schneider and Luc Fransen. The first reflects on integrating economic, ecological, and social considerations into more sustainable business models (Cho et al., 2020; Schneider, 2015). The second proposes forms of national-institutional configurations that affect corporate social responsibility differently in different countries (Fransen, 2013; Fransen et al., 2019). This chapter connects the two scholars' discussions while searching for answers about corporate sustainability engagement using an SD motivations framework that encompasses timing and geographic considerations (Simões-Coelho & Figueira, 2021).

For practitioners, this study helps uncover the reasons to embrace sustainability and indicates that this path may lead to improved business results. The cases of large CG-MNEs can disseminate knowledge and best practices. Thus, it is expected that both managers and researchers will be able to appreciate and profit from this study.

2. LITERATURE REVIEW

2.1. Sustainable Development and Corporate Engagement

SD was a term coined in 1987 by the World Commission on Environment and Development or Brundtland Commission. Its final report defines SD as meeting the present's needs without compromising the future (UN WCED, 1987). Brundtland's report put together a more comprehensive concept of sustainability, going beyond the environment and adding development, a term borrowed from the field of economics – "the 'environment' is where we live, and 'development' is what we all do in attempting to improve our lot within that approach. The two are inseparable" (UN WCED, 1987, p. 7).

This concept was further explored and detailed in the three major SD global conferences that have happened since. These conferences were integrated into a series of international treaties and protocols that advanced the SD agenda globally. Each generated specific agreements – the Agenda 21 from Rio 92, the Johannesburg Declaration in 2002, and the Future We Want from Rio+20. With the Millennium Goals, the Island States Pathway, the Sustainable Management of Forest Statement, and the 1972 Declaration of Human Environment, they compose the documents the United Nations Sustainable Development Goals (UN SDGs) Knowledge Platform considers the most critical conventions on SD as a whole (United Nations Organization, 2020).

These agreements and conventions increasingly integrated the companies into the realm of proposed solutions for global sustainability. Many new regulations or instruments were imposed by governments or suggested by the business community to address SD, among them, the creation of a Climate Change Exchange in Chicago, USA, the development of ISO 14000 to standardize environmental management, the imposition of health companies' flexibility measures to ensure medication supply for less-developed countries via the TRIPS Agreement (Luke, 2013), among others. However, the global UN Sustainable Development conferences counted on the meek participation of businesses until Rio+20.

In this 2012 gathering, prior to the beginning of the UN member countries summit, a Corporate Sustainability Forum was held with more than 2,000 business leaders, multilateral and civil society organizations, together with UN agencies (UN Global Compact, 2012). It is, thus, a novel agenda for some companies while others embraced it early and evolved their business along with it. Conventional businesses follow a market logic that targets profits and seem incapable of embracing SD's complexities (Schneider, 2015). Most of the corporations in operation were founded and prospered before the emergence of the ESG concept, but management increasingly accepts it as global resources' scarcity becomes more evident (Luke, 2013). Corporations have become pivotal for global sustainability to advance this agenda and reduce their environmental impact (Diesendorf, 1999; Schneider, 2015), making them a central focal point for legislators' and stakeholders' pressure alike.

In line with these pressures and their gained SD knowledge, some companies adapted to new, more sustainable business models (Bryson & Lombardi, 2009). The business community also created new structures to support the sustainability precepts. The World Business Council for Sustainable Development (WBCSD. was founded in 1995 and grew to direct membership of 225 global companies and 6,500 others associated with 60 country organizations in every continent (WBCSD, 2024). In parallel, there have been several initiatives to improve certification and reporting in sustainability. The most successful initiatives in the 2010s have been the B Corporations certification, which initially attracted small businesses around the world but has been able to gather the interest and accredit large multinationals (B Corporation. 2020) and the Global Reporting Initiative, which created a standard for corporate sustainability reporting (Asif et al., 2011; Searcy & Buslovich, 2014). As the SD in business trend grew, the major stock exchanges have been encouraged to promote indices and platforms for sustainable investing along with companies, investors, and regulators (UN Partnership Programme, 2020). The most visible and valued index internationally is the Dow Jones Sustainability Index, which evaluates companies and stocks from different countries and exchanges (Robinson et al., 2011).

To be aligned with the global sustainability benchmark, companies and instruments had to adjust to the 2015-launched UN SDGs framework. There has been a specific concern to address businesses across the platform. The SDGs are a set of principles and targets within the UN's 2030 sustainability agenda that aim to bring together governments, corporations, and civil society to help humankind overcome its matters and create value for humanity (United Nations Organization, 2015). These principles are gathered as the 17 SDGs and 169 specific targets. Businesses are an essential part of different SDGs. Reaching the targets will largely depend on their adjustment to this new order, together with governments, non-governmental organizations (NGOs), and individuals.

Unlike the early days of the SD discussions, corporate participation was organic, mainly through the WBCSD. As part of the SDGs is translated into international, national, or subnational legislation, they become compulsory for companies. Two SDGs are directly related to the business world: SDG 12 focuses on production and consumption and includes a specific target of "adopting sustainable business practices and reporting." In contrast, SDG 17 consists of two targets on multi-stakeholder partnerships to make sure it entices enough focus and traction. But the whole agenda can be, directly or indirectly, addressed by the corporations. In parallel, the ESG framework was derived from discussions held and promoted within the WBCSD, by consulting firms, and business events, particularly the World Economic Forum (Cruz & Matos, 2023).

Among other instruments, the UN created a comprehensive guide for the Food, Beverages, and Consumer Goods Industries to address the 17 SDGs. Called the SDGs Industry Matrix, this guide (UN and KPMG. 2016) was launched in February 2016 to help businesses prepare for this new world. However, it is also a reference for lawmakers, pressure groups, and other stakeholders in their interactions with corporations. The guide can also function as a manual to companies when there is growing awareness of stakeholders and media regarding socio-environmental aspects such as climate change, lack of hydrological resources, destruction of biodiversity, ethnic conflicts, and urban violence (Lemme, 2010). It brings recommendations of certification schemes to improve corporate sustainability, such as Fairtrade or the Saboo Standard for social certification, and examples of companies that are part of the Global Compact, the United Nations' led corporate sustainability initiative for companies that acknowledge the need to operate in a more sustainable mode (Oliveira et al., 2008) and voluntarily commit to programs with the human rights, labor, environment, social, and anticorruption principles. Each SDG has a "Leading by Example section" with one or more multinational companies listed, including AB InBev, Arcor Group, Cargill, The Coca-Cola Company, General Mills, Lego Group, Malawi Mangoes, Nestlé, SABMiller, Tetra Pak, and Unilever, among others.

The 193 countries officially represented in the General Assembly approved the SDGs unanimously in September 2015. Immediately after, global, national, and subnational indicators started to be negotiated for each of the 169 targets. As countries adopt legislation based on the SDGs and have their laws enforced, associated with resources to ensure corporate compliance, sustainability efforts may prove more widespread and effective (Chen et al., 2014). However, while comprehensive, the UN's type of guidance can be perceived as soft since adherence to it is not required but rather optional, and regulation can be very lax in several countries, especially in the less developed ones (Epstein & Buhovac, 2014).

2.2. Corporate Sustainability and the ESG

The working definition by Diesendorf is used throughout this project – "Sustainability and sustainable futures are treated here as the goals or endpoints of a process called Sustainable Development" (1999, p. 22). So, sustainability is a term used as a short format for SD. The influence of the sustainability concept has increased significantly over time, turning it into a core element of government and international organizations' policies (Mebratu, 1998). When sustainability was adopted as a social practice in the mid-1900s, it seemed "antithetical to the work of trained professional managers" (Luke, 2013, p. 87).

Criticism grew in parallel with this new influence, and some believe that the SD discourse aims to preserve the privilege of corporations instead of preserving the world (Luke, 2013), being more concerned with their financial performance than contributing to the planet's well-being (Barauskaite & Streimikiene, 2021). Still, SD is increasingly critical to granting companies a continuous license to operate in the global scenario, requiring a shift in their corporate model and strategic direction that flowed into the ESG concept. Schneider (2015) proposes a new logic to businesses, which can become more sustainable than conventional companies in two different ways, a framework still considered nowadays (Cho et al., 2020). Either as a comprehensive end-goal SD company or a financial performance one with environmental and social performance means to get there, as per Fig. 13.1.

Market-centered companies have the ultimate goal of contributing to the company's financial performance by being SD-conscious on the way. Sustainability-centered ones are organizations that have narrowed into a wholesome means-equation, as in the Triple Bottom Line (TBL) concept. The TBL derives from the well-known bottom-line expression used to describe a company's net results (Lemme, 2010). According to the TBL acronym creator (Elkington, 2004), its agenda focuses not only on the economic value that may be added but also on the environmental and social value added or even destroyed depending on the decisions taken by the companies. The TBL concept is widely used to address themes such as circular economy to sustainable business (Khan et al., 2021) and is also called the golden triangle.

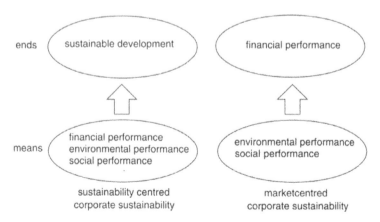

Fig. 13.1.   Types of Corporate Sustainability. *Source*: Schneider, 2015.

Aiming for TBL, several companies have joined the Global Compact, the pact that includes the UN and corporations toward SD (United Nations Organization, 2020). Most of them disclose their sustainability practices in annual reports. This pragmatic approach may bring positive results for companies, improving goodwill and protecting their image with their stakeholders – consumers, media, NGOs, shareowners, governments – and may even be a strategy to increase the perception of more quality relative to competitors, contributing to the long-term performance of companies (Lemme, 2010). Different studies have also used the acronym ESG to portray the connection between financial success and increased sustainability (Beckmann et al., 2014; Cupertino et al., 2019; Stellner et al., 2015), which relate to corporate survival in the long run.

A successful company must be capable of self-perpetuation, outliving its executives and members (Fleck, 2009). One of the characteristics of successful corporations is to inspire respect via the positive reputation they build throughout their existence. A company can only be viewed positively in the XXI century if it grows and advances sustainably (Barnett & Pollock, 2012). Eberle et al. (2013) show how companies are increasingly concerned with adverse communication effects on their business. To that end, they must count on the goodwill of their stakeholders by changing their practices. Goodwill is built through time and depends on how well a company is known and how much its actions make it look good or bad (Brown, 1995). Clients assess a company's reputation as a sign to predict future action; thus, a positive reputation can reduce risks (Ruth & York, 2004). Simultaneously, there are situations when consumers cannot assess the quality of a certain product before a purchase, but a positive reputation may serve as a sign of this corporation's products' basic quality (Rose & Thomsen, 2004), leading to increased sales.

Together with reputation gains, another longer-term positive result may be shareowner value. Different indexes around the world have been working to capture the possible financial reward of embracing more sustainable business. An example is the Dow Jones Sustainability Index, created as a business tool that helps investors evaluate long-term shareholder value and risk management related to the TBL – economic, environmental, and social developments (Epstein & Roy, 2003). Multinational organizations have recognized that it may be necessary for their business to turn them more sustainable. However, companies need strong calls for change to progress in their status quo. "The findings [of a longitudinal 25 years study] show that, internally, leadership and the business case are the [main] drivers, whilst the most important external drivers are reputation, customer demands and expectations, and regulation and legislation" (Lozano, 2015, p. 32). Thus, both innovation and legitimacy are means to achieve progress while ensuring the company's long-term survival.

The capability of being accepted by public opinion is one of the reputational dimensions, called the "social license to operate" (Sustainable Business Council, 2013). The larger the losses, the more incentive companies have to engage with social responsibility (Brammer & Pavelin, 2005) and develop new business models (Boons et al., 2013). The social license to operate is a manifestation of Institutional Theory (Webb et al., 2020), and the new business models appear as a response to the need to compete via innovation in processes and products, as predicted by Innovation Theory. These theories are dissected in the next section.

2.3. Institutions, Innovation, and Corporate Survival

Institutional theory exposes the roots for adopting governmental and unwritten communal principles to ensure legitimation (North, 1990). Innovation Theory shows that the economy evolves through incremental (Schumpeter, 1980; Sweezy, 1943) or radical changes that end up disrupting previous arrangements (Christensen, 1997, 2006), as companies must adapt continuously to continue existing.

The quest for complying with institutional consensus, or legitimacy, forces leaders to adopt formal policies within their organizations (Meyer & Rowan, 1977) and has become a strong motivation toward SD. These policies become fundamental to corporate survival through social judgment's subjective approval (Bitektine, 2011). The institutionalization of SD via the United Nations and most national governments made it a desirable business track. The UN created the basis for institutionalizing corporate social responsibility and sustainability and influenced governments and companies to follow the same route (Brammer & Pavelin, 2005). These institutional values became the new, positive "myths" to be observed by organizations (Barbieri et al., 2010), which adopted the sustainable models and practices considered better in the contemporary social system. North (1990) described this movement in his comprehensive work focusing on the overall social environment and governance, institutions create the ground rules that will impact organizations. For him, the institutions are the "rules of the game" in any given society, as they restrain all society's interactions in politics, economy, or social relations. The institutionalization process, however, is unequal in different societies (Fransen, 2013), such as in the asymmetries of an emerging and a developed market. Incremental changes on top of previous institutions will eventually modify the whole edifice (North, 1990).

On its way to becoming institutionalized, SD itself has been constructed on top of the corporate responsibility history (Harlow et al., 2013). Companies are influenced by institutionalization and must adapt to benefit from government policies (Silva-Rêgo & Figueira, 2019). Some firms lag and resist it or just "greenwash" their initiatives (Milne & Gray, 2013). Within companies, the process for accepting and adopting SD practices may be better understood as SD becomes more institutionalized. The complexity of generating positive economic, social, and environmental results all at once is not trivial, given the uncertainty that innovation, especially radical innovation, brings (Barbieri et al., 2010).

Sustainable innovations will often require radicalness, going beyond just products, processes, and eco-innovation, as they must include social and economic objectives oriented to the future (Boons et al., 2013). Adapting may be the only possibility, and organizations that can turn the ESG into a market advantage can ensure survival (Wang et al., 2023). The economic theorist Joseph Schumpeter discussed innovation in 1911, describing it broadly, including developing new products, changing production and transportation methods, conquering new markets, and altering organizational structures. Innovation does not necessarily mean inventing but rather applying new technologies, materials, methods, and energy sources (Schumpeter, 1980). In the late 1930s, he and his followers proposed that innovation was an activity of individuals called entrepreneurs (Sweezy, 1943), coining a role that became identified with creativity and inventiveness. Theorists have since compiled increasingly complex and comprehensive theories of innovation on top of this foundation (Downs & Mohr, 1979; Sears & Baba, 2011), agreeing that innovation requires creative energy toward valuable new outcomes.

One of the innovation aspects brought by Schumpeter was that of Creative Destruction, which would be capitalism's ability to continuously destroy its status quo and give birth to new structures that will later be destroyed and reconstructed (Schumpeter, 2008). Christensen (1997) described the Disruptive Innovation theory as broad transformations that radically change the economy and society through a technological or organizational breakthrough. Disruptive innovation starts with performances below the mainstream practices. However, they accelerate the market and surpass the old technology, turning it obsolete in the long run. For him, innovating should be every managers' end goal as merely surviving is the opposite of great results (Christensen, 2006).

To comply with its corporate purpose, innovation should be learned by exploring new possibilities while exploiting previous certainties (Sarasvathy, 2001). Included as corporate strategy, innovation should be a tool to allow for the adoption of sustainable practices throughout the organization, embedded in a long-term orientation program with a sense of urgency (Turner & Pennington, 2015) to ensure survival. In summary, SD would be increasingly more institutionalized in the global society, and as companies feel the need to join the sustainability efforts, it also becomes a source of innovation that some will seize as an opportunity for growth. The scheme in Figure 13.2 condenses how Institutional and Innovation theories, together with the SD concept, act as forces to shape corporate sustainability on a background of corporate survival.

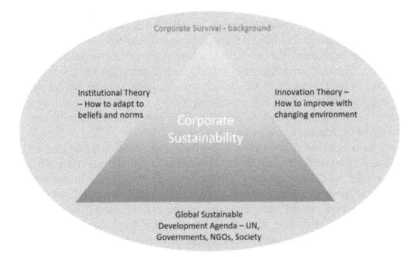

Fig. 13.2. Corporate Survival Background. *Source*: Prepared by the authors.

Sustainable innovations should be radical and oriented to the future (Charter et al., 2008) to ensure company survival. However, SD seems to have entered the companies via an institutionalization process before evolving into competitive innovation. Field literature revealed that the motivations for corporate sustainability most prevalent in the literature are Legitimacy, Social Insurance, Market Success, and Process Improvement (Bansal & Roth, 2000; Brammer & Pavelin, 2005; Darnall, 2003; Epstein, 2008; Godfrey, 2005; Godfrey et al., 2009; Simões-Coelho & Figueira 2021; Windolph et al., 2014).

Legitimacy and Social Insurance are connected to Institutional Theory, as these motivations derive from a need to comply with the local business environment's rules, regulations, and social expectations (Fransen, 2013). Market Success and Process Improvement include innovations that allow sustainability to become a tool for competitive advantage and companies' performance (Hall & Wagner, 2012). The latter motivations foster the development of new business models (Boons et al., 2013) with the advancement of sustainable innovations, whether disruptive or incremental. These new business models also comply with Schneider's (2015) prediction of companies with SD as their means or end-goals, beyond the conventional sole profit-oriented model.

3. METHOD

This study was designed using the traditional method of gap finding and filling to develop the questions, as there is no settled Sustainability Theory to be challenged. It is a field that still requires incremental research and the creation of complex theory through collaboration and interaction beyond individual researchers' capabilities (Van de Ven, 2007). The objectives were developed to focus on the gaps found in corporate sustainability literature from CG-MNEs, being the main questions summarized as: What motivates companies to engage with the SD agenda in different regions of the world? How does engagement evolve through time in CG-MNEs from an emerging and developed economy?

From the beginning, the work was designed as process research (Van de Ven, 2007), allowing for qualitative or quantitative methods. However, qualitative methods were most often the best choice. Multiple sources were employed to triangulate information. The case study method (Yin, 2009) and protocols (Eisenhardt, 1989; Eisenhardt & Graebner, 2007) were the choices for the field research with companies.

This study's unit of analysis is the CG-MNE, a multinational corporation that targets and communicates directly to consumers. For analytical consistency, the single focus is consumer goods corporations since business-to-business, infrastructure, or other types of companies, as well as local firms, may have different needs and respond to different pressures (Aguinis & Glavas, 2012; Dickinson-Delaporte et al., 2010) and, thus, may not allow for direct comparison among them. The United Nations acknowledged the differences by creating a SD guide for several industries – Consumer Goods, Financial Services, and Transportation, among others (UN Global Compact, 2015). Each has a specific set of guidelines and exemplary cases that can work as a manual for newcomers or smaller companies.

Also, the focus on multinational enterprises derives from the fact that companies located in more or less developed countries may face different levels of pressure to implement a sustainability agenda (Nidumolu et al., 2009). It is due both to activists' pressure groups, more organized in developed countries (Surroca et al., 2013) and the more strict implementation requirements of the global UN-led agreements for the same richer countries (Amran et al., 2014).

Thus, this study links the companies' agenda to their territory of operations. Two CG-MNE cases were chosen, taking into consideration that the corporations selected must be members of the Global Compact, present themselves as SD-engaged ones, and be recognized by other rankings, memberships, and awards. Beyond that, they must operate directly in every macro-region of the world, marketing to consumers. One of the companies must be headquartered in a developed country and the other in an emerging one. The two countries selected were the USA and Brazil, respectively.

The researchers elected these two countries due to their previous working knowledge of them and their extensive business and academic contacts in both. Brazil has 48 participants in the list of Global Compact consumer goods companies, and the US has 59 (UN Global Compact, 2019). In the former country, 28 are corporations, and the remainder are small and medium-sized businesses. In the case of the US, 39 are corporations. Corporations were the target for case studies since the research unit was the CG-MNEs.

Among them, the selection criteria for the case studies were (a) Being originally from one of the two selected countries and headquartered in the same market; (b) Having operations in all macro-regions of the world, according to the UN classification; (c) Directly managing its subsidiaries (not operating primarily through franchises); (d) Marketing to consumers, as expected for a consumer goods company; (e) Producing periodic report(s) with information about the mission, vision, operations, and sustainability strategy and initiatives. It provides statistical as well as qualitative information about the company's figures and principles; and (f) Self-identifying and being recognized as companies that reach for corporate sustainability. They must be part of the Global Compact and participate in other visible activities, membership, or awards in the SD area. The companies selected for the case studies were The Coca-Cola Company and Natura & Co.

Natura & Co emerged as a "best-in-class" consumer goods multinational corporation in sustainability engagement. Besides being a Global Compact member, it was the first publicly traded corporation in the world certified as a B-Company (B Lab, 2014; Watson, 2014). It has also been part of the Dow Jones Sustainability Index since 2014 (S&P Global, 2021) and the São Paulo Stock Exchange B3's Corporate Sustainability Index since it was created (B3 Stock Exchange, 2020). It is renowned globally as a company that seeks sustainability (Vilha & Quadros, 2006) while based in Latin America, where fewer studies are produced than in most other areas of the world (Ciravegna et al., 2013), making it an attractive research object.

On the other hand, The Coca-Cola Company was chosen for being among the most visible companies in the Global Compact (UN Global Compact, 2019); its global capillarity, being present in virtually every corner of the world; and for participating in a large number of sustainability pacts and organizations (The Coca-Cola Company, 2020). Besides that, the company or its bottling partners have been listed in the Dow Jones Sustainability Index in different years (S&P Global, 2021). Through time, they have been recognized and awarded several sustainability awards around the world, ranging from the International Water Association (The Coca-Cola Company, 2012) to Best Place to Work (Comparably, 2020) to several recognitions by the Clinton Global Initiative (Clinton Foundation, 2021), among others.

For the cases studied, semi-structured in-depth interviews with key managers were conducted, as presented in Table 13.1. The interview script was developed, taking into consideration the findings presented in the literature explored and the research objectives. For those interested, the interview script is available upon request to the corresponding author. During the interview stage, questions were slightly rearranged to follow a logical order for the interviewee and respect their professional background. In total, 18 interviews were conducted: 7 with executives of Natura, 9 with The Coca-Cola Company, and with two independent scholars with extensive executive and academic knowledge in the field and familiar with both companies, Dr. Helio Mattar[i] and Dr. Thomas Lovejoy[ii].

4. RESULTS AND DISCUSSION

The study questions versed on (1) what motivates companies' engagement in different regions of the world and (2) how engagement evolves within Consumer Goods MNEs from an emerging and a developed economy. To answer those questions, it elected authors that worked toward a model of broad corporate motivations for sustainability (Bansal & Roth, 2000; Brammer & Pavelin, 2005; Darnall, 2003; Epstein, 2008; Godfrey, 2005; Godfrey et al., 2009; Windolph et al., 2014; Simões-Coelho & Figueira, 2021). These motivations were Legitimacy, Market Success, Process Improvement, and Social Insurance. Each of them addresses different aspects of the reasons behind companies' engagement globally.

These motivations were then validated against scientific field articles from every region of the world to derive the findings and were later tested in case studies with CG-MNEs. The main findings by Simões-Coelho and Figueira (2021) were that: (1) Scientific interest in corporate sustainability was on the rise since it appeared as a topic in the early 2000s; (2) Legitimacy was the most prevalent motivation, followed by Process Improvement and Market Success, and lastly by Social Insurance; (3) Legitimacy and Process Improvement appeared early as an academic interest, followed by Market Success and Social Insurance; (4) The most significant number of articles were global ones, but, as a macro-region, the one that counted with more interest on corporate SD was Europe, followed by Asia, North America, Africa, and Latin America; and (5) The more developed regions had more studies in Market Success and Process Improvement than less developed ones.

Table 13.1.   Interviews.

No.	Position	Company	Duration
1	Chief Executive Officer	Natura	55 min
2	Marketing, Innovation, and Sustainability Vice-President	Natura	43 min
3	Director of Corporate Affairs	Natura	38 min
4	Manager of New Markets' Strategy	Natura	44 min
5	Sustainability Manager	Natura	50 min
6	Chief Executive Officer *(Former Executive)*	Natura	54 min
7	Director of Corporate and Governmental Affairs *(Former Executive)*	Natura	63 min
8	President and Chief Operations Officer	Coca-Cola	65 min
9	Chief Communications, Sustainability, and Strategic Partnerships Officer	Coca-Cola	60 min
10	Chief Growth Officer	Coca-Cola	40 min
11	Sustainability Vice-President	Coca-Cola	70 min
12	Group Director	Coca-Cola	70 min
13	President for Latin America	Coca-Cola	75 min
14	Global Policy and Sustainability Vice-President	Coca-Cola	45 min
15	Global Safety Assessments and Regulatory Affairs Vice-President	Coca-Cola	60 min
16	Chief Marketing Officer for Sparkling Beverages	Coca-Cola	120 min
17	Dr. Helio Mattar	Independent Scholar	59 min
18	Dr. Thomas Lovejoy	Independent Scholar	31 min
Total interview time			1,042 min

Source: Prepared by the authors.

These findings derived the framework in Figure 13.3, containing two main axes along with the motivations. One axis suggests that some motivations appear longitudinally, some at an earlier and others at a later stage. The other indicates that different markets/countries adopt different motivations depending on their sophistication or competitiveness level. Longitudinally, the findings led to consider that motivations change over time; early motivations are connected to compliance, and later ones aim for competition. Regionally, the beliefs were that motivations vary based on socio-economic development – the more developed the market, the more motivation to embed innovative initiatives toward business growth; motivations in each market are independent of a corporation's national origin, and motivations will change as the development level of a country changes.

The cases concentrate on understanding how corporate sustainability was adopted and expanded in the two companies. The first case study highlighted the leadership effect on SD engagement, as previously signaled in the literature (Lozano, 2015). The framework of Simões-Coelho and Figueira (2021) purposefully excluded the leadership factor to ensure analysis in a level playing field, independent of individual belief. However, it is recognized and understood as a possible propulsion or repressing force to corporate sustainability and must be considered when it appears as a compelling element in a case.

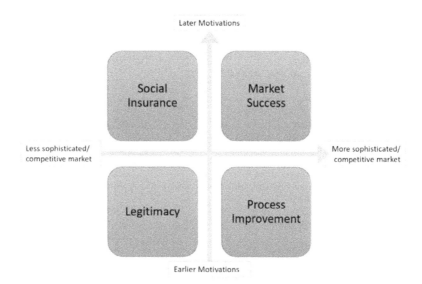

Fig. 13.3.   Motivations' Framework. *Source*: Simões-Coelho & Figueira (2021).

The corporations were selected among the Global Compact members (UN Global Compact, 2019) as a proxy for their commitment to SD. They are sizeable international Consumer Goods Companies, among the market leaders both in domestic and global markets, which operate in every one of the world's macro-regions (United Nations Statistics Division, 2012) and publish periodical financial and sustainability reports.

Despite these similarities and their business success, the two companies operate in different markets and, naturally, have different business stories. The Coca-Cola Company has been an international company since the 1920s (The Coca-Cola Company, 2021), when it started to plan a global strategy and sponsored its first Olympic Games in 1928. Natura is a product of the much more recent globalization wave of emerging countries' companies (Gu & Lu, 2011). It only started direct international operations in 1994 in South America's neighbors Argentina and Chile (Natura & Co, 2021) and took more than 25 years to strengthen international operations to surpass their domestic revenues, according to its CEO (Personal Communication). The American company has had most of its revenues from international operations for decades.

TCCC has also been a publicly traded company for over one century, and its last dominant shareowner was chairman Robert Woodruff in the 1950s (The Coca-Cola Company, 2021). At Natura & Co, the founders are still very present as members of the company's board (Natura & Co, 2020). Even though they only own approximately one-third of the company, they still significantly influence Natura & Co's directives. More data on these two companies are given in Fig. 13.4.

	The Coca-Cola Company	Natura & Co
Financial Information (US$)		
Revenues	37 Bn	10 Bn
Int'l Revenues	~70%	~55%
Market Cap*	216 Bn	12 Bn
Control	No dominant	No dominant
Company Info		
Country of Origin	USA	Brazil
Industry	Beverages	Beauty
Foundation	1886	1969
Int'l Presence	200+ countries	100+ countries
Direct Employees	86,000	34,000
Indirect Employees	700,000	6,000,000
Market		
Brands Operated	500+	Undisclosed (hundreds, under 4 companies)
Leadership Position		
Domestic	1st	1st
Global	1st	4th
Regional Sales	29% Europe/M. East/Africa	60% Latin America
	27% Latin America	23% Europe
	24% Asia/Pacific	12% Asia/Pacific
	18% North America	3% North America
	2% Global Ventures	2% Africa
Sustainability		
Pacts Membership		
Global Market	Yes	Yes
B Corps	No	Yes
Bonsucro	Yes	No
Animal Welfare (several)	Yes	Yes
Human Rights (several)	Yes	Yes
Sustainability Indexes		
Main Home Country	DJSI – some years	B3 Sust. Index – every year
International	No	DJSI
NGOs Cooperation	Several	Several
Schneider type of Co.	Market-Centered	Sustainability-Centered
Proposed typology	Protocol	Native

Fig. 13.4. Data on Case Studies Companies. *Source*: Prepared by the authors.

Their sustainability history also followed different paths. At Natura & Co, all sources consulted on developing the case study pointed out the embeddedness of SD into its operations since the company's creation. At TCCC, the efforts toward fully compromising with this agenda are still underway, as pointed out by the company's president and COO himself (Personal Communication).

Both companies have engaged in a complete corporate sustainability agenda. However, the end goal appears to be different between the companies. While Natura & Co reached a Triple Bottom Line modus operandi, TCCC narrowed its focus on the financial rewards, with the social and environmental aspects treated as means to reach this end goal. According to Schneider's (2015) model reviewed by Cho et al. (2020), the former would be a sustainability-centered company, while the latter can be described as a market-centered company.

As this study proposes a new typology for corporate engagement with SD, given the two cases and the literature analyzed, it appears that companies can pursue either a Native or a Protocol sustainability engagement. The difference between them is the level of agenda integration within a business. In the Native company, SD is engrained in its DNA. One indication is the company being market- or sustainability-centered (Schneider, 2015), but there are other dimensions to consider. National origin did not play a role in the two cases, maybe because they were already corporate sustainability references before this research started and are international companies that play by global rules. However, both theoretical (Amran et al., 2014; Nidumolu et al., 2009) and field literature (Achabou et al., 2017; Escobar & Vredenburg, 2011; Surroca et al., 2013) report that there may be differences in the way companies handle sustainability in accordance with each country's development level, independently of their national origins.

Benito et al. (2022) describe how the transformation of the world in the 21st century affects firms. Managers are expected to create and implement strategies in response to social, environmental, and technological changes as well as political institutions. Depending on the arrangements found in each location, companies like Natura and Coca-Cola adjust their policies to comply with the region's geopolitics or institutions. This level of local engagement would also directly reflect the whole organization's sustainability dimensions (Lozano, 2023), contributing to how the CG-MNE is seen by each market where it operates.

Many leaders adopt an SD agenda in pursuit of legitimacy (Meyer & Rowan, 1977), social approval (Bitektine, 2011), or personal ethics and honorability (Aguinis & Glavas, 2012; Aßländer, 2013). Nevertheless, studies have shown that leadership, together with customer demand and regulation, is one of the main reasons to embrace sustainability (Lozano, 2015). It is also a key factor for a business to become a Native sustainable company. In the Natura & Co case, the leadership factor was crucial for ensuring the level of commitment to the SD agenda achieved by the company and recognized by all stakeholders. According to the company's former Corporate and Governmental Affairs Director, "Due to a certain leadership profile, Natura really took off... [as] sustainability became part of the company's executive profile" (personal communication).

In the Coca-Cola Company case study, leadership has given different importance levels to the topic over time. Stakeholders recognize the company's efforts toward the TBL, but sustainability is not yet ingrained in each business executive practice. With the increasing pressure exerted by global leadership as reported by the COO and the CSO (Personal Communication) and the growing pursuit for sustainability reflected in the company's reports (The Coca-Cola Company, 2022), this seems to be changing toward a long-term policy. The Sparkling Beverages CMO said: "As a leading company and a leading system, we need to live up to our standards and leadership. (...) Because, after all, this is what sustainability is about, at least our sustainability" (personal communication).

In the model proposed below, there are three types of companies portrayed. The companies that consider SD for guiding their practices and strategies are named Protocol and Native ones, depending on the level of integration with the business. The companies that do not consider sustainability a key asset are present in the model as Non-SD-Oriented ones. These are firms that strive to grow revenues and profit, tackling additional issues as required by legislation. They address sustainability only as demanded and have previously been named "Conventional Companies" in the literature (Cho et al., 2020; Schneider, 2015). The Non-SD-Oriented companies were not the subject of this study. Thus, they are defined by the exclusion of the sustainability attributes.

Protocol and Native companies, on the other hand, incorporate the SD agenda beyond its institutional aspects and innovate from this foundation. The corporate sustainability motivations framework already indicated that companies with a more extended sustainability history in more competitive markets would be more inclined to adopt sustainable strategies. The comparison between the Natura and the Coca-Cola case studies allowed to detail better the attributes that would make SD further engrained into the firm's culture and philosophy.

A Protocol sustainable company must count on attributes that are among the ones that helped to select this work's case studies, including (1) self-identity as a company striving for sustainability; (2) membership to Global Compact or similar pacts; (3) publication of periodical SD reports; (4) participation in rankings, accreditations, and awards that form evidence of public recognition of corporate sustainability; and (5) sustainable projects driving part of its innovation initiatives. The findings allow inferring that this would be the initial stage of an SD-centered firm.

A Native sustainable company counts on the same attributes of a Protocol one but goes beyond. The SD agenda is naturally part of the day-to-day business as if written in its corporate DNA. The additional attributes for a Native company would be primarily (1) long-term SD-focused leadership, (2) executive rewards system dependent on sustainability goals, (3) sustainable directives enforced on top of financial priorities, and (4) fully sustainable business cases for growth and innovation. In this scenario, all innovation comes from sustainability, leaving no room for conventional revenues-seeking-only new products and services.

This theoretical generalization differs from Schneider's (2015) side-by-side evolution model. The process from being a Non-SD-Oriented to a Protocol to a Native CG-MNE is viewed as a continuum, where additional attributes increase the engagement with corporate sustainability and transform how a company operates. Figure 13.5 summarizes the proposed typology. The Native stage would be the highest one in this typology. However, as cautioned by Dr. Mattar, even the most SD-engaged companies have not yet reached the ideal operation to be considered fully sustainable (Personal Communication). So, it is possible that the attributes related to each stage may change in the future as standards and expectations become stricter.

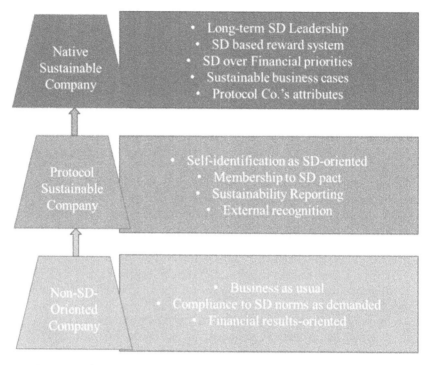

Fig. 13.5. Summary of Attributes – Typology for Corporate Engagement with Sustainability. *Source*: Prepared by the authors.

5. CONCLUSIONS

This study concentrates on consumer goods multinational companies' motivations and engagement for corporate sustainability. To understand the dynamics of this once-considered antithetical connection (Luke, 2013) and propose an engagement model, the work first elected the motivations for sustainability found in a previous study that reviewed field cases from every world region (Simões-Coelho & Figueira, 2021). Then, it reviewed and compared two case studies conducted with CG-MNEs from a developed and an emerging country. Empirical evidence from the cases indicates that the engagement with sustainability changes through time, mostly from compliance to institutions into differentiations aimed at success in each market. It also suggests that the motivations and engagement change according to each local operation's development level, independently from the company's country of origin.

Two main quests can delimit the overall research questions that operationalized this work. The first concerns local differences in relation to global companies' priorities. The second, to understand the pace of this engagement in different companies. To each of those quests, this study responded with a theoretic abstraction that can operationalize scientific studies and organizational reflection. Besides, a relevant topic was raised, versing about the leadership factor, which cannot be disregarded, especially in extreme belief or disbelief in the corporate sustainability agenda.

Two main theories and a SD framework are the foundations for this study. The findings reflect the Institutional and Innovation theories while striving to advance the knowledge of corporate sustainability. The study proposes that companies move from adopting ESG due to institutional regulation (North, 1990) to innovating for competitive reasons (Barbieri et al., 2010; Boons et al., 2013). Natura & Co built its credentials due to the SD institutionalization throughout the business while creating new products and implementing new processes with a sustainability mindset. As predicted in the literature (Bitektine, 2011), The Coca-Cola Company rejuvenated its corporate brand with similar messages to obtain society's subjective approval.

The motivations' research also reinforced longitudinal and regional considerations to corporate sustainability engagement. The previous field studies analyzed, and the case studies with Natura & Co and TCCC also filled part of the gaps related to national-institutional arrangements and corporate sustainability (Fransen, 2013; Fransen et al., 2019) and brought new insights about the differences between a developed country MNE and this relatively new phenomenon of an emerging market's one (Gu & Lu, 2011). As a whole, this study provides theoretical contributions to corporate sustainability, especially embodied in the proposed new model. They can help both practitioners within multinational or local enterprises and scholars in corporate sustainability.

Treating the Natura & Co case's leadership factor is another, as it may model future studies with the same or other companies. Yet another is the matter of issue identification for the development of sensible corporate sustainability strategies, discussed in the TCCC case, which may subsidize studies in the areas of business as well as communications. Finally, the study proposes a theoretical generalization for how CG-MNEs and other multinational companies might evolve as they integrate sustainability into their business, leading to the proposed typology. From an externally imposed agenda to an internalized source of growth and innovation opportunities, these companies may move from conventional to becoming Protocol and then Native sustainability companies. Besides supporting studies in corporate sustainability engagement, these discussions and the models may also function as a roadmap to practitioners who intend to strategically develop their organizations, as SD institutionalization requires.

However, the limitations of this study are manifold. Among the most significant ones: Only two case studies were conducted; Only one segment was addressed – CG-MNEs; Only companies recognized in SD engagement were studied; Only two countries of origin, an emerging and a developed one; The interviewees' corporate level for the cases was mainly limited to senior officers from each companies' HQ; The longitudinal storyline of each company was reconstructed via documentation, as the timing for observation was restricted; The great majority of the literature was in English only (with few exceptions of Portuguese and Spanish studies indexed in English). Thus, these limitations and the contributions of the work lead to a series of future study opportunities.

There is a plethora of studies that can be derived from this work. As all the literature was indexed in English, other languages may bring different insights. Also, more CG-MNEs from different countries may provide relevant additional information to corroborate or reform the findings. Studies on companies in other segments, industries, and countries may reveal different realities and engagement formats. The study concentrated on reputable companies for their ESG work. Adding non-reputable companies may bring new perspectives, too.

As interviews were primarily conducted with high-level business executives from the two companies' headquarters, more comprehensive observations can be made reaching employees at different organizational levels and in different locations and countries. In the same way, more extended longitudinal studies will be important to define and refine strategic paths for changing institutional arrangements.

NOTES

i. Dr. Mattar holds a Ph.D. in Industrial Engineering from Stanford University. He was a well-known businessman and, since 2000, has been fully dedicated to a Non-governmental Organization (NGO) that focuses on consumer awareness. He presides over the conscious consumerism Akatu Institute and is a member of several global councils and boards, including Dow Chemical's United States (US) and Unilever's United Kingdom (UK) sustainability boards.

ii. Dr. Lovejoy is considered the "godfather of biodiversity," a term he coined. He earned his Ph.D. at Yale University, was a University Professor at George Mason University and a senior fellow at the United Nations Organization. He was one of the environmental sustainability movement's world leaders, having advised three American presidents (Reagan, Bush, and Clinton) and several organizations and companies on environmental issues worldwide.

REFERENCES

Achabou, M. A., Dekhili, S., & Hamdoun, M. (2017). Environmental upgrading of developing country firms in global value chains. *Business Strategy and the Environment*, *26*(2), 224–238. https://doi.org/10.1002/bse.1911

Aguinis, H., & Glavas, A. (2012). What we know and don't know about corporate social responsibility: A review and research agenda. *Journal of Management*, *38*(4), 932–968. https://doi.org/10.1177/0149206311436079

Amran, A., Periasamy, V., & Zulkafli, A. (2014). Determinants of climate change disclosure by developed and emerging countries in Asia Pacific. *Sustainable Development*, *22*(3), 188–204. https://doi.org/10.1002/sd.539

Asif, M., Searcy, C., Garvare, R., & Ahmad, N. (2011). Including sustainability in business excellence models. *Total Quality Management and Business Excellence*, *22*(7), 773–786. https://doi.org/10.1080/14783363.2011.585784

Aßländer, M. (2013). Honorableness or beneficialness? Cicero on natural law, virtues, glory, and (corporate) reputation. *Journal of Business Ethics*, *116*(4), 751–767. https://doi.org/10.1007/s10551-013-1819-7

B Corporation. (2020). *About B Corps*. Retrieved from https://bcorporation.net/about-b-corps

B Lab. (2014). *B impact report – Natura SA*. Retrieved from https://bcorporation.net/directory/natura-cosmeticos-sa

B3 Stock Exchange. (2020, July 18). *Natura & Co Holding S.A.* Retrieved July 19, 2020, from http://www.b3.com.br/en_us/

Bansal, P., & Roth, K. (2000). Why companies go green: A model of ecological responsiveness. *Academy of Management Journal, 43*(4), 717–736.

Barauskaite, G., & Streimikiene, D. (2021). Corporate social responsibility and financial performance of companies: The puzzle of concepts, definitions and assessment methods. *Corporate Social Responsibility and Environmental Management, 28*(1), 278–287.

Barbieri, J., Vasconcelos, I., Andreassi, T., & Vasconcelos, F. (2010). Inovação e sustentabilidade: novos modelos e proposições. *RAE – Revista de Administração de Empresas, 50*(2), 146–155.

Barnett, M., & Pollock, T. (2012). *The Oxford handbook of corporate reputation.* Oxford University Press. https://doi.org/10.1177/0001839213518022

Beckmann, M., Hielscher, S., & Pies, I. (2014). Commitment strategies for sustainability: How business firms can transform trade-offs into win-win outcomes. *Business Strategy and the Environment, 23*(1), 18–37. https://doi.org/10.1002/bse.1758

Benito, G., Cuervo-Cazurra, A., Mudambi, R., Pedersen, T., & Tallman, S. (2022). The future of global strategy. *Global Strategy Journal, 12*(3), 421–450.

Bitektine, A. (2011). Toward a theory of social judgments of organizations: The case of legitimacy, reputation, and status. *Academy of Management Review, 36*(1), 151–179. https://doi.org/10.5465/amr.2009.0382

Boons, F., Montalvo, C., Quist, J., & Wagner, M. (2013). Sustainable innovation, business models and economic performance: An overview. *Journal of Cleaner Production, 45,* 1–8. https://doi.org/10.1016/j.jclepro.2012.08.013

Brammer, S., & Pavelin, S. (2005). Corporate reputation and an insurance motivation for corporate social investment. *Journal of Corporate Citizenship,* (Winter), 39–51.

Brown, S. (1995). The moderating effects of insupplier/outsupplier status on organizational Buyer attitudes. *Journal of the Academy of Marketing Science, 23*(3), 170–181. https://doi.org/10.1177/0092070395233002

Bryson, J. R., & Lombardi, R. (2009). Balancing product and process sustainability against business profitability: Sustainability as a competitive strategy in the property development process. *Business Strategy and the Environment, 18*(2), 97–107. https://doi.org/10.1002/bse.640

Charter, M., Gray, C., Clark, T., & Woolman, T. (2008). Review: The role of business in realising sustainable consumption and production. In *Perspectives on radical changes to sustainable consumption and production* (p. 470). Greenleaf Pub.

Chen, T., Larsson, A., & Mark-Herbert, C. (2014). Implementing a collective code of conduct – CSC9000T in Chinese textile industry. *Journal of Cleaner Production, 74,* 35–43. https://doi.org/10.1016/j.jclepro.2014.03.026

Cho, C., Kim, A., Rodrigue, M., & Schneider, T. (2020). Towards a better understanding of sustainability accounting and management research and teaching in North America: A look at the community. *Sustainability Accounting, Management and Policy Journal, 11*(6), 985–1007.

Christensen, C. (1997). *The innovator's dilemma: When new technologies cause great firms to fail.* Harvard Business Review Press.

Christensen, C. (2006). The ongoing process of building a theory of disruption. *Journal of Product Innovation Management, 23*(1), 39–55.

Ciravegna, L., Lopez, L., & Kundu, S. (2013). Country of origin and network effects on internationalization: A comparative study of SMEs from an emerging and developed economy. *Journal of Business Research, 67*(5), 916–923. https://doi.org/10.1016/j.jbusres.2013.07.011

Clinton Foundation. (2021). *Clinton global initiative.* Retrieved from https://www.clintonfoundation.org/search/node/coca-cola

Comparably. (2020). *The Coca-Cola Company awards.* Retrieved from https://www.comparably.com/companies/the-coca-cola-company/awards

Cruz, C., & Matos, F. (2023). ESG maturity: A software framework for the challenges of ESG data in investment. *Sustainability, 15*(3), 2610.

Cupertino, S., Consolandi, C., & Vercelli, A. (2019). Corporate social performance, financialization, and real investment in US manufacturing firms. *Sustainability, 11*(7), 1836. https://doi.org/10.3390/su11071836

Darnall, N. (2003). Motivations for participating in a US voluntary environmental initiative: the multi-state working group and EPA's EMS pilot program. In M. Sharma, S., Starik (Ed.),

Research in corporate sustainability: The evolving theory and practice of organizations (pp. 1–46). Edward Elgar Publishing Ltd.

Dickinson-Delaporte, S., Beverland, M., & Lindgreen, A. (2010). *Building corporate reputation with stakeholders: Exploring the role of message ambiguity for social marketers.* https://doi.org/10.1108/03090561011079918

Diesendorf, M. (1999). Sustainability and sustainable development. In D. Dunphy, J. Benveniste, A. Griffiths, & P. Sutton (Eds.), *Sustainability: The corporate challenge of the 21st century* (Vol. 2, pp. 19–37). Allen & Unwin.

Downs, G., & Mohr, L. (1979). Toward a theory of innovation. *Administration & Society, 10*(4), 379–408.

Eberle, D., Berens, G., & Li, T. (2013). The impact of interactive corporate social responsibility communication on corporate reputation. *Journal of Business Ethics, 118*, 731–746.

Eisenhardt, K. (1989). Building theories from case study research. *Academy of Management Review, 14*(4), 532–550. https://doi.org/10.5465/AMR.1989.4308385

Eisenhardt, K., & Graebner, M. (2007). Theory building from cases: Opportunities and challenges. *Academy of Management Journal, 50*(1), 25–32. https://doi.org/Article

Elkington, J. (2004). Enter the triple bottom line. In A. Henriques & J. Richardson (Eds.), *The triple bottom line: Does it all add up?* (Vol. 1, pp. 1–16). Earthscan.

Epstein, M. (2008). Implementing corporate sustainability: Measuring and managing social and environmental impact. *Strategic Finance, 89*(7), 25–31.

Epstein, M., & Buhovac, A. (2014). Making sustainability work: Best practices in managing and measuring corporate social, environmental, and economic impacts. In *Ecological economics* (2nd ed, pp. 13–16). Greenleaf Publishing.

Epstein, M., & Roy, M. (2003). Making the business case for sustainability. *Journal of Corporate Citizenship*, (Spring), 79–96.

Escobar, L., & Vredenburg, H. (2011). Multinational oil companies and the adoption of sustainable development: A resource-based and institutional theory interpretation of adoption heterogeneity. *Journal of Business Ethics, 98*(1), 39–65. https://doi.org/10.1007/s10551-010-0534-x

Fleck, D. L. (2009). Archetypes of organizational success and failure. *BAR – Brazilian Administration Review, 6*(2), 78–100. https://doi.org/10.5465/AMBPP.2005.18778485

Fransen, L. (2013). The embeddedness of responsible business practice: Exploring the interaction between national-institutional environments and corporate social responsibility. *Journal of Business Ethics, 115*(2), 213–227. https://doi.org/10.1007/s10551-012-1395-2

Fransen, L., Kolk, A., & Rivera-Santos, M. (2019). The multiplicity of international corporate social responsibility standards: Implications for global value chain governance. *Multinational Business Review, 27*(4), 397–426.

Gallardo-Vázquez, D., & Sanchez-Hernandez, M. (2014). Measuring corporate social responsibility for competitive success at a regional level. *Journal of Cleaner Production, 72*, 14–22. https://doi.org/10.1016/j.jclepro.2014.02.051

Garcia, A. S., Mendes-Da-Silva, W., & Orsato, R. J. (2019). Corporate sustainability, capital markets, and ESG performance. In W. Mendes-Da-Silva (Ed.), *Individual behaviors and technologies for financial innovations* (pp. 287–309). Springer. https://doi.org/10.1007/978-3-319-91911-9_13

Gjølberg, M. (2010). Varieties of corporate social responsibility (CSR): CSR meets the "Nordic Model." *Regulation and Governance, 4*(2), 203–229. https://doi.org/10.1111/j.1748-5991.2010.01080.x

Godfrey, P. (2005). The relationship between corporate philanthropy and shareholder wealth: A risk management perspective. *Academy of Management Review, 30*(4), 777–798. https://doi.org/10.5465/AMR.2005.18378878

Godfrey, P., Merril, C., & Hansen, J. (2009). The relationship between corporate social responsibility and shareholder value: An empirical test of the risk management hypothesis. *Strategic Management Journal, 30*, 425–445. https://doi.org/10.1002/smj

Gu, Q., & Lu, J. (2011). Effects of inward investment on outward investment: The venture capital industry worldwide 1985–2007. *Journal of International Business Studies, 42*(2), 263–284. https://doi.org/10.1057/jibs.2010.51

Hall, J., & Wagner, M. (2012). Integrating sustainability into firms' processes: Performance effects and the moderating role of business models and innovation. *Business Strategy and the Environment, 21*(3), 183–196. https://doi.org/10.1002/bse.728

Harlow, J., Golub, A., & Allenby, B. (2013). A review of utopian themes in sustainable development discourse. *Sustainable Development, 21*(4), 270–280. https://doi.org/10.1002/sd.522

Khan, I., Ahmad, M., & Majava, J. (2021). Industry 4.0 and sustainable development: A systematic mapping of triple bottom line, circular economy and sustainable business models perspectives. *Journal of Cleaner Production, 297*, 126655.

Lemme, C. F. (2010). O valor gerado pela sustentabilidade corporativa. In D. Zylberstajn & C. Lins (Eds.), *Sustentabilidade e geração de valor: A transição para o século XXI* (pp. 37–63). Elsevier.

Lozano, R. (2015). A holistic perspective on corporate sustainability drivers. *Corporate Social Responsibility and Environmental Management, 22*(1), 32–44. https://doi.org/10.1002/csr.1325

Lozano, R. (2023). Analysing organisations' engagement with and impacts to sustainability. *Business Strategy and the Environment*. https://doi.org/10.1002/bse.3445

Luke, T. W. (2013). Corporate social responsibility: An uneasy merger of sustainability and development. *Sustainable Development, 21*, 83–91. https://doi.org/10.1002/sd.1558

Mebratu, D. (1998). Sustainability and sustainable development. *Environmental Impact Assessment Review, 18*(6), 493–520. https://doi.org/10.1016/S0195-9255(98)00019-5

Meyer, J., & Rowan, B. (1977). Institutionalized organizations: Formal structure as myth and ceremony. *JSTOR, 83*(2), 340–363.

Milne, M., & Gray, R. (2013). W(h)ither ecology? The triple bottom line, the global reporting initiative, and corporate sustainability reporting. *Journal of Business Ethics, 118*(1), 13–29. https://doi.org/10.1007/s10551-012-1543-8

Natura & Co. (2020). Annual report 2019. São Paulo.

Natura & Co. (2021). O mundo é mais bonito com você | Natura Brasil. Retrieved February 27, 2021, from https://www.natura.com.br/

Nidumolu, R., Prahalad, C., & Rangasawmi, M. (2009). Why sustainability is now. *Harvard Business Review, 87*(9), 56.

North, D. (1990). *Institutions, institutional change, and economic performance.* Cambridge University Press.

Oliveira, J., Ogliari, C., Pupo, F., Contreras, F., Coelho Neto, G., Smaha, H., … Santos, V. (2008). A implementação do pacto global pelas empresas do paraná. *RGSA – Revista de Gestão Social Ambiental, 2*(3), 92–110.

Pless, N., Maak, T., & Stal, G. (2012). Promoting corporate social responsibility and sustainable development through management development. *Human Resource Management, 51*(6), 873–904. https://doi.org/10.1002/hrm.21506

Robinson, M., Kleffner, A., & Bertels, S. (2011). Signaling sustainability leadership: empirical evidence of the value of DJSI membership. *Journal of Business Ethics, 101*(3), 493–505. https://doi.org/10.1007/s10551-011-0735-y

Rose, C., & Thomsen, S. (2004). The impact of corporate reputation on performance: Some Danish evidence. *European Management Journal, 22*(2), 201–210. https://doi.org/10.1016/j.emj.2004.01.012

Ruth, J., & York, A. (2004). Framing information to enhance corporate reputation: The impact of message source, information type, and reference point. *Journal of Business Research, 57*(1), 14–20. https://doi.org/10.1016/S0148-2963(02)00270-9

S&P Global. (2021). *Dow Jones world sustainability index.* Retrieved from https://www.spglobal.com/spdji/en/indices/esg/dow-jones-sustainability-world-index/#data

Sarasvathy, S. (2001). Causation and effectuation: Toward a theoretical shift from economic inevitability to entrepreneurial contingency. *Academy of Management Review, 26*(2), 243–263. https://doi.org/10.5465/AMR.2001.4378020

Schneider, A. (2014). Reflexivity in sustainability accounting and management: Transcending the economic focus of corporate sustainability. *Journal of Business Ethics, 127*, 525–538. https://doi.org/10.1007/s10551-014-2058-2

Schumpeter, J. A. (1980). *Theory of economic development.* Routledge. Retrieved from https://www.amazon.com/Theory-Economic-Development-InterestBusiness/dp/0878556982

Schumpeter, J. A. (2008). *Capitalism, socialism and democracy.* Harper Perennial.

Searcy, C., & Buslovich, R. (2014). Corporate perspectives on the development and use of sustainability reports. *Journal of Business Ethics, 121*(2), 149–169. https://doi.org/10.1007/s10551-013-1701-7

Sears, G., & Baba, V. (2011). Toward a multistage, multilevel theory of innovation. *Canadian Journal of Administrative Sciences, 28*(4), 357–372. https://doi.org/10.1002/CJAS.198

Silva-Rêgo, B., & Figueira, A. (2019). New institutional economics: Contributions to international business studies. *International Journal of Emerging Markets*, *14*(5), 1102–1123. https://doi.org/10.1108/IJOEM-07-2018-0372

Simões-Coelho, M., & Figueira, A. (2021). Why do companies engage in sustainability? Propositions and a framework of motivations. *BAR-Brazilian Administration Review*, *18*.

Sotorrío, L., & Sánchez, J. (2008). Corporate social responsibility of the most highly reputed European and North American firms. *Journal of Business Ethics*, *82*(2), 379–390. https://doi.org/10.1007/s10551-008-9901-2

Stellner, C., Klein, C., & Zwergel, B. (2015). Corporate social responsibility and Eurozone corporate bonds: The moderating role of country sustainability. *Journal of Banking & Finance*, *59*, 538–549. https://doi.org/10.1016/j.jbankfin.2015.04.032

Surroca, J., Tribó, J., & Zahra, S. (2013). Stakeholder pressure on MNEs and the transfer of socially irresponsible practices to subsidiaries. *Academy of Management Journal*, *56*(2), 549–572. https://doi.org/10.5465/amj.2010.0962

Sustainable Business Council. (2013). *Social licence to operate paper*. Auckland, New Zealand.

Sweezy, P. M. (1943). Professor Shumperter's theory of innovation. *The Review of Economics and Statistics*, *25*(1), 93–96.

The Coca-Cola Company. (2012). *IWA award*. Retrieved from https://www.coca-colacompany.com/press-releases/iwa-award-coke-wins-with-water-recovery-system

The Coca-Cola Company. (2020). *Business & sustainability report*. Atlanta, USA. Retrieved from https://www.coca-

The Coca-Cola Company. (2021). The Coca-Cola Company: Refresh the world. Make a difference. Retrieved February 27, 2021, from https://www.coca-colacompany.com/home

The Coca-Cola Company (2022). *Business and sustainability report*. Retrieved from https://www.coca-colacompany.com/content/dam/journey/us/en/reports/coca-cola-business-and-sustainability-report-2022.pdf

Turner, T., & Pennington, W. (2015). Organizational networks and the process of corporate entrepreneurship: how the motivation, opportunity, and ability to act affect firm knowledge, learning, and innovation. *Small Business Economics*, *45*(2), 447–463. https://doi.org/10.1007/s11187-015-9638-0

UN and KPMG. (2016). *Food, beverage and consumer goods. SDG industry matrix*. New York, NY. Retrieved from https://sustainabledevelopment.un.org/content/documents/9786CRT046599SDG_Food_Bev_24Feb_WEB_FINAL.pdf

UN Global Compact (2012). *Rio+20 corporate sustainability forum*. Retrieved from https://www.unglobalcompact.org/library/1041

UN Global Compact (2015). *SDG industry matrix*. Retrieved from https://www.unglobalcompact.org/library/3111

UN Global Compact (2019). *Retail participants*. Retrieved from https://www.unglobalcompact.org/

UN Partnership Programme (2020). *Sustainable stock exchanges*. Retrieved from https://sseinitiative.org/about/

UN WCED (1987). *Our common future. Report of the world commission on environment and development*. New York, NY. https://doi.org/10.1080/07488008808408783

United Nations Organization (2015). *SDGs knowledge platform*. Retrieved from https://sustainabledevelopment.un.org/

United Nations Organization (2020). *UN global compact*. Retrieved from https://www.unglobalcompact.org/

United Nations Statistics Division (2012). *Composition of macro geographical (continental) regions, geographical sub-regions, and selected economic and other groupings*. United Nations. Retrieved from http://unstats.un.org/unsd/methods/m49/m49regin.htm

Van de Ven, A. (2007). *Engaged scholarship: A guide for organizational and social research*. Oxford University Press.

Vilha, A., & Quadros, R. (2006). Development of new competencies and practices the innovation management to sustainable development: The study of natura. In *PICMENT 2006 proceedings* (pp. 908–916). Istanbul, Turkey.

Wang, W., Sun, Z., Wang, W., Hua, Q., & Wu, F. (2023). The impact of environmental uncertainty on ESG performance: Emotional vs. rational. *Journal of Cleaner Production*, *397*, 136528.

Watson, B. (2014, December 12). Natura joins B Corps: Will other big business embrace sustainability certification? *The Guardian*, 12–14. Retrieved from https://www.theguardian.com/sustainable-business/2014/dec/12/b-corps-certification-sustainability-natura

WBCSD. (2024). *World Business Council for sustainable development*. Retrieved from https://www.wbcsd.org/

Webb, J., Khoury, T., & Hitt, M. (2020). The influence of formal and informal institutional voids on entrepreneurship. *Entrepreneurship Theory and Practice, 44*(3), 504–526.

Windolph, S., Harms, D., & Schaltegger, S. (2014). Motivations for corporate sustainability management: Contrasting survey results and implementation. *Corporate Social Responsibility and Environmental Management, 21*(5), 272–285. https://doi.org/10.1002/csr.1337

Yin, R. (2009). *Case study research: designs and methods – Fourth Edition. Applied social research methods series* (Vol. 5). Sage Inc. https://doi.org/10.1097/FCH.0b013e31822dda9e

INDEX